Digitalization of Decentralized Supply Chains During Global Crises

Atour Taghipour
Normandy University, France

IGI Global
PUBLISHER of TIMELY KNOWLEDGE

A volume in the Advances in Logistics, Operations, and Management Science (ALOMS) Book Series

Published in the United States of America by
IGI Global
Business Science Reference (an imprint of IGI Global)
701 E. Chocolate Avenue
Hershey PA, USA 17033
Tel: 717-533-8845
Fax: 717-533-8661
E-mail: cust@igi-global.com
Web site: http://www.igi-global.com

Library of Congress Cataloging-in-Publication Data

Names: Taghipour, Atour, 1974- editor.
Title: Digitalization of decentralized supply chains during global crises / Atour Taghipour, editor.
Description: Hershey : Business Science Reference, 2021. | Includes bibliographical references and index. | Summary: "This book provides new approaches of digitalization of decentralized supply chains and industries to help researchers, educators, consultants and practitioners to deal with global crises and to improve the global performance of supply chains"-- Provided by publisher.
Identifiers: LCCN 2021000179 (print) | LCCN 2021000180 (ebook) | ISBN 9781799868743 (hardcover) | ISBN 9781799868750 (paperback) | ISBN 9781799868767 (ebook)
Subjects: LCSH: Business logistics--Technological innovations. | Decentralization in management.
Classification: LCC HD38.5 .D546 2021 (print) | LCC HD38.5 (ebook) | DDC 658.70285--dc23
LC record available at https://lccn.loc.gov/2021000179
LC ebook record available at https://lccn.loc.gov/2021000180

This book is published in the IGI Global book series Advances in Logistics, Operations, and Management Science (ALOMS) (ISSN: 2327-350X; eISSN: 2327-3518)

British Cataloguing in Publication Data
A Cataloguing in Publication record for this book is available from the British Library.

Advances in Logistics, Operations, and Management Science (ALOMS) Book Series

ISSN:2327-350X
EISSN:2327-3518

Editor-in-Chief: John Wang, Montclair State University, USA

MISSION

Operations research and management science continue to influence business processes, administration, and management information systems, particularly in covering the application methods for decision-making processes. New case studies and applications on management science, operations management, social sciences, and other behavioral sciences have been incorporated into business and organizations real-world objectives.

The **Advances in Logistics, Operations, and Management Science** (ALOMS) Book Series provides a collection of reference publications on the current trends, applications, theories, and practices in the management science field. Providing relevant and current research, this series and its individual publications would be useful for academics, researchers, scholars, and practitioners interested in improving decision making models and business functions.

COVERAGE

- Services management
- Computing and information technologies
- Organizational Behavior
- Information Management
- Decision analysis and decision support
- Risk Management
- Finance
- Marketing engineering
- Production Management
- Political Science

IGI Global is currently accepting manuscripts for publication within this series. To submit a proposal for a volume in this series, please contact our Acquisition Editors at Acquisitions@igi-global.com or visit: http://www.igi-global.com/publish/.

The Advances in Logistics, Operations, and Management Science (ALOMS) Book Series (ISSN 2327-350X) is published by IGI Global, 701 E. Chocolate Avenue, Hershey, PA 17033-1240, USA, www.igi-global.com. This series is composed of titles available for purchase individually; each title is edited to be contextually exclusive from any other title within the series. For pricing and ordering information please visit http://www.igi-global.com/book-series/advances-logistics-operations-management-science/37170. Postmaster: Send all address changes to above address.

Titles in this Series

For a list of additional titles in this series, please visit:
http://www.igi-global.com/book-series/advances-logistics-operations-management-science/37170

Global Perspectives on Change Management and Leadership in the Post-COVID-19 Era
Ebtihaj Al-Aali (University of Bahrain, Bahrain) and Meryem Masmoudi (University of Bahrain, Bahrain)
Business Science Reference • ©2021 • 374pp • H/C (ISBN: 9781799869481) • US $215.00

Handbook of Research on Innate Leadership Characteristics and Examinations of Successful First-Time Leaders
Matthew Waritay Guah (South Carolina State University, USA)
Business Science Reference • ©2021 • 500pp • H/C (ISBN: 9781799875925) • US $285.00

Handbook of Research on Recent Perspectives on Management, International Trade, and Logistics
Güner Koç Aytekin (Ufuk University, Turkey) and Çağlar Doğru (Ufuk University, Turkey)
Business Science Reference • ©2021 • 490pp • H/C (ISBN: 9781799858867) • US $345.00

Handbook of Research on Multidisciplinary Perspectives on Managerial and Leadership Psychology
Rick D. Johnson (Johnson Professionals, Inc., USA)
Business Science Reference • ©2021 • 742pp • H/C (ISBN: 9781799838111) • US $285.00

Transforming Corporate Governance and Developing Models for Board Effectiveness
Qaiser Rafique Yasser (Centre for Rural Economy, Pakistan) and Abdullah Al-Mamun (University of Wollongong, Australia)
Business Science Reference • ©2021 • 345pp • H/C (ISBN: 9781799866695) • US $195.00

Encyclopedia of Organizational Knowledge, Administration, and Technology
Mehdi Khosrow-Pour D.B.A. (Information Resources Management Association, USA)
Business Science Reference • ©2021 • 2734pp • H/C (ISBN: 9781799834731) • US $3,950.00

For an entire list of titles in this series, please visit:
http://www.igi-global.com/book-series/advances-logistics-operations-management-science/37170

IGI Global
PUBLISHER of TIMELY KNOWLEDGE

701 East Chocolate Avenue, Hershey, PA 17033, USA
Tel: 717-533-8845 x100 • Fax: 717-533-8661
E-Mail: cust@igi-global.com • www.igi-global.com

Editorial Advisory Board

Table of Contents

Foreword xii

Preface xiii

Acknowledgment xxiv

Chapter 1
Accelerating the Digitalization of the Supply Chain: An Empirical Research About COVID-19 Crisis 1
Mohammed Merimi, Faculty of International Business, Normandy University, France
Atour Taghipour, Faculty of International Business, Normandy University, France

Chapter 2
Digitalization to Reduce Tasks Without Added Value or Human Contact in a Pandemic 25
Md. Masudul Hassan, Department of Agribusiness, Atish Dipankar University of Science and Technology, Bangladesh
Samira Islam Resmi, Department of Agribusiness, Atish Dipankar University of Science and Technology, Bangladesh

Chapter 3
Digital, Decentralized Supply Chain and Its Implication for B2B Marketing: A Case Study From the Indian Medical Equipment Industry 46
Subhasis Ray, Xavier Institute of Management, India

Chapter 4
Manufacturer Service-Oriented Strategy: A New Source of Competitive Advantage in Homogenous Industrial Markets 64
Youssef Elhaoussine, Beijing Normal University-Hong Kong Baptist University United International College, China

Chapter 5
The Influence of Digitization on Supply Chain Sustainable Performance 81
Kiran M. B., Pandit Deendayal Petroleum University, India

Chapter 6
Semantically Enhanced Web Service for Global Supply Chain Disruption Management 107
Kamalendu Pal, City, University of London, UK

Chapter 7
Security Issues of Blockchain-Based Information System to Manage Supply Chain in a Global Crisis 143
Kamalendu Pal, City, University of London, UK

Chapter 8
The Perspectives of Supply Chain Management Using Natural Knowledge From 3D Blockchain Technologies and Avatar-Based and Geographic Information Systems (GIS) 174
Vardan Mkrttchian, HHH University, Australia
Dmitry Davydov, Penza State University, Russia
Viacheslav Voronin, Moscow State Technological University "Stankin", Russia

Compilation of References 193

Related References 218

About the Contributors 249

Index 253

Detailed Table of Contents

Foreword xii

Preface xiii

Acknowledgment xxiv

Chapter 1
Accelerating the Digitalization of the Supply Chain: An Empirical Research About COVID-19 Crisis 1
Mohammed Merimi, Faculty of International Business, Normandy University, France
Atour Taghipour, Faculty of International Business, Normandy University, France

The chapter proposes ways to improve the digitalization of supply chains during global crises. After a survey conducted on a sample of 49 logistics professionals, the authors find that today it has become necessary to accelerate the deployment of an advanced digitalization of the supply chain as a whole. Due to the problems encountered during pandemic crises throughout history, especially the COVID-19 crisis, and in today's computerized world, it is needed to transform the supply chains towards 100% digital. In order to do that, first the authors need to study the fluctuations in supply and demand during crises in order to understand the general effect of pandemics on the supply chain. Thereafter, it is necessary to adopt and improve the appropriate IT systems, especially to digitalize the interaction between buyers and suppliers. This will change the purchasing contracts because the buyers have more transparency on the situation of their suppliers since access to information is easier in a digital environment where everything is connected.

Chapter 2
Digitalization to Reduce Tasks Without Added Value or Human Contact in a Pandemic 25
Md. Masudul Hassan, Department of Agribusiness, Atish Dipankar University of Science and Technology, Bangladesh
Samira Islam Resmi, Department of Agribusiness, Atish Dipankar University of Science and Technology, Bangladesh

Digitalization is the use of technological innovations within the business context with a major influence on products, services, business processes, sales channels, and supply channels. The associated potential advantages include, among others, increased sales or productivity, innovations in price creation, and new sorts of client interaction. Global enterprises are facing supply chain issues, and consequently, potentially higher operational costs, lower inventory, and the prospects of lower demand will make them reluctant to disburse resources and time to connect in M&A and financing activities, predominantly if valuations of targets remain high. Digitalization of the supply chain (DSC) could be a way that companies can start to strategize and accomplish trade strength against supply chain disturbance. The main focus of this chapter is that digitalization enhances prosperity without human contact in a pandemic, will alter labor markets, and impacts business models.

Chapter 3
Digital, Decentralized Supply Chain and Its Implication for B2B Marketing: A Case Study From the Indian Medical Equipment Industry 46
Subhasis Ray, Xavier Institute of Management, India

This chapter discusses the possible effects of decentralized, digital supply chains on B2B marketing. Traditional buying and selling functions will change once large organizations decide to procure from digital platforms. Using the case study of medikabazaar.com, an Indian start-up, the chapter shows that while medical supply purchase will become decentralized, digital platforms will create a new centralization of suppliers and have a significant impact on industrial buying particularly for high value medical equipment purchase in small towns or small hospitals. Organizational buying process will be impacted and companies that choose to supply products directly to hospitals will have to change their marketing strategy suitably.

Chapter 4
Manufacturer Service-Oriented Strategy: A New Source of Competitive Advantage in Homogenous Industrial Markets 64
Youssef Elhaoussine, Beijing Normal University-Hong Kong Baptist University United International College, China

This chapter develops a new hybrid manufacturing service-based marketing strategy for manufacturers evolving in a homogenous market. First, by using the Porter's value chain model, it will outline how manufacturers develop their competitive advantages in a normal context and then run the same theoretical analysis in the context of a homogenous market where it is difficult for manufacturers to create a difference. In addition, a qualitative research in the form of semi-conducted interviews with factory executives will confirm the homogeneity of strategies among competitors and outline the importance of developing new strategic directions. The conclusion will show that in order to create competitive advantages without using too many resources, marketing, service management, and technology could work together and lead manufacturers to adopt a more service-based marketing management orientation.

Chapter 5
The Influence of Digitization on Supply Chain Sustainable Performance 81
Kiran M. B., Pandit Deendayal Petroleum University, India

This chapter intends to explore the influence of digitization on supply chain sustainable performance. An attempt has been made in this chapter, first, to define supply chain management and its practical relevance, then to highlight the different components of the supply chain, and finally, how Industry 4.0 technologies can be used in designing these components so that all the components of the supply chain work in a coordinated manner and that they are effective in achieving the objectives of supply chain sustainability.

Chapter 6
Semantically Enhanced Web Service for Global Supply Chain Disruption Management..........107
Kamalendu Pal, City, University of London, UK

The recent coronavirus pandemic has now unleashed a global supply chain crisis across a huge number of organizations, stemming from a lack of understanding and flexibility of the multiple layers of their global supply chains and a lack of diversification in their sourcing strategies. One of the technical options to mitigate the pandemic is to automate business processes by which heterogeneous data integration is encouraged. The convergence of Semantic Web with service-oriented computing is manifested by Semantic Web services technology. It addresses the major challenge of automated, interoperable, and meaningful coordination of web service composition in industrial applications – such as apparel business. Automatic service composition may dramatically improve the development efficiency of web service applications. This chapter proposes an approach to automatically process semantic service composition (SSC) using description logics (DLs) to provide well-defined semantics. Also, this chapter explains the role of ontologies in the architecture of the Semantic Web.

Chapter 7
Security Issues of Blockchain-Based Information System to Manage Supply Chain in a Global Crisis 143
Kamalendu Pal, City, University of London, UK

Global supply chain crisis management has become increasingly crucial for tackling unusual incidents (e.g., natural disaster, terrorism, pandemic). While crisis management has focused on a few organizations involved in supply chain operations (manufacturers, governments, carriers, and the consuming public), it has primarily received a functional focus. Due to their decentralized network structure, supply chains are prone to suffer from disruptive events solved by supply chain crisis management. This chapter presents the blockchain technologies' possibilities and limits used in an integrated IoT-based information system architecture. The chapter describes how the scalability limits of blockchain technology affect the proposed architecture performance that uses it. Also, the chapter presents a review of the academic literature, pointing out how some solutions use a centralization process to improve response time and security of the blockchain-based architecture. Finally, the chapter provides security threat models, which consider by blockchain protocols in IoT networks.

Chapter 8
The Perspectives of Supply Chain Management Using Natural Knowledge From 3D Blockchain Technologies and Avatar-Based and Geographic Information Systems (GIS) 174
Vardan Mkrttchian, HHH University, Australia
Dmitry Davydov, Penza State University, Russia
Viacheslav Voronin, Moscow State Technological University "Stankin", Russia

The blockchain restores control and ownership of information back to its rightful owner, thus eliminating dependencies on central authorities and third parties. These material chains are immensely complex; they can be subject to the laws and regulations of more than 200 countries and territories, and they are heavily influenced by many different factors ranging from freight consolidation to the timing of hundreds of concurrent shipments. This chapter is about algorithmic modeling of supply chain management using natural knowledge from a 3D-hybrid blockchain as a dragon chain.

Compilation of References 193

Related References 218

About the Contributors 249

Index 253

Foreword

Without a doubt, global crisis increases uncertainty and disruption in this world. Face to these disruptions, supply chains need to maintain their competitiveness. The digitalization of the supply chain is one of the best answers to these problems, that enables companies to address the new challenges of the supply and demand side in global crisis.

This book studies the digital transformation of supply chains, which is an answer to a real need expressed by academics and practitioners. Supply chain digitalization is now a real need for all companies in the sector of service and the sector of manufacturing. In addition, there is a scarcity of books covering the topic of digital transformation of supply chains and this book fills a major gap in this domain. The book analyzes, the concept of digitalization from different aspects. The book deals with different essential processes of supply chains. The focus of this book is also on the decentralized supply chains to propose the original solutions for independent actors of supply chains.

The parts of the book are well-linked and integrated altogether and offer a holistic and overarching perspective of supply chain digitalization. Hence, readers of this book will benefit extensively from this approach and the intertwined theoretical and applied approach followed when covering various aspects of digitalization of supply chains during global crisis. I am confident that this book will be very popular amongst academics and practitioners. In addition, it will be extremely valuable to both undergraduate and postgraduate students reading for Supply Chain Management. To conclude, this book is a welcome addition. I recommend it highly to anybody interested to the topic of Digitalization of Supply Chains.

Sharareh Taghipour
Ryerson University, Canada

Preface

In 2019, during the last days of the year, a highly infectious virus that causes fatal respiratory illnesses, recognized as COVID19, was reported to the World Health Organization (WHO) by Chinese authorities. On January 30, 2020, the WHO declared the COVID-19 outbreak a global health emergency and On March 11, 2020, the WHO declared COVID-19 a global pandemic. One year later this pandemic has caused the death of near to 2,800,000 people, while infecting near to 128 million across our planet and continue to treat this world.

Apart from being a sanitary crisis, at the economic level, the global pandemic has caused supply chain disruption around the world, causing huge uncertainties in both supply and demand parts of supply chains. On one side, the demand for some products and services has reduced (examples: in the sector of good production the demand for new manufactured automobiles; in the sector of service the demand for hotels). On the other side, manufacturers around the world are facing shortages of raw materials and parts, because of an interruption in the production, disruptions to transportation and labor shortage. In this context, organizations start to reexamine their production and service systems based on digitization of operations to not only mitigate the risk of a pandemic, but also to build a resilient supply chain, while continuing to reduce costs and maximizing profits with the objective to remain competitive. For example, many companies and restaurants during the global pandemic integrated, easy-to-deploy robotics solutions to respect social distancing while continuing their business.

The literature of supply chain management can be classified into two types of supply chain: centralized and decentralized supply chains. In centralized supply chains new technology, which theoretically optimizes supply chain performance, is already adapted. On the other side, in decentralized supply chains, each member is a separate economic entity that makes its operational decisions independently. The question that can be asked is how the decentralized actors can integrate new technologies to compete in a risky environment such as a global pandemic.

The advent of new technologies, whatever the type of supply chains, allows them to complete their processes faster, more flexible and efficient. These technologies will transform the traditional way of manufacturing and providing services. Following there exist some examples how this technology can offer competitive advantages to industries.

- **Reducing tasks without added value or human contact in a pandemic:** Cobots (collaborative robots) or AGV (Automated Guided Vehicles) can assist operators or employees in strenuous, dangerous or without any added value tasks.
- **Improving productivities of humans:** Augmented reality can help operators to see digital instruction for assembling complex components. MES (Manufacturing Execution System) can also be used to supervise machines and operators with full traceability of manufacturing information according to the continuous improvement initiatives.
- **Improving productivities of machines:** Big Data in mass production can be used to collect and analyze the data in order to optimize the productivity of machines. Industrial Internet Sensors allow to respond to the need to supervise the productivities of machines.
- **Optimizing the available capacity:** Digital Twin, which is the virtual representation of a product, can be used for the design, simulation, monitoring, optimization or maintenance of the product.
- **Reducing the time of research and development:** Additive manufacturing, in addition to Digital Twin, can be used to accelerate the time of production of prototypes by avoiding designing and manufacturing the molds.
- **Reducing the cycle time:** Process Simulation Software is used to find optimal conditions for an examined process. Additive manufacturing, in addition to Digital Twin also can help to reduce the cycle time.
- **Reducing inventories:** Scanners of the points of sales can assist to compute the level inventories and to improve demand forecasting.
- **Reducing no-quality:** The quality can be improved by using the intelligent robots. Augmented reality or Cobots can assist the operators in their operations.

The purpose of this book is to provide the new and innovative ways of adoption of new technologies such as collaborative robots, manufacturing execution system, augmented reality, big data, digital twin, mobile technologies, etc. in decentralized supply chains in a global pandemic.

- Digital transformation strategies in supply chains
- Inter-organizational information sharing in decentralized supply chains
- Digital supply chain using decentralized block chains
- The influence of digitalization on supply chain sustainable performance
- Electronic forecasting in decentralized supply chains
- A digital supply chain for managing the disruption risks and resilience
- Digitalization to reduce tasks without added value or human contact in a pandemic
- Reducing tasks without added value or human contact in a pandemic
- Improving productivities of humans-machines using intelligent solutions
- Digital supply chain twin to simulate and optimize the time and capacity while avoiding the risk
- Industry 4.0 technologies and their applications in fighting COVID-19 pandemic
- Secure information sharing in digital supply chains
- Measuring supply chain performance of a digital supply chain network
- A theoretical framework of digital supply chain integration
- Digital information at the intersection of Big Data Analytics and supply chain management

A DESCRIPTION OF THE TOPIC IN THE WORLD TODAY

Efforts to address supply chain digitalization are scattered across a few aspects. Reviewing the existing literature on supply chain digitalization reveals that only focus is on a single aspect of supply chain digitalization. (Shiyong et al., 2016) explains in his book that Industry 4.0 places a three-pronged focus on integration across the entire value chain:

- **Horizontal integration:** Throughout the value chain, people and machines communicate in concrete time immediately to the operations center. Organizations are also connected to each other, fostering partnerships and industrial networks.
- **Vertical integration:** The piloting of systems and subsystems through the reconfiguration and flexibility of production networks.
- **Time integration:** Throughout the product lifecycle, connected objects record product usage, design data and manufacturing.

Ridha Derrouiche and Samir Lamouri (2020) believe that the gradual shift to Supply Chain 4.0 fulfills the promise of a more autonomous and flexible enterprise for organizations seeking productivity. The organizations are investing in new mechanisms for automation and empowerment of their means of production. Big data, connected objects and artificial intelligence are welcomed at all levels of the production chain. Thus, Ridha Derrouiche, and Samir Lamouri assume that the transition to digitalization offers organizations new potential in terms of reducing production costs, inventory management, time savings, among others. Thanks to an optimal tuning of Industry 4.0 solutions (connected objects, collection, and analysis of field data, etc.), companies can now place the customer at the heart of the supply chain by adjusting production to their needs.

Deniaud et al. (2020) focus on the Transition 4.0 strategy that each link in the supply chain must designate in order to fully maximize it. In this situation, they offer a decision support tool that agrees to prioritize and determine the growth strategy to adopt for a change to Supply Chain 4.0. Fel et al. (2020) question the role of Industry 4.0 in the repatriation of production to France. They prove that the growth of Industry 4.0 is angry to encourage relocations and recognize both the suitable factors and the obstacles to this movement. They similarly analyze the effects of such an action on the supply chain.

A DESCRIPTION OF THE TARGET AUDIENCE

Digitalization of supply chain is the only key success for companies during a global pandemic. In particular, the book provides a comprehensive review and understanding of how these techniques and principles can contribute to the effective and efficient digitalize the supply chains and more especially during global crisis.

A DESCRIPTION OF THE EACH CHAPTER

Accelerating the Digitalization of the Supply Chain: An Empirical Research About the COVID-19 Crisis

Digitalization defined as an enabler by leveraging digital technologies, is a new stage in the organization of supply chains. This concept, which is a new evolution of the concept of Industry 4.0, first defined by Shiyong et al. (2016), took on importance after the Covid-19 pandemic. During this pandemic, humanity is experiencing one of the greatest crises in the world, affecting all sectors of the global economy. The

Covid-19 has disrupted world trade, resulting in a blockage of the supply chain and subsequently losses of the competitive advantages. Our study proposes ways to improve the digitalization of supply chains during global crises. After a survey conducted on a sample of 49 logistics professionals, we find that today it has become necessary to accelerate the deployment of an advanced digitalization of the supply chain as a whole. In order to do that, first we need to study the fluctuations in supply and demand during crises, in order to understand the general effect of pandemics on the supply chain. Thereafter, it is necessary to adopt and improve the appropriate IT systems, more especially to digitalize the interaction between buyers and suppliers. This will change the purchasing contracts, because the buyers have more transparency on the situation of their suppliers, since access to information is easier in a digital environment, where everything is connected. However, due to the problems encountered during pandemic crises throughout history, especially the Covis-19 crisis, and in today's computerized world, it is needed to transform the supply chains towards 100% digital. Especially with the arrival of the 5G, digitization will become a necessity in the near future. Finally, researchers need to conduct research on the security of digital tools, as well as the connection of company networks and information systems, because we are on a part of the company that contains sensitive information that can be used by a company's competitors to eliminate it.

Digitalization to Reduce Tasks Without Added Value or Human Contact in a Pandemic

Digitalization is that the use of technological innovations within the business context with a major influence on product, services, business processes, sales channels, and supply channels. The associated potential advantages include, among others, increased sales or productivity, innovations in price creation, and new sorts of client interaction (Urbach & Ahlemann, 2019, p.7). Value as digitalization and sensible automation progress, several can see their jobs altered. Advances in automation and digital technologies can mean that individuals can more and more work side by side with robots, sensible automation and artificial intelligence. Humans and machines combined will generate additional price than either one alone. Supply chains area unit a backbone of economies and society, and mostly act with nature. The interactions in these supply chain ecosystems area unit terribly advanced and triggered by mutual interrelations and feedbacks between supply chains, nature, society, and also the economy (Christopher and Towill 2000). In a dynamic environment, supply chains are networks of independent firms. The aim of supply chain management is to bring these businesses together in a fast-paced environment (Taghipour & Frayret, 2011). Supply chain management is important for managing the use of resources and information by using coordination mechanisms to organize independent companies (Taghipour, 2014). The speedy expansion of Internet provides the world enormous achievements both in social and economic life in the twenty-first century. Digitalization has an influential impact on the economy. The Supply chains and operations management community has created impressive methodical fundamentals, techniques and tools for sustainability and digitalization of Supply chains for the last three decades. The COVID-19 pandemic has exposed a series of novel challenges for Supply chains and operations management which lead to an understudied research and academic area (Ivanov, D; 2020). Digitalization plays a vital role on recent competitive market and it is linked with the utilization of digital technologies to alter business model and to convey new value-producing opportunities to the modern business environment in an aim to move towards a digital business (Mihardjo et al. 2019).Isolation measures executed universally to contain the outbreak have hit financial activity difficult, whereas the sharp disintegration in business and consumer confidence, compounded by recent financial market turmoil, will proceed to decrease optional spending and investment. One major uncertainty concerns the duration of the current outbreak and the plausibility of further waves. The east to west development of the epicenter of the emergency which has immersed Europe and presently parts of the US, highlights how nations are a distinctive stage in managing with the outbreak, meaning that supply and demand issues in specific markets could have long tail impacts for worldwide businesses. Global enterprises are facing supply chain issues, consequently potentially higher operational costs, lower inventory and the prospects of lower demand will be reluctant to disburse resources and time to connect in M&A and financing activities, predominantly if valuations of targets remain high. Digitalization of supply chain could be a way that companies can start to strategize and accomplish trade strength against supply chain disturbance. In this context, enormous information analytics can assist firms in streamlining their supplier selection process, cloud-computing is progressively being used to encourage and manage supplier connections and logistics and shipping forms can be significantly improved through automation and the internet of things.

The coronavirus (COVID-19) outbreak depicts that pandemics and epidemics can badly bring havoc on supply chains around the world (Queiroz et al. 2020). The aim of this chapter is to look at the Digitalization to reduce tasks without added value or human contact in a pandemic.

Digital, Decentralized Supply Chain and Its Implication for B2B Marketing: A Case Study From the Indian Medical Equipment Industry

The COVID19 pandemic has created huge disruptions in the business world. The world economy has almost stopped functioning and when it bounces back, it will be a new normal. One of the business functions that will change in size, shape and character are the global supply chains. In a flat, globalized world, supply chains were located in areas that provided cost advantage to companies. China, for example, was a major supply hub of global economy in the pre-COVID world. Companies now realize that concentrating supply chains can be a matter of risk in terms of business continuity. Diversification of supply chain risks is happening in two ways- 1) de-centralization in control and configuration and b) digitization including the use of AI-ML (Artificial Intelligence and Machine Learning). In this chapter, I focus on the effects of digitalizing supply chains on B2B marketers. B2B companies are suppliers to all corporations and in a digitalized supply chain, the buyer and seller will face new issues and challenges. Using the case study of an Indian start-up medikabazaar.com (MBR), I show how hospital purchases may change when procurement goes digital and what implications it has for B2B marketers. MBR has created a digital platform for medical supplies in India, thus disrupting the usual process of medical establishments buying from multiple vendors. The study shows that digital, decentralized supply chain will a) significantly impact the purchase of high value medical equipment and b) create both de-intermediation (removal of existing intermediaries from the procurement process) and re-intermediation (introduction of new intermediaries) impacting buyer behaviour and buying process in industrial marketing. It also suggests possible ways existing products and brands can fight back against digital platforms.

Manufacturer Service-Oriented Strategy: A New Source of Competitive Advantage in Homogenous Industrial Markets

The main goal of branding strategies is to help businesses to make a difference in their market. Brand strategy efforts helps companies to grow and develop by gaining more customers and market shares (Keller and Lehmann, 2006). When the market is flourishing, such efforts are not always required. Companies can take advantage of the organic market growth. However, when a market is becoming more saturated or when competition become fiercer, brand strategy efforts are critical. They must be planned judiciously in order to achieve the intended difference in the market.

Compare to consumer brands in a B2C market, manufacturers in a B2B market have less opportunities to make the difference over their competitors. Manufacturers are intrinsically production and efficiency oriented. Their quest to gain competitive advantages is usually accomplished through production efficiency or in other words by producing the best product while optimizing the use of resources. In the context of manufacturers, or producers of parts and equipment that may be marketed by another company, competitive advantages generated by production efficiency are usually translated into price driven competitiveness. And all functions of the value chain participate actively toward this endeavor. In short, the manufacturer able to produce a suitable enough product at the best price should have more chance to win more market share.

However, after an era of expansion, several manufacturer markets could be considered becoming homogenous. In such market conditions, manufacturers have difficulties to achieve competitive advantages as customers are not able to differentiate one manufacturer offer from the other. Manufacturers need to acknowledge this situation and focus on areas of the value chain where a sustainable difference can be achieved. This article will introduce a new brand strategy by first analyzing theoretically and through a qualitative research conducted in the printing industry in China how manufactures in homogenous market develop competitive advantages and then propose a change in posture from producer to service provider in order to help building suitable competitive advantages. In order to be sustainable, the implications of this change and recommendation for further research will be proposed.

The Influence of Digitization on Supply Chain Sustainable Performance

An effort has been made in this work to explore the importance of digitization in the context of supply chain management. Specifically, the work focuses in highlighting the influence of digitization on supply chain sustainable performance. The following are the objectives: to study the components of a company's supply chain; to understand the problems or issues; to understand how digitization technologies work; how digitization can help, components of a company's supply chain, in achieving sustainable objectives.

Semantically-Enhanced Web Service for Global Supply Chain Disruption Management

Recent coronavirus pandemic has now unleashed a global supply chain crisis across a huge number of organizations, stemming from a lack of understanding and flexibility of the multiple layers of their global supply chains and a lack of diversification in their sourcing strategies. One of the technical options to mitigate pandemic is to automate business processes by which heterogeneous data integration is encouraged. The convergence of semantic web with service-oriented computing is manifested by Semantic Web Services technology. It addresses the major challenge of automated, interoperable, and meaningful coordination of Web Service composition in industrial applications – such as apparel business. Automatic service composition may dramatically improve development efficiency of web service applications. This chapter proposes an approach to automatically process Semantic Service Composition (SSC) using Description Logics (DLs) to provide well-defined semantics. Also, this chapter explains the role of ontologies in the architecture of the semantic web.

Security Issues of Blockchain-Based Information System to Manage Supply Chain in Global Crisis

Global supply chain crisis management has become increasingly crucial for tackling unusual incidents (e.g., natural disaster, terrorism, pandemic). While crisis management has focused on a few organizations involved in supply chain operations (manufacturers, governments, carriers, and the consuming public), it has primarily received a functional focus. Due to their decentralized network structure, supply chains are prone to suffer from disruptive events solved by supply chain crisis management. This chapter presents the blockchain technologies' possibilities and limits used in an integrated IoT-based information system architecture. The chapter describes how the scalability limits of blockchain technology affect the proposed architecture performance that uses it. Also, the chapter presents a review of the academic literature, pointing out how some solutions use a centralization process to improve response time and security of the blockchain-based architecture. Finally, the chapter provides a classification of security threat models, which consider by blockchain protocols in IoT networks.

The Perspectives of Supply Chain Management Using Natural Knowledge From 3D Blockchain Technologies and Avatar-Based and Geographic Information Systems (GIS)

The Production supply chain consists of many participants like Producer, Consumer (people who buy the product and consume them), Wholesalers and Retailers. This system consists of many levels of mediator parties as well which have different policies of commission. Due to the difference in these policies, the Producers do not get their fair share of price. Due to the varying prices, consumers also suffer as they do not get the right quality of product for the right price (Youssef Tliche, Atour Taghipour, Beatrice Canel, 2020). There are no central records maintained regarding the transactions between the participants which could lead to many serious problems. To tackle the above-mentioned issues, we need a holistic approach which can provide solutions to most of the above issues. Here, Blockchain based solution can be used to achieve: Traceability (we can trace the whereabouts of the product, origin of the product, etc.), Transparency (so that a sense of trust is achieved), Fairness (by removing the intermediaries), Assurance of products safety and pricing (so that nobody has to bear the loss).

A CONCLUSION OF HOW THE BOOK IMPACTS

The book is written to cover the interests of a wide variety of audiences ranging from academic researchers, students and practitioners. It features numerous methods and technics for the digitalization of supply chains.

This work is an excellent book that pool together the literature related to digitalization of supply chains, and presents some new methods and algorithms as well. This book is clearly written and makes good use of tables and diagrams to illustrate the digitalization of supply chains.

I recommend this book for a variety of audiences: professors, researchers, students and practitioners who are interested to obtain a good understanding of the current state of digitalization of supply chains and to implement them in the service and goods industries.

REFERENCES

Christopher, M., & Towill, D. R. (2000). Supply chain migration from lean and functional to agile and customised. *Supply Chain Management*, *5*(4), 206–213. doi:10.1108/13598540010347334

Deniaud, I., Marmier, F., & Michalak, J. L. (2020). Méthodologie et outil de diagnostic 4.0: Définir sa stratégie de transition 4.0 pour le management de la chaîne logistique. *Logistique & Management*, *28*(1), 4–17. doi:10.1080/12507970.2019.1693914

Derrouiche, R., & Lamouri, S. (2020). *Supply Chain 4.0*. Academic Press.

Fel, F., Cayla, J., & Carbone, V. (2020). L'industrie 4.0 peut-elle favoriser une relocalisation de la production en France? *Logistique & Management*, *28*(1), 18–28. doi:10.1080/12507970.2019.1683477

Ivanov, D. (2020). Predicting the impacts of epidemic outbreaks on global supply chains: A simulation-based analysis on the coronavirus outbreak (COVID-19/SARS-CoV-2) case. *Transportation Research Part E, Logistics and Transportation Review*, *136*, 101922. doi:10.1016/j.tre.2020.101922 PMID:32288597

Keller, K. L., & Lehmann, D. R. (2006). Brands and branding: Research findings and future priorities. *Marketing Science*, *25*(6), 740–759. doi:10.1287/mksc.1050.0153

Mihardjo, L., Sasmoko, S., Alamsjah, F., & Elidjen, E. (2019). Digital leadership role in developing business model innovation and customer experience orientation in industry 4.0. *Management Science Letters*, *9*(11), 1749–1762. doi:10.5267/j.msl.2019.6.015

Queiroz, M. M., Ivanov, D., Dolgui, A., & Wamba, S. F. (2020). Impacts of epidemic outbreaks on supply chains: Mapping a research agenda amid the COVID-19 pandemic through a structured literature review. *Annals of Operations Research*, 1–38. PMID:32836615

Shiyong, W. (2016). Implementing smart factory of industrie 4.0: An outlook. *International Journal of Distributed Sensor Networks*, *12*(1). doi:10.1155/2016/3159805

Taghipour, A. (2014). Improving the Plan of a Manufacturing Network with Non-Integrated Business Units. *International Journal of Applied Logistics*, *5*(2), 1–11. doi:10.4018/ijal.2014040101

Taghipour, A., & Frayret, J. M. (2011). A new heuristic search with local optimization to manage a supply chain. *Meta*, 15.

Tliche, Y., Taghipour, A., & Canel-Depitre, B. (2020). An improved forecasting approach to reduce inventory levels in decentralized supply chains. *European Journal of Operational Research*, *287*(2), 511–527. doi:10.1016/j.ejor.2020.04.044

Urbach, N., Ahlemann, F., Böhmann, T., Drews, P., Brenner, W., Schaudel, F., & Schütte, R. (2019). The impact of digitalization on the IT department. *Business & Information Systems Engineering*, *61*(1), 123–131. doi:10.100712599-018-0570-0

Acknowledgment

The editor would like to acknowledge the help of all the people involved in this project and, more specifically, to the authors and reviewers that took part in the review process. Without their support, this book would not have become a reality.

First, the editor would like to thank each one of the authors for their contributions. Our sincere gratitude goes to the chapter's authors who contributed their time and expertise to this book.

Second, the editor wishes to acknowledge the valuable contributions of the reviewers regarding the improvement of quality, coherence, and content presentation of chapters. Most of the authors also served as referees; we highly appreciate their double task.

Atour Taghipour
Normandy University, France

Chapter 1
Accelerating the Digitalization of the Supply Chain:
An Empirical Research About COVID-19 Crisis

Mohammed Merimi
Faculty of International Business, Normandy University, France

Atour Taghipour
Faculty of International Business, Normandy University, France

ABSTRACT

The chapter proposes ways to improve the digitalization of supply chains during global crises. After a survey conducted on a sample of 49 logistics professionals, the authors find that today it has become necessary to accelerate the deployment of an advanced digitalization of the supply chain as a whole. Due to the problems encountered during pandemic crises throughout history, especially the COVID-19 crisis, and in today's computerized world, it is needed to transform the supply chains towards 100% digital. In order to do that, first the authors need to study the fluctuations in supply and demand during crises in order to understand the general effect of pandemics on the supply chain. Thereafter, it is necessary to adopt and improve the appropriate IT systems, especially to digitalize the interaction between buyers and suppliers. This will change the purchasing contracts because the buyers have more transparency on the situation of their suppliers since access to information is easier in a digital environment where everything is connected.

DOI: 10.4018/978-1-7998-6874-3.ch001

INTRODUCTION

The Coronavirus is a reminder of the globalization of the outsourcing of activities, the development of collaborative models (Taghipour, 2009), customer and supplier integration (Mbiatem et al., 2018), the continuous search for competitiveness, and the development and research of new technologies. This made the Supply Chain at the same time the real engine for companies, a distinguishing factor face to face of their customers and one of their greatest risks in case of weakness. The COVID-19 pandemic is a health crisis, but its consequences are also economic.

Today's supply chains are highly sophisticated and innovative and are critical to the competitiveness of many organizations. But their global correlations and interactions make them increasingly fragile on a scale of risk, with more potential fading points and a smaller margin of error to reduce business disruptions and delays (Taghipour, 2014a). Efforts over the years to optimize the supply chain to reduce costs, decrease inventory and increase asset utilization have mainly squeezed out the room and flexibility needed to control delays and disruptions. The COVID-19 pandemic crisis demonstrated that many companies are unaware of how fragile they are to global shocks of abundance because of the relationships within their supply chain.

Advantageously, new technologies and techniques are making their approach, greatly improving visibility and clarity throughout the supply chain and promoting greater resilience and agility, without the collective costs associated with traditional risk management approaches (Ren et al., 2016). The traditional view of the linear supply chain and its improvement for organizations is giving way to digital supply networks, where functional silos are broken down within the enterprise and all parties are connected to the entire supply network, allowing for complete visibility, responsiveness, participation, agility and improvement (Taghipour, 2014b). Increasingly, these digital supply networks are generated and created in order to anticipate disruptions and reorganize themselves appropriately to mitigate their impact.

In 2016, a study conducted by GT Nexus and Capgemini revealed that 70% of governments had approached projects related to digital change. The document states that by 2021, the general use of data between suppliers, companies and customers will have evolved considerably. Indeed, the field of supply chain has the characteristic of being strongly divided. Both from the actors' point of view (different providers) and from the IT point of view (each one works with its own application). Excellent communication will therefore allow for simplification and fluidity of the information sharing between the different parties as well as the logistic flows (Tliche et al., 2019). Particularly thanks to techniques that allow real-time monitoring of processes. Thus, what brings us to know the supply problems in connection with the covid-19 crisis, and why it is necessary to accelerate the digitalization of the supply chain?

In this chapter, first, we will review the literature, then present and analyze the results of our questionnaire, the recommendations, and limitations of the study.

Background

Today's world has faced unprecedented pandemics (Larson and Nigmatulina, 2009), which have had serious negative outcomes on the company as a whole, but also on the efficiency of operations and supply chain (SC) management (OSCM) business models. Such impacts agitators frequently produce ripple effects (Ivanov 2020). While supply chains around the world have already been suffering from pandemics and epidemics, they have recently been severely impacted by an unprecedentedly disruptive pandemic, namely Covid-19 (Boccaletti et al. 2020), which is being investigated as a new type of coronavirus that is highly contagious with destructive consequences (Ivanov and Dolgui 2020).

1. Supply Chain and the Pandemic

a. Pandemic Covid-19

The pandemic with the new coronavirus SARS-COV (coronaviral disease 2019; formerly 2019-nCoV), an outbreak originally focused in Hubei Province in the People's Republic of China, has spread worldwide. On January 30, 2020, the WHO Emergency Committee reported a global health emergency based on increased case notification rates in China and other countries. Contingency detection rates are increasing daily and can be monitored in real time on the official Johns Hopkins University website. As of mid-February 2020, China is bearing the heavy burden of mortality, while the impact in other Asian countries, North America, and Europe remains low so far.

Coronaviruses are single stranded, enveloped, positive RNA viruses that infect not only humans but also animals. Coronaviruses were first known in 1966 by Bynoe and Tyrell, who noticed the viruses in patients with common colds.

Although the COVID-19 pandemic is primarily considered a health crisis, it is also an economic crisis. In the U.S., the industrial supply system has evolved over the years from a local base to a global network of relatively few multinational companies. The evolution of the COVID-19 health crisis proves the vulnerability of the entire industrial and food supply system, offering researchers little opportunity to explore this system and its underlying assets in real time.

COVID-19 has brought the industrial and food supply chain into the public arena as organizations and consumers in the supply chain respond to the health crisis. Consumers have stockpiled products in the face of real and anticipated deficiencies

(Hall et al., 2020). Within the supply chain, sudden changes in production-related regulations and demand have led to business disruptions, such as changes in working conditions in processing plants and hampering productivity (Hall et al., 2020; Corkery and Yaffe-Bellany, 2020; Glaa et al., 2014).

b. Supply Chain Problems during the Pandemic

The negative impacts of COVID-19 on the supply chain have alarmed academics (Govindan et al. 2020) and industry experts (such as Deloitte; Forbes; Business Insider; Fortune; Harvard Business Review; Institute for Supply Chain Management). The COVID-19 epidemic is already having a large-scale impact on OSCM. Fortune (2020), in an article published on February 21, 2020, reported that 94% of Fortune 1000 companies were facing Supply Chain disruptions due to the pandemic (Covid-19). As for Deloitte (2020), the publication argued that the full impact of the epidemic on the supply chain remained unexplored. Past pandemics show valuable information regarding supply chains. The World Economic Forum - WEF (2020) highlighted the need for organizations and companies to reorient and adapt their supply chains to meet future business challenges. For example, the short-term priority may be "movement of workers" and "transport and production", while in the long term, methods, strategies, and capabilities related to data sharing and digital readiness would be implemented and developed for oversight committees (World Economic Forum - WEF 2020).

In a situation where serious disruptions, such as the global or partial closure of craftsmen, airports operating with severe restrictions, and a lack of medical equipment and supplies, are consigned to the universal supply chains (Ivanov, 2020), many industries such as electronics, automotive, consumer goods, medical equipment, etc., have been affected. Indeed, as China is known as the factory of the world, the disruption of supply chains due to Covid-19 around the world started in China before spreading elsewhere. The significant impact of this challenge requires strong supply chain resilience actions and strategies (Pournader et al. 2020). On the other hand, OSCM responses to such pandemics should include making universal supply chains readier and more integrated for digitalization (World Eco- nomic Forum-WEF 2020). Digitization of scientific committees could strengthen and improve quality in the face of pandemic-related disruptions by increasing the flexibility of the model for managing ecological phenomena (Ivanov, 2020) under any circumstances.

Thus, according to (Aldrighetti et al. 2019) it is fair to say that recent improvements have been made in the literature regarding supply chain response. Thus, as well as pandemic operations (Paul and Venkateswaran 2020; El-Nemr et al., 2021), according to (Ivanov 2020), the consequences of epidemics on the supply chain need to be adequately studied and analyzed. To this end, operational management (OM) and operational research (OR) approaches such as complexity and network theories, e.g. Markov chains, Bayesian networks, ecological modeling, network theory (Li and Zobel 2020), also simulation (discrete event simulation, agent-based simulation, system dynamics) (Ivanov 2020), as well as optimization (strong optimization, random programming, mixed linear programming, heuristics, dynamic programming) (Amiri-Aref et al. 2019). All these approaches could bring interesting and relevant elements to address this complex epidemic situation. On the other hand, empirical theories such as dynamic capacities, contingency theory, resource-based visions (RBV), organizational information processing theory (OIPT) with applications to resilience, according to (Dubey et al. 2020) could be used in parallel with OM/OR approaches to examine the impacts of epidemics on the supply chain.

2. Digitalization of the Supply Chain

Within the company, the impacts of digitalization are not limited to the configuration of the supply chain. They also affect business lines and know-how. Within the company, the principle is the same: new forms of organization are being put in place, with the necessary existence of new players guaranteeing the availability of big data practices, data storage and IT architecture. This evolution is the result of changes within the enterprise's ecosystem.

a. The Need for Digitalization in the Supply Chain

Companies are now facing increased globalized competition. To remain competitive and efficient, the digitalization of the supply chain has become mandatory. The benefits and advantages of digital technology for the supply chain are no longer in dispute. The digital supply chain goes far beyond the mere concept: conclusive results are multiplying. For example, Nexans (world leader in cable solutions) is promoting its range of TMS (Transportation Management System) adoption with several objectives: risk control, cost reduction and process automation.

The vast majority of organizations say they are experimenting, to varying degrees, a digital modification of their supply chain, but only a few of them believe they have arrived at a good destination. The wave is thick, of those that shake up the ancient models. According to the "Panorama of Digitalization 2019-2020", carried out by the Supply Chain and Logistics Association (Aslog), 90% of companies are exploring a "direct to Customer" model to cope with the arrival of new competitors, and among them, 40% have already opted for an omnichannel rather than multi-channel approach.

While more complex to implement, it is also the approach that best improves the customer experience and leads to the immediate corollary of this observation:

88% of the companies surveyed see their supply chain evolve, and more than 6 out of 10 say they are experiencing "strong impacts" in areas such as production, warehousing, transport, or customer service.

On the other hand, according to (Jim Kilpatrick & Lee Barter; 2020) "While COVID-19 may be the trigger for organizations to rethink their global supply chain management model and strategy and advance the adoption of digital supply network models and capabilities, short-term measures will be required to address the immediate challenge.

b. Supply Chain and Industry 4.0

Ridha Derrouiche & Samir Lamouri (2020) believe that the gradual shift to Supply Chain 4.0 fulfills the promise of a more autonomous and flexible enterprise for organizations seeking productivity. These organizations are investing in new mechanisms for automation and empowerment of their means of production. Big data connected objects and artificial intelligence are welcomed at all levels of the production chain. Thus, Ridha Derrouiche & Samir Lamouri assume that the transition to digitalization offers organizations new potential in terms of reducing production costs, inventory management, time savings, among others. Thanks to an optimal tuning of Industry 4.0 solutions (connected objects, collection, and analysis of field data, etc.), companies can now place the customer at the heart of the supply chain by adjusting production to their needs.

(Shiyong et al., 2016) explains in his book that Industry 4.0 places a three-pronged focus on integration across the entire value chain:

- Horizontal integration: throughout the value chain, people and machines communicate in concrete time immediately to the operations center. Organizations are also connected to each other, fostering partnerships and industrial networks.
- Vertical integration: the piloting of systems and subsystems through the reconfiguration and flexibility of production networks.
- Time integration: Throughout the product lifecycle, connected objects record product usage, design data and manufacturing.

(Deniaud et al., 2020) focus on the Transition 4.0 strategy that each link in the supply chain must designate in order to fully maximize it. In this situation, they offer a decision support tool that agrees to prioritize and determine the growth strategy to adopt for a change to Supply Chain 4.0. (Fel et al. 2020) question the role of Industry 4.0 in the repatriation of production to France. They prove that the growth of Industry 4.0 is angry to encourage relocations and recognize both the suitable factors and the obstacles to this movement. They similarly analyze the effects of such an action on the supply chain.

EMPIRICAL RESEARCH

Methodology

We chose a quantitative analysis methodology in this study. The data is collected through a Google Forms survey and distributed on LinkedIn in order to target professionals in the logistics field of business.

This analysis will help us get better insights on this field of business, and also allow us to identify the problems, and the behaviors of organizations facing the destabilization of their supplies after the lockdown.

After data collection, we will proceed with the descriptive statistics analysis of the variables, this analysis will allow us to identify several relevant information and answer our problematic.

And finally, we will analyze different solutions proposals. These proposals will be based on a scientific reflection and combine answers from our questionnaire and elements from articles published in this field, in particular the article "Impacts of epidemic outbreaks on supply chains: mapping a research agenda amid the COVID-19 pandemic through a structured literature review".

Objectives of our Study

The objective of our questionnaire is to find out the negative effects of the pandemic on companies, and how they have tried to solve these problems. Finally, to know what the digitalization of the Supply Chain allows to bring in terms of solutions that ensure the stability of the stocks of the company during the crisis. In order to achieve our objective, we have elaborated a list of short and clear questions addressed to professionals in the logistics business, as well as to all the people in the company who have experienced the stock movements during the first lockdown and de-confinement, in order to define our problem and try to propose appropriate solutions.

Results and Analysis

1. Target

In order to make the answers to our questionnaire more relevant and meaningful, we decided to target a socio-professional category that has experienced first-hand the movements of stocks during and after the crisis, but we ended up having answers from professionals who haven't had to deal with the stocks movements directly but had relevant information to provide about how the crisis was managed at their company. After distributing the questionnaire on the social network LinkedIn and sending it to our contacts to answer, we managed to collect 47 answers that seemed significant due to the nature of our target (Table1).

Table 1. Professions

Supply chain professions	**Number of answers**
Buyer	14
Consultant	2
Education	3
Engineer DevOps	1
Export Business Developer	1
Forwarder	2
IT	1
Manager in operations	2
Seller	7
supplier	6
Supply chain	8
Total	**47**

Figure 1. Questioned function in the studied supply chains

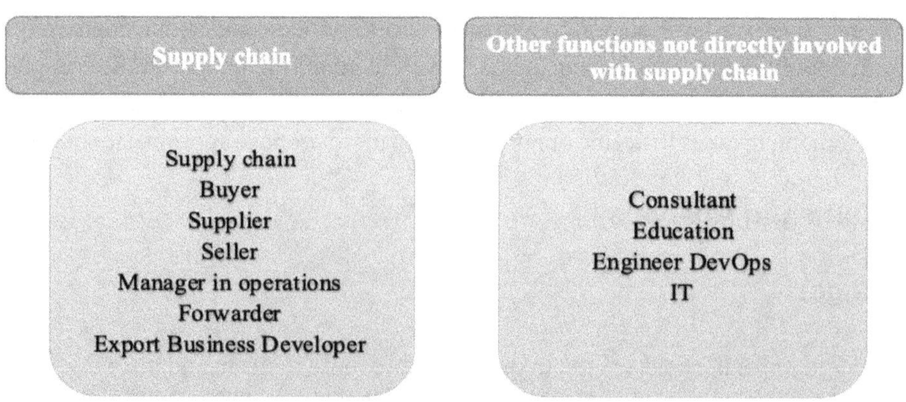

From the table above, we notice that our target is strongly present in the answers with 14 Buyers, 8 in Supply chain, 6 Suppliers, 7 Sellers, 2 Forwarders, 2 Managers in operations and finally Export Business developer with a subtotal of 40 respondents and accounting for 85% of total responses.

In our analysis, we have made a small distinction between jobs that are directly related to logistics and flow management, and jobs that are not directly related to the supply chain (Figure 1).

Based on this distribution, we notice that 85% of our answers come from respondents who have concrete experience in the supply chain field. This will make the obtained answers more relevant to our study.

2. Supply Problems During the First Lockdown

Everyone agrees that the Covid-19 pandemic crisis has disrupted the supply chain, especially at the supply level, this is well expressed by the majority of companies through publications on the web, as well as several articles published, especially the one published by the audit and consulting firm Deloitte on Risk Management and Disruption related to the supply chain. "by Jim Kilpatrick & Lee Barter.

On our part to confirm the existence of the problems and after surveying our target, we had the following results (figure 2).

Figure 2. Supply chain problem

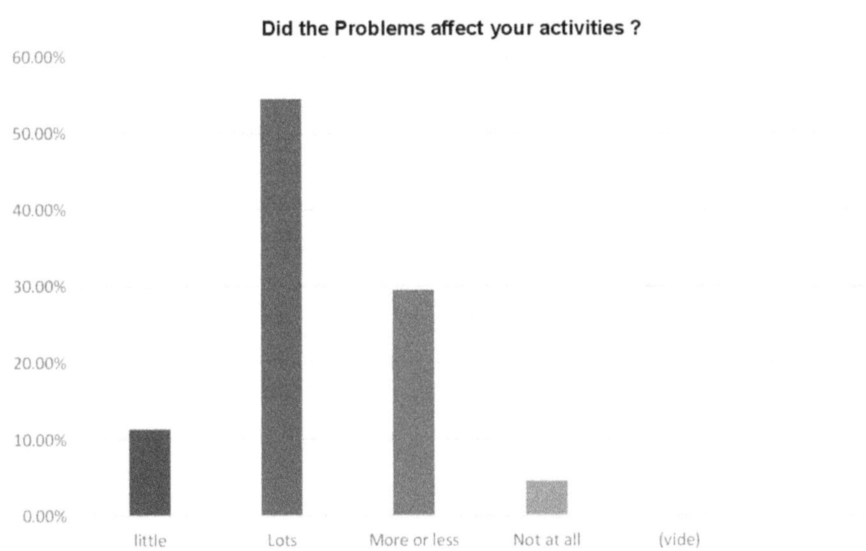

On our part to confirm the existence of the problems and After surveying our target, we had the following results (figure 2).

The majority of responses with a percentage of 87.2% indicate the existence of problems due to the supply chain blockage during and after the first containment. only 12,8% did not have problems during this period.

3. Supply Chain Issues

The majority of respondents (16 answers) have had problems of Delay & Delivery Time, 15 respondents have had a supply & Out-of-stock problems, this means that most of the problems encountered are focused on these issues. but also, we found other problems in the supply chain such as Suppliers problems, production problems, order management, transports costs and customers problems (Table 2).

Table 2. Supply chain issues

Problems	Number of people who have had this problem
Delay & Delivery Time	16
Supply &Out-of-stock	15
Suppliers problems	4
Production problems	2
Order Management	1
Transports Costs	1
Customers problems	2

The majority of respondents (16 answers) have had problems of Delay & Delivery Time, 15 respondents have had a supply & Out-of-stock problems, this means that most of the problems encountered are focused on these issues. but also, we found other problems in the supply chain such as Suppliers problems, production problems, order management, transports costs and customers problems.

The problems of delivery and supply delays are the most frequent problems encountered during and after the lockdown, this is absolutely normal because customers cannot have a visibility on their suppliers that allows them to see production or delivery delays at real time in order to anticipate possible solutions. This brings us back to the connection between the different actors of the supply chain and their performance during crises in general.

4. The Impact of Supply Chain Issues

Through our questionnaire we find that 54.55% of the respondents said that the problems encountered during and after the containment have a great impact on their supply chain, so we have 29% find that these problems are more or less impacting, and the rest see that these problems do not affect their activity very much (Figure 3).

Figure 3. Impact of supply chain problems

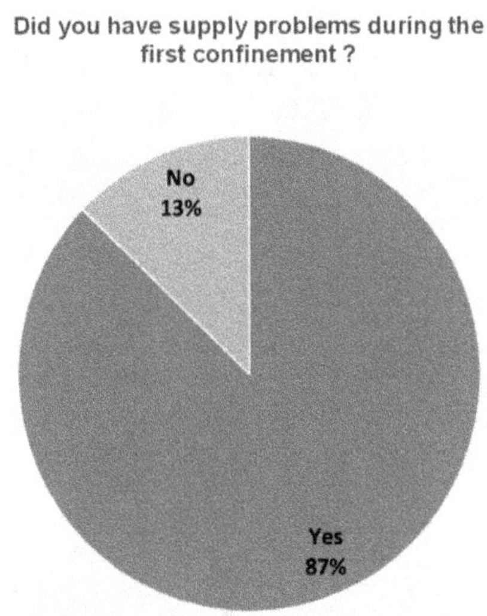

The problems cited by the professionals surveyed in our study, are common problems that always happen in the supply chain, but the Covid-19 pandemic has increased the rate of risk associated with supply chain problems. The traditional method of supply chain management has not been able to mitigate the magnitude of the problems, and the damage is considerable on companies at all levels (Financial, Brand Image, market share ...), hence the need for the generalization of digitalization in the supply chain. This will allow a connection between the different actors of the supply chain and improve visibility, in order to better forecast the possible alternatives (Tliche et al., 2020).

5. Safety Stock was Able to Cover the Disrupted Supply After the First Lockdown

Each year companies adopt strategies to reduce their stocking costs throughout the supply chain, they try to calculate their demand based on previous demand and refine the results to have a safety stock that removes the risk of normal fluctuation related to offer and demand (Lebosse et al., 2017)

With the magnitude of fluctuation of offer and demand related to Covid-19, the majority of the companies do not have the capacities to secure their stocks. the parameters of the security stock which were historically developed several times, have to be revised one more time, especially with the succession of crises and the decrease of the performance of the logistic chain to cope with the different problems which are accentuated with the disruption of the demand and the offer at world level.

We notice that the results of our study, show that the professionals of the Supply chain meet problems to minimize the risks supplies and secure their stocks in front of the demand, we have 47,83% of the respondents stated that their security stocks were not sufficient to counter the fluctuation, against 39,13% their security stocks were able to cope with the disruption in supply (Figure 4).

Figure 4. Safety stock

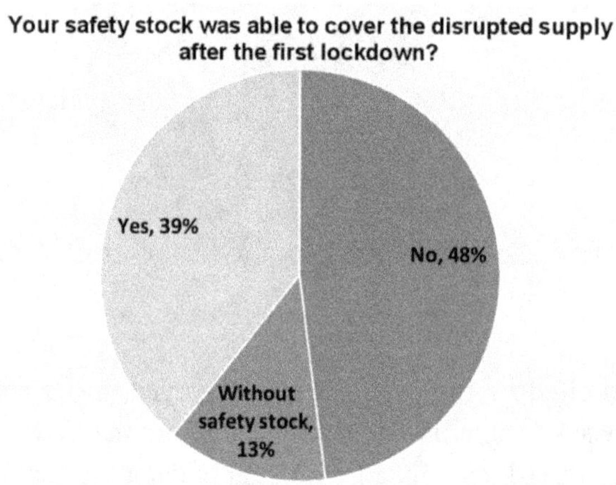

So, professionals are looking for their part to face the different risks by trying to find some solutions that are workarounds only most of the time or have no use at all. the majority of the professionals (74,47%) questioned in our survey did not find solutions for problems encountered during and after Lockdown (Figure 5).

Figure 5. Finding solutions for this situation

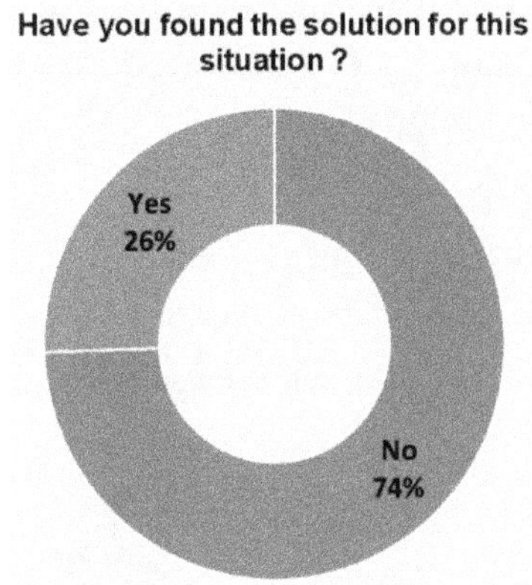

6. Finding Solutions for this Situation

Following paper represents the finding solutions (Table 3)

Table 3. Finding solutions

Finding solutions
Adapting our forecasts to the situation, alerting suppliers to our needs
Buy more each time
Digital P o D
offer alternatives to our customers
Sell the stock to the customer as it was sellable
Special transport
suggesting other products and making commercial offers with our customers
Supplier contracts were well negotiated
There is currently no answer to this question.
There is no answer so far
Upgrade to new packaging and double the sources of supply
We keep in our safety stock what seem essential for our business to keep on going based on our predictions and annual budget.

7. The Usefulness of the Suggested Solutions

27.78% of our respondents consider the solutions to deal with the pandemic as definitive and useful to counter disruptions in the supply chain during the crisis,

27.78% consider that these solutions are not sustainable (Loivet et al., 2020) and are just workarounds, we also find that 22.22% consider that the solutions put in place are somewhat useful and finally 11.11% see that these solutions are not in any way useful for the company (Figure 6).

Figure 6. Usefulness of the suggested solution

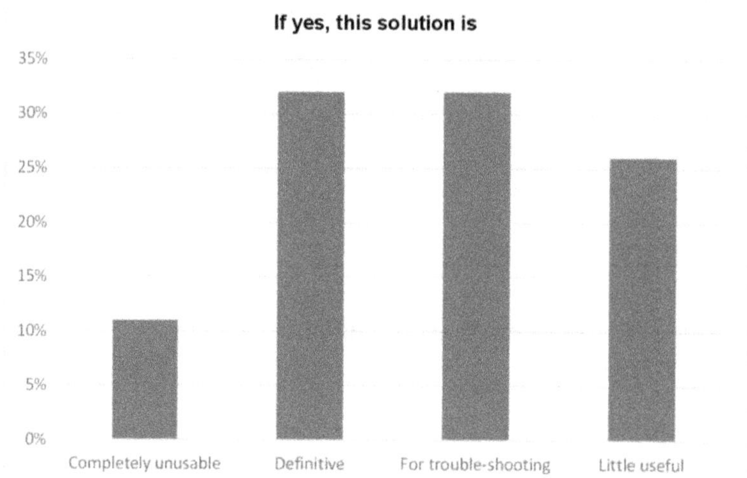

It is noticeable that some of the people surveyed have found solutions to deal with the destabilization of the supply chain, and although they have found these solutions, they judge them to be a little effective or even not useful to solve their problems.

8. Can the Digitalization Supply Chain Offer Solutions to Better Manage the Covid-19 Crisis?

The professionals surveyed in our study affirm with a percentage of 87.23% the usefulness of the supply chain in solving the different problems encountered during the covid-19 crisis. This is quite normal because it offers several advantages, increases performance, and removes loopholes (Figure 7).

Figure 7. Digitalization of supply chain

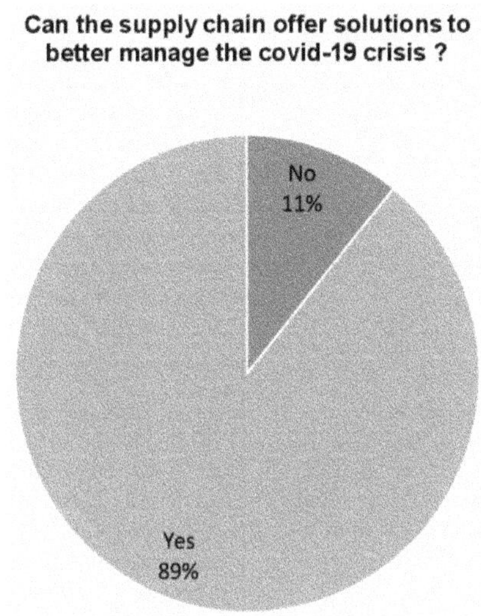

9. How the Digitalization of the Supply Chain can Help Logistics Professionals in Their Work?

Some respondents to our questionnaire have given some answers that we will explain and try to analyze (Table 4).

Table 4. Impact of digitalization of SC during crisis

How digitalization of SC can Help in work during crisis?	Analysis
Blockchain system	Indeed, to talk about the digitalization of the supply chain, we have to discuss the security of information, the servers that will be storing and what someone can hack or take over the system because it can cause huge losses to the company. So, the blockchain That makes it difficult for one user to gain control of, or game, the network.
Digital SCM results in more data, higher planning abilities and shorter reaction times.	The digitization of the SC allows the sharing of data between the actors of the supply chain easily because everyone can access the data in real time, it also offers more capacity for planning and forecasting that helps to minimize the response time to various problems.

continued on following page

Table 4. Continued

How digitalization of SC can Help in work during crisis?	Analysis
Digitalization is good for supply chain, but disruption is more or less in liaison with forecasts accuracy	In fact, forecasts are very important to face the fluctuation of demand and supply, but we must not forget that in order to forecast well it is necessary to consider all the possible variables, so it is necessary to have all the information relative to the market and the suppliers. The digitalization of the supply chain provides these elements in a short time and this makes the reaction of the company and the adaptation of the forecasts to the changing situation faster.
Digitalization is only one component of the supply chain ... It is still in its infancy, and needs to mature... To be followed of course	The digitalization of the Supply chain is in the beginning, this is clear because until now, there are not many research articles on this subject, but with the Covid-19 this subject has become a trend. Let's not forget that almost all companies rely now on information systems, which is the corner stone of future digitalization projects.
Digitalization of the supply chain facilitates access to information, minimizes delays	This is among the advantages of digitalization.
Digitalization would help in our cases of the suppliers were working but the pandemic made them stop, we had to inform our customer as it was direct impact on his production lines	Digitalization allows us to connect customers with their suppliers, which gives us visibility on their production chain to know the delays and to adapt according to changes.
Digitization will give you real time statute on your stock, delivery time and supplier's stock but it can't give you oversight of borders closing unfortunately	A very good point because the macroeconomic environment of companies is very complex. It is difficult to anticipate such measures from governments and their impact on our business.
Digitization will help all the departments of the company to stay in touch and to keep an eye on what they currently have in stock in real time and what is going to miss. So, it will be easier for everyone to anticipate. I think that anticipation is the key in the current context to avoid any disruption due to the virus.	The digitalization of the supply chain allows the anticipation of operational decisions, this is an essential element to avoid problems and reduce their impact.
Even if the digitalization of the logistic chain is in the beginning, it has so far shown an important efficiency	The supply chain has shown its efficiency, but it should be known that there are many areas for improvement such as data security.
I give as an example the Amazon company, which is part of the first generation that uses supply chain digitalization, which allows to reduce delivery times and reduce operating costs in order to reach record production levels.	Amazon is today an example of the efficiency of the supply chain.
It takes less time with digital tools to process orders	Time is money, and digitalization saves time at all levels.
It will give better visibility	
It will make time short, Real time Control	Time is money, and digitalization saves time at all levels, better control of traffic flows.

continued on following page

Table 4. Continued

How digitalization of SC can Help in work during crisis?	Analysis
Makes information accessible	Today living in a world of information, who holds the information holds the power. The digitalization of the supply chain makes access to information easier and makes the company more able to react to challenges.
Timely follow-up of the supply chain and can be automatic follow-up notification to the buyer and supplier when inventory disturbances start to appear	For all logistics professionals, supplier monitoring is a priority because they are responsible for the availability of merchandise, products or raw materials. For this reason, the digitalization of the supply chain for them facilitates several tasks that allow them to negotiate more and have control over suppliers.

SOLUTIONS AND RECOMMENDATIONS

- Accelerating the digitalization of the supply chain, because it allows to have a visibility on the suppliers, to gain time, to acquire the information in real time (Taghipour, 2018).
- The need to implement more sophisticated simulation techniques (Currie et al. 2020; Cauhois et al., 2017).
- Optimization of supply chain processes.
- The impact of the covid-19 crisis on the supply chain, in particular on production systems, confirms that the 4.0 industry and digital manufacturing can play a critical role for SC resilience and ripple effect control (Ivanov and Dolgui 2019), because during the crisis, companies that adopt this digital industrial management mode, which is part of Industry 4.0, are best positioned during the pandemic crisis, and in the planning of future recovery processes (Dubey et al. 2019; Ivanov and Dolgui 2020; Ivanov and Das 2020).
- Study the fluctuations in supply and demand during crises to try to understand the general effect of pandemics on the supply chain.
- We need to strengthen the resilience of the supply chain including through increased SC viability (Ivanov and Dolgui 2020).
- Researchers must focus on the digital aspect of the supply chain in order to adopt and improve the use of IT systems.
- Develop new key performance indicators to assess the digitalized supply chain.

- With the digitalization of the supply chain, contracts will change, negotiations will focus on access to supplier information. this engages the theory of trust between customers and suppliers.
- Control stocks, supply, transport, flow of goods.
- Ensure the security and storage of information in servers.
- Planning worldwide scenarios.
- Focus on production schedule agility.
- Update inventory management policy and planning parameters.
- Know and use other sources of supply.
- Explore the extended supply network.
- Use the 20/80 method to focus on flagship products that contain more risk.

LIMITS AND RESEARCH VOICES

Like all research, by bringing together its contributions to the promotion of knowledges, we also make a report on its limitations, which in turn translates into opportunities and leads to be explored by other researchers.

- The first limitation of the empirical part of the study is that a sample of 47 professionals does not allow us to generalize the results obtained for all professionals in the supply chain. So, we suggest that we take a larger sample for further studies, and try to have more time to search and push the target to answer your questionnaire. because in our case it was difficult to get more answers. So, we decided to send messages directly to our targets which took a lot of time. in the future we must plan more time to get more answers.
- The second limit of our work consists in targeting professionals in the supply chain, because there are other targets that can be interesting, especially the members of the management committee, because they are the ones who plan the long-term strategies according to the challenges and problems encountered.
- The third limitation is that our study does not focus on a specific industry or sector, because the needs may differ according to the nature of the activity carried out, and the digitalization of the supply chain must study in an advanced stage the specificities of each industry or sector, in order to find the most suitable solutions for each situation.

CONCLUSION

Due to the problems encountered during pandemic crises throughout history, especially the Covis-19 crisis, and in today's computerized world, we must start to develop the supply chain towards 100% digital. Especially with the arrival of the 5G, digitization will become a necessity in the near future. Researchers need to conduct research on the security of digital tools, as well as the connection of company networks and information systems, because we are on a part of the company that contains sensitive information that can be used by a company's competitors to eliminate it. So, the question is: "is the digitalization of the supply chain secure?".

REFERENCES

Aldrighetti, R., Zennaro, I., Finco, S., & Battini, D. (2019). Healthcare supply chain simulation with disruption considerations: A case study from Northern Italy. *Global Journal of Flexible Systems Managment, 20*(1), 81–102. doi:10.100740171-019-00223-8

Amiri-Aref, M., Farahani, R. Z., Hewitt, M., & Klibi, W. (2019). Equitable location of facilities in a region with probabilistic barriers to travel. *Transportation Research Part E, Logistics and Transportation Review, 127*, 66–85. doi:10.1016/j.tre.2019.04.010

Boccaletti, S., Ditto, W., Mindlin, G., & Atangana, A. (2020). Modeling and forecasting of epidemic spreading: The case of Covid-19 and beyond. *Chaos, Solitons, and Fractals, 135*, 109794. doi:10.1016/j.chaos.2020.109794 PMID:32288357

Cauchois, R., Taghipour, A., Kang, D., Zoghlami, N., & Abed, M. (2017). Advanced Solutions for a Supply Chain with Stochastic Information. *Journal of Advanced Management Science, 5*(1).

Corkery, M., & Yaffe-Bellany, D. U. S. (2020). Food Supply Chain Is Strained as Virus Spreads. *The New York Times*.

Currie, C. S., Fowler, J. W., Kotiadis, K., Monks, T., Onggo, B. S., Robertson, D. A., & Tako, A. A. (2020). How simulation modelling can help reduce the impact of COVID-19. *Journal of Simulation, 14*(2), 83–97. doi:10.1080/17477778.2020.1751570

Deniaud, I., Marmier, F., & Michalak, J. L. (2020). Méthodologie et outil de diagnostic 4.0: Définir sa stratégie de transition 4.0 pour le management de la chaîne logistique. *Logistique & Management, 28*(1), 4–17. doi:10.1080/12507970.2019.1693914

Derrouiche, R., & Lamouri, S. (2020). *Numéro spécial: Supply Chain 4.0*. Academic Press.

Dubey, A. D., & Tripathi, S. (2020). Analysing the sentiments towards work-from-home experience during covid-19 pandemic. *Journal of Innovation Management, 8*(1), 13–19. doi:10.24840/2183-0606_008.001_0003

Fel, F., Cayla, J., & Carbone, V. (2020). L'industrie 4.0 peut-elle favoriser une relocalisation de la production en France? *Logistique & Management, 28*(1), 18–28. doi:10.1080/12507970.2019.1683477

Govindan, K., Mina, H., & Alavi, B. (2020). A decision support system for demand management in healthcare supply chains considering the epidemic outbreaks: A case study of coronavirus disease 2019 (COVID-19). *Transportation Research Part E, Logistics and Transportation Review, 138*, 101967. doi:10.1016/j.tre.2020.101967 PubMed

Hall, D., Lister, J., & Mercer, H. (2020). *Privatised and Unprepared: The NHS Supply Chain*. Academic Press.

Ivanov, D. (2020). Viable supply chain model: Integrating agility, resilience and sustainability perspectives—lessons from and thinking beyond the COVID-19 pandemic. *Annals of Operations Research*, 1–21. doi:10.100710479-020-03640-6 PMID:32836614

Ivanov, D., & Das, A. (2020). Coronavirus (COVID-19/SARS-CoV-2) and supply chain resilience: A research note. *International Journal of Integrated Supply Management, 13*(1), 90–102. doi:10.1504/IJISM.2020.107780

Ivanov, D., & Dolgui, A. (2020). Viability of intertwined supply networks: Extending the supply chain resilience angles towards survivability. A position paper motivated by COVID-19 outbreak. *International Journal of Production Research, 58*(10), 2904–2915. doi:10.1080/00207543.2020.1750727

Kilpatrick, J., & Barter, L. (2020). *COVID-19: Managing supply chain risk and disruption*. Deloitte.

Larson, R. C., & Nigmatulina, K. R. (2009). Engineering responses to pandemics. *Information, Knowledge, Systems Management, 8*(1-4), 311–339. doi:10.3233/IKS-2009-0145 PMID:20543252

Lebosse, S., Taghipour, A., & Canel-Depitre, B. (2017). Quick response to fluctuations in supply chains: A review. *Journal of Advanced Management Science, 5*(5).

Li, Y., & Zobel, C. W. (2020). Exploring supply chain network resilience in the presence of the ripple effect. *International Journal of Production Economics, 228*, 107693. doi:10.1016/j.ijpe.2020.107693

Loivet, W., Taghipour, A., & Kang, D.-S. (2020). The Rise of Green Supply Chain Management: Between Complexity and Necessity, Journal of Economics. *Business and Management, 8*(1), 1–7.

Mbiatem, J., Taghipour, A., & Canel-Depitre, B. (2018, August). Supplier Selection Approaches for Decision Makers. In *Proceedings of the 8th International Conference on Information Communication and Management* (pp. 108-112). Academic Press.

Nadia, E. N., Beatrice, C. D., & Atour, T. (2021). The Determinants of Hotel Room Rates in Beirut: A Hedonic Pricing Model. *International Journal of Trade, Economics and Finance, 12*(2).

Paul, S., & Venkateswaran, J. (2020). Designing robust policies under deep uncertainty for mitigating epidemics. *Computers & Industrial Engineering, 140*, 106221. doi:10.1016/j.cie.2019.106221

Pournader, M., Kach, A., & Talluri, S. (2020). A review of the existing and emerging topics in the supply chain risk management literature. *Decision Sciences, 51*(4), 867–919. doi:10.1111/deci.12470

Ren, Z., Taghipour, A., & Canel-Depitre, B. (2016, October). Information sharing in supply chain under uncertainty. In *2016 6th International Conference on Information Communication and Management (ICICM)* (pp. 67-71). IEEE. 10.1109/INFOCOMAN.2016.7784217

Shiyong, W. S., Wan, J., Li, D., & Zhang, C. (2016). Implementing smart factory of industry 4.0: An outlook. *International Journal of Distributed Sensor Networks, 12*(1), 3159805. doi:10.1155/2016/3159805

Taghipour, A. (2009). Évaluation de la collaboration dans une chaîne d'approvisionnement. *Revue française de gestion industrielle, 28*(1), 25-42.

Taghipour, A. (2014a, June). Globally improvement of upstream planning in manufacturing networks. In *2014 International Conference on Logistics Operations Management* (pp. 15-19). IEEE. 10.1109/GOL.2014.6887441

Taghipour, A. (2014b). Improving the Plan of a Manufacturing Network with Non-Integrated Business Units. *International Journal of Applied Logistics, 5*(2), 1–11. doi:10.4018/ijal.2014040101

Taghipour, A. (2018). A Contemporary Approach to Plan Independent Logistics Actors. In *Contemporary Approaches and Strategies for Applied Logistics* (pp. 337–364). IGI Global. doi:10.4018/978-1-5225-5273-4.ch014

Tliche, Y., Taghipour, A., & Canel-Depitre, B. (2019). Anticipation of Demand in Supply Chains. In *Hierarchical Planning and Information Sharing Techniques in Supply Chain Management* (pp. 1–45). IGI Global. doi:10.4018/978-1-5225-7299-2.ch001

Tliche, Y., Taghipour, A., & Canel-Depitre, B. (2020). An improved forecasting approach to reduce inventory levels in decentralized supply chains. *European Journal of Operational Research, 287*(2), 511–527. doi:10.1016/j.ejor.2020.04.044

Tyrrell, D. A. J., & Bynoe, M. L. (1966). Cultivation of viruses from a high proportion of patients with colds. *Lancet*, *287*(7428), 76–77. doi:10.1016/S0140-6736(66)92364-6 PMID:4158999

ADDITIONAL READING

Cisneros-Cabrera, S., Pishchulov, G., Sampaio, P., Mehandjiev, N., Liu, Z., & Kununka, S. (2021). An approach and decision support tool for forming Industry 4.0 supply chain collaborations. *Computers in Industry*, *125*, 103391. doi:10.1016/j.compind.2020.103391

Ivanov, D. (2021). Lean resilience: AURA (Active Usage of Resilience Assets) framework for post-COVID-19 supply chain management. *International Journal of Logistics Management*, *ahead-of-print*(ahead-of-print). Advance online publication. doi:10.1108/IJLM-11-2020-0448

Lorentz, H., Aminoff, A., Kaipia, R., & Srai, J. S. (2021). Structuring the phenomenon of procurement digitalisation: Contexts, interventions and mechanisms. *International Journal of Operations & Production Management*, *41*(2), 157–192. doi:10.1108/IJOPM-03-2020-0150

Mahfod, J., Khoury, B., Canel-Depitre, B., & Taghipour, A. (2021). Logistics Providers in Syria Humanitarian Operations. In *Demand Forecasting and Order Planning in Supply Chains and Humanitarian Logistics* (pp. 171–197). IGI Global. doi:10.4018/978-1-7998-3805-0.ch006

Taghipour, A., & Frayret, J. M. (2012). Mutual adjustment search with incentive for supply chain planning coordination. *International Journal of Computer Integrated Manufacturing*, *25*(10), 946–962. doi:10.1080/0951192X.2011.646307

Taghipour, A., & Frayret, J. M. (2013). Dynamic mutual adjustment search for supply chain operations planning co-ordination. *International Journal of Production Research*, *51*(9), 2715–2739. doi:10.1080/00207543.2012.737952

Taghipour, A., & Frayret, J. M. (2013). Coordination of operations planning in supply chains: A review. *International Journal of Business Performance and Supply Chain Modelling*, *5*(3), 272–307. doi:10.1504/IJBPSCM.2013.055729

Tliche, Y., Taghipour, A., & Canel-Depitre, B. (2019). Downstream Demand Inference in decentralized supply chains. *European Journal of Operational Research*, *274*(1), 65–77. doi:10.1016/j.ejor.2018.09.034

Vosooghidizaji, M., Taghipour, A., & Canel-Depitre, B. (2020). Supply chain coordination under information asymmetry: A review. *International Journal of Production Research*, *58*(6), 1805–1834. doi:10.1080/00207543.2019.1685702

Wamba, S. F., & Queiroz, M. M. (2020). Industry 4.0 and the supply chain digitalization: A blockchain diffusion perspective. *Production Planning and Control*, 1–18. doi:10.1080/09537287.2020.1810756

KEY TERMS AND DEFINITIONS

Blockchain: Blockchain technology is most simply defined as a decentralized, distributed ledger that records the provenance of a digital asset.

Data Analysis: Data Analysis is the process of systematically applying statistical and/or logical techniques to describe and illustrate, condense and recap, and evaluate data.

Digitalization: Digitalization is the use of digital technologies to change a business model and provide new revenue and value-producing opportunities; it is the process of moving to a digital business.

Efficient Supply Chain: An efficient supply chain makes the best use of its resources—financial, human, technological or physical. By doing so minimizes costs for materials and packaging and reduces time wastage.

Empirical Research: Empirical research is defined as any research where conclusions of the study is strictly drawn from concretely empirical evidence.

Fifth-Generation Wireless (5G): 5G is the latest iteration of cellular technology, engineered to greatly increase the speed and responsiveness of wireless networks.

Random Programming: The term random refers to any collection of data or information with no determined order, or is chosen in a way that is unknown beforehand.

Resilience: The capability of a strained body to recover its size and shape after deformation caused especially by compressive stress.

Supply Chain: A supply chain is defined as the entire process of making and selling commercial goods, including every stage from the supply of materials and the manufacture of the goods through to their distribution and sale. Successfully managing supply chains is essential to any company hoping to compete.

Chapter 2
Digitalization to Reduce Tasks Without Added Value or Human Contact in a Pandemic

Md. Masudul Hassan
https://orcid.org/0000-0001-9865-1976
Department of Agribusiness, Atish Dipankar University of Science and Technology, Bangladesh

Samira Islam Resmi
https://orcid.org/0000-0001-8081-7229
Department of Agribusiness, Atish Dipankar University of Science and Technology, Bangladesh

ABSTRACT

Digitalization is the use of technological innovations within the business context with a major influence on products, services, business processes, sales channels, and supply channels. The associated potential advantages include, among others, increased sales or productivity, innovations in price creation, and new sorts of client interaction. Global enterprises are facing supply chain issues, and consequently, potentially higher operational costs, lower inventory, and the prospects of lower demand will make them reluctant to disburse resources and time to connect in M&A and financing activities, predominantly if valuations of targets remain high. Digitalization of the supply chain (DSC) could be a way that companies can start to strategize and accomplish trade strength against supply chain disturbance. The main focus of this chapter is that digitalization enhances prosperity without human contact in a pandemic, will alter labor markets, and impacts business models.

DOI: 10.4018/978-1-7998-6874-3.ch002

INTRODUCTION

Digitalization is that the use of technological innovations within the business context with a major influence on product, services, business processes, sales channels, and supply channels. The associated potential advantages include, among others, increased sales or productivity, innovations in price creation, and new sorts of client interaction (Urbach & Ahlemann, 2019, p.7). Value as digitalization and sensible automation progress, several can see their jobs altered. Advances in automation and digital technologies can mean that individuals can more and more work side by side with robots, sensible automation and artificial intelligence. Humans and machines combined will generate additional price than either one alone. Supply chains area unit a backbone of economies and society, and mostly act with nature. The interactions in these supply chain ecosystems area unit terribly advanced and triggered by mutual interrelations and feedbacks between supply chains, nature, society, and also the economy. (Christopher and Towill 2000; Lee 2004;Goldsby *et al.* 2006; Eckstein *et al.* 2015;Gunasekaran *et al.* 2016;Dubey *et al.* 2018; Fadaki *et al.* 2020). In a dynamic environment, supply chains are networks of independent firms. The aim of supply chain management is to bring these businesses together in a fast-paced environment (Taghipour & Frayret, 2011). Supply chain management is important for managing the use of resources and information by using coordination mechanisms to organize independent companies (Taghipour, 2014). The speedy expansion of Internet provides the world enormous achievements both in social and economic life in the twenty-first century. Digitalization has an influential impact on the economy. The Supply chains and operations management community has created impressive methodical fundamentals, techniques and tools for sustainability and digitalization of Supply chains for the last three decades. The COVID-19 pandemic has exposed a series of novel challenges for Supply chains and operations management which lead to an understudied research and academic area (Ivanov, D; 2020). Digitalization plays a vital role on recent competitive market and it is linked with the utilization of digital technologies to alter business model and to convey new value-producing opportunities to the modern business environment in an aim to move towards a digital business (Mihardjo *et al.* 2019).Isolation measures executed universally to contain the outbreak have hit financial activity difficult, whereas the sharp disintegration in business and consumer confidence, compounded by recent financial market turmoil, will proceed to decrease optional spending and investment. One major uncertainty concerns the duration of the current outbreak and the plausibility of further waves. The east to west development of the epicenter of the emergency which has immersed Europe and presently parts of the US, highlights how nations are a distinctive stages in managing with the outbreak, meaning that supply and demand issues in specific markets could have long tail impacts for worldwide businesses. Global enterprises are facing supply chain issues, consequently potentially higher operational costs, lower inventory and the prospects of lower demand will be reluctant to disburse resources and time to connect in M&A and financing activities, predominantly if valuations of targets remain high. Digitalization of supply chain could be a way that companies can start to strategize and accomplish trade strength against supply chain disturbance. In this context, enormous information analytics can assist firms in streamlining their supplier selection process, cloud-computing is progressively being used to encourage and manage supplier connections and logistics and shipping forms can be significantly improved through automation and the internet of things (McKenzie, B. 2020).

The coronavirus (COVID-19) outbreak depicts that pandemics and epidemics can badly bring havoc on supply chains around the world (Queiroz *et al.* 2020). The aim of this chapter is to look at the Digitalization to reduce tasks without added value or human contact in a pandemic. In this chapter, following topics will be focused:

1. Digitalization enhances prosperity without human contact in a pandemic.
2. Digitalization will alter labor markets.
3. Digitalization impacts business models.
4. Factors influencing digitalization to reduce tasks in supply chain management.
5. Impediments of digitalization of supply chain to reduce task.

Keywords: Digitalization, Supply Chain, sustainability, Technological Innovations, Supply channels, Operations management, COVID-19, Pandemic, Artificial intelligence.

DIGITALIZATION ENHANCES PROSPERITY WITHOUT HUMAN CONTACT IN A PANDEMIC

The diverse ways in which digital technologies engage with social, environmental, ethical, legal, and economic frameworks necessitate a far-sighted and broad view of how they can optimize benefits to society while mitigating harms in the pandemic.

The creation of digital collaboration in the pandemic period was influenced by nine values:

1. **Inclusiveness –** Leaving no one behind in order to achieve the Sustainable Development Goals by enhancing equality of ability, access, and outcomes (High-Level, U. S. G. S.,2019).
2. **Respect –** Respect for human rights and integrity, diversity, the protection and security of personal data and computers, as well as national and international law (High-Level, U. S. G. S.,2019).

3. **Human centeredness** – optimizing human benefits while ensuring that humans stay in control of decisions (High-Level, U. S. G. S.,2019).
4. **Human flourishing** – fostering long-term economic development, social good, and self-realization opportunities (High-Level, U. S. G. S.,2019).
5. **Transparency** – Promoting transparent access to data and activities (High-Level, U. S. G. S.,2019).
6. **Collaboration** – Upholding open standards and interoperability to make collaboration simpler (High-Level, U. S. G. S.,2019).
7. **Accessibility** – Designing devices and services that are accessible, easy, and dependable for a wide range of users (High-Level, U. S. G. S.,2019).
8. **Harmony** – The use of emerging technology by governments and companies in ways that win the trust of peers, stakeholders, and people, while avoiding exploiting or exacerbating divides and conflicts; and,
9. **Sustainability** – Advancing the goal of a zero-carbon, zero-waste economy that does not jeopardize future generations' ability to meet their own needs (High-Level, U. S. G. S.,2019).

Effect of Digitalization of Finance and Accounting in Business Activity

Implementing digitalization brings greater flexibility, contributing specifically to the creation of Shared Service Centers (SSCs) for activities with a high repetition rate. The digital revolution is opening up to finance and accounting too though slowly.

In their financial divisions, only 22 percent of German businesses use artificial intelligence. 60 percent of policy makers in finance and accounting agree that the job of their divisions will be significantly influenced by artificial intelligence. More than half (60%) of the major German companies with operations in more than 10 countries use at least one SSC for funding purposes. 70 percent of the operations outsourced to SSC are in the field of finance and accounting. According to the PWC report, the bulk of these SSCs are located in Germany and abroad. Digital technology such as big data, business analytics, and AI are being opened up by the financial industries, but many businesses are also very vigilant about the application of these innovations (Ilcus, M. A. (2018).)

Key to Winning Digitalization in the Financial Sector

Contactless financial services and digitalization in the post-COVID era would be an unavoidable development. Enhanced digitalization can also satisfy the increasing need of financial institutions to reduce costs and risks. Despite the pandemic's negative effect on its activities, the local branch of Ping an Bank in Wuhan reported an improved result. The pandemic has boosted consciousness among financial institutions of digital transformation and FinTech. After the contagious epidemic subsides, it is possible banks will accelerate research and application of fin tech. It is clear that we were asked to point out that the number of Chinese banks affected in February by the COVID-19 pandemic was less than half of the total number of transactions registered in the country in the first two months. Intelligent marketing, risk management, goods, day-to-day activities and office work include non-contact financial services. Also during extraor, banking-related business continues without any interruption. Smart credit has been an important way for banks to fund small and micro enterprises. Many banks primarily target small businesses operating in sectors such as e-commerce, takeouts, logistics, and pharmacy. Based on government data, banks can build financing platforms for SMEs. A systematic program that calls for sophisticated planning is digital transformation. In financial organizations, the implementation of emerging technology, such as AI and big data, plays a key role in developing fintech-related initiatives. Sooner or later, the pandemic will pass, but innovation will continue, which explains why financial institutions are emphasizing and increasingly evolving digital transformation and contactless finance. By linking core companies and upstream and downstream companies, banks can also establish online supply-chain financing networks to promote industries in manufacturing and trading. Cooperation with the government and industry may also be encouraged by the government (Ye Wangchun, 2020). Supply chain operations are typically coordinated and scheduled hierarchically, either through the central and aggregated control of a corporate planning unit, which necessitates a high level of information exchanges, or through the inefficient upstream planning approach, in which operations are planned and the derived dependent demand is sent to suppliers. When independent members refuse to share information such as cost, profit margin, inventory level, or capacity utilization, a high level of information exchange creates problems. Decentralized approaches to coordination of operations planning decisions based on some minimal information sharing have been proposed as a solution to these problems. Decentralized approaches to coordination of operations planning decisions based on some minimal information sharing have been proposed in many academic disciplines to address these challenges (Taghipour & Frayret, 2013;Taghipour, 2014).

Digitalization and Public Health

From prevention and wellness promotion to curative treatments and self-management, emerging technology and the digital world give new ways to recognize needs and deliver healthcare (EU report, 2019). As such, the ability to improve healthcare services in ways that can lead to the efficiency, accessibility, efficacy, and equity of healthcare priorities of the health system. In this context, digitalization should be regarded as a means, a collection of instruments, not a public health objective (Odone *et. al,* 2019). A main challenge is to ensure that all individuals benefit from the advantages of emerging technology. As public health practitioners must ensure that creativity and technology help to reduce our world's inequities, instead of being another reason why people are left behind.

Mobile applications have the ability to help contact tracing strategies to control and reverse the spread of COVID-19. The use of apps has assisted health authorities in a number of countries worldwide in tracking and reducing the ongoing COVID-19 pandemic, has enabled the coordination of medical follow-up of patients, and has given direct guidance to people to play their part in disease control (Kleinman, 2020). These apps' added benefit is that they can monitor contacts that may not be recognized or remembered by an individual. Contact tracing and alert aims to help public health authorities to quickly recognize as many contacts as possible with a reported case of COVID-19, to ask for self-quarantine if possible, and to test and isolate them quickly if symptoms occur. Contact tracing is typically carried out by public health authorities on a manual basis. This is a time-consuming approach in which cases are interviewed to assess who recall being in touch with from 48 h before the onset of symptoms right up to the point of self-isolation and diagnosis. In this method, digital resources such as mobile apps with tracing features can be of significant benefit, identifying both known and unknown contacts of a reported case and possibly assisting in their follow-up, particularly in environments with large numbers of cases where public health authorities can become overwhelmed. In the battle against COVID-19, many Member States in the EU and EEA have introduced or plan to launch initiatives involving contact tracing applications. Policy concerns relating to privacy and data protection have been posed by the use of these technologies, identifying different practices in different countries in particular between Asia and Europe. The adoption of (encouraged or compulsory) digital tools, the digital infrastructure allowed and activated by the national government, and the possibility of data sharing are the key conditions and dilemmas for enhancing digital contact tracing strategies. In this regard, EU Member States should urgently converge on effective app solutions that reduce the processing of personal data and acknowledge that interoperability between these apps can help public health authorities, especially after the reopening of the EU's internal borders (Fig. 1).

Outside Europe, several data collection technologies have been developed by China, South Korea, Taiwan and Singapore to control the spread of the virus. In order to identify positive situations, China implemented a government-mandated QR code that indicates the citizen's level of danger. Singapore urged individuals to install an app that uses Bluetooth signals between nearby devices called "Trace

Figure 1. Key participants in the healthcare open innovation ecosystem
Source: (iNNOVAHEALTH. 2012).

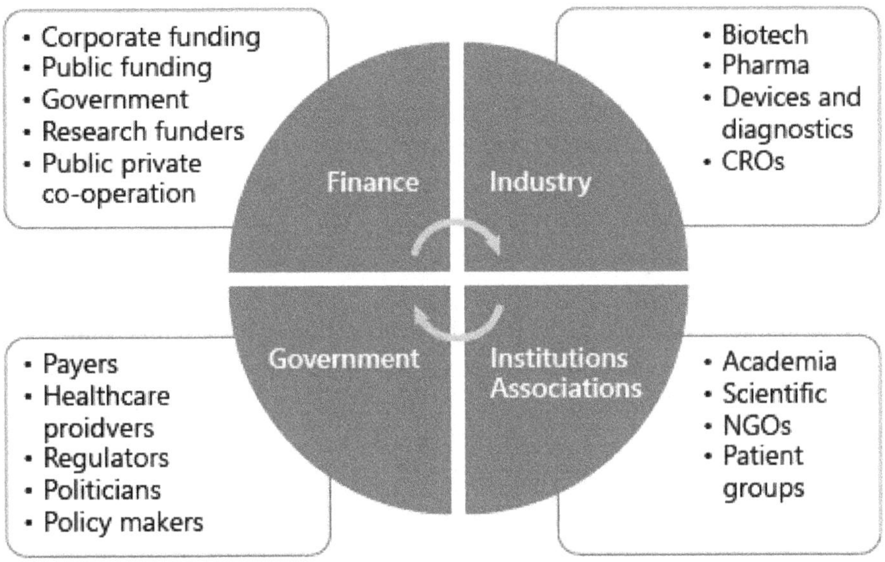

Together." Similarly, Hong Kong needs all new arrivals to download the "Stay home Safe" app, while the "Corona 100 m" app in South Korea tracks all GPS personal data and movements that the government can use. A similar technique was used by Taiwan, where the contact tracing scheme enables the government to contact people by leaving their devices at home to ensure that they do not avoid monitoring. Instead, apps produced in Europe are focused on voluntary use, without the responsibility of the government. As of June 2020, for example, Italy has created the 'Immuni' software, which is recommended, but not mandatory. This software uses a Bluetooth signal to recognize potential exposure to positive circumstances. The "Stop Covid" French app functions similarly and is focused on voluntary use, as is the "Corona-Warn-App" German app. A new approach to digital communication tracing between Europe and Asia is obviously in place. This may be attributed to differences at the political level, but also to the characteristics of the population, where the collectivist spirit of Asian countries can promote collective action and efforts to deal with the spread of the virus. However we should bear in mind that such initiatives will only help to contain the UK COVID-19 outbreak if they are successfully implemented and are part of a larger package of social distance, infection control, and hygiene measures (Griffin, 2020) interventions.

DIGITALIZATION WILL ALTER LABOR MARKETS

Changes in demand for goods and services, as well as technology and globalization, have influenced labor markets.

- **Job creation:** new industries, goods, and services;
- **Job change:** digitalization, human-machine interfaces, and new management styles;
- **Job loss:** automation and robotics;
- **Job shift:** digital networks, crowd sourcing, and the 'sharing' economy

These four effects of digitalization are laced with macroeconomic implications arising from changes in labor markets, pay, social inequality, and the quality of newly developed, improved, or "shifted" employment, among other things (Degryse, C. 2016).

In Case of Industry Sector

The first was the steam engine, the second was electrification and mass production, the third was the computer, and the fourth is the digital revolution (Kowalski 2015), which combines advances in information technologies with robotization, task automation, the internet of things, 3D printing, driverless cars, and – Drones, cyber-weapons, surveillance, and other defense and anti-terrorism technologies (Degryse, C. 2016). Operational planning is a task that all manufacturing and logistical firms must complete. Its coordination with supply chain partners aims to synchronize resource usage to reduce inefficiencies, such as unnecessary inventory holding, or to increase revenue through better resource utilization (Taghipour & Frayret, 2013;Taghipour, 2009).

'While advances in robotics produce tangible machines that are often easily associated with specific jobs (for example, a hamburger-making robot or a precision assembly robot), progress in software automation will likely be much less visible to the public; it will often take place deep inside corporate walls, and it will have more holistic impacts on organizations and the people they employ' (Ford 2015: 105). Similarly, 3D printing, which is often misunderstood as a toy, is a part of this movement that will, in the not-too-distant future, raise a slew of new questions for society. 'In the years ahead, breakthroughs in robotics and automation will improve productivity and performance, translating into economic benefits for manufacturers,' according to Roubini (2015). Software developers, engineers, research scientists, and other staff with the skills and education needed to function in the brave new manufacturing age would benefit from this wave of growth. Ford is persuaded that this is where the future lies, explaining the phenomenon of offshoring, in which highly skilled technical jobs (lawyer, radiologist, tax analyst, software programmer, and so on) are gradually moved to low-wage countries, such as India, where tax experts specialize in US tax law (Ford, 2015, p. 118) (Degryse, C. 2016).

Irani (2015), on the other hand, takes a skeptical view of the 'second age of the machine.' Allowing themselves to be blinded by Google, Facebook, and other engineers, she claims, authors fail to see that algorithms do not substitute labor, but rather displace it. 'McAfee and Brynjolfsson neglect the labor of cultural data workers, as if algorithms trained, tuned, and enhanced themselves, as if by magic.' As a consequence, she observes, there are armies of employees employed in the background about which the main platforms say nothing: 'Google's self-driving car doesn't just go wherever its passengers like.' A human worker must drive around, scan, and map the car's universe, including everything from curb heights to intersection angles, in order for it to "drive itself" (Degryse, C. 2016).

In Case of Services Sector

The services sector is the part of the Fourth Revolution that is currently attracting more media coverage. 'The same forces that shook up the manufacturing sector – globalization and labor-saving technological progress – are now beginning to shake up the services sector, increasing the risk of a severe job crisis – an outcome that has so far been avoided' (Roubini 2015).

Transport, distribution and sales services, guest accommodation, small repairs and plumbing, tool hire services, but also banking, printing, estate agents, technical coaching, accounting, translation, child care and personal care, secretarial services, healthcare, and so on are among the sectors affected. It is sufficient to observe everyday lives: to read the papers, consult train schedules, read mail, contact clients and suppliers, call a taxi, leaf through catalogues, order and pay for purchases, consult the weather forecast, check our bank balance, pay taxes, and so on, all through applications on our smart phones or tablets. These services were created by traditional businesses who saw digitalization as a way to expand the services they provide, make them easier to access, and simplify consumers' preferences and modes of consumption: online newspapers, public transportation schedules, fully digital ticket purchases, bank account management, and so on (Degryse, C. 2016).

The job stakes in these digitalized services provided by 'traditional' firms are hardly fresh, with the primary issue being the displacement of workers by these digitalized services. For a long time, the cashier at the bank has been replaced by an automat for the vast majority of transactions; shops distribute digital versions of their catalogue through the internet, allowing consumers to order and pay for their purchases directly on a website in the absence of personal contact with sales employees; department stores have developed home shopping apps; newspapers provide news on demand. In these areas, 'digitalization' has occurred over time, whether or not it has been followed by job losses and/or a worsening of working conditions (the press sector is emblematic of this degradation, with journalists famously subject to increasing levels of pressure(Bittner 2011), (Degryse, C. 2016).

JOB PROSPECTS IN THE DIGITAL ECONOMY

Table 1.

Jobs that are most at risk of being automated or digitalized	Automated/digitalized workers face the least risk.	New jobs
✓ Job in the office and clerical duties ✓ Some areas of financial services ✓ Sales and trade ✓ Transportation, ✓ logistics Manufacturing industry ✓ Construction ✓ Some forms of services (translation, tax consultancy, etc.)	✓ Arts, education, and the media ✓ Legal assistance ✓ Human resource management, ✓ management ✓ Some facets of financial services in business ✓ Providers of medical services Engineers, scientists, and computer staff ✓ Various programs are available (social work, hairdressing, beauty care, etc.)	**'Top of the scale'** ✓ Data analysts, Data miners, and data architects are all types of people who deal with data. ✓ Developers of software and applications Experts in networking, artificial intelligence, and other fields. ✓ Designers and manufacturers of smart machines, robots, and 3D printers ✓ E-commerce and ✓ digital marketing experts
		'Bottom of the scale' ✓ Employed on digital channels are digital 'galley slaves' (data entry or filter workers) and other 'mechanical Turks.' ✓ In the 'collaborative' market, Uber drivers, casual odd-jobs (repairs, home maintenance, pet care, etc.)

Source: Christophe Degryse (ETUI 2016) based on Frey & Osborne, Ford, Valsamis, Irani, Head, Babinet data.

The supply chain planning systems described in the literature can be divided into two types: centralized and decentralized planning systems. Theoretically, centralized systems can improve supply chain performance, but their implementation necessitates a high level of information sharing among supply chain partners. When independent partners refuse to share information, this causes problems. Decentralized systems are intended for supply chains where each member is a separate economic entity that makes its operational decisions independently, but with some minimal information sharing, to address these difficulties (Taghipour & Frayret, 2012). Digitalization is one of the most important drivers of technological change in the near future, and the creation and use of digital logic circuits, as well as its derivative technologies, such as the computer, smart phone, and the Internet, are at the heart of this growth. Production, service delivery, and even the private sphere are all affected by digital technology. As electronic devices and microprocessors link people with people, machines with staff, and machines with machines, connectivity opens up entirely new dimensions.

DIGITALIZATION IMPACTS BUSINESS MODELS

Automating and digitizing tasks and procedures may be extremely beneficial to businesses. Aside from obvious outcomes like lower labor costs, outputs may include higher reliability and lower maintenance costs; new quality standards with less human errors; and improved productivity and performance.

Activity in the field of innovation, new strategy, turbulence in technology factors directly influence business models activity due to digitalization._

Activity in the Field of Innovation

All activities undertaken by a company to add value to its goods and services are described as innovation activity in an organization. As a result, the use of innovations like social media and big data, which are seen as groundbreaking by most SMEs, can have an effect on business models experimentation. When a firm explicitly pursues an internal driver like creative behavior (Hurley and Hult, 1998; Utterback and Abernathy, 1975), it is expected that it will lead to experimentation, and hence budget allocation and team activities related to business models will be sponsored. Companies with a high degree of innovation – whether in product, marketing, or organizational innovation – are usually expected to outperform their competitors. Companies who excel at creativity – whether it's product, marketing, or organizational – are likely to be willing to do new things with their business models (Bouwman, H. *et. al*, 2018).

New Strategy

The term "strategy" is commonly used to refer to business plans or business models. On a more operational stage, business models require the execution of a plan in the business logic. As a result, a firm's orientation toward strategic decisions would allow them to be implemented in the business models, making business models experimentation important (Casadesus-Masanell and Ricart, 2010; Chesbrough, 2010; Chesbrough and Rosenbloom, 2002). Say for example; SME experimentation with its business models would be aided by openness to strategy debate (Bouwman, H. *et. al*, 2018).

Turbulence in Technology

Turbulence in technology has a direct impact on industry (Johnson *et al.,* 2008). Over the last few decades, the assessment and development of technical advances has become the fastest growing trend in industry. Business must constantly adapt to IT implementations, so they can investigate how emerging innovations impact their business models. Furthermore, they will test out IT applications and see what effect they have on their business models. This holds valid, notwithstanding, for modern IT technologies such as social media and big data (Bouwman, H. *et. al*, 2018).

In terms of what they sell (their value propositions, e.g., Gandhi, *et. al*, 2018) and how they sell it (their value demonstrations, e.g., Syam & Sharma, 2018), digital technologies have changed the way business-to-business firms act in business markets, and they have also posed new requirements to a firm's capabilities (Ritter, T., & Pedersen, C. L. 2020).

Digitization Creates an Inclusive Digital Economy

Any individual can potentially link to someone else, obtain and generate information, or engage in commercial or social activity, thanks to mobile internet and increasingly powerful and low-cost computing. Similarly, there are less technological obstacles to global economic activity at scale for organizations of any size. Economic inclusion can be aided by digital technologies by eliminating information barriers, broadening access, and lowering the level of skills necessary to participate in the economy (World Bank Group,2016). Naturally, this does not imply that all and everything should be linked and digitized. It also does not suggest that the social and economic effects of emerging technologies are always positive or inclusive. Digital technology has the ability to both generate opportunities and worsen inequity. Creating an equitable digital economy would necessitate a collective effort from a wide variety of stakeholders from all walks of life.

The ability of digital technologies to empower traditionally marginalized people and drive inclusive economic development is illustrated by financial inclusion. (UNCDF). E-commerce illustrates how emerging technology paired with supportive policies can lead to equitable economic growth – it has thrived in countries where starting a company is relatively simple and historically disadvantaged populations have access to the internet. As more individuals and small businesses buy and sell internationally, more friendly rules for cross-border e-commerce are required, just as they are for inclusive mobile finance (UNCTAD, 2015).

Employee flexibility, autonomy, and responsibility will increase as a result of digitalization: where, when, and how people work will be independent of their physical location. This will have an impact on remuneration quality and fairness, working hours, lifelong learning, and social security and pension savings.

FACTORS INFLUENCING DIGITALIZATION TO REDUCE TASKS IN SUPPLY CHAIN MANAGEMENT

Developing Digital Capabilities in your Workforce

83 percent of chief executives are not optimistic that their company will develop and execute the future operating models required to enable digital transformation, according to the 2019 KPMG Global CEO Outlook report. In shifting that view, the supply chain leader has a unique opportunity. COVID-19 has shown that one of the greatest value levers that corporations have to pull is keeping the supply chain right. For development, talent and technology are both important. Digital transformation affects every corner of industry, but with regard to the scale, shape and capacity of the workforce, it will be highly noticeable. For resilience, up skilling workers for a digital era are important. In a nutshell: Individuals are at the center of every business, and their choices and behavior decide its success or failure (KPMG, 2020).

A Stronger Workforce for Digital

Companies need to be able to deliver real-time communication and responsiveness to meet fast-changing consumer needs, which will take professional staff to adjust to an ever-changing environment. A couple of examples of digital skills:

Manufacturing

Enterprises do not afford to wait for market shifts to be felt in sales results. Sensors installed into smart products in the field in the future will immediately feed information back to manufacturers about the habits of their consumers and the efficiency of their devices. Before the consumers themselves are even aware of it, consumer needs can well be expected. It's just one piece of the puzzle to update, redeploy and retain permanent workers. On the one hand, effective companies extend to their workforces the logic of as-a-service' procurement. This means, in some situations, outsourcing operating activities to contracting partners or even rivals. For some it means digitizing the experience and expertise of workers, developing common algorithmic systems that can improve decision-making (KPMG, 2020).

Transportation

More smart phone applications and devices that specialize in automated load monitoring and freight matching for contact-free deliveries will certainly be used by truck drivers. Software-as-a-service businesses, for instance, provide their clients with the ability to monitor shipments in real time. The need for truck drivers to constantly check in with dispatchers and brokers throughout the journey is removed by these automated monitoring systems. Start-ups are shaking up the industry, from self-driving companies that have made automating trucking their task, to systems designed to match cargo-delivery needs to truck availability (KPMG, 2020).

Track and Trace Advanced

By monitoring raw materials and finished goods all the way from point-of-origin to the final point-of-sale, this gives companies unprecedented visibility and control of their supply chains. Advanced track and trace systems allow for real-time monitoring of assets and inventory, and instant location analysis. Where changes in the scheduled freight route or climate control are observed, the monitoring technology enables time and place verification and control measurements to be independently checked. This allows the rationalization and optimization of fleets to maximize profitability. An example of this is the pharmaceutical supply chain, where track and trace technology, along with conditions of the drug, enables the detection of past and present locations. Drug enforcement laws about such items as humidity and temperature range are assessed and recorded during the entire transportation journey. Remediation events are caused if they fall out of the permissible range. Any node of the supply chain can be monitored through the supply chain, from producer to packager to retail store, and perhaps back again for returns or recalls. Track and trace also helps battle drugs that are counterfeited, stolen or adulterated (KPMG, 2020).

Block Chain

21st century supply chains are quicker, more interconnected and need larger volumes of data to be exchanged. The dynamics of these environments generate operational threats, difficulties in terms of reconciliation, and opportunities for fraud and security issues. Many leaders apply blockchain to ensure the quality and protection of products as they move through regional and global boundaries, effectively a distributed digital ledger. Products pass through a lot of procedures and intermediaries. In the blockchain, every product hand-off is registered, providing a permanent history of a product, from creation to sale. In modern supply chains, this eliminates delays, mistakes, and prices, while also creating visibility, a great commodity (KPMG, 2020).

Predictive Analytics

The facts that supply chain risk and mitigation plans are focused on historical data and hindsight is a major contributor to underperformance. New predictive modeling is likely to help foster informed choices, facilitating action rather than response. When the client is still disappointed if a delivery is not made in full or on time, it's too late. It doesn't solve the problem by adding money and time to repair disruptions after the fact. Many leading supply chain managers use data analytics, machine learning (ML) and other technologies, such as pandemics, financial, geopolitical and environmental events, to forecast future supply chain disruptions. This will assist companies with logistics planning, inventory management, output planning and constructive risk management issues. Organizations can see the broader picture by scenario planning and make successful trade-off choices on topics such as how much stock to hold, and where, or how to balance inventory costs against consumer satisfaction costs. In order to identify sweet spots between seemingly contradictory goals, simulations can be run easily, based on real-time inventory data, consumer demand, and supplier capacity. These scenarios, increasingly allowed by AI and automation, can help prescribe rather than just predict. Companies are able to recognize strategic and concentrated supplies that are at risk by evaluating historical incidents and hypothesizing potential risks, and most significantly, recognize when existing internal risk capacities prove inadequate (KPMG, 2020).

Cognitive Decision Centers (CDCs)

Investing in CDCs gives a cross-functional view of the supply chain, from one end of distribution and marketing to the other end of financing and procurement. Usually, each of these roles is separate, and each is promoted against goals identified in its own terms, without regard to the larger strategic ambitions of the company. Moreover, their interests never match. It ultimately negatively affects the performance of the others as each role aims to optimize against its respective main performance indicators. Tomorrow's CDCs are likely to use state-of-the-art artificial intelligence to collect and analyze cross-functional data, enabling decision-makers within an enterprise to recognize conflict points and model multiple trade-offs in the search of the best scenario. Simply put, CDCs are about maximizing efficiency across the enterprise, not the performance of specific business units (KPMG, 2020).

IMPEDIMENTS OF DIGITALIZATION OF SUPPLY CHAIN TO REDUCE TASK

The primary challenges in developing digital supply chain, according to (Xu, J., 2014), are collecting all necessary data from several disparate sources, ensuring its accuracy, and developing a software infrastructure and framework that can use the data to manage and execute the supply chain. Since the chain's duration includes both internal and external partners, it will be sluggish and error-prone. Furthermore, current large volumes of inventory may not be sufficient to satisfy demand, distribution infrastructure may be inadequate, and product quality may be difficult to monitor (Büyüközkan, G., & Göçer, F.,2018). The following are some of the impediments for digital supply chain:

- **Lack of preparation:** Insufficient demand planning, guidance, and resources (Xu, J., 2014), (Schrauf, S., & Berttram, P.,2016).
- **Lack of cooperation:** Insufficient collaboration with external associates and internal feature feedback (Xu, J., 2014), (Padmos, D *et. al.*, 2016), (Penthin, S., & Dillman, R. 2015).
- **Demand forecasting error:**
- Overly optimistic demand, inventory, development, and other data forecasts (Xu, J., 2014), (Carter, P. L. *et. al.*, 2009), (Richey, R. G. *et. al.*, 2016).
- **Lack of knowledge exchange:** Corporations' aversion to exchanging information (Xu, J., 2014).
- **The pursuit of the silver bullet:** The assurance that all will be well (Xu, J., 2014), (Hines, T., 2004).
- **Lack of knowledge:** Experience and expertise in supply chain management are lacking(Xu, J., 2014),(Hines, T., 2004).
- Lack of the necessary flexibility and agility in supply chain management (Xu, J., 2014), (Hines, T., 2004). (Richey, R. G. *et. al.*, 2016), (Penthin, S., & Dillman, R. 2015).
- **High volatility:** In supply chain management, there is a lack of expertise and skills in coping with volatility (Xu, J., 2014), (Hines, T., 2004), (Padmos, D *et. al.*, 2016).
- **Overconfidence in suppliers:** Depending on particular suppliers in specific locations (Xu, J., 2014), (Hines, T., 2004).
- **Lack of integration:** There is a lack of awareness of how to combine digital and non-digital supply chain management (Xu, J., 2014), (Hines, T., 2004), (Padmos, D *et. al.*, 2016), (Penthin, S., & Dillman, R. 2015).

CONCLUSION

Digitalization has changed every area of industry in the covid-19 pandemic situation. Logistics and supply chain are no exception. Digital transformation can be described as the strategic and prioritized transformation of business competencies, processes, practices, and models in order to fully leverage the opportunities and innovations of emerging technology and their impact. A focus change from the traditional supply chain to the digital supply chain is an evolving global trend in supply chain management today. Organizations can use technological tools like IoT, CC, and BD to turn their current supply chain structure's 'traditional paper-based' or 'hybrid mix of technology' backed processes into collaborative digital models with greater flexibility, agility, and transparency. Unlike traditional supply chain systems, which have resulted in static organizational arrangements, inaccessible data, and fractured relationships with partners, a digital supply chain allows for process automation, flexibility, and digital asset management. Various technologies, such as RFID, GPS, and ST, are examples of this trend. The purpose of a supply chain is to get the right item to the right customer at the right time, in the right place, in the right quantity, in the right condition, and at the right (low) price. To satisfy today's consumer needs, this could be achieved using a digital supply chain.

REFERENCES

Bittner, A. K. (2011). *Managing change: Innovation and trade unionism in the news industry*. EFJ.

. Bouwman, H., Nikou, S., Molina-Castillo, F. J., & de Reuver, M. (2018). The impact of digitalization on business models. *Digital Policy, Regulation and Governance*.

Büyüközkan, G., & Göçer, F. (2018). Digital supply chain: Literature review and a proposed framework for future research. *Computers in Industry*, *97*, 157–177. doi:10.1016/j.compind.2018.02.010

Carter, P. L., Monczka, R. M., Ragatz, G. L., & Jennings, P. L. (2009). Supply chain integration: Challenges and good practices. *CAPS Research*, 95-99.

Casadesus-Masanell, R., & Ricart, J. E. (2010). From strategy to business models and onto tactics. *Long Range Planning*, *43*(2-3), 195–215. doi:10.1016/j.lrp.2010.01.004

Chesbrough, H., & Rosenbloom, R. S. (2002). The role of business model in capturing value from innovation: Evidence from Xerox Corporation's technology spin-off companies. *Industrial and Corporate Change*, *11*(3), 529–555. doi:10.1093/icc/11.3.529

Christopher, M., & Towill, D. R. (2000). Supply chain migration from lean and functional to agile and customized. *Supply Chain Management*, *5*(4), 206–213. doi:10.1108/13598540010347334

Degryse, C. (2016). *Digitalisation of the economy and its impact on labour markets*. ETUI research paper-working paper.

Dubey, R., Altay, N., Gunasekaran, A., Blome, C., Papadopoulos, T., & Childe, S. J. (2018). Supply chain agility, adaptability and alignment: Empirical evidence from the Indian auto components industry. *International Journal of Operations & Production Management*, *38*(1), 129–148. doi:10.1108/IJOPM-04-2016-0173

Eckstein, D., Goellner, M., Blome, C., & Henke, M. (2015). The performance impact of supply chain agility and supply chain adaptability: The Moderating Effect of Product Complexity. *International Journal of Production Research*, *53*(10), 3028–3046. doi:10.1080/00207543.2014.970707

Fadaki, M., Rahman, S., & Chan, C. (2020). Leagile supply chain: Design drivers and business performance implications. *International Journal of Production Research*, *58*(18), 5601–5623. doi:10.1080/00207543.2019.1693660

Ford, M. (2015). *Rise of the robots: technology and the threat of a jobless future*. Basic Books.

Gandhi, S., Thota, B., Kuchembuck, R., & Swartz, J. (2018). Demystifying data monetization. *MIT Sloan Management Review*, 1–9.

Goldsby, T. J., Griffis, S. E., & Roath, A. S. (2006). Modeling lean, agile, and leagile supply chain strategies. *Journal of Business Logistics*, *27*(1), 57–80. doi:10.1002/j.2158-1592.2006.tb00241.x

Gunasekaran, A., Tiwari, M. K., Dubey, R., & Wamba, S. F. (2016). Big data and predictive analytics applications in supply chain management. *Computers & Industrial Engineering*, *101*, 525–527. doi:10.1016/j.cie.2016.10.020

High-Level, U. S. G. S. (2019). *Panel on Digital Cooperation*. The Age of Digital Interdependence Report.

Hines, T. (2004). *Supply chain strategies: Customer driven and customer focused*. Routledge.

Hurley, R. F., & Hult, G. T. M. (1998). Innovation, market orientation, and organizational learning: An integration and empirical examination. *Journal of Marketing*, *62*(3), 42–54. doi:10.1177/002224299806200303

Ilcus, M. A. (2018). Impact of Digitalization in Business World. *Revista de Management Comparat International*, *19*(4), 350–358. doi:10.24818/RMCI.2018.4.350

iNNOVAHEALTH. (2012). *Building on Open Innovation Ecosystem in Europe for Healthcare*. Cyprus EU Presidency.

Irani, L. (2019). Justice for Data Janitors. In *Think in Public* (pp. 23–40). Columbia University Press. doi:10.7312/marc19008-003

Ivanov, D. (2020). Viable supply chain model: Integrating agility, resilience and sustainability perspectives—lessons from and thinking beyond the COVID-19 pandemic. *Annals of Operations Research*, 1. doi:10.100710479-020-03640-6 PMID:32836614

Johnson, M. W., Christensen, C. M., & Kagermann, H. (2008). Reinventing your business model. *Harvard Business Review*, *86*(12), 57–68.

Kowalski, W. (2015, July). The European digital agenda: Unambitious and too narrow. *Social Europe*, *6*. https://www.socialeurope.eu/2015/07/european-digitalagenda-unambitious-narrow

KPMG International Cooperative. (2020). *Building supply chain resilience through digital transformation.* Retrieved from https://assets.kpmg/content/dam/kpmg/xx/pdf/2020/06.

Lee, H. L. (2004). The tripple-A supply chain. *Harvard Business Review*, *82*(10), 102–112. PMID:15559579

McKenzie, B. (2020). Beyond COVID-19: Supply chain resilience holds key to recovery. *Retrieved*, *24*, 2020.

Mihardjo, L., Sasmoko, S., Alamsjah, F., & Elidjen, E. (2019). The influence of digital customer experience and electronic word of mouth on brand image and supply chain sustainable performance. *Uncertain Supply Chain Management*, *7*(4), 691–702. doi:10.5267/j.uscm.2019.4.001

Padmos, D., Alexander, M., Brody, P., Chadam, J., Cookson, C., Little, J., & Meadows, B. (2016). *Digital supply chain: it's all about that data.* Ernst and Young.

Penthin, S., & Dillman, R. (2015). *Digital SCM.* Academic Press.

Queiroz, M. M., Ivanov, D., Dolgui, A., & Wamba, S. F. (2020). Impacts of epidemic outbreaks on supply chains: Mapping a research agenda amid the COVID-19 pandemic through a structured literature review. *Annals of Operations Research*, 1–38. PMID:32836615

Richey, R. G. Jr, Morgan, T. R., Lindsey-Hall, K., & Adams, F. G. (2016). A global exploration of big data in the supply chain. *International Journal of Physical Distribution & Logistics Management*, *46*(8), 710–739. doi:10.1108/IJPDLM-05-2016-0134

Ritter, T., & Pedersen, C. L. (2020). Digitization capability and the digitalization of business models in business-to-business firms: Past, present, and future. *Industrial Marketing Management*, *86*, 180–190. doi:10.1016/j.indmarman.2019.11.019

Roubini, N. (2015). *Labor in the Digital Age (Part 1 and Part 2).* Roubini Global Economics.

Schrauf, S., & Berttram, P. (2016). *Industry 4.0: How digitization makes the supply chain more efficient, agile, and customer-focused.* Strategy & Recuperado de https://www. strategyand. pwc. com/media/file/Industry4.0.pdf

Syam, N., & Sharma, A. (2018). Waiting for a sales renaissance in the fourth industrial revolution: Machine learning and artificial intelligence in sales research and practice. *Industrial Marketing Management*, *69*, 135–146. doi:10.1016/j.indmarman.2017.12.019

Taghipour, A. (2009). Évaluation de la collaboration dans une chaîne d'approvisionnement. *Revue française de gestion industrielle, 28*(1), 25-42.

Taghipour, A. (2014). Improving the Plan of a Manufacturing Network with Non-Integrated Business Units. *International Journal of Applied Logistics*, *5*(2), 1–11. doi:10.4018/ijal.2014040101

Taghipour, A. (2014). Production Network Planning Based on Constraint Relaxation and Discount Approach. *Lecture Notes on Information Theory*, *02*(03), 279–282. doi:10.12720/lnit.2.3.279-282

Taghipour, A., & Frayret, J. M. (2011). A new heuristic search with local optimization to manage a supply chain. *Meta*, 15.

Taghipour, A., & Frayret, J. M. (2012). Mutual adju tment search with incentive for supply chain planning coordination. *International Journal of Computer Integrated Manufacturing*, *25*(10), 946–962. doi:10.1080/0951192X.2011.646307

Taghipour, A., & Frayret, J. M. (2013). Dynamic mutual adjustment search for supply chain operations planning co-ordination. *International Journal of Production Research*, *51*(9), 2715–2739. doi:10.1080/00207543.2012.737952

Taghipour, A., & Frayret, J. M. (2013). Coordination of operations planning in supply chains: A review. *International Journal of Business Performance and Supply Chain Modelling*, *5*(3), 272–307. doi:10.1504/IJBPSCM.2013.055729

UN Capital Development Fund (UNCDF). (n.d.). Available online: https://www.uncdf.org/financial-inclusion)

United Nations Conference on Trade and Development (UNCTAD). (2015). *Information Economy Report 2015 Unlocking the Potential of E-Commerce for Developing Countries*. https://unctad.org/en/PublicationsLibrary/ier2015_en.pdf

Urbach, N., & Ahlemann, F. (2019). *IT Management in the Digital Age: A Roadmap for the IT Department of the Future*. Springer., doi:10.1007/978-3-319-96187-3

Utterback, J. M., & Abernathy, W. J. (1975). A dynamic model of process and product innovation. *Omega*, *3*(6), 639–656. doi:10.1016/0305-0483(75)90068-7

World Bank Group. (2016). *World development report 2016: digital dividends*. World Bank Publications.

Xu, J. (2014). *Managing digital enterprise: ten essential topics*. Springer. doi:10.2991/978-94-6239-094-2

Chapter 3
Digital, Decentralized Supply Chain and Its Implication for B2B Marketing:
A Case Study From the Indian Medical Equipment Industry

Subhasis Ray
Xavier Institute of Management, India

ABSTRACT

This chapter discusses the possible effects of decentralized, digital supply chains on B2B marketing. Traditional buying and selling functions will change once large organizations decide to procure from digital platforms. Using the case study of medikabazaar.com, an Indian start-up, the chapter shows that while medical supply purchase will become decentralized, digital platforms will create a new centralization of suppliers and have a significant impact on industrial buying particularly for high value medical equipment purchase in small towns or small hospitals. Organizational buying process will be impacted and companies that choose to supply products directly to hospitals will have to change their marketing strategy suitably.

DOI: 10.4018/978-1-7998-6874-3.ch003

INTRODUCTION

The COVID19 pandemic has created huge disruptions in the business world. The world economy has almost stopped functioning and when it bounces back, it will be a new normal. One of the business functions that will change in size, shape and character are the global supply chains. In a flat, globalized world, supply chains were located in areas that provided cost advantage to companies. China, for example, was a major supply hub of global economy in the pre-COVID world. Companies now realize that concentrating supply chains can be a matter of risk in terms of business continuity. Diversification of supply chain risks is happening in two ways- 1) de-centralization in control and configuration and b) digitization including the use of AI-ML (Artificial Intelligence and Machine Learning). In this chapter, I focus on the effects of digitalizing supply chains on B2B marketers. B2B companies are suppliers to all corporations and in a digitalized supply chain, the buyer and seller will face new issues and challenges. Using the case study of an Indian start-up *medikabazaar.com* (MBR), I show how hospital purchases may change when procurement goes digital and what implications it has for B2B marketers. MBR has created a digital platform for medical supplies in India, thus disrupting the usual process of medical establishments buying from multiple vendors. The study shows that digital, decentralized supply chain will a) significantly impact the purchase of high value medical equipments and b)create both de-intermediation (removal of existing intermediaries from the procurement process) and re-intermediation (introduction of new intermediaries) impacting buyer behaviour and buying process in industrial marketing. It also suggests possible ways existing products and brands can fight back against digital platforms.

BACKGROUND

Industrial marketing refers to the sales and marketing of industrial goods to different organizations which then use such goods for further processing or re-sell them in the market. B2B marketing has a broader scope and covers commercial transaction between two organizations. For the purpose of this chapter, both terms have been used interchangeably.

The healthcare industry in India is poised for a major change in the post COVID world. Even before the pandemic, the Indian government's medical insurance scheme for almost half of its 1.3 billion population, 'Ayushman Bharat', was seen as a boost for the hospital sector. The scheme would enable affordable healthcare for millions but also provide increased revenue outlook for the medical industry. Rising income of a young and growing population and burden of chronic diseases also meant demand for better healthcare and wellbeing related products and services. During COVID19, the Indian government has announced special procurement schemes for made-in-India ventilators and personal protective equipments for the first time in the country's history. The country's push and policy for self-reliance *(Atma-nirbhar Bharat)*, 'make-in India', have created new impetus to the domestic medical equipment manufacturing and hospital supplies industry. However, the pandemic also created huge problems for purchasing managers in hospitals. Many small and medium enterprises were shut down during the nine week lockdown in the whole country and the partial lockdowns that went on till August, 2020, causing disruptions in hospital supplies. As caseloads started increasing, hospitals started switching to online procurements. At the time of writing this chapter, Medikabazaar.com (MBR) was India's no. 1 B2B platform for hospitals and doctors. Taking advantage of the pandemic situation, the company pushed for digital procurement for doctors and hospitals. A large number of medical products were made available through the company's website. In the process, the dynamics of buying and selling hospital and medical supplies changed.

Buyers in B2B markets go through a pre-defined process before finalizing their supplier. Organizational buying process has eight steps: problem recognition, general need description, product specifications, supplier search, proposal acquisition and analysis, supplier selection, order routine and performance review. The roles of decision makers in such purchases have been clearly identified in the literature. The concept of the 'buying centre', a group of people collectively involved in the industrial procurement process within the buying organization is also well established. Within the buying centre, one may find various roles of the purchasers during the purchase process: Initiator, influencer, gatekeeper, decider, purchaser and user. Initiators start the procurement process by raising a request/indent for a new purchase. Influencers are individuals who influence the final choice of a product or service based on their expertise and power. Gatekeepers control the flow of information between the buyer and seller. Deciders are the final decision makers in a purchase situation. Purchasers carry out the routine tasks like soliciting for proposals and sending purchase orders. Users refer to the executives who actually use a purchased product.

Introduction of an online platform is likely to change the buying behaviour and hence the marketing strategy for buyers and sellers respectively. Thus, the research objective of this chapter is to understand how the buying process and buying roles will change when customers adopt digital, decentralized procurement and what are the implications for suppliers' (i.e. B2B marketers) marketing strategy?

LITERATURE REVIEW

Supply chain refers to a network of companies, products and processes that work seamlessly to provide customer value. Suppliers are external companies supplying goods and services to help organizations build products and services. The term chain signifies the interlinkage across products supplied and the producers supplying them. It is thus obvious that quality of supplies and suppliers will determine the final quality of the product and success and sustainability of an organization. Managing supply chain has become much more than giving purchase orders, receiving goods and paying for them. The literature on supply chain management has evolved significantly over the last three decades. In line with the goal of this chapter, this section reviews extant literature on digital, decentralized supply chains and the relation between supply chain management and industrial /B2B marketing.

With the advent of the Internet and now Artificial Intelligence, Machine Learning and Industry 4.0, supply chain management has adopted digital tools, techniques and processes. The construct, role and elements of Industry 4.0 has changed supply chain management (Garay-Rondero et al., 2019). A digital supply chain is *'a smart, value-driven, efficient process to generate new forms of revenue...and to leverage novel technological and analytical methods'* (Buyukozkan & Gocer, 2018). This digitalization of the supply chain is not about digital goods or services but the way the processes are handled including self-driving vehicles, robotics, cloud services, bid data, sensors and 3-D printing (Agrawal & Narain, 2018). The main drivers of digital supply chain are technology, digitization, integration and collaboration (Iddris, 2018). Moving from a physical process of goods procurement to an Internet based platform can also be termed as a digital supply chain. The COVID19 pandemic is likely to increase this trend where buying organizations will rely on increased digitalization in supply chain to avoid business disruptions. Digital supply chains, by their very notion, makes companies more agile, economical even though there are inherent challenges in such supply chains (Agrawal & Narain, 2018). However, along with technology, digital supply chains will also impact other organizational functions like finance, marketing and strategy (Ageron et al., 2020).

Supply chains are becoming more complex and customers are demanding faster deliveries (Jung et al., 2008). The issue of centralization and decentralization in supply chains have received renewed attention in the context of the pandemic. The outbreak of the pandemic in China, the world's factory, has raised questions about supply chain outsourcing and centralization. Centralization decisions have been driven by the need for efficiency and cost. However one also needs to look at incentive compatibility and informational decentralizability while taking such decisions (Lee & Whang, 1999). Organizational barriers and information flow will also determine if decentralization is at all feasible (Lee & Billington, 1993). From a risk management perspective, multiple sourcing is preferred subject to availability of adequate and efficient suppliers (Tang et al., 2014) as decentralized decisions are generally inefficient and lead to inferior performance (Liu et al., 2007). Being a multilevel, multi-agent activity, decentralized supply chains will require more scrutiny in terms of resources (Walsh & Wellman, 2003). In suppler-retailer situations, it is clear that decentralization decision will depend on price and lead time sensitivity (Zhu, 2015) as well as local incentive systems (Geunes et al., 2016). However, in high tech industries that require close supplier collaboration, decentralization will require a hybrid approach (Lu et al., 2012). Giannoccaro (2018) approaches the topic of decentralization from a behavioural supply chain management perspective and finds that problem solving ability of managers and resistance to change will be two determinants in such cases though complex decision making problems will always require high centralization.

Suppliers form an integral part in B2B marketing and there is a close overlap between managing supply chain and managing industrial buyers and sellers. Electronic business has influenced supply chain (Croom, 2005) as inter-organizational processes have undergone significant change. E-marketplaces, digital platforms for product purchase has also changed the way buyers procure goods and services helping the latter to automate many of their transactional deals and procurement related processes. E-market place transition goes through three distinct phases – creation, integration and globalization (Lavassani et al., 2008; Alrubaiee et al., 2012)). Companies need to integrate their internal and external procurement activities and share strategic information to make use of the e-marketplaces (Eng, 2004). The focus of existing literature in B2B marketing and supply chain management is on buyer –seller relationship (Ellram, 2019). Shift to a more digitalized procurement process will impact key account management (Ryals & Humphries, 2007; LaMBRer & Enz, 2017) and consequent theory development (Hadjikhani & LaPlaca, 2013). A systems perspective of the market may help us understand the shift better (Vargo & Lusch, 2011; Kozlenkova et al., 2015) as well as be the key to improve customer satisfaction and collaboration in the demand-supply chain (Cambra-Fierro & Polo-Redondo, 2008; Formentini & Romano, 2016). Further, operational planning requires great co-ordination with supply chain partners (Taghipour & Frayret, 2013) in an environment of information asymmetry for appropriate supplier selection approaches (Mbiatem, 2018; Tliche et al., 2019; Vosooghidizaji et al., 2020).

The review of existing literature shows that digital and decentralized supply chain have caught researchers' attention but the interrelation between these chains and B2B marketing as not been explored fully. There is also scant literature on what existing vendors can/should do when a platform based supplier comes to the market. When physical procurement moves to e-marketplace based procurement, several changes can be expected from the seller side. Most of the research so far has focussed on the buyer side issues though even here, not much is known about changes in organizational buying behaviour and their impact on selling strategy and technique. Moreover, as Iddris(2018), points out there is need for qualitative study to further explore digital supply chain along all its dimensions. This chapter aims to fill this gap.

RESEARCH OBJECTIVE AND METHODOLOGY

Based on the research gap identified in the previous section, the research objective of this chapter is to identify possible impact/changes in buying and selling of industrial goods due to shift from a physical procurement model to a single e-marketplace based procurement. With this objective in mind, the author aims to answer the research question, "In the context of e-marketplace based procurement, how will changes in organizational buying behaviour impact marketing strategy of B2B marketers?"

Digitalized supply chain is an emerging issue that requires an interpretive approach to understand the customer experience (Flyvbjerg, 2006; Siggelkow, 2007). Many of the technologies and processes are new in developing countries and hence the case study method is suitable to study such new and evolving phenomenon (Edmondson & McManus, 2007). Since we are exploring 'how' customer behaviour will be changed due to digital procurement, an interpretive approach using a single case study is suitable. (Pedersen et al., 2013). As the candidate case, we study MedikaBazaar.com, India's first and largest platform for medical supplies. Since medical supplies have been in focus during the pandemic, a study of the digitalization of such supply chains can help us provide theoretical generalization about the impact of such change for both buyers and sellers in B2B market. Data for the case was collected from various media reports on medicabazaar.com, the author's interaction with the founder, videos on the company and data available at the company website.

CASE STUDY

Hospitals procure a multitude of products and services from several vendors. This may include high value purchases for intensive care units as well as costly equipments related to X-ray, ultrasonography or cancer care. Other items could be for regular patient use like beds and furniture while consumables consist of items like syringes, disinfectants and oxygen. Hospitals have a centralized purchasing department and several purchase processes for various items. Given the criticality of many of hospital supplies, sellers need to make innovative products, build relationships and deliver value for ongoing business. To sustain growth and operational excellence, it is important for hospitals to optimize their cost and efficiency of medical procurement.

MBR (www.medikabazaar.com) was established in 2015 by Vivek Tiwari and Ketan Malkan to provide hospitals and other medical establishments a one-stop shop for all their needs, almost like Amazon in consumer markets. Being the first in the Indian medical market, the company had to invest significant amount in creating awareness through direct contacts and digital media. Medical establishments can search for different products and suppliers, order them from MBR at specified time and prices and receive them on time. In 2020, MBR was connected to more than 30,000 such buying organizations and delivered products and services through 22 fulfilment centres. The company had the largest digital medical product catalogue in India having 300,000 products and it partnered with top brands and vendors to satisfy the needs of the medical establishments. Some of the product categories sold by MBR included- consumables and disposables (e.g. syringes), laboratory equipments, medical devices, medicine, dental products, medical implants, surgical instruments, hospital infrastructure and rehabilitation aids. Although this chapter just focusses on hospital procurement, MBR also sold to other institutions e.g. COVID prevention related products to educational institute and government organizations. MBR claimed to provide a complete solution for an interested hospital- identifying the right products, providing product comparisons, recommendation based on customer needs, instant quotations and buying options, building a requirement catalogue for the customer, providing historical analysis of usage and cost, financing, and price alerts for identified products.

Some of the challenges identified by the company included vendor registration with the hospitals and creating exclusive contracts with sellers. Vendor registrations, particularly in government hospitals, were a tedious and time –consuming process in India. As the company gained traction in the Indian markets, several global brands like Roche and 3M came on the platform. On its side, the company also explored possible sale of recycled and refurbished products to interested customers.

One of MBR's innovation was VIZI, a software based tool based on artificial intelligence and machine learning. Customers could buy the software based tool for a nominal fee. Once customer consumption data (use of various medical products) is entered into the tool, it could analyse historical data and generate projections which could then be used to purchase supplies from MBR. The company claimed that VIZI could provide cost savings of 30% to customers because of its superior processing and analytic power. MBR thus claimed to provide transparent, efficient supply chain management solution for its customers. During an online interaction with the author, the CEO of the company said that the real market potential was in India's smaller cities. Small hospitals and clinics could now access quality healthcare products at an affordable price from MBR instead of relying on a limited number of traders or distributors. Another innovation of the company involved using drones to provide last mile delivery of critical medical supplies. Apart from reduced delivery time, drones could also help in reducing human contact in the supply chain and the consequent risk of infection.

DISCUSSION

Introduction of a digital platform for platform for procurement will lead to several changes in the buying process of a hospital. In the background section of this chapter we have discussed about the eight steps in the organization buying process and the role of buying centres during such process. Below, the author examines the impact of a new supplier like MBR on such processes as well as the impact for other selling organizations (different brands) in such a changed scenario. For the purpose of simplicity we will consider only high value purchases (machines and equipments) done by hospitals. Industrial purchases can be classified into three groups- buying a product for the first time (new buy), buying a product that is being used with some alterations and modification (modified re-buy) and repeat purchase of a product (straight rebuy). Each of these situations will undergo change when buying happens through a single, digital platform like MBR.

Step1: Problem Recognition

The first step in the organizational buying process is problem recognition when members in the buying organization identify the need for a fresh procurement. In the case of a new buy, a digital platform will require significant time to understand customer pain points. Hospitals will still have to rely on existing vendors to help them understand which new solutions could be useful and take a more informed decision. Modified rebuy situations may not change much as users are likely to continue with existing vendors and brands if possible. In rebuy situations, depending on the contractual conditions, there is little incentive for hospitals to change vendors as transaction cost for on boarding a new vendor is likely to be high. As part of the buying centre, actual users in the buying centre will gain more power in the purchase process. From a marketing standpoint, independent sellers need to increase their effort to engage with customers early on and get their buy-in for suggested products. The online media could be used to push more information to willing customers as an additional marketing tool. This scenario may change as MBR's AI-ML based tool VIZI gets more acceptance from target customers.

Stage 2: General Need Description

At this stage in the industrial buying process, the general need of the customer is articulated clearly. For example, if there is a problem (stage 1) in getting high quality X-rays done, the purchase manager, based on her knowledge, at this stage will spell out the general features of a new X-ray machine that may solve the problem. The impact of a new digital supplier is likely to be low across all purchase scenarios at this stage as the customer knowledge about the solution is shaped by her previous experience and knowledge about such products. Medical product brands should increase focus on continuous education programmes for their customers to handle such situations.

Stage 3: Product Specification

At this stage of the buying process, the customer arrives at more specific technical requirements for the product sought. Taking the example of the X-ray machine discussed above, the customer may highlight the safety aspect or energy consumption of the product in relation to an industry standard or even a known brand like, say, Siemens. The impact of a new supplier like MBR is likely to be high, especially in case of new buy, as customers can also use the MBR digital product catalogue to find out compatible brands and the technical specification of the products. To hold their turf, established brands and existing vendors need to focus on online/offline demonstration and simulation to establish their brand superiority particularly in relation to the brands sold by MBR. In situations of modified re-buy and straight rebuy, the customer is likely to continue with existing brand choice given the high value of purchase and sensitivity of operating high end equipments in a hospital.

Stage 4: Supplier Search

Once the technical specification of the product is finalized by the members of a buying centre, the buyer starts looking for suppliers who can supply such products. Typically, in high end industrial selling, large brands start working with customers from Stage 3 so that customers are convinced of their unique product specification. In such cases, the customer's brand choice is narrowed down to a few leading brands. This set of possible vendors is also known as the consideration set. Once MBR is established as a viable new supplier, this position is likely to change. With its large digital catalogue and tie up with leading global brands like 3M and Roche, MBR can positively influence buying behaviour in case of new purchases. Even for repeat purchases, the customer may look for equivalent brands as there is enough knowledge inside the buying organization about the product and functioning. To counter competitor like MBR, established vendors need to take the role of a channel steward where they not only distribute products through partners but lead the go-to-market strategy through superior execution. Like the case of many B2C products, hospitals may also prefer to buy products from companies who has distribution network close by and can provide better service support.

Stage 5: Proposal Acquisition and Analysis

At this stage of the buying process, customers have a clear idea about the technology and product specifications. They would then advertise for interested vendors to submit their proposals in pre-defined formats. The proposals or quotations received are then analysed for their techno-commercial feasibility and how they match with the customer demand. Vendors need to give their proposal to prospective customers mentioning specific products and their prices. For high end product procurement, vendors like MBR can often provide multiple solutions from brands registered with them and thus enjoy a better advantage at this stage. Even in cases where the customer goes for a straight rebuy, MBR will have an advantage in providing a better rate because of their cost advantage. Thus digital, decentralized supply chain will be helpful for companies like MBR at this stage of the buying process. Product brands need to provide a comprehensive cost-benefit analysis to prospective buyers to gain advantage. They may consider mentioning their own servicing and maintenance capabilities too.

Stage 6: Supplier Selection

Based on the proposals received and their techno-commercial feasibility, buyers decide on a possible vendor to procure their products. This stage in industrial buying may also involve further rounds of negotiation as well as clarification on products and prices. Both MBR and standalone suppliers will not have any specific advantage here and the same holds true for modified rebuys and straight rebuy situation. Product brands need to continue their existing marketing investment and relationship building activities by providing necessary information and clarification to the customers.

Stage 7: Order Routine

This stage involves customers specifying conditions of order execution like delivery schedule, on site installation, provision of onsite service engineers, inspection and payment schedule. For high value industrial purchases, order routine is a function of the supplier brand and specific requirements from the customer. Hence, supplier brands will decide the impact of MBR type of vendors on the purchase process.

Large brands like GE, Phillips and Siemens are likely to remain unaffected at this stage due to their technical expertise and quality. However, for smaller or newer brands in the market going with suppliers like MBR may make more sense. One must note that for medical equipment business much of the order routine is driven by customer history with big brands and MBR will find it considerably difficult to wield additional advantage at this stage. However, for straight rebuy cases, MBR may have an advantage in supplying to customers. For standalone brands, the best strategy here would be to continue and improve their performance related to delivery and servicing to maintain their brand equity.

Stage 8: Performance Review

This is the last stage in the buying process and refers to the good practice of reviewing supplier performance for future business. Many customers do this periodically and reward/blacklist their suppliers based on their performance over the last few years. A supplier who delivered late in the last cycle of delivery may be replaced with another who assures timely delivery. Being a new player in the market MBR will find it difficult to score at this stage as customers would be hard-pressed to compare their performance with traditional product suppliers. However, for straight rebuy situations, because of the routineness of such transactions, MBR may have an advantage over other vendors. This stage could be a game changer for traditional standalone brands who could provide evidence of their long standing history with the customer, excellent relationships nurtured over time and proof of performance. In industrial markets all these factors go a long way in creating win-win synergies for buyers and sellers.

The impact of introducing a digital procurement platform on buying and selling of medical equipments is indicated in Table 1.

Buying Centre Impact

As discussed in the background section of this chapter, buying centre refers to a group of individuals who together influence and decide on a purchase. Marketers need to map the individuals in a specific buying centre and pitch their products depending on their requirement. For example, in a hospital, the radiologist (influencer) may influence the choice of an X-ray machine even though a technician (user) is the end user. The hospital CEO remains the decider while the purchase manager plays the role of a gatekeeper (controlling flow of information to the seller) as well as the primary point of contact for the seller. How will introduction of digital platforms like MBR change the scenario? This author believes that the role of the buying centre will not be seriously affected with the only exception being the CEO or

Table 1. Impact of introducing a digital procurement platform on buying and selling of medical equipments

Buying Process Steps	New Buy	Modified Rebuy	Straight Rebuy	Sales/Marketing Implication for medical product brands
Problem Recognition	Low	Low	Low	• Increase solution selling • Provide user with more online information
General Need Description	Low	Low	Low	• Provide continuous customer education to doctors and technologists
Product specification	*High*	Low	Low	• Provide online and offline demo
Supplier Search	*High*	Low	*High*	• Increase distribution reach and quality
Proposal Analysis	*High*	Low	*High*	• Provide better cost-benefit analysis
Supplier Selection	Low		Low	• Continue existing marketing effort
Order Routine	Brand dependant/Low	Low	*High*	• Increase delivery and service performance
Performance Review	Brand Dependant/Low	Low	*High*	• Provide historical proof of cost and efficiency

CFO (decider). As CEO/CFOs are concerned with return on investment for hospital supplies, MBR could significantly influence them by bringing in the logic of cost optimization and supply chain efficiency. Use of MBR tool like VIZI can provide useful dashboards to top management to understand macro procurement trends in their own organization, benchmark with other competitors and adopt a suitable procurement strategy.

Role of Buyers in Small City Hospitals

MBR has admitted that its key focus will be smaller cities and smaller hospitals. Our analysis also supports this strategy. Independent hospitals (as opposed to national chains) in smaller cities are likely to be under-served by large product brands/ their distributors and thus MBR's impact will be proportionately higher in converting such customers. As discussed above, smaller hospitals will also have fewer members in their buying centre and deciders (owner/ CEOs) will have much more decision making power.

Summing up, introduction of digital platform based supply options will decentralize the purchase process but also recentralize it at the point of platform. Thus central purchasing teams in hospitals can now stop identifying and interacting with multiple vendors (decentralization) but this activity will now be carried out by vendors like MBR (recentralization). This will have significant impacts on the marketing strategies of vendors should they decide to continue selling to hospitals instead of selling to/ through MBR. For high value purchases, MBR will impact the purchasing process at several steps of the buying process including product specification, supplier search, proposal acquisition and analysis. This holds true for both new buys and straight rebuys. Marketers will have to suitable fine-tune their strategies if they want to compete in this newly configured marketplace.

Limitation and Future Research Direction

Introduction of decentralized, digital platforms will disrupt the supply chains permanently. In the case of medial equipments, high value purchases will be impacted in the way vendors are chosen by hospitals as shown in this chapter. However, this research has several limitations. It only considers high value purchases and not supply of regular low cost consumables like syringes. Second it does not fully consider the situation in smaller cities where buying process and buying centres are different. Third, it assumes that big brands in the industry will continue to go solo rather than tying up with platforms like MBR. Future research can consider all such factors as well as some additional ones. First, our experience in the consumer markets show that many platforms like Amazon start developing private labels for established categories which are largely commoditized. There may be a chance that MBR may decide to go this way. Already, as our case shows, it has started creating markets for refurbished products where it will have higher pricing power. Second, many consumer brands try to recover their loss due to online retailers by agreeing to be the contract manufacturer for such retailers. Future research can explore if large brands like GE will consider manufacturing white label products for digital platforms like MBR.

CONCLUSION

This chapter discussed the impact of platform based suppliers on supply chain and marketing. It uses the case of medikabazaar.com, a digital platform for medical supplies that has disrupted the medical supply industry in India. Using the theoretical framework of buying process and buying centres, it argues that several stages of industrial buying process will be disrupted. It also suggests that existing players can adopt strategies to counter the advance of digital decentralized supply chains. While digitalization of supply chain is a given in the global economy, the decentralization aspect can be contested. As we show in this paper, there could be possible re-intermediation of the supply chain in the form of platform based business models like medikabazaar.com. Platforms will allow de-centralizing by letting more number of suppliers in the buying process but will aggregate such suppliers and supplies in a way that benefits them and their customers.

REFERENCES

Ageron, B., Bentahar, O., & Gunasekaran, A. (2020, July). Digital Supply Chain: Challenges and future directions. *Supply Chain Forum International Journal (Toronto, Ont.)*, *21*(3), 133–138.

Agrawal, P., & Narain, R. (2018). Digital supply chain management: An Overview. *IOP Conference Series. Materials Science and Engineering*, *455*(1).

Alrubaiee, L., Alshaibi, H., & Al-bayati, Y. (2012). Relationship between B2B e-commerce benefits, e-marketplace usage and supply chain management. *Global Journal of Management and Business Research*, *12*(9).

Büyüközkan, G., & Göçer, F. (2018). Digital Supply Chain: Literature review and a proposed framework for future research. *Computers in Industry*, *97*, 157–177. doi:10.1016/j.compind.2018.02.010

Cambrra-Fierro, J. J., & Polo-Redondo, Y. (2008). Creating satisfaction in the demand-supply chain: The buyers' perspective. *Supply Chain Management.*

Croom, S. R. (2005). The impact of e-business on supply chain management. *International Journal of Operations & Production Management*, *25*(1), 55–73. doi:10.1108/01443570510572240

El Nemr, Canel, & Taghipour. (2021). The Determinants of Hotel Room Rates in Beirut: A Hedonic Pricing Model. *International Journal of Trade, Economics and Finance*, *12*(2).

Ellram, L. M., & Murfield, M. L. U. (2019). Supply chain management in industrial marketing–Relationships matter. *Industrial Marketing Management*, *79*, 36–45. doi:10.1016/j.indmarman.2019.03.007

Eng, T. Y. (2004). The role of e-marketplaces in supply chain management. *Industrial Marketing Management*, *33*(2), 97–105. doi:10.1016/S0019-8501(03)00032-4

Flyvbjerg, B. (2006). Five misunderstandings about case-study research. *Qualitative Inquiry*, *12*(2), 219–245. doi:10.1177/1077800405284363

Formentini, M., & Romano, P. (2016). Towards supply chain collaboration in B2B pricing. *International Journal of Operations & Production Management*, *36*(7), 734–756. doi:10.1108/IJOPM-03-2015-0124

Garay-Rondero, C. L., Martinez-Flores, J. L., Smith, N. R., Morales, S. O. C., & Aldrette-Malacara, A. (2019). Digital supply chain model in Industry 4.0. *Journal of Manufacturing Technology Management, 31*(5), 887–933. doi:10.1108/JMTM-08-2018-0280

Geunes, J., Romeijn, H. E., & van den Heuvel, W. (2016). Improving the efficiency of decentralized supply chains with fixed ordering costs. *European Journal of Operational Research, 252*(3), 815–828. doi:10.1016/j.ejor.2016.02.004

Giannoccaro, I. (2018). Centralized vs. decentralized supply chains: The importance of decision maker's cognitive ability and resistance to change. *Industrial Marketing Management, 73*, 59–69. doi:10.1016/j.indmarman.2018.01.034

Hadjikhani, A., & LaPlaca, P. (2013). Development of B2B marketing theory. *Industrial Marketing Management, 42*(3), 294–305. doi:10.1016/j.indmarman.2013.03.011

Iddris, F. (2018). Digital supply chain: Survey of the literature. *International Journal of Business Research and Management, 9*(1), 47–61.

Jung, H., Chen, F. F., & Jeong, B. (2008). Decentralized supply chain planning framework for third party logistics partnership. *Computers & Industrial Engineering, 55*(2), 348–364. doi:10.1016/j.cie.2007.12.017

Kozlenkova, I. V., Hult, G. T. M., Lund, D. J., Mena, J. A., & Kekec, P. (2015). The role of marketing channels in supply chain management. *Journal of Retailing, 91*(4), 586–609. doi:10.1016/j.jretai.2015.03.003

Lambert, D. M., & Enz, M. G. (2017). Issues in supply chain management: Progress and potential. *Industrial Marketing Management, 62*, 1–16. doi:10.1016/j.indmarman.2016.12.002

Lavassani, K., Movahedi, B., & Kumar, V. (2008, May). Transition to B2B e-Marketplace enabled supply chain: Readiness assessment and success factors. In CONF-IRM 2008 Proceedings (p. 59). Academic Press.

Lee, H., & Whang, S. (1999). Decentralized multi-echelon supply chains: Incentives and information. *Management Science, 45*(5), 633–640. doi:10.1287/mnsc.45.5.633

Lee, H. L., & Billington, C. (1993). Material management in decentralized supply chains. *Operations Research, 41*(5), 835–847. doi:10.1287/opre.41.5.835

Liu, L., Parlar, M., & Zhu, S. X. (2007). Pricing and lead time decisions in decentralized supply chains. *Management Science, 53*(5), 713–725. doi:10.1287/mnsc.1060.0653

Lu, S. Y., Lau, H. Y., & Yiu, C. K. (2012). A hybrid solution to collaborative decision-making in a decentralized supply-chain. *Journal of Engineering and Technology Management, 29*(1), 95–111. doi:10.1016/j.jengtecman.2011.09.008

Mbiatem, J., Taghipour, A., & Canel-Depitre, B. (2018, August). Supplier Selection Approaches for Decision Makers. In *Proceedings of the 8th International Conference on Information Communication and Management* (pp. 108-112). Academic Press.

Pedersen, E. R. G., Henriksen, M. H., Frier, C., Søby, J., & Jennings, V. (2013). Stakeholder thinking in sustainability management: The case of Novozymes. *Social Responsibility Journal, 9*(4), 500–515. doi:10.1108/SRJ-08-2012-0101

Ryals, L. J., & Humphries, A. S. (2007). Managing key business-to-business relationships: What marketing can learn from supply chain management. *Journal of Service Research, 9*(4), 312–326. doi:10.1177/1094670507299380

Scuotto, V., Caputo, F., Villasalero, M., & Del Giudice, M. (2017). A multiple buyer–supplier relationship in the context of SMEs' digital supply chain management. *Production Planning and Control, 28*(16), 1378–1388. doi:10.1080/09537287.2017.1375149

Siggelkow, N. (2007). Persuasion with case studies. *Academy of Management Journal, 50*(1), 20–24. doi:10.5465/amj.2007.24160882

Taghipour, A. (2017). *Contemporary Approaches and Strategies for Applied Logistics: A contemporary approach to plan independent logistics actors*. IGI Global.

Taghipour, A., & Frayret, J. M. (2013). Dynamic mutual adjustment search for supply chain operations planning co-ordination. *International Journal of Production Research, 51*(9), 2715–2739. doi:10.1080/00207543.2012.737952

Tang, S. Y., Gurnani, H., & Gupta, D. (2014). Managing disruptions in decentralized supply chains with endogenous supply process reliability. *Production and Operations Management, 23*(7), 1198–1211. doi:10.1111/poms.12160

Tliche, Y., Taghipour, A., & Canel-Depitre, B. (2019). Downstream Demand Inference in decentralized supply chains. *European Journal of Operational Research, 274*(1), 65–77. doi:10.1016/j.ejor.2018.09.034

Tliche, Taghipour, & Canel. (2018). *Anticipation of Demand in Supply Chains in Hierarchical Planning and Information Sharing Techniques in Supply Chain Management*. IGI Global.

Vargo, S. L., & Lusch, R. F. (2011). It's all B2B… and beyond: Toward a systems perspective of the market. *Industrial Marketing Management*, *40*(2), 181–187. doi:10.1016/j.indmarman.2010.06.026

Vosooghidizaji, M., Taghipour, A., & Canel-Depitre, B. (2020, December). Information Asymmetry in Supply Chain Coordination: State of the Art. *Journal of Industrial and Intelligent Information*, *8*(2), 38–43. doi:10.18178/jiii.8.2.38-43

Vosooghidizaji, M., Taghipour, A., & Canel-Depitre, B. (2020). Supply chain coordination under information asymmetry: A review. *International Journal of Production Research*, *58*(6), 1805–1834. doi:10.1080/00207543.2019.1685702

Walsh, W. E., & Wellman, M. P. (2003). Decentralized supply chain formation: A market protocol and competitive equilibrium analysis. *Journal of Artificial Intelligence Research*, *19*, 513–567. doi:10.1613/jair.1213

Zhu, S. X. (2015). Integration of capacity, pricing, and lead-time decisions in a decentralized supply chain. *International Journal of Production Economics*, *164*, 14–23. doi:10.1016/j.ijpe.2015.02.026

KEY TERMS AND DEFINITIONS

Buying Centre: Group of individuals in an organization involved in its purchasing process.

Decentralized Supply Chain: A system of procuring goods and services required in an organization from multiple sources or vendors.

Industrial Buying: Purchase of products by organizations for their own use or re-sell.

New Buy: A product purchased by an organization for the first time.

Platform: A digital platform providing goods and services to organizations.

Vendor: Individuals or organizations supplying products to another individual or organization.

Chapter 4
Manufacturer Service-Oriented Strategy:
A New Source of Competitive Advantage in Homogenous Industrial Markets

Youssef Elhaoussine
Beijing Normal University-Hong Kong Baptist University United International College, China

ABSTRACT

This chapter develops a new hybrid manufacturing service-based marketing strategy for manufacturers evolving in a homogenous market. First, by using the Porter's value chain model, it will outline how manufacturers develop their competitive advantages in a normal context and then run the same theoretical analysis in the context of a homogenous market where it is difficult for manufacturers to create a difference. In addition, a qualitative research in the form of semi-conducted interviews with factory executives will confirm the homogeneity of strategies among competitors and outline the importance of developing new strategic directions. The conclusion will show that in order to create competitive advantages without using too many resources, marketing, service management, and technology could work together and lead manufacturers to adopt a more service-based marketing management orientation.

DOI: 10.4018/978-1-7998-6874-3.ch004

INTRODUCTION

The main goal of branding strategies is to help businesses to make a difference in their market. Brand strategy efforts helps companies to grow and develop by gaining more customers and market shares (Keller and Lehmann, 2006). When the market is flourishing, such efforts are not always required. Companies can take advantage of the organic market growth. However, when a market is becoming more saturated or when competition become fiercer, brand strategy efforts are critical. They must be planned judiciously in order to achieve the intended difference in the market.

Compare to consumer brands in a B2C market, manufacturers in a B2B market have less opportunities to make the difference over their competitors. Manufacturers are intrinsically production and efficiency oriented (Mudambi et al., 1997). Their quest to gain competitive advantages is usually accomplished through production efficiency or in other words by producing the best product while optimizing the use of resources. In the context of manufacturers, or producers of parts and equipment that may be marketed by another company, competitive advantages generated by production efficiency are usually translated into price driven competitiveness. And all functions of the value chain participate actively toward this endeavor. In short, the manufacturer able to produce a suitable enough product at the best price should have more chance to win more market share.

However, after an era of expansion, several manufacturer markets could be considered becoming homogenous. In such market conditions, manufacturers have difficulties to achieve competitive advantages as customers are not able to differentiate one manufacturer offer from the other. Manufacturers need to acknowledge this situation and focus on areas of the value chain where a sustainable difference can be achieved. This article will introduce a new brand strategy by first analyzing theoretically and through a qualitative research conducted in the printing industry in China how manufactures in homogenous market develop competitive advantages and then propose a change in posture from producer to service provider in order to help building suitable competitive advantages. In order to be sustainable, the implications of this change and recommendation for further research will be proposed.

SOURCE OF COMPETITIVE ADVANTAGE IN CLASSIC MANUFACTURING

Before considering the effect of such a homogenous market on the conception of competitive advantages, it is important to first comprehend simply how price advantage could be achieved in manufacturing markets. In order to do so, a value chain's model (Porter, 1985) is presented in figure 1. Through a conceptual analysis, the contribution from all five primary activities and four supporting activities on creating competitive advantage will be performed and analyzed theoretically. Then, this exploration will be put in the context of a homogenous market where manufacturers should have difficulties creating differences between each other.

Figure 1. Porter generic value chain (Porter, 1985)

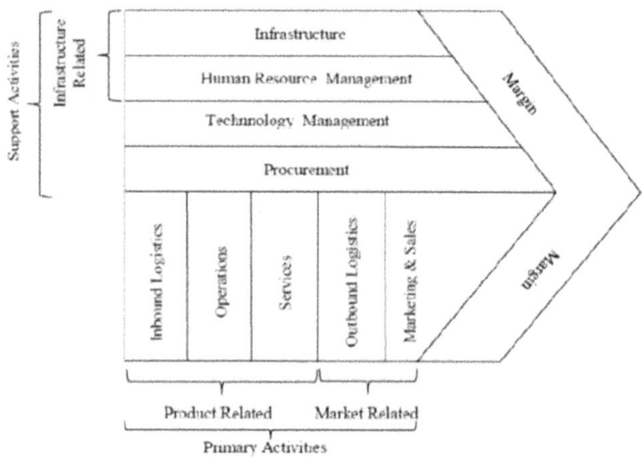

In manufacturing markets:

- Inbound logistics, which includes all receiving, warehousing and inventory management of raw materials for production, helps factories to build price leverage by optimizing and distributing materials to various departments.
- Operation or production, which encompass all efforts needed to convert raw materials into a finished product or service, is controlled by the factories and represent the core of their activities. The leverage would be represented by engineering efforts to optimize production process.
- Services as well as Marketing and Sales are represented in the form of intangible activities. Price leverage can be achieved in reducing efforts (i.e. reducing direct sales or reducing service scope).
- Outbound logistics, which happens after all operations are completed and the end-product is ready for customers, could also develop leverage by optimizing product transit from the manufacturer to the customers (Taghipour, 2012; Tliche et al., 2019). In international trade, the latter part is even more important as goods needs to cross borders.
- Procurement is an important cost center directly related to a price competitive advantage. All factory purchases of fix assets or consumables will have an

impact of the marginal cost of the production output. The main example are raw materials, machineries, and spare parts, Price leverage is achieved by getting cheaper and consistent products.

- Technology level defines how processes are efficient. Whether a task is performed by hand or by automation will affect the marginal cost of the production output.
- Human resource is particularly relevant in countries where labor cost in the manufacturing industry was considered to be low and represented a comparative advantage in the global marketplace. But today the trend has changed and start to reverse.
- Infrastructure represents fix assets purchased by the manufacturer. In some cases, factories locate or relocate to cheaper real estate areas.

Therefore, what would happen if by reaching market homogeneity, price-based competitive advantage could no more be created?

On the surface, it would mean that all manufacturers offer the same deals and values to all customers. To be more specific, it would mean that most primary and secondary parts of the value chain mentioned earlier are becoming uniform across the market and do not provide competitive advantages. The following development shows how this could be interpreted within all value chain functions:

- For inbound logistics, once optimized, it becomes very difficult to improve its process if the manufacturer does not develop.
- For operation or productions, manufacturer use similar machinery and production process across the industry. A large amount of resources would be required to invest in better engineering and production machinery, if it is available.
- For marketing and sales, the competitive advantage promoted and sold to the market is based on the performance of other functions. If the benefits of the offer are similar across competitors, then a competitive advantage would be difficult to achieve.
- For service, an industrial offer usually includes a tangible component based on the value of the actual product as well as a service intangible component based on the action that could be performed before, during and after the purchase of the tangible product. Therefore, service deployment depends on how the manufacturer's management team perceives the importance of service within its offer. If all competitors are providing the same array of services, the differentiation between them is unlikely.
- For outbound logistics, in a homogenous market or not, a manufacturer selling to customers usually outsource this function. Transportation arrangements

and paperwork are handled by forwarders. Their offer is based on the current demands and a price reduction is very difficult to achieve due to the fact that forwarders operate on very small margin.

- For procurement, all competitors have more or less similar costs for raw material and inventory management. In order to get an advantage, a manufacturer would require to have enough resource to achieve economy of scales in buying more raw materials, or maximizing use of inventory space.
- For technology related to production, the situation is similar to the operation or production function. However, for technology related to other function of the value chain, the development and the use of a more efficient decision system process can be achieved at relatively low cost.
- For human resource, the salary and related cost (i.e. training, incentive) can be reduced but this could affect other functions. Lower paid employees are less motivated or more reluctant to provide extra efforts to help building competitive advantage.
- For infrastructure, the cost will depend of the location for the manufacturer. The leverage could be achieved by relocating, but this strategy is easily adoptable by competitors.

From a preliminary examination, the consequence of this market homogeneity could leave the possibility to develop competitive advantages only to manufacturer with the financial means and the sheer size to use economy of scales on the primary and secondary activities of the value chain. Among other things, their size and money guaranty that they can achieve strong leverage with suppliers and logistic parties. In addition, it means that they can also finance technological development to improve production process and get a return on their investment. Furthermore, they could pay employees better and improve their dedications to the tasks. This interpretation emphasizes the fact that there is a direct relationship between financial resources and competitive advantage in manufacturer markets. Therefore, is there any other way requiring fewer financial resources to obtain a competitive advantage?

The second overview of the Porter's framework still permits to outline two possible functions for manufacturers in homogenous markets to develop 'cheaper' competitive advantages: marketing and services management. Both activities have something in common: they have an intangible perspective. Marketing is represented by the intangible evaluation around the brand identity created for the market and service management is intangible by nature. What is interesting about intangible value is that their evaluation and worth are inconsistent across customers. For example, customers might agree on how much worth a special packaging (a tangible value). However, they might have different evaluation on how much worth a consulting session to improve quality (an intangible value). Another example; in a manufacturing context, customers might have similar evaluation on the cost of a tangible product characteristic. But they might have difficulties to assess consistently the value of a good customer service before, during and after the production. Although they are not in the core of manufacturer activities, intangible values could have the ability to create salient competitive advantages and therefore be useful for manufacturer in homogenous markets. From this theoretical perspective, manufacturers would need to embrace those two functions of the values chain and follow a more service-marketing orientation.

SEMI-CONDUCTED INTERVIEWS AND HOMOGENOUS MARKET PERSPECTIVE

In order to confirm the hypothesis stating that manufacturers evolving in a homogenous market should adopt a more service-marketing orientation in order to develop cost efficient competitive advantages, a round of in-depth interviews have been performed with factory executives from the printing consumable aftermarket industry in China. This industry is an example of a market that went through the up and down of the product life cycle and is now in the middle of a homogenous phase where competing manufacturers have difficulties to develop distinctive positioning. From a preliminary interview with the Director of the industry media, Recycling Time Media (aka RT Media is in charge of publishing periodically magazine, broadcasting online TV Channel and organize worldwide trade exhibitions around the world for the printing aftermarket industry. Their headquarter is located in Zhuhai, China), an overview of the market dynamic was established and confirms the struggles facing Chinese manufacturers. It was outlined that this industry has known a large expansion with the development of printers within households and service SMEs. It produced recycled or brand new generic compatible cartridges that offer an alternative to costlier OEM cartridge. This development was also favored by the emergence of e-commerce sales channel, which allowed thousands of retailers (small and big) around the world to purchase those products from manufacturers or wholesalers and sell them to end users. However, after many years of prosperity, the market reached a certain level of maturity pushing manufacturers to develop new strategies to survive. The fight over market shares and customers became more intense leading manufacturer with limited options.

Therefore, in order to assess those strategic options taken by manufacturers in this industry, a set of 5 separate interviews with Chinese factory executives from large to small size, were conducted in Zhuhai in either the interviewee office or a neutral location. First, the interviewer introduced himself. The purposes of the interview were to identify what strategies are currently used by manufacturers evolving in a homogenous market and observe what areas are overlooked. The result and analysis of those interviews will help to identify the current situation and potentially to identify new strategic directions in order to develop cost efficient competitive advantages in a homogenous market.

During the interview. the interviewer mentioned to each interviewee that the interview consists of approximately 20 questions and should last around 45 to 60 minutes. Then, the purpose of the interview was presented as an investigation on Chinese manufacturer brand strategy in the printing aftermarket. It was outlined that in order to guaranty confidentiality, all information mentioning the manufacturer or information that could help recognizing the manufacturers will be removed from any publication or public use of the present article.

The questioning sequence was constructed using the marketing mix and the flower of service frameworks, which outline the different decision centers involved in marketing strategies. Such decision will define how a factory will be positioned in the market and perceived differently from other competitors. The semi-conducted interview was sequenced in several sequences described below:

Step 1: Contextual and Introduction sequence

The first set of questions were asked in order to set up the interview background and establish a marketing and sales context with the interviewee. The orientation of the first sequence was toward obtaining information about clients, and the general effort made to obtain and retain them. The questions were as follow:

- How many clients do you have currently? Could you describe them?
- How did you find your customers?
- Do customers switch to your competitors? What do you think are the reasons for customers to switch?

Step 2: Basic brand element sequence

The second set of questions aimed at understanding the basic branding elements enacted by the manufacturer. Visual branding represent the basics for a brand to be perceived differently by customers. The answer will show if the company tries a minimum to be different from other competitor and sets the way for the following sequences. The questions were as follow:

- What is the logo and the name of your factory? How did you choose or design those elements? What are the colors of your company? If any, where can I see those colors in your factory?

Step 3: Marketing Mix Sequence

The third sequence asked more specific questions about the manufacturer's offer. It follows the four P's of the Marketing mix: Product, Price, Promotion and Place. Each question allows comparing the different manufacturers and observing how they position themselves in the market. The questions were as follow:

- ◦ Can you describe your product portfolio? (*Product*)
- ◦ How do you set your prices? How do you position your price compared with your competitors? (*Price*)
- ◦ What do you do to communicate and attract new customers? (*Promotion*)
- ◦ Which channel do you use to sell your products? (*Place*)

Step 4: Flower of service sequence

Since industrial or B2B offers are not only focusing on the tangible product itself but also on intangible services, the fourth sequence question was design to capture the service implementation of manufacturers. It follows the 8 petals of the Flower of Service framework: Consultation, Order Taking, Hospitality, Safekeeping, Payment, Information, Billing and Exception. Similar to the previous sequence, it allows further comparison between the different manufacturers and observing how they position themselves in the market. The questions were as follow:

- ◦ Besides producing for your customer, what do you do for them? (*Consultation*)
- ◦ Could you describe briefly the order process in your factory? (*Order taking*)
- ◦ Where do you meet with your customer? (*Hospitality*)
- ◦ What do you do to make your customers trust your production and your company? (*Safekeeping*)
- ◦ What are the payment methods customers can use when dealing with you? (*Payment*)
- ◦ During the order process, how to communicate with your current customer? *Information*)
- ◦ What part of the export procedures do you perform on the behalf of your customers? (*Billing*)
- ◦ What special request can you handle for you customers? (*Exception*)

Step 5: Summary sequence

Finally, the interviewee is asked to address the main goal of the interview and offer direct answers on what they do in order to establish a difference with competitors. The previous sequences helped to recall important information to that effect. In addition, a hypothetical question was asked to see what resources would be considered to increase the difference with other manufacturers and competitively. This question helps to understand what is the main strategic focus of manufacturers. The questions were as follow:

- ◦ What makes you different from your competitors

- What resources would you required to be more competitive? And how would you use it?

From the various interviews, it was possible to identify three main patterns across all interviews. First, customers have difficulties to differentiate one manufacturer from others, especially because the prices, the products and the services offered are often similar. All answers from the marketing mix and the flower of service sequences showed that manufacturers do similar actions. Second, in order to achieve a difference, manufacturers would need a large amount of resources. The most cited were money and technology for production in order to be more price competitive and develop better product quality. It was outline that it is however a difficult endeavor since profit margin are very low. Finally, the best strategy to gain and retain customers (in respect to its cost effectiveness) is to develop a strong interpersonal relationship at executives' level. However, this implies a larger effort from senior management to create this bound since more junior management experience higher turnover.

Furthermore, there were several important points that were not mentioned but are relevant due to their absence. First, there was the lack of brand strategy or identity from manufacturers. Besides the basic brand elements such as name, logo and color codes, no other significant branding strategy was mentioned. Of course, all manufacturers mentioned that they have the best product and the best prices. However, this does not qualify as brand strategy because it represents as similar positioning across competitors. As mentioned earlier, the purpose of a brand strategy is to create a noticeable difference for the customers and most importantly that the customers accept and recognized it when deciding to select a manufacturer.

Second, although the flower of services shows that there were several possibilities to offer services to customers (represented by the eight petals), manufacturers only focused on the basics such as providing export paperwork, organizing logistics and of course treating customers to dinners when they visit. Some mentioned that they could help customers designing their packaging but those services were based on a specific demand from the customers, they were not part an already stated offer. Those services seem narrow and other perspectives could be considered since B2B interactions requires more than an exchange of product with money. For example, manufacturers could offer better access to quality control during production. They could also offer warehousing space for customers who purchase goods from different industries in the same geographic area. They could offer more payment terms. They could assist their customers in other activities such as designing retail outlet. They could create more efficient communication channels to manage customers before, during and after the production. Many more possibilities are available; however, they need identified, designed and performed according to the manufacturers' possibilities and the customers' demands.

As a conclusion, those interviews showed a certain homogeneity and restraint inside the market where the strategy of factories become uniform and where customers can hardly perceive the difference between manufacturers 'offers. Manufacturers seem to act and direct their strategies in the same ways. Their focus is mostly on developing competitive advantages through price, improving quality through better production efficiency and potentially developing relationship though interpersonal connections. However, these directions do not allow to develop competitive advantages since most competitors are following them. Besides, developing those directions requires financial resources that are not always constantly available.

Therefore, from this analysis, the main problematic is not about knowing how to create a competitive advantage, but rather knowing how to create one that won't require too much of their resources. This specific problematic is due to the fact that manufacturers operate on a low profit margin range, and any increase on cost or loss in revenue could threaten the fragile stability of the company and could lead to a critical situation. In fact, such problematic is not specific to this industry, it could be generalized to any market that present the same characteristics of a homogenous B2B market. So, a new service and marketing strategy could offer the opportunity to develop such a differentiation between manufacturers while being cost effective.

SOLUTIONS AND RECOMMENDATIONS: ADOPTION OF MANUFACTURING SERVICE-BASED STRATEGY

The marketing of services involves considerations and tasks that are different from those involved in the marketing of tangible products. In building intangible service values, manufacturers need to adopt a service management process in order to reduce the several gaps involved in services marketing. Of course, customers are looking for the best product, but in manufacturing, since the process of finding and purchasing the right product is complex, customers are also looking to get the best 'supply chain experience' possible while purchasing (Mahfod et al., 2019 ; Loivet et al., 2020). In the context of a homogenous market, where the salience of product values (tangible value) are diminished, services and the values they carry become preeminent. From that perspective, the same process uses in service marketing could be used to improve the manufacturer's brand and develop competitive advantages.

In that direction, service marketing theories and practices needs to be considered. The purpose will be to align the manufacturer offer with the customer's expectations (Parasuraman, 2004). To do so, a manufacturer's management team will need to consider the experience around the purchase of the physical product. This does not mean they should forget their main priority, which is producing the best possible output for their client. The idea is rather for a manufacturer to pose as a service provider while producing goods. Such shift toward service marketing strategy offers plenty possibilities in developing values (Matthyssens, 2006). If the tangible values could no more carry competitive values efficiently, several services dimensions, such as the service scope, the service encounters, the servicescape, and most importantly the employees in contact with the customers, could carry them.

Interestingly, the last dimension mention above is believed to be the most important in this context. This is confirmed by the trend where manufacturers use their sales teams to develop strong interpersonal bond with customers (Abdul-Muhmin, 2005). The objective then, for a manufacturer service-based strategy, would also be to try to synthetize and homogenize the interpersonal interaction or encounters with customers in order to associate them to the manufacturer. Nowadays, the interpersonal relationship is too dependent on the individual. In other word, customers see the benefit of a factory by judging the agent they are in contact with. But if these agents leave the company, the interpersonal values go with them and do not remain in the manufacturer brand. In order to build a sustainable advantage, it is important that the value created remain with the manufacturer or its 'brand'.

IMPLICATIONS FOR MANUFACTURERS

Adopting Service-Based Strategy

So, what would be the implications in order to implement this strategy? In addition to external marketing activities, the development of internal and interactive marketing becomes important for manufacturers. These two marketing directions aimed at developing a sustainable and effective service marketing strategy. As manufacturers are historically producer, their main marketing focus was on external marketing in order to communicate about their offer to the market. To accomplish the shift in service-based marketing strategy proposed in this article, the two other form of marketing activities must be considered. Their definition and their implication in the context of manufacturers will help to develop a new manufacturing service-based strategy.

First, internal marketing is an interaction process between the organization and its employees. It aims at understanding and fulfilling employee's needs when doing their job, which in return will enhance employee motivation, retention and performance with customers. By satisfying the needs of internal customers, an organization increases its efficiency to satisfy external customers (Ahmed and Rafiq, 2003). In order to do so, manufacturers need to create a process in the form of a dialogue between the internal customers (frontline employees or agents) and the executives (decision makers for all functions of the value chain). Second, interactive marketing requires a constant monitoring of customers through multiple communication and delivery channels or contact points (Shankar and Malthouse, 2006). Manufacturers need to develop processes to perform this information monitoring in order to tailor their offer to the idiosyncratic needs of industrial customers (Simon & Schumann, 2001).

In both internal and interactive marketing activities, the dialogue with internal or external customers is information-based and required appropriate medium to carry the information. Therefore, a new process is needed to monitor efficiently these interactions with the aim to provide better values.

Role of Information Technology

Technology has been outlined as an important factor in service firms. One way for manufacturers to perform this ultra-dynamic monitoring and control the quality of their output, is to adopt a constant monitoring of information using appropriate information technology tools. Figure 2 shows that IT is at the center to build an osmosis between external, internal and interactive marketing activities required in implementing service marketing-oriented strategy (Parasuraman, 2004).

Figure 2. Pyramid model of services marketing (Parasuraman, 2004)

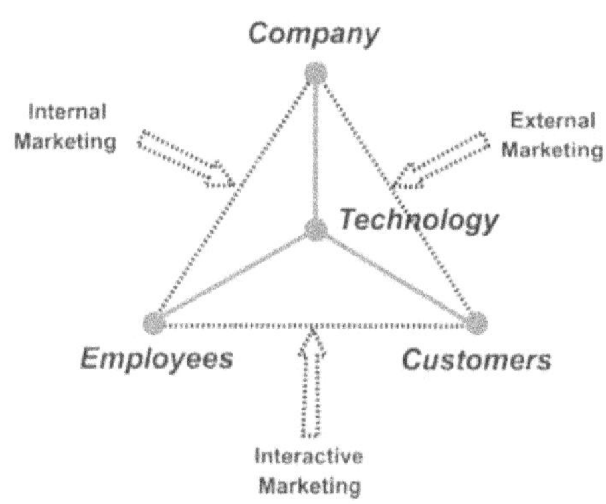

In an internal marketing perspective, information technology could help creating a more inclusive communication process between manufacturer's decision centers and frontline employees. An IT system could collect and provide up-to-date data from all the functions of the value chain and make the data pool available to all internal customers so they could make educated decisions. In an interactive marketing perspective, the pursue of synthesizing and homogenizing the interpersonal interaction or encounters between frontline employees and customers usually involved the use of a Customer Relationship Management (CRM) information system. This has the advantage to provide data and monitoring between customers and a company, in here manufacturers (Alipour and Mohammadi, 2011).

However, instead of limiting CRM to external customers, a CRM system should also consider centralizing all information and offering internal customers with up-to-date information from all functions of the value chain, transforming a classic CRM system into an Internal and External Customer Relation Management system (or IECRM). Such orientation would give to manufacturers' executives a better control and monitoring of the intangible value they want to provide to their customers. And since the quantity and the dynamic nature of data to process represents a real challenge, they would need to deploy an adapted larger range of information technology tools: software and hardware.

In CRM, the emphasis is mostly put on the software part. But the management of data coming from a multitude of different activities in the value chain, at different time, collected from different people, for different purpose and at large quantity requires manufacturers to think about more suitable hardware and on how to use them as constant learning tools to manage internal and external customers. From this perspective, the efficiency of the CRM system depends on how it is used and how it is updated. While interacting with a CRM system, users either collect information (output) and/or provide information (input). However, if an IECRM system is considered, the input becomes more complex and require therefore hardware devices allowing efficient input. In IECRM, executives would be required to set up process to assess internal customer's experience and needs. And internal customers would be required to provide data not only to executives but also to external customers.

In today's world, the new trend of professional IT hardware development goes to device that provide mobility and versatility. In IECRM, both values are useful when frontline employees are in roaming and require to provide and consult rich information. Such devices can help to assist customers and they can provide evaluation to executives in order to assess the situation and possibly outline new internal needs. An example could be virtual reality or enhance reality device. Their innovative added values are based on providing a higher level of rich media information. In IECRM, this could be very useful when the customer, the frontline employees or support services want to check prototype or run simulations to assess results. For the customer it is a way to predict quality before starting production. And for frontline employees, it is a way to assess the situation and predict unexpected needs. In here, IT hardware serves as tools that allow a better managing data with the purpose to identify, create, deploy and monitor various intangible values.

Managing Service Quality

A final aspect to consider, for manufacturers deciding to manage intangibles values and considering the implementation of service-based marketing strategy with the implications mentioned above, one problem remains: the assessment of quality. In the presented service-based strategy, Manufacturers will produce their traditional tangible values and deploy their new intangible values. Although they have experience in handling and assessing quality for tangible values, intangible values are different (Parasuraman, 2004). They have a heterogeneous nature based on the situation and the customer. Their delivery requires a constant assessment of the output. In order to allow the manufacturer service-based strategy to be efficiently implemented and create sustainable competitive advantage, it should undergo the same process of quality management assessment as any other business area,

However. the body of literature on total quality management (TQM) has focused on manufacturing (Mahmood et al., 2014; Singh and Ahuja, 2014), service firms (Arasli, 2012; Talib et al., 2013; Psomas and Jaca, 2016; Jyoti et al., 2017), in mass services (Woon, 2000), in service and manufacturing separately (Prajogo, 2005; Bouranta et al., 2019). In addition, comparison between manufacturing TQM and service TQM has been covered (Silvestro, 1998; Sureshchandar et al., 2001; Prajogo, 2005).. Furthermore, research on TQM also used to help assessing and developing internal and external customer's satisfaction (Singh et al., 2006; Sit et al., 2009; Bouranta et al., 2019).

In the context presented in this article, where a manufacturer poses as a service provider, the process to assess TQM may be different and could offer a new direction in research. The focus could be on the criteria to assess. Can the same criteria used in the study of TQM for manufacturing and for service firm be combined and mixed? For example, soft TQM practices are intangible and are primarily related to leadership, employee empowerment and culture, while hard TQM practices refer to quality improvement tools and techniques, such as quality management systems, cost of quality and statistical process control, benchmarking (Fotopoulos and Psomas, 2009). Or is it necessary to develop new ones? The door is open to new research that will surely provide strong managerial implications for manufacturers and manufacturer in general.

REFERENCES

Abdul-Muhmin, A. G. (2005). Instrumental and interpersonal determinants of relationship satisfaction and commitment in industrial markets. *Journal of Business Research, 58*(5), 619–628. doi:10.1016/j.jbusres.2003.08.004

Ahmed, P. K., & Rafiq, M. (2003). Internal marketing issues and challenges. *European Journal of Marketing, 37*(9), 1177–1186. doi:10.1108/03090560310498813

Alipour, M., & Hallaj Mohammadi, M. (2011). The effect of Customer Relationship Management (CRM) on achieving competitive advantage of manufacturing tractor. *Global Journal of Management and Business Research, 11*(5).

Arasli, H. (2012). Towards business excellence in the hospitality industry: A case for 3-, 4-, and 5-star hotels in Iran. *Total Quality Management & Business Excellence, 23*(5-6), 573–590. doi:10.1080/14783363.2012.669539

Bouranta, N., Psomas, E., Suárez-Barraza, M. F., & Jaca, C. (2019). The key factors of total quality management in the service sector: A cross-cultural study. *Benchmarking, 26*(3), 893–921. doi:10.1108/BIJ-09-2017-0240

Fotopoulos, C. B., & Psomas, E. L. (2009). The impact of "soft" and "hard" TQM elements on quality management results. *International Journal of Quality & Reliability Management, 26*(2), 150–163. doi:10.1108/02656710910928798

Jyoti, J., Kour, S., & Sharma, J. (2017). Impact of total quality services on financial performance: Role of service profit chain. *Total Quality Management & Business Excellence, 28*(7-8), 897–929. doi:10.1080/14783363.2016.1274649

Keller, K. L., & Lehmann, D. R. (2006). Brands and branding: Research findings and future priorities. *Marketing Science, 25*(6), 740–759. doi:10.1287/mksc.1050.0153

Loivet, W., Taghipour, A., & Kang, D. S. (2020). The Rise of Green Supply Chain Management: Between Complexity and Necessity. *Journal of Economics, Business and Management, 8*(1), 1–7.

Mahfod, J., Canel-Depitre, B., & Taghipour, A. (2019). Quality Function Deployment in Supplier Evaluation. *Journal of Advanced Management Science, 7*(4), 131–135. doi:10.18178/joams.7.4.131-135

Mahmood, S., & Ahmed, A. (2014). Relationship between TQM dimensions and organizational performance. *Pakistan Journal of Commerce and Social Sciences, 8*(3), 662–679.

Matthyssens, P., Vandenbempt, K., & Berghman, L. (2006). Value innovation in business markets: Breaking the industry recipe. *Industrial Marketing Management, 35*(6), 751–761. doi:10.1016/j.indmarman.2005.05.013

Mudambi, S. M., Doyle, P., & Wong, V. (1997). An exploration of branding in industrial markets. *Industrial Marketing Management, 26*(5), 433–446. doi:10.1016/S0019-8501(96)00151-4

Parasuraman, A. (2004). Assessing and improving service performance for maximum impact: Insights from a two-decade-long research journey. *Performance Measurement and Metrics, 5*(2), 45–52. doi:10.1108/14678040410546064

Porter, M. (1985). *The value chain. The Value Chain and Competitive advantage: creating and sustaining superior performance.* Academic Press.

Prajogo, D. I. (2005). The comparative analysis of TQM practices and quality performance between manufacturing and service firms. *International Journal of Service Industry Management, 16*(3), 217–228. doi:10.1108/09564230510601378

Psomas, E. L., & Jaca, C. (2016). The impact of total quality management on service company performance: Evidence from Spain. *International Journal of Quality & Reliability Management, 33*(3), 380–398. doi:10.1108/IJQRM-07-2014-0090

Silvestro, R. (1998). The manufacturing TQM and service quality literatures: Synergistic or conflicting paradigms? *International Journal of Quality & Reliability Management, 15*(3), 303–328. doi:10.1108/02656719810198917

Simon, H., & Schumann, H. (2001). *Pricing opportunities in the digital age.* Academic Press.

Singh, K., & Singh Ahuja, I. (2014). Effectiveness of TPM implementation with and without integration with TQM in Indian manufacturing industries. *Journal of Quality in Maintenance Engineering, 20*(4), 415–435. doi:10.1108/JQME-01-2013-0003

Singh, P. J., Feng, M., & Smith, A. (2006). ISO 9000 series of standards: Comparison of manufacturing and service organizations. *International Journal of Quality & Reliability Management, 23*(2), 122–142. doi:10.1108/02656710610640916

Sureshchandar, G. S., Rajendran, C., & Anantharaman, R. N. (2001). A conceptual model for total quality management in service organizations. *Total Quality Management, 12*(3), 343–363. doi:10.1080/09544120120034492

Taghipour, A. (2012). *Supply Chain Management: Coordination of Operations Planning*. Lambert Academic Publishing.

Talib, F. (2013). An overview of total quality management: Understanding the fundamentals in service organization. *International Journal of Advanced Quality Management, 1*(1), 1–20.

Tliche, Y., Taghipour, A., & Canel-Depitre, B. (2019). Downstream Demand Inference in Decentralized Supply chains. *European Journal of Operational Research, 274*(1), 65–77. doi:10.1016/j.ejor.2018.09.034

Woon, K. C. (2000). TQM implementation: Comparing Singapore's service and manufacturing leaders. *Managing Service Quality, 10*(5), 318–331. doi:10.1108/09604520010345777

Chapter 5 The Influence of Digitization on Supply Chain Sustainable Performance

Kiran M. B.
https://orcid.org/0000-0001-5855-8670
Pandit Deendayal Petroleum University, India

ABSTRACT

This chapter intends to explore the influence of digitization on supply chain sustainable performance. An attempt has been made in this chapter, first, to define supply chain management and its practical relevance, then to highlight the different components of the supply chain, and finally, how Industry 4.0 technologies can be used in designing these components so that all the components of the supply chain work in a coordinated manner and that they are effective in achieving the objectives of supply chain sustainability.

INTRODUCTION

An effort has been made in this work to explore the importance of digitization in the context of supply chain management. Specifically, the work focuses in highlighting the influence of digitization on supply chain sustainable performance. The following are the objectives.

1. To study the components of a company's supply chain
2. To understand the problems or issues
3. To understand how digitization technologies work

DOI: 10.4018/978-1-7998-6874-3.ch005

4. How digitization can help, components of a company's supply chain, in achieving sustainable objectives

Background

A Supply chain consists of the company, suppliers, customers, logistics, and all other entities which are involved in the transformation of raw materials into a finished product, which is delivered to the customer. Today, a company's supply chain is facing multiple challenges, such as the timely acquisition of raw materials, acquiring materials of the right quality, accurately forecasting customer demand, understanding customer's requirement, timely payment of suppliers, identifying right suppliers, managing work in process, managing company's inventory, etc. Managing supply chain challenges is very much essential for the success of any organization (Fair, 1989; Blinder, 1986; Atour Taghipour,2018). As far as the author's knowledge goes, practitioners and researchers require a resource, which comprehensively covers the effect of digitization on supply chain sustainability. In this context, the proposed work assumes special significance.

MAIN FOCUS OF THE CHAPTER

The objective of any company must be to design its supply chain and ensure it achieve excellence during operation. The components of a company's supply chain are shown in Figure 1.0.

With the advent of Industry 4.0 technologies (viz. mobile, internet of things, augmented reality, 3D printing, sensors, Big-Data, etc.) (Ornig, 2016), researchers have started using these technologies in designing the various components of the supply chain. The idea is to make all the components of the supply chain efficient, flexible, quick, and also work in a coordinated manner for meeting the expectations of the customer. In the following paragraphs, an effort has been made to highlight how Industry 4.0 technologies can be used in not only making the particular component to excel but also to contribute to the excellence of the entire supply chain. The following paragraphs show how digital technologies have been used in designing the different supply chain components.

1. **Planning:** Organizations will have to plan so that they can design the right supply chain for meeting the requirements of customers. Accurately forecasting the demand of a product is very important as it helps the company in identifying buying the right type of materials, in the right amount, at the right time at the right place, and the right price. This is done by establishing contracts with

Figure 1. Components of a company's supply chain

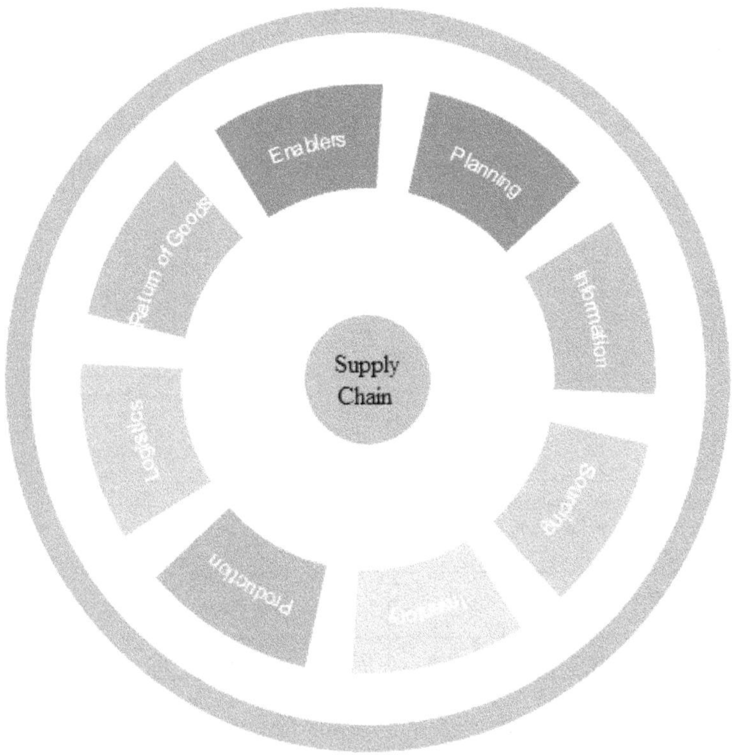

the right suppliers. An accurate forecast would also help suppliers in knowing what type of materials are required by whom, when, and in what quantities. So that the supplier can not only plan but also sell the raw materials required by the company at competitive prices. Thus, suppliers require the company's forecast and sales data so that they can make the right decisions at the right time.

The biggest challenge the supply chain managers face today, is in dealing with volatility in the supply chain (Handfield et al., 2013; Wieland et al.,2016; Solen Lebosse et al.,2017). Volatility in the supply chain is mainly due to – misaligned corporate functions- different components of the supply chain having different goals (Chang et al., 2016), long lead times- the inability of the suppliers to supply materials in time (Owen,2007), inaccurate forecasting- not having a complete understanding of the market and customers, supply chain disruptions- may be due to the advent of new technology or new government regulations. Supply chain volatility may also come from government policies, changes in the price of raw materials, and short product life cycles. Thus, managing supply chain volatility is a complex function. To overcome the volatility in the supply chain, many new practices have been developed, because of its practical importance (Engelhardt,2012; Yi et al.,2011; Gligor et al.,2014; Prater, 2001). Christopher et al. (2017) indicated in his research work that the existing methods for managing volatility in the supply chain are insufficient. To deal with this problem of handling supply chain volatility, the following practices have been followed (Table 1).

Table 1. Best practices to be followed by the company for managing volatility in supply chain

Sl.No	Best Practices	Benefits to the company
1	Shared company goals across departments	All stakeholders are on the same page
2	Providing incentives to customers, for sharing the data related to their requirements	for building accurate sales forecasts
3	Know supply lead time deviation at the earliest	To reduce long supply lead times
4	Designing reliable business processes	To meet customer demand
5	Changing the organizational culture	People openly communicate problems Focus on the implementation of lessons learned Focus on a permanent solution to a problem rather than providing a temporary solution
6	Essential to have a long-term partnership with the competitors	for managing severe market competition.

In addition to these, many supply chain managers are also facing a challenge of limited bandwidth/or resources. Hence, they cannot study the impact of all factors affecting the supply chain volatility. They are more interested in knowing which of the above factors require more focus. That is, which of the above factors are more critical relative to others. To solve this problem, one researcher has used the Analytical hierarchy process (AHP) (Saatyet al., 1980). AHP helps supply chain managers in the decision-making process. Many researchers have applied AHP in solving the problem of supplier selection in supply chain management (Ramanathan et al.,2007; Shaw et al.,2012). Some of the researchers have used AHP in analyzing the performance of the supply chain systems (Chan, 2003; Sharma et al.,2007). Thus, it is clear that managing a supply chain is a complex function and it is very much essential for managers to have the necessary experience and a holistic perspective for solving supply chain related problems. If a company's forecast is low then the company cannot fulfill the customer order, as a result, there would be lost sales. Similarly, if the forecast is very high then this would result in excess products in the company's warehouse which results in loss of revenue.

With the advent of digital technologies, companies will have to design a strategy for implementing digitization. The strategy should cover aspects such as the need for the company to go in for digital transformation, the components of the company's supply chain that require digital transformation, the associated time frame, and the selection of appropriate technology for implementing the digital transformation of the components of the company's supply chain. Technology selection must ensure that all the components of the company's supply chain work seamlessly with one another.

2. **Information:** Companies require information about materials, goods, people, suppliers, and other entities of the supply chain (Figure 2) so that the right decisions can be made at the right time. For example, the company may be interested in knowing whether a supplier has already dispatched raw materials, and at what time the materials will arrive at the company. This information is very much crucial. Many subsequent decisions are affected by this piece of information. With the introduction of the Internet of things (IoT) in 1999, IoT was first applied as IoT enabled manufacturing in automobile companies for process monitoring and post-sales management (Kirk,2015; Zhang et al.,2011).

Figure 2. (a) Elements of information (b) Details of information elements in the supply chain

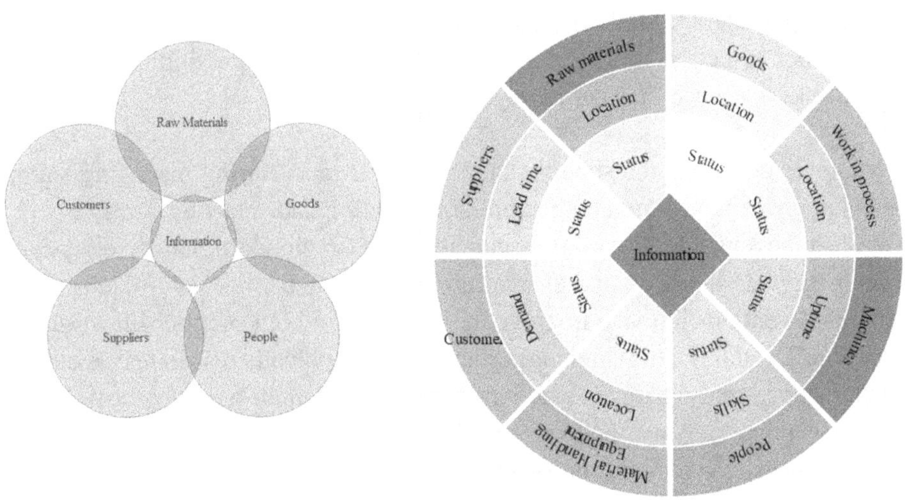

With the advent of Industry 4.0, this was known as a Cyber-physical system. With the advent of sensors and Radiofrequency identification devise (RFID) information about all the elements of the supply chain can be made available in real-time. This would greatly help suppliers, manufacturers, and customers in taking the right decisions. Also, this would enhance the visibility and transparency across the entire supply chain. With the advent of the latest technologies such as the internet of things (IoT), all the elements of a company's supply chain will be exchanging information in real-time as opposed to a conventional system where exchanging information happens one agent at a time. In many conventional systems because of the lack of availability of the right information at the right time, many mistakes used to happen. Such as, mistakes in delivering products or raw materials, which would result in wastage of effort, time, and cost. Thus, with the introduction of IoT, many of the existing supply chain models need to be redesigned.

To solve the privacy and security problems associated with RFID technology, researchers have developed models that use both RFID and IoT. By implementing these technologies, a company's supply chain will be made aligned to Industry 4.0 principles. That is, the elements of a company's supply chain start exchanging information not only in real-time but also will be smart enough to safeguard the privacy and security of the information.

3. **Sourcing**: is the process of locating, evaluating, and engaging with the suppliers for providing raw materials and services. Earlier, business houses used to own the entire supply chain. Like in the case of Ford motors. Starting from raw materials to the finished products (cars). Nowadays, business houses, manufacturing products, are more focused and they depend on many suppliers and contractors for the supply of raw materials and spare parts. Conventional supplier selection and evaluation methods have the possibility of making mistakes because they are purely manual.

Whatever decisions the supply chain managers take, during managing supply chains largely depends upon both supplier evaluation and selection decision.

With the advent of Industry 4.0, researchers have developed digital-based systems for both supplier selection and evaluation. These systems not only require fewer human interventions but also improve the accuracy in both supplier selection and evaluation. To address, the challenges such as geographically distributed, dynamic, and interactive supply chains researchers have proposed multi-agent systems (MAS). Many researchers are working on a multi-agent system (MAS) technology that will provide better visibility and transparency concerning supplier selection and evaluation between manufacturers and suppliers. Researchers have also worked on exploring the effect of economic and environmental factors on supplier selection and evaluation (Ghadimi et al.,2018).

MAS system has the following components in the architecture (Pezhman et al.,2019):

1. User interface layer
2. Technical /or Business logic layer
3. Data layer

The interface layer (UI) consists of forms that will be used by both manufacturers and suppliers for filling in the necessary data. This was implemented using Java technology. Both Java swing-based GUI and web-based UI available. The business logic layer contains the business validation objects for performing the necessary business validations. Data layer stores the vendor selection and evaluation details. The data layer has a supplier knowledge base, and the manufacturer's database as well.

MAS system achieves connectivity between manufacturers and suppliers through the internet. Thus, suppliers can be added or removed by using the MAS system. MAS system allows any component of the supply chain can be added or removed and thus it helps in addressing the connectivity aspect. Using MAS, different components of the supply chain may exchange information in real-time using the Internet. This would keep all the components of the supply chain with the latest information. Thus, it ensures transparency across the supply chain. Thus, MAS ensures decentralization and components of the supply chain can interact with one another over the Internet. MAS would help the company in ranking its suppliers based on defined criteria of evaluation. Thus, by using MAS, the productivity of the entire supply chain is improved.

4. **Inventory**: Organizations will have to carry enough quantities of raw materials, semi-finished products, and finished products so that customer's requirements are met at the right time. Proper management of inventory is very important for the success of the company.

Types of Inventories

1. Raw materials, Semi finished & finished product
2. Spare parts
3. Raw materials, Semi finished & finished product

Though having inventory is good but if not maintained at the right level would result in an excessive tie-up of investment, a large space is required, there is also an associated inventory carrying cost. With the advent of lean philosophy, companies wanted to do away with this traditional inventory-based system. As per the lean philosophy, inventory is a type of waste. Hence, companies want to eliminate this waste. This new concept known as Just-in-Time (JIT) supply chain has drawn attention from many production managers. JIT has many advantages – reduced inventory, reduced costs, improved product quality, reduced lead time, superior competitive advantages. One of the researchers has reported working on incorporating Industry 4.0 technologies into green and lean supply chains.

4. Spare parts

Spare parts Inventory management is very much essential for Aircraft. Spare parts inventory management includes activities like –demand forecasting, optimized system parameters, and estimation of replenishment quantities. Many researchers have been working on inventory management using the Internet of Things (IoT) (Kilpi et al., 2009). How IoT can be used in managing inventory through location tracking was studied by Atzori et al. (2010). Few researchers have studied how IoT can help in improving the accuracy of inventory details (Da Xu et al.,2014; Sun,2012). Lee et al. (2015) have studied new ways to reduce the inventory cost by vendor-managed inventory system. Few researchers have studied the application of IoT and RFID in managing the inventory (Zheng et al., 2017).

Aircraft component reliability directly affects the number of spare parts required. RFID can also be used in the unique identification of spare parts. RFID with a Global positioning system (GPS) using IoT architecture can provide real-time data of spare parts (Gnimpieba et al., 2015). For performing spare parts inventory management, researchers had three objectives- maximizing availability, reducing inventory cost, and minimizing environmental impact. Most of the research studies (Yongquan et al., 2016) use historical data for analysis and condition monitoring information for spare parts inventory management. Data mining and machine learning are also useful in predicting the remaining life-time of components and hence the demand for spare parts. The IoT-based architecture provides visibility, efficiency, and effectiveness in managing incoming raw materials, storage, and outgoing raw materials and thus helps in managing inventory.

Location of parts, lead time, ordering cost, and inventory carrying cost may be used as indicators for monitoring and controlling inventory system. Data mining tools combined with Big data are useful in optimizing inventory in manufacturing companies. Every item stored in inventory carries RFID tags and as such generates huge data. By applying data mining techniques in IoT architecture helps in data classification and the management of inventory.

Jing Chen et al. (2019) studied how Industry 4.0 technology can be used in managing the inventory of maintenance, repair, and operation parts (MRO) of a manufacturing company. He showed how digital technologies-Data analytics, machine learning, additive manufacturing, and the Internet of Things can be used in the inventory management of MRO. He showed how the clustering of MRO components would help in devising appropriate strategies for managing inventories. In his research, he identified the characteristics of MRO components. Based on the usage of MRO components, he classified components into four groups erratic, lumpy, smooth, and intermittent. For each group, he devised different inventory strategies. Using Big data, machine learning, and IoT helped in improving demand forecasting of MRO components. Using Additive manufacturing lead time for low volume components are reduced. For component deliveries of MRO components, small shuttles are used for achieving efficiency in transportation.

Cyber-physical system (CPS) (Figure 3) wherein a manufacturing process is controlled by an embedded computer, wireless network, and a feedback loop. In a cyber-physical system, whenever the quantity of components in a bin becomes equal to the reorder level, by using RFID and cloud-based system, an order will be placed for replenishment. In this way, inventory management is possible in real-time.

Figure 3. Cyber-physical system components

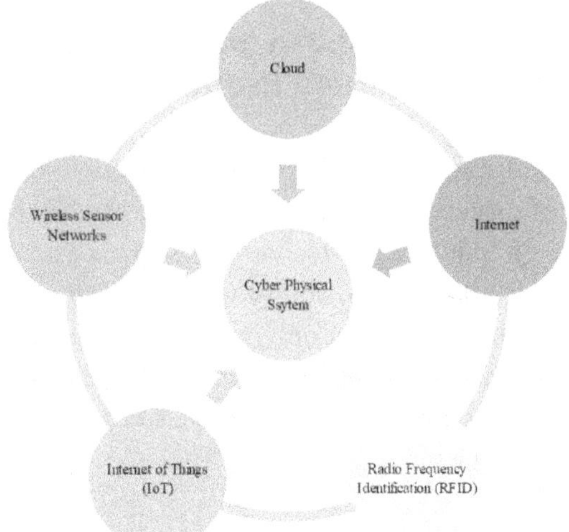

5. **Production:** Managers are responsible for buying the right type of raw materials, in the right quantities, at the right place, and at the right time. In conventional manufacturing system, this was a very big challenge. They are also responsible

for ensuring the products are made as per the designed production schedule, inspected, and delivered a quality product to the customer at the right time.

Benefits by Using Industry 4.0 in Manufacturing in Reducing Defects, While Manufacturing Complex Products:

With the advent of Industry 4.0, companies have started using digital technologies for reducing production costs and in-turn the cost of the final product. Digitization in manufacturing has helped companies in reducing scrap by using simulation facilities available with computer numerical control machines. Before machining, the simulation can be done to check whether the program is correct or not. By doing so, defective products will not be produced. The cost of manufacturing can be optimized by using technologies like Just in time manufacturing, activity-based costing, and total quality management. The advent of additive manufacturing has made it possible to produce parts having complex geometry. Additive manufacturing creates a physical object employing digital input. The advantage is that rapid design simulation is possible through additive manufacturing. This gives agility to new product development. Additive manufacturing (AM) is used in the making of – casting patterns and cores, Jigs, Fixtures, repair of parts. The main disadvantage of additive manufacturing is that the AM machines are very costly. Also, AM manufactured components will have low surface quality and low dimensional accuracy (Hoover et al., 2002).

Benefits by Using Industry 4.0 in Improving Efficiency While Inspecting Manufactured Products:

In traditional manufacturing systems, the product inspection was purely post-process in nature. Majority of inspection was done based on statistical sampling.

With the advent of Industry 4.0 technologies, the cost of inspection can be brought down by using a Machine vision-based inspection system. Also, machine vision-based systems can be used not only in post-processed mode but also in in-process and online modes. Many of the earlier inspection systems are only fit to be used in sampling inspection. But, the vision-based systems can also be used in 100% inspection of manufactured products.

Benefits by Using Industry 4.0 in Making Manufacturing of Products Eco-Friendly:

Experts believe that the implementation of Industry 4.0 technologies will bring down carbon emission substantially. With the advent of Industry 4.0, new business models such as Manufacturing as a service (MaaS) came into being. This will change the way the manufacturers deliver their products to their customers. Manufacturing by using smart machines would result in less waste, increased resource utilization, higher productivity, and reduced cost of manufacturing.

The manufacturing system needs to be efficient for becoming cost-effective (Veer Shivajee et al.,2019; Hartmann,2015). Veer Shivajee et al. (2019) have analyzed automobile manufacturing companies and have shown how manufacturing conversion costs can be reduced by using digitization and real-time data. Industry 4.0 technologies are being used throughout the product development life cycle. Digital manufacturing using Industry 4.0 has dramatically changed the way manufacturing is being done. Also, it has resulted in increased flexibility and improved efficiencies. One of the biggest advantages of digital manufacturing is breaking the barrier and integrating the different components of manufacturing. Digital simulation is one of the main functions of digital manufacturing (Ribeiro et al.,2019). Digital simulation helps in studying the process design and product quality even before buying the raw materials. Thus, a lot of time, effort, and money can be saved and better-quality products can be produced at a reduced cost. Using autonomous robots in digital manufacturing has reduced set-up times. Robots along with artificial intelligence can work independently with no human intervention. Thus, higher efficiencies are possible (Fitzgerald,2017; Bal, 2012). Autonomous robots are capable of working round the clock with a consistent quality of work. Autonomous robots are also used in digital manufacturing for performing a simulation of autonomous workstations.

Cloud computing (Hackett,2008; Columbus,2015) is giving flexibility to digital manufacturing. Cloud computing (Table 2) provides different services.

Table 2. Cloud-based services in digital technology

Cloud-based services	Service description	Service benefits
SaaS	Software as a service	Software as a Service provide applications- (e.g. CAD, FEA, etc.) over the internet
PaaS	Platform as a service	Provides developers the necessary platform for building cloud-based applications.
IaaS	Infrastructure as a service	provides high computing resources (e.g. servers, storage, etc.) over the internet.

Internet of Things (IoT) has made digital manufacturing more reliable. That is in digital manufacturing, sensors are used for collecting data from the shop floor so that up-to-date information about the shop floor is made available to all stakeholders in real-time. By making up-to-date information about the machines and manufacturing processes has made it possible for analyzing the information in off-line.

Big data analytics is used in digital manufacturing for analyzing the vast data that is being created in manufacturing. It would help production managers in analysis and decision making. Big data analytics is being used by production managers in predicting the future. Big data is being used in planning stages from line balancing to production schedules.

Performance measures used in smart manufacturing are as follows.

- Cost measures: Training cost, the unit cost of a product, energy cost, maintenance cost, Research, and development cost. Product development cost, rework cost, WIP cost
- Quality measures: warranty claim, mean time between failures, process visualization control
- Productivity: optimized production, overall equipment effectiveness, Equipment utilization, line efficiency, optimized plant layout, optimized work station design, production test procedures
- Time: Mean flow time, processing time, makespan, cycle time, lead time, machine uptime

Employees in the smart factory are also using eye trackers and wearable sensors are being used for improved communication between operators and the digital factory. Industry 4.0 makes operators safe, productive at the workplace, and employee satisfaction (Golan et al., 2019).

Most companies have failed in achieving sustainable goals, because of their inability to easily switch over from manufacturing one product to another (Annie Francie et al.,2014; Zhigang et al., 2016). Manufacturing companies are facing challenges (e.g. skill gaps, budget constraints, etc.) while implementing Industry 4.0 technologies (Tae KyungSung, 2018). The main advantage of Industry 4.0 in manufacturing is that the production managers will have real-time access to all the details related to the supply chain. Thus, Industry 4.0 technologies will give better visibility to the production manager (SurajitBag et al., 2020). They showed how Big data analytics are useful in achieving sustainable supply chain goals. Many companies who have started using remanufacturing and recycling practices have suffered production losses, due to uncertainties in the supply of raw materials and excess storage of work in process (Inderfurth,2005). Uncertainties in the manufacturing environment will affect the decisions managers will take. Uncertainties will also affect the quality of decisions made by managers. Accuracy in sales forecasting of recycled products will be reduced in the case of volatile situations. This will harm the company's profit margin. Also, due to high uncertainties, companies have the habit of keeping increased inventories to meet customer demand. With the rapid change in technologies, having high inventories have the risk of becoming obsolete.

Decision-making during uncertainties becomes easier with the use of data analytics and hence managers have started using Big data analytics.

Smart Manufacturing

Smart manufacturing enables the machine-to-machine communications and data transfer through the wireless network, using IoT-based technologies (Federico et al., 2018). Implementing innovative technologies in manufacturing also involves facing many new challenges. The main advantage of Industry 4.0 technologies in manufacturing is that it will make the system more efficient and effective (Arnesh et al., 2018). Data collected from heterogeneous sensors (Figure 4) may be in different formats and hence there is a need to store all data centrally. The centrally stored data is then pre-processed for eliminating noise and spurious values. This step is very much essential as this will enhance the quality of the data. The data is then filtered before constructing a data warehouse. The data warehouse is used by managers for decision making.

Figure 4. Data warehouse architecture

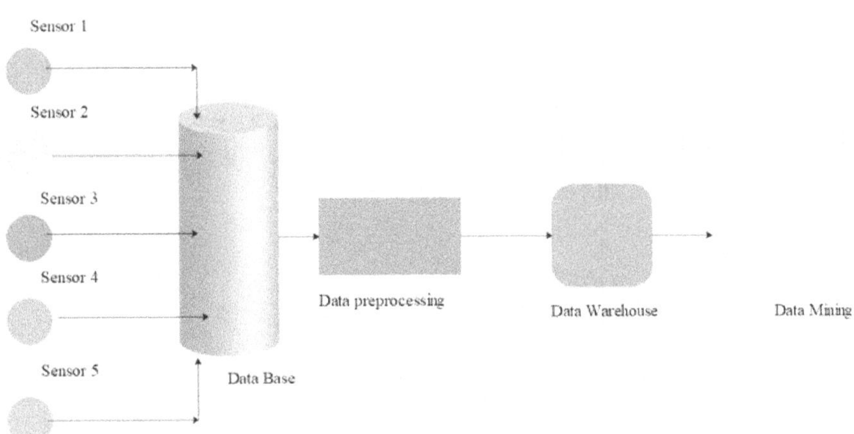

IoT based artificial intelligence is being used for activities such as vehicle routing, production scheduling, controlling the movements of automated guided vehicles, etc. (Alem, 2018). Thus, IoT-enabled technologies will help in integrating the physical world with the cyber world. Despite standardization, still a lot of challenges the manufacturing companies will have to deal with while implementing IoT technologies.

For managing IoT projects, experienced project managers are required because of the complexities involved in managing projects. Project managers will have to use the latest project management tools for managing project risks. Project risks can be technical and non-technical. Project managers must ensure that the IoT based projects are completed within time, within budget, and at the same time meeting all the stakeholder's expectations. The success of the project depends to a large extent on the active involvement of all the concerned people. Project managers will have to communicate with all team members so that there will not be any communication gap or misunderstanding in understanding project objectives. Project managers will have to focus on resource development. They may establish tie-ups with universities and research organizations for skill development and for ensuring the availability of people with the right skills at the right time.

6. **Logistics:** Logistics include activities like receiving customers' orders, goods are delivered as per schedule, and payments are received from customers in time. However, there were many drawbacks with the existing logistics systems. With the advent of Industry 4.0 technologies, industries have started implementing them for overcoming the problems associated with the existing logistics systems. Digitization is very useful for creating a reliable method for the transportation of raw materials, finished products, and services (Evans,2017). Digitization has also helped in reducing carbon emission (Marwyk et al.,2016). Also, this has created high visibility among manufacturers, suppliers, customers, and other entities of the supply chain. A digital logistics system has important characteristics (Figure 5)-cooperation, connectivity, adaptiveness, integration, autonomous control, and cognitive improvement.

Figure 5. Characteristics of digital logistics system

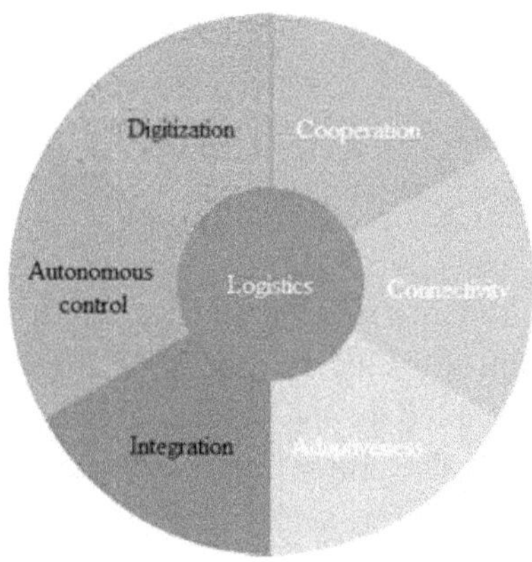

a. **Co-operation:** When different elements of the supply chain (e.g. Manufacturer, supplier, etc.) work with cooperation through digitization, there is a high possibility of improved efficiency and reliability in the supply chain.
b. **Connectivity:** this refers to having a well-defined interface so that all the elements of the supply chain can interact with one another digitally in a seamless fashion. That is, all the components will have interfaces so that they can interact with one another (Owen,2007; Alldredge et al.,2015). The objective of connectivity is to enable the system to include any new device as a component without any difficulty.
c. **Adaptiveness:** refers to the ability of the system/or components, connected digitally, to adapt or change itself with the changes in the environment (Canetta et al., 2011). The case study presented in (Canetta et al., 2011) shows how the transport providers of FMCG companies in Turkey have adapted themselves in response to the change in consumer behavior.
d. **Integration:** refers to the ability of the system to work as a coordinated set of interdependent components, when connected digitally.
e. **Autonomous control:** refers to the ability of the system, with the help of digitization, to take decisions independently.
f. Digitization in logistics has made it smarter and reduced the number of mistakes that used to happen in the conventional system. Also, the decisions will be taken by the system with minimal human interventions.

When a digital logistics system is implemented with digital technologies (viz. mobile, sensors, cloud, augmented reality, 3D printing, Big Data, etc., would help organizations plan, synchronize logistics operations, and transparency among all the elements of the supply chain.

7. **Return of Goods:** Managers are responsible for designing a proper channel so that the defective raw materials could be returned to the suppliers as per the contract. Similarly, if the product is defective, then either the product should be subjected to reworking or be scrapped. With the introduction of digital technologies like additive manufacturing, maintenance of the jet engine is being done. Repair of turbo engine blades, by additive manufacturing, has been reported. With the availability of machine vision and artificial intelligence, it is possible to classify the machined components into acceptable, rejected, or reworkable. This would greatly help in ensuring quality products reaching the customers. By using digital transformation technologies, it is possible to rank the suppliers.

Reverse logistics helps in solving many environmental problems (Tang et al.,2012). It is collecting the used parts or components from the customers. The used products are subjected to recovery processes. Recovery processes include remanufacturing and recycling and finally disposing of the products which are not repairable. Inventory and production planning of return goods is highly complicated because of uncertainties associated with return goods.

Industry 4.0 greatly helps in analyzing the economic and environmental aspects of closed loop-based supply chain systems. Industry 4.0 also helps in information sharing across organizations. Many researchers have studied closed-loop supply chain systems (Behret et al.,2009; Kumar et al.,2014). Dev et al. (2017) studied the closed-loop supply chain systems in detail by constructing a discrete event model and then did a simulation. They reported that there exists a trade-off between continuous and periodic review policies for total inventory carrying cost and variance in order with K (Equation 1). Where,

$$K = \text{change in value of return rate / demand ratio} \tag{1}$$

Wang et al. (2017) have studied the economic benefits of reverse logistics. His research showed that there is a time delay because of losses during reprocessing and returns. Not many researchers have worked on integrating returns with inventory and production planning. This is very much required while evaluating closed-loop supply chains for economic and environmental factors. Zhong et al. (2015) have analyzed RFID-based technology for tracking logistics in manufacturing shops and warehouses. They could able to track the material flow from store to warehouse. Kumar et al. (2014) have researched the health care system for managing inventory using RFID in a closed-loop supply chain.

Normally, the information is collected through RFID is passed into the Enterprise Resource Planning software of a manufacturing company with the help of a cyber-physical system. RFID middleware connects RFID hardware and the cyber-physical system. Besides, the RFID middleware also does the following functions.

- Collection of data from RFID readers
- Filtering of data
- Directing the data to go to the appropriate IT-based system

Data collected employing RFID devices are connected to the reverse SC Model with the help of the cyber-physical system. The reverse supply chain consists of a manufacturer, new material supplier, recycled material supplier, and the customer. The recycled material supplier collects used items from customers. Thus, the manufacturer has the option of buying material either from a new material supplier

Table 3. Key enablers for achieving sustainable objectives for supply chain

Sl No.	Description	Requirements
1	Organizational transformation	requires a change in the mindset of people towards sustainability
2	Availability of managers having required skills	Understanding of Project management tools and techniques, Project management experience
3	A high degree of cooperation among all the components of the supply chain	Availability of proper Interfaces
4	The adaptability of an organization for meeting uncertainties	The ability of the organization to change itself for meeting the uncertainties in the market conditions
5	Responsible organization	Organizations have to become responsible for implementing practices like remanufacturing, reuse, and recycling.
6	Motivation from top management	Encouraging organization by allocating necessary funding for implementing innovative technologies/practices
7	Transformational leadership	Availability of strong leaders – knowledgeable in company philosophy and objectives
8	Open-mindedness	Sharing knowledge about sustainability and innovative practices and information with all the elements of the supply chain.
9	Efficient transportation	Necessary of using cfficient transportation system for protecting the environment
10	Innovative solutions	Necessary for creating high technology R&D labs for designing and developing innovative solutions.
11	IoT/ RFID/Big Data/Artificial Intelligence, based solutions	Implementing high technology solutions/ applications using RFID etc. for improving efficiency and effectiveness of the organization
12	Renewable Energy	Using renewable energy wherever possible.
13	Good Employee-Employer relationship	It is essential to create a very good working relationship between employers and employees of the organization
14	Strict Legislation	Strict rules and regulations are required for enforcing the sustainability of the supply chain.
15	Good community relationship	Building good community relationships and to become socially responsible
16	Operator friendly workstation design	To improve the working conditions of the operators
17	International collaboration	To promote foreign direct investment
18	Providing subsidies by Government	The government should give subsidies to organizations for adopting renewable energy systems

or a recycled material supplier. The advantage of using recycled material is that it is normally cheaper than the new material. Bass (1969) proposed a model which states that users of innovation uses not only mass media information but also use word of mouth.

The reverse supply chain architecture consists of many entities- new material suppliers, recycled material suppliers, manufacturers, and customers connected overcloud. Applications related to production-production planning, production scheduling, etc. are connected to the cyber-physical network through production service providers under the Industry 4.0 environment.

8. **Enabling:** This activity helps in ensuring that the supply chain works as per the expectations of the company and helps in meeting the organization's goals. This is monitoring the different entities of the supply chain so that all entities work in a coordinated manner and that the customer's expectations are met by delivering the right quality products at the right time. Internet of Things (IoT), is a new technology that can monitor the status of different elements of the supply chain. That is, using IoT, it is possible to provide better visibility among manufacturers, suppliers, customers, and other stakeholders.

Also, IoT helps a supply chain in achieving resilience. Supply chain resilience is the ability of the supply chain to recover from disruptions by maintaining continuity of operations at the desired level of control with connectedness over structure and function. IoT also utilizes sensors and Radio Frequency Identification Devise (RFID) for providing visibility across all the elements of the supply chain. Collaboration among all the stakeholders (viz. manufacturer, supplier, customer, etc.) for achieving the flexibility of the supply chain(Table 3). Researchers have also explored the possibility of using concepts like lean production and six-sigma for increasing supply chain resilience.

Today, manufacturing organization has the objective of achieving both economic and environmental sustainability. That is to achieve sustainability in the supply chain, require designing new products, processes, and services (Pankaj et al.,2020; Daiane et al., 2018). Many researchers (Yanni Gao et al.,2018; Nadia El Nemr et al., 2020) have been working on developing sustainable strategies for the supply chain management. The main objective of developing sustainable strategies is to achieve both economic and environmental sustainability.

FUTURE RESEARCH DIRECTIONS

The proposed research work shows that the application of Industry 4.0 for supply chain sustainability is still in infancy. Industry 4.0 is being used mainly in very few sectors, such as automobile, transportation, aerospace, machine tools, and health care. There is a lot of scope for applying Industry 4.0 in domains like agriculture, Pharma companies, Defense, Smart city development, and Textiles.

CONCLUSION

With the advent of digital technologies, the supply chain is greatly benefitted. The supply chain has become smart, autonomous, adaptive, efficient, secured, and agile. As the result, there is better visibility and transparency among all the elements of the supply chain. A digital supply chain can make smart and accurate decisions, with minimum human intervention. The digital supply chain is making customers happy as there are better transparency and responsiveness. The supply chain should have the objective of meeting both economic and environmental sustenance. For executing IoT based projects experienced project managers are required for completing the projects successfully.

The selection of the right technology is very much essential, for completing IoT based projects. Top management commitment is very much essential in all stages of a project. Project managers will have to ensure the availability of the right organizational culture. Also, managers will have to ensure active people are involved in all stages of the project. Firms will have to be more responsible by implementing best practices such as reuse, recycling, repair, refurbishment, etc. The government will have to ensure the availability of the right rules and regulations for enforcing sustainability objectives. Government and business houses should work on a cooperative basis in using digital technologies for providing maximum comfort and value to society.

REFERENCES

Alldredge, K., Newaskar, P., & Ungerman, K. (2015). *The digital future of consumer-packaged-goods companies*. McKinsey & Co., White Paper.

Atzori, L., Lera, A., & Morabito, G. (2010). The internet of things: A survey. *Computer Networks*, *54*(16), 2787–2805. doi:10.1016/j.comnet.2010.05.010

Bag, Wood, Xu, Dhamija, & Kayikc. (2020). Big data analytics as an operational excellence approach to enhance sustainable supply chain performance. *Resources, Conservation and Recycling*, 153.

Bal, S., & Tact, B. (2012). Clouds for Different Services. *IJCSI International Journal of Computer Science*, *9*, 273–277.

Bass, F. M. (1969). A new product growth model for consumer durable. *Management Science*, *15*(5).

Behret, H., & Korugan, A. (2009). Performance analysis of the hybrid system under quality impacts of returns. *Computers & Industrial Engineering*, *56*(2), 507–520.

Blinder, S. (1986). Can the Production Smoothing Model of Inventory Behavior be Saved? *The Quarterly Journal of Economics*, *101*(3), 431–440. doi:10.2307/1885691

Canetta, L., Salvade, A., Schnegg, P. A., Müller, E., & Lanini, M. (2011). RFID-ERP Key data integration challenges. In L. Canetta, C. Redaelli, & M. Flores (Eds.), *Digital Factory for Human-Oriented Production Systems* (pp. 73–95). Springer. doi:10.1007/978-1-84996-172-1_5

Chan, F. T. S. (2003). Performance measurement in a supply chain. *International Journal of Advanced Manufacturing Technology*, *21*(7), 534–548. doi:10.1007001700300063

Chang, E., West, M., & Hanzic, M. (2006). A digital ecosystem for extended logistics enterprises. *e-Networks in an Increasingly Volatile World Proceedings of the 11th International Workshop on Telework*, 32-40.

Chen, Finkenstaedt, & Liu. (2019). Maintenance Repair and Operations Parts Inventory Management in the Era of Industry 4.0. *IFAC-PapersOnLine*, *52*(13), 171–176.

Christopher, M., & Holweg, M. (2017). Supply chain 2.0 revisited: A framework for managing volatility-induced risk in the supply chain. *International Journal of Physical Distribution & Logistics Management*, *47*(1), 2–17. doi:10.1108/IJPDLM-09-2016-0245

Colakovic, A., & Hadzialic, M. (2018). Internet of Things (IoT): A review of enabling technologies, challenges, and open research issues. *Computer Networks*, *144*, 17–39. doi:10.1016/j.comnet.2018.07.017

Columbus L. (2015). 10 Ways Analytics Are Accelerating Digital Manufacturing. *Forbes*.

Da Xu, L., He, W., & Li, S. (2014). Internet of things in industries: A survey. *IEEE Transactions on Industrial Informatics*, *10*(4), 2233–2243. doi:10.1109/TII.2014.2300753

Dev, N. K., Shankar, R., & Choudhary, A. (2017). Strategic design for inventory and production planning in a closed-loop hybrid system. *International Journal of Production Economics*, *183*, 345–353. doi:10.1016/j.ijpe.2016.06.017

El Nemr, N., Canel, B., & Taghipour, A. (2020). Luxury Hotels' Eco-Friendly Activities & Customers' Preferences and Willingness to Pay for Green Hotels. *Journal of Advanced Management Science*, *8*(1). Advance online publication. doi:10.18178/joams.8.1.7-14

Engelhardt & Nowitzki. (2012). Improving value chain flexibility and adaptability in build-to-order environments. *International Journal of Physical Distribution & Logistics Management*, *42*, 318–337.

Fair, R. C. (1989). The production-smoothing model is alive and well. *Journal of Monetary Economics*, *24*(3), 353–370.

Fitzgerald, J. (2017). Using autonomous robots to drive supply chain innovation. *Deloitte Perspective*, 215–227.

Gao, Y., Li, Z., Taghipour, A., Canel, B., & Kang, D. S. (2018). Supply Chain Coordination: A Review. *Journal of Advanced Management Science*, *6*(4), 213–217. doi:10.18178/joams.6.4.213-217

Ghadimi, & Wang, Lime, & Heavey. (2019). Intelligent sustainable supplier selection using multi-agent technology: Theory and application for Industry 4.0 supply chains. *Computers & Industrial Engineering*, *127*, 588–600.

Ghadimi, P., Toosi, F. G., & Heavey, C. (2018). Multi-agent systems approach for sustainable supplier selection and order allocation in a partnership supply chain. *European Journal of Operational Research*, *269*(1), 286–301.

Gligor, D. M., & Holcomb, M. (2014). The road to supply chain agility: An RBV perspective on the role of logistics capabilities. *International Journal of Logistics Management*, *14*(25), 160–179.

Gnimpieba, Z. D. R., Nait-Sidi-Moh, A., Durand, D., & Fortin, J. (2015). Using the Internet of Things technologies for a collaborative supply chain: Application to tracking of pallets and containers. *Procedia Computer Science*, *56*, 550–557.

Golan, M., Cohen, Y., & Singer, G. (2019). A framework for the operator– workstation interaction in Industry 4. *International Journal of Production Research*, *58*(8), 2421–2432.

Handfield, R. B., Straube, F., Pfohl, H. C., & Wieland, A. (2013). *Trends and Strategies in Logistics and Supply Chain Management: Embracing Global Logistics Complexity to Drive Market Advantage*. DVV Media Group.

Hartmann, B., King, W. P., & Narayanan, S. (2015). *Digital Manufacturing: the revolution will be virtualized*. McKinsey.

Hoover, W. E. Jr, Eloranta, E., Holmstrom, J., & Huttunen, K. (2002). *Managing the Demand-Supply Chain: Value Innovations for Customer Satisfaction*. John Wiley & Sons.

Inderfurth, K. (2005). Impact of uncertainties on recovery behavior in a remanufacturing environment: A numerical analysis. *International Journal of Physical Distribution & Logistics Management*, *35*(5), 318–336.

Jianga, Z., Zhou, T., & Zhang, H. (2016, November). Reliability and cost optimization for remanufacturing process planning. *Journal of Cleaner Production*, *135*(1), 1602–1610.

Kilpi, J., Töyli, J., & Vepsäläinen, A. (2009). Cooperative strategies for the availability service of repairable aircraft components. *International Journal of Production Economics*, *117*(2), 360–370.

Kirk, R. (2015). Cars of the future: The Internet of Things in the automotive industry. *Network Security*, *9*, 16–18.

Kouedeu, A. F., Kenné, J.-P., Dejax, P., Songmene, V., & Polotski, V. (2014). Production Planning of a Failure-Prone manufacturing/Remanufacturing System with production-Dependent Failure Rates. *Applied Mathematics*, *5*(10), 10. doi:10.4236/am.2014.510149

Kumar, A., & Rahman, S. (2014). RFID-enabled process re-engineering of closed-loop supply chains in the health care industry of Singapore. *Journal of Cleaner Production*, *85*, 382–394.

Lebosse, S., Taghipour, A., & Canel-Depitre, B. (2017). Quick Response to Fluctuations in Supply Chains: A Review. *Journal of Advanced Management Science*, *5*(5), 394–400.

Lee, I., & Lee, K. (2015). The Internet of Things (IoT): Applications, investments, and challenges for enterprises. *Business Horizons*, *58*(4), 431–440.

Montori, Bedogni, Di Felice, & Bononi. (2018). Machine-to-machine wireless communication technologies for the Internet of Things: Taxonomy, comparison and open issues. *Pervasive and Mobile Computing*, *50*, 56–81.

Mülling, D., Neutzling, A. L., Seuring, S., & do Nascimentod, L. F. M. (2018). Linking sustainability-oriented innovation to supply chain relationship integration. *Journal of Cleaner Production*, *172*, 3448–3458. doi:10.1016/j.jclepro.2017.11.091

Ornig, H. J. (2016). *Leading into the Future: The so What? on Exponential Technology and Leadership*. Balboa Press.

Owen, J. M. (2007). *The Scientific Article in the Age of Digitization*. Springer.

Pankaj, Ansari, & Kant. (2020). A Pythagorean fuzzy AHP approach and its application to evaluating the enablers of sustainable supply chain innovation. *Sustainable Production and Consumption, 23*, 77-93.

Prater, E., Biehl, M., & Smith, M. A. (2001). International supply chain agility—Tradeoffs between flexibility and uncertainty. *International Journal of Operations & Production Management, 21*, 823–839.

Qrunfleh, S., & Tarafdar, M. (2013). Lean and agile supply chain strategies and supply chain responsiveness: The role of strategic supplier partnership and postponement. *Supply Chain Management*, *18*, 571–582.

Ramanathan, R. (2007). Supplier selection problem: Integrating DEA with the approaches of the total cost of ownership and AHP. *Supply Chain Management*, *12*, 258–261.

Ribeiro da Silva, E., Shinohara, A. C., Pinheiro de Lima, E., Angelis, J., & Machado, C. G. (2019). Reviewing Digital Manufacturing concept in the Industry 4.0 paradigm. *Procedia CIRP*, *81*, 240–245.

Saaty, T. L. (1980). *The Analytic Hierarchy Process: Planning, Priority Setting, Resource Allocation*. McGraw-Hill International Book Co.

Sharma, M. K., & Bhagwat, R. (2007). An integrated BSC-AHP approach for supply chain management evaluation. *Measuring Business Excellence*, *11*, 57–68.

Shaw, K., Shankar, R., Yadav, S. S., & Thakur, L. S. (2012). Supplier selection using fuzzy AHP and fuzzy multi-objective linear programming for developing the low carbon supply chain. *Expert Systems with Applications*, *39*, 8182–8192.

Shivajee, V., Singh, R. K., & Rastogi, S. (2019). Manufacturing conversion cost reduction using quality control tools and digitization of real-time data. *Journal of Cleaner Production*, *237*, 117678.

Sun, C. (2012). Application of RFID technology for logistics on the internet of things. *AASRI Procedia*, *1*, 106–111.

Sung, T. K. (2018). Industry 4.0: A Korea perspective. *Technological Forecasting and Social Change*, *132*, 40–45.

Taghipour. (2018). *Operations, and Management Science, Hierarchical Planning and Information Sharing Techniques in Supply Chain Management.* IGI Global. . doi:10.4018/978-1-5225-7299-2

Tang, C. S., & Zhou, S. (2012). Research advances in environmentally and socially sustainable operations. *European Journal of Operational Research*, *223*(3), 585–594.

Telukdarie, A., Buhula, E., Baga, S., Gupta, S., & Luo, Z. (2018). Industry 4.0 implementation for multinationals. *Process Safety and Environmental Protection*, *118*, 316–329. doi:10.1016/j.psep.2018.06.030

Wang, W., Wang, Y., Mo, D., & Tseng, M. M. (2017). Managing component reuse in remanufacturing under product diffusion dynamics. *International Journal of Production Economics*, *183*, 551–560.

Wieland, A., Handfield, R. B., & Durach, C. F. (2016). Mapping the landscape of future research themes in supply chain management. *Journal of Business Logistics*, *37*, 205–212.

Yi, C. Y., Ngai, E. W. T., & Moon, K. L. (2011). Supply chain flexibility in an uncertain environment: Exploratory from five case studies. *Supply Chain Management*, *16*, 271–283.

Yongquan, S., Xi, C., He, R., Yingchao, J., & Quanwu, L. (2016). Ordering decision-making methods on spare parts for a new aircraft fleet based on a two-sample prediction. *Reliability Engineering & System Safety*, *156*, 40–50.

Zhang, Y., Qu, T., Ho, O., & Huang, G. Q. (2011). Real-time work-in-progress management for the smart object-enabled ubiquitous shop-floor environment. *International Journal of Computer Integrated Manufacturing*, *24*(5), 431–445.

Zheng, M., & Wu, K. (2017). Smart spare parts management systems in semiconductor manufacturing. *Industrial Management & Data Systems, 117*(4), 754–763.

Zhong, R. Y., Huang, G. Q., Lan, S., Dai, Q. Y., Chen, X., & Zhang, T. (2015). A big data approach for logistics trajectory discovery from RFID-enabled production data. *International Journal of Production Economics, 165*, 260–272.

ADDITIONAL READING

Abbey, J. D., Meloy, M. G., Guide, V. D. R. Jr, & Atalay, S. (2015). Remanufactured product in closed-loop supply chains in consumer goods. *Production and Operations Management, 24*(3), 488–503. doi:10.1111/poms.12238

Abdulmalek, F. A., & Rajgopal, J. (2007). Analyzing the benefits of lean manufacturing and value stream mapping via simulation: A process sector case study. *International Journal of Production Economics, 107*(1), 223–236. doi:10.1016/j.ijpe.2006.09.009

Ablanedo-Rosa, J. H., & Alidaee, B. (2010). Quality improvement supported by the 5S an empirical study of Mexican organizations. *International Journal of Production Research, 48*(23), 7063–7087. doi:10.1080/00207540903382865

Anand, G., & Kodali, R. (2008). A conceptual framework for lean supply chain and its implementation. *Int. J. Value Chain Manag., 2*(3), 313–357. doi:10.1504/IJVCM.2008.019517

Azevedo, S. G., Carvalho, H., Duarte, S., & Machado, V. C. (2012). Influences of green and lean upstream supply chain management practices on business sustainability. *IEEE Transactions on Engineering Management, 59*(4), 753–765. doi:10.1109/TEM.2012.2189108

Bai, C., Sarkis, J., & Dou, Y. (2015). Corporate sustainability development in China: Review and analysis. *Industrial Management & Data Systems, 115*(1), 5–40. doi:10.1108/IMDS-09-2014-0258

Belekoukias, I., Garza-Reyes, J. A., & Kumar, V. (2014). The impact of lean methods and tools on the operational performance of manufacturing organizations. *International Journal of Production Research, 52*(18), 5346–5366. doi:10.1080/00207543.2014.903348

KEY TERMS AND DEFINITIONS

Company: The organization that produces the product desired by the customer by using raw materials obtained from the supplier.

Customer: The organization who will buy a company's product.

Manufacturing: The process of transforming raw material into finished products.

Supplier: The organization that supplies raw materials, cutting tools, cutting fluids, etc.

Chapter 6
Semantically Enhanced Web Service for Global Supply Chain Disruption Management

Kamalendu Pal
https://orcid.org/0000-0001-7158-6481
City, University of London, UK

ABSTRACT

The recent coronavirus pandemic has now unleashed a global supply chain crisis across a huge number of organizations, stemming from a lack of understanding and flexibility of the multiple layers of their global supply chains and a lack of diversification in their sourcing strategies. One of the technical options to mitigate the pandemic is to automate business processes by which heterogeneous data integration is encouraged. The convergence of Semantic Web with service-oriented computing is manifested by Semantic Web services technology. It addresses the major challenge of automated, interoperable, and meaningful coordination of web service composition in industrial applications – such as apparel business. Automatic service composition may dramatically improve the development efficiency of web service applications. This chapter proposes an approach to automatically process semantic service composition (SSC) using description logics (DLs) to provide well-defined semantics. Also, this chapter explains the role of ontologies in the architecture of the Semantic Web.

DOI: 10.4018/978-1-7998-6874-3.ch006

INTRODUCTION

The pandemic has also created temporary "manufacturing deserts", whereby a city, region or whole country's output drops so substantially, they become a no-go zone to source anything apart from essential items such as food stuffs and pharmaceuticals. All manufacturing business today appreciates the value and consequence of building an effective supply chain as part of enterprise proliferation and profitability (Pal, 2017). There exist different types of industry specific supply chain (e.g. automobile, pharmaceutical, agriculture, apparel). In simple, supply chain is a system with organization, people, technology, activity, information and resource involved in, to deliver a product or service from suppliers to customers. In this way, supply chain activity transforms natural resources, raw materials and components into final products, and delivers them to customers. Therefore, a supply chain is a network of facilities and distribution options that performs the functions of material procurement, transformation of these materials into intermediate and finished products, and distribution of these finished products to customers (Pal, 2017). Supply Chain Management (SCM) aims at improving the allocation, management and control of logistical resources.

The first signs of SCM were perceptible in Toyota Motor Manufacturing's Just-In-Time (JIT) procurement system (Shingo, 1988). Particularly, JIT was used to control suppliers to the factory just in the right quantities, to the right location, and at the right time, in order to optimize system-wide costs and customer affordability. The main goal was to reduce inventory level drastically, and to regulate the suppliers' interaction with the production line more effectively. It consisted of two distinct flows through the supply chain organizations: material and information. The scope of the manufacturing supply chain begins with the source of supply and ends at the point of consumption. It extends much further than simply a concern with the physical movement of materials. Equal emphasis is given to supplier management, purchasing, inventory-management, manufacturing management, facilities planning, customer service, information flow, transport and physical distribution. Some of the important business processes, along manufacturing supply chain, are shown in Figure 1.

Manufacturing supply chain management tries to bring suppliers and customers together in one concurrent business process. Its main objective is to synchronize the needs of the customer with the flow of raw material from purchasers. This balances Constraint Satisfaction Problem (CSP) with appropriate customer service, minimum inventory holding cost and optimal unit cost. In this complex CSP environment, the design and operation of an effective supply chain is of fundamental importance for global manufacturing business (Taghipour, 2020) (Radhouri et al., 2018) (Cliché et al., 2020).

It is worth noting that purchasing process does not finish when the customer places an order using an existing sales channel. Customer queries, before or after order placement, are inevitable. At the same time, the seller might want to contact customers with purchase confirmation and shipping information. Customer service encompasses all points of contact between the seller and the customer and is an important output of SCM. It results from the accumulated value of all business processes along the supply chain. These business processes are responsible for offering an acceptable level of customer service. Moreover, these business processes are also interdependent, if one business function fails to provide the expected level of customer service then chain is disrupted, and the scheduled workload in other areas is destabilized. Consequently, customer satisfaction is the casualty.

Figure 1. Diagrammatic representation of supply chain business processes

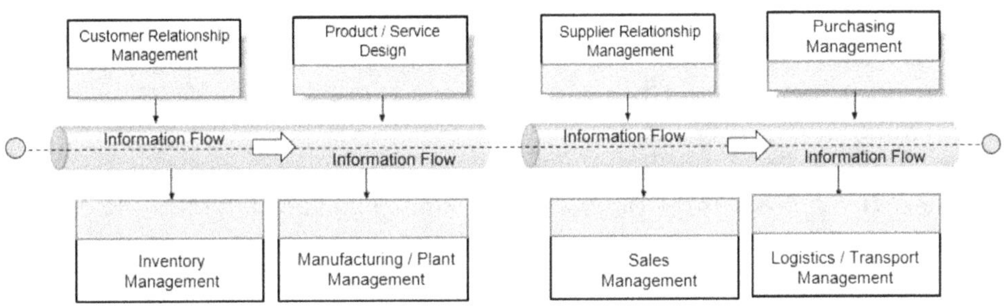

To provide better quality of customer service at no additional cost or workload, all business processes along the supply chain must be balanced. This requires trade-offs throughout the supply chain. It is essential to think in terms of a single interconnected chain rather than narrow functional business processes when considering effective trade-offs. Seamless integration along the supply chain is challenged when there is a conflict between a company's functional behaviours and objectives, as is often the case. For example, suppliers typically want manufacturers to purchasing in bulk quantities, in stable volumes, and with flexible delivery dates. However, although most manufacturers desire long production shifts, they need to flexible to their customers' requirements and fluctuating market demands. Thus, the suppliers' objectives are in direct conflict with the manufacturers' wish for flexibility. Indeed, since manufacturing decisions are typically made without accurate information about customer demand, the ability of manufacturers to match supply and demand depends largely on their ability to change supply volume as information about demand arrives. In the same way, the manufacturers' goal of making bulk production batches typically conflicts with the objects of both distribution and warehouse facilities layout to reduce material inventory. To make the situation worse, this latter goal of reducing inventory typically implies an extra cost in transportation and distribution.

System fluctuations over time are also critical criteria that need to be considered. Even when the requisition is accurately known because of prior contractual agreements, say strategic decisions need to take demand and cost variations due to changes in market trends, market and sales logistics, competitive movement and the like. These time-varying demand and cost criteria make it more complex to figure out the most appropriate supply chain strategy – the one that optimizes system-wide management costs and complies with customer needs. Global optimization indicates that it is not only essential to optimize across supply chain resources, but also across business activities connected with the supply chain. In addition, SCM is capturing, storing, and analyzing data that has high volume, greater velocity, and comes from a variety of sources (e.g. machines, radio frequency identification tags, geographical positioning system data, text files, and so on). These data sources are putting very high demand on SCM for a strong data infrastructure, the right analytical tools to manipulate it, and people skilled in the use of analytics.

Figure 2. Heterogeneous information systems along global manufacturing chain

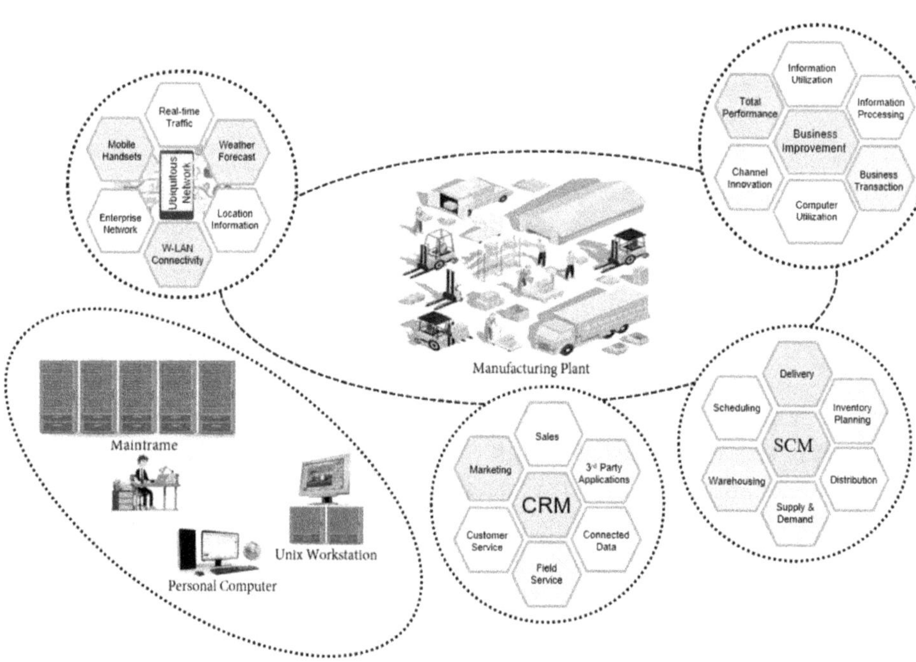

Accomplishing manufacturing supply chain superiority in today's globalized world is a very hard challenge for many manufacturers. Effective SCM can be a competitive advantage that needs synergistic relationships between distributed business-partners with the aim of maximizing customer experience and providing a profit for each supply chain partner (Fugate et al., 2006) (Kalakota & Whinston, 1997). The design of collaborative business processes is vital for successful SCM and enabled by internet technologies (Li, 2002). The main objectives of SCM can be categorized as follows:

- Lowering material holding cost by using appropriate Material Requirement Planning (MRP), which needs to reflect JIT inventory management in the production line.
- Reducing overall production costs by streamlining the product flow with the production process and enhancing information flow between business-partners.
- Improving customer satisfaction by offering quick delivery and flexibility through the seamless cooperation with distributors, warehouse operators, and other customer centric services.

In the presuppositions mentioned above, the most central demand is that the enterprises in manufacturing supply chain need to communicate effectively. There has been a great deal of research literature on supply chain effective communication mechanisms (Pal, 2018) (Pal, 2019) (Gunasekaran & Ngai, 2004) (Ramanathan & Gunasekaran, 2014) however their perspectives and proposed approaches very greatly. One common theme is that competitive success relies on operation-managers' ability to recognize market-demands in the business environment and then to lay-down organizational, and where appropriate, manufacturing supply chain resources to appropriately meets customers' demands. This is a most important requirement of SCM real-world business solution.

Meanwhile manufacturing supply chain business is consisted of various enterprises, while almost each enterprise has its own software system applications and corporate dedicated databases (e.g. enterprise legacy system). In this way, a new business-operating environment has emerged. There are plenty of information and data intersecting and even repeating with each other, which calls for whole business heterogeneous information systems integration.

The information technology (IT) progress and the increasing use of world wide web-based applications in day-to-day business operation has created possibilities for software-based manufacturing supply chain management (Pal, 2019). There are several development originating from different quarters of software-based business processes automation issues, ranging from ERP (Enterprise Resource Planning) to CRM (Customer Relationship Management), WMS (Warehouse Management Systems), MPC (Manufacturing Planning and Control), and MES (Manufacturing Execution System), facilitating various aspect of the manufacturing chain operations. It provides a new way to store, process, distribute and exchange information both within companies and with customers and suppliers in the manufacturing chain. This environment has increasing demands for information or knowledge exchange among business-partners along manufacturing supply chain. Therefore, in information-rich manufacturing chain, the effective interaction among enterprises mainly depends on the interaction among the information systems of enterprises, which is usually realized by enterprises information systems integration.

However, system heterogeneity among enterprise systems is caused by the difference of developers, application platform, development platform, and communication protocol and data format used for exchange of information. Integration of heterogeneous data source is the typical problem in information systems integration.

Despite these efforts, web service discovery is still a complex task and is difficult to implement manually. Hence, Semi-automated or fully dynamic web service discovery hence presents a real research challenge. To address the problem, this chapter describes the functionalities of a hybrid knowledge-based service matchmaking framework, SWSDF, which uses Structured Case-Base Reasoning (S-CBR) and Rule-Based Reasoning (RBR). The remainder of the chapter is organized as follows. Section 2 outlines the overview and motivations of this chapter. It includes a brief introduction of semantic enrichment of web service using ontology; semantic web service frameworks; and ontology-based service description of a business scenario. In addition, it also provides a formal web service description for the business case using Description Logic (DL). Section 3 describes the overview of S-CBR and its relevance for semantic web services research. Section 4 presents briefly the system architecture of SWSDF and its service similarity assessment algorithm. This includes a material management business scenario and the service concept similarity assessment algorithm; including its evaluation procedure. Section 5 presents a review of relevant research approaches for web service discovery. Section 6 ends with concluding remarks.

BACKGROUND OF DATA INTEGRATION PROBLEM

In today's digital age, data is the supply chain operation's lifeblood. It enables business organizations to innovate, make smart and timely decisions, and maintain a quality level of manufacturing supply chain operational service. To provide certain level of operational service, business needs to capture data, clean them if it is appropriate, integrate different business activities data, and process them to make corporate decisions.

Despite these efforts, web service discovery is still a complex task and is difficult to implement manually. Hence, Semi-automated or fully dynamic web service discovery hence presents a real research challenge. To address the problem, this chapter describes the functionalities of a hybrid knowledge-based service matchmaking framework, SWSDF, which uses Structured Case-Base Reasoning (S-CBR) and Rule-Based Reasoning (RBR). The remainder of the chapter is organized as follows. Section 2 outlines the overview and motivations of this chapter. It includes a brief introduction of semantic enrichment of web service using ontology; semantic web service frameworks; and ontology-based service description of a business scenario. In addition, it also provides a formal web service description for the business case using Description Logic (DL). Section 3 describes the overview of S-CBR and its relevance for semantic web services research. Section 4 presents briefly the system architecture of SWSDF and its service similarity assessment algorithm. This includes a material management business scenario and the service concept similarity assessment algorithm; including its evaluation procedure. Section 5 presents a review of relevant research approaches for web service discovery. Section 6 ends with concluding remarks.

OVERVIEW AND MOTIVATION

Web services have become the popular choice for the implementation of service delivery systems, which are distributed and interoperable. These services are built by a set of core technologies that provide these functionalities for communication, description, and discovery of services. The standards that cater these functionalities are Simple Object Access Protocol (SOAP), Web Services Description Language (WSDL), and Universal Description, Discovery, and Integration (UDDI) (OASIS, 2004). These XML-based standards use common Internet Protocols for the exchange of service requests and responses. (Extensible Markup Language, XML, is a common platform-independent data format across the enterprise) Figure 3A shows the relationship of these technologies as a standards stack for web services; and Figure 3B describes briefly service publishing, service requesting and service finding mechanisms using a simple diagrammatic representation.

When a service provider creates a new service, it describes the service using standard WSDL, which defines a service in terms of the messages to be exchanged between services and how they can be found by specifying the location of the service with an appropriate Universal Resource Locater (URL). To make the service available to consumers, the provider registers the service in a UDDI registry by supplying the details of the service provider, the category of the service, and technical details on how to bind to the service. The UDDI registry will then maintain pointers to the WSDL description and to the service. When a consumer wants to use a service, it queries the UDDI registry to find the service that matches its needs and obtains the WSDL description of that service, as well as the access point of the service. The consumer uses the WSDL description to construct a SOAP message to be transported over HTTP (Hyper Text Transmission Protocol) with which to communicate with the service.

Web services are loosely coupled software components that are published, located and invoked across a network-computing infrastructure. Software-based web services are the building blocks for Service Oriented Computing (SOC), and they can be composed to provide a coarse-grained functionality and to automate business processes. In addition, technological improvements are providing more advanced communication facilities (e.g. online vendor managed inventory replenishment, payment using mobile hand-held devices). Business service facilities are providing more flexibility to its end-users and at the same time managing these business processes are becoming more complex. In SCM, many applications can be built by calling different web services available on the web or corporate intranets. These applications are highly dependent on discovering of correct web services. In particular, the description of web service consists of the technical parameters, constraints and policies that define the terms to invoke the web service. A web service definition needs four important things – *name, description, input* and *output*. Name provides business service name and it is used as a unique identifier; description represents the brief outline of the service; the input consists of number of parameters; and the output is also represented by a set of service parameters. SOAP based protocol

Figure 3. Diagrammatic representation of web service technologies: A. Web service standards stack; B. Web service relationships diagram

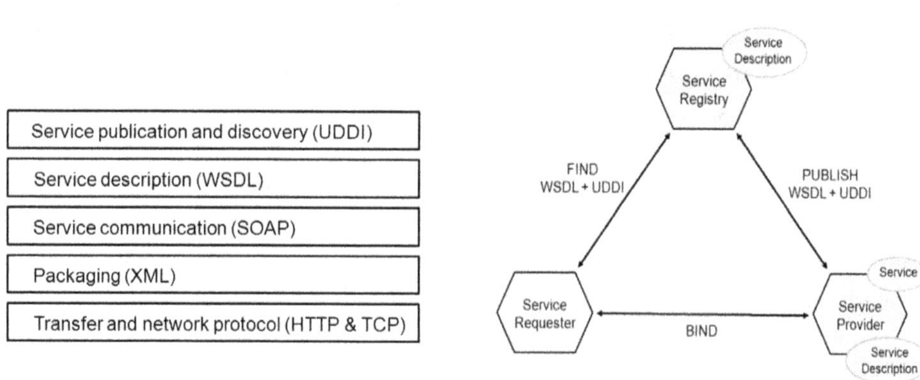

provides the mechanism to exchange structured information in a decentralized and distributed information system.

In this way, web services aim to use the Web as a worldwide infrastructure for distributed computation purposes in order to carry out seamless integration of business processes. However, as the set of available web services increases, it becomes crucial to have automated service discovery mechanisms to help in finding services that match a requester's requirement. Finding appropriate web services depends on the facilities available for service providers to describe the capabilities of their services and for service requesters to describe their needs in an unambiguous form that is ideally machine-readable. In order to achieve this objective, ordinary web service description need to be enriched using domain ontology (or semantic markup). The next section introduces the concept of ontology and semantic annotation mechanisms of web services.

Semantic Enrichment of Web Service using Ontology

The word ontology has its origin in philosophy, and it relates the philosophical study of the nature of existence. In information management, the term ontology has a particular meaning: "An ontology is an explicit specification of a conceptualization" (Gruber, 1993). Studer et al. (Studer et al., 1998) advocated that this specification is also formal, i.e. an ontology is an *explicit* and formal specification of conceptualizing an environment (Antoniou & Harmelen, 2008) for a particular area of interest in a human understandable, and machine-readable format, which consists of objects, concepts, relationships, axioms, individuals and assertions (Guarino & Giaretta, 1995).

Ontologies are often considered as bare building blocks for heterogeneous software system integration. The use of ontologies in computing has gained popularity in recent decades for two specific reasons: they facilitate interoperability, and they enhance computer-based reasoning practice. Particularly in computer science and information science, knowledge reuse is facilitated by the use of explicit ontology, as opposed to implicit ontology (i.e. knowledge encoded into software systems). Hence, suitable ontology languages are required to realize explicit ontologies with respect to three important aspects:

- *Conceptualization*: The language should choose an appropriate reference model, such as Unified Modelling Language (UML) based class model (OMG, 2009), and provide corresponding ontology constructs to represent factual knowledge. For example, defining the classes and related relationships in a particular area of interest, and asserting relations among classes.

- *Vocabulary*: In addition to factual knowledge, the language needs to have vocabulary (i.e. assigning symbols to concepts) and grammar rules in order to represent the vocabulary explicitly.
- *Axiomatization*: In order to capture the semantics for inference, rules and constraints are required in addition to factual knowledge. One can use these rules to produce new facts from existing knowledge.

Information sharing among supply chain business partners using information systems is an important enabler for SCM. Many research works are devoted to answering the question of 'what information to share'. Li and co-researchers (Li et al, 2006) offer four types of data to be shared across the supply chain, namely, *order*, *demand*, *inventory*, and *shipment*. Lambert and his fellow researcher (Lambert & Cooper, 2000) suggest supply chain issues that need to be managed, such as customer service management, inventory management, and so on. In addition, they emphasize the importance of focusing on business processes, rather than individual functions. Consequently, information about these issues needs to be shared in order to achieve efficiency and effectiveness in the supply chain. In this way, information sharing activities require that human and/or machine agents agree on common and explicit ontologies (or business related taxonomies) so as to exchange information and derive knowledge to achieve collaborative objectives of business operations. In order to share knowledge across different communities, three requirements need to be considered when developing explicit ontologies: *extensibility* – reuse existing concepts and develop ontologies in an incremental way; *visibility* – publishing information and knowledge on the Web based on common ontological grounds between information publishers and consumers; and *inferenceability* – enable logical inference on facts through axiomatization.

The semantic web inherits the power of interoperability and it can function as a distributed collaborative knowledge-base for a particular application domain. Moreover, to encode the ontology in information systems different knowledge representation techniques (e.g. graph-based, logic-based representation and other formal representation mechanisms) are used. A part of supply chain inventory management ontologies is shown in Figure 4.

In this diagrammatic representation, a procurement officer is a managerial role aimed on sourcing, procurement, and supply management for an enterprise. Corporate procurement can take place globally due to the economic benefits of the described supply chain. In this process, product costing, transportation facilities, country specific risk associated for a procurement process are all part of the procurement manager's decision-making activities. The top-level basic concepts (i.e. relevant entities or classes) are *country*, *profile*, *description*, *material*, and so on. The concept *profile* is further specialized as *costing* and *resource*. In the same way, concept *material*

Figure 4. A partial state of the world represented by supply chain inventory management ontology

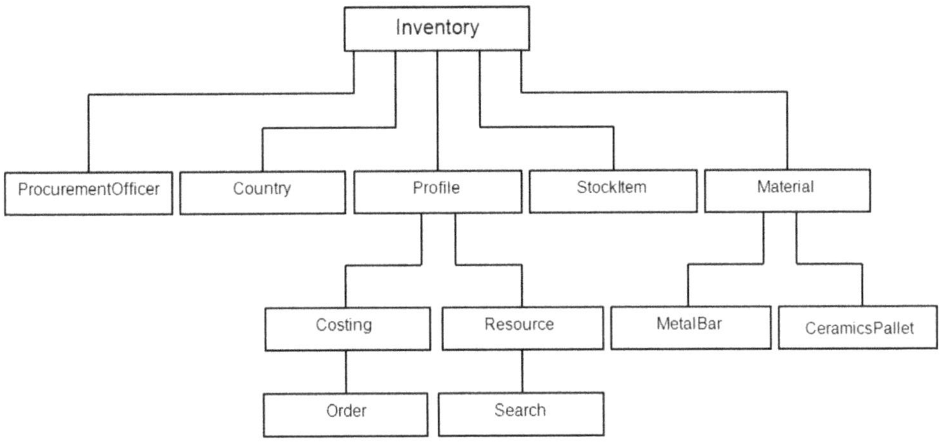

is specialized as *metatl bar*, and *ceramics pallet*. A supply chain business process may be atomic, composed of only one logistical service, or it may be a composite process, containing a series of services that together form a workflow.

These ontologies are presented in OWL (Ontology Web Language) description format; and they can form as the basis for the semantic representation of supply chain related services. The details of logical formalism and consistency checking mechanisms are beyond the scope of this chapter. However, a part of the inventory management ontology formalism is described in Table-1, using description logics (Baader & Nutt, 2003); and some of its core concepts are adopted from the service modeling approach, which has been used for the semantic service description in SWSDF. The objective of the ontology-based semantic similarity algorithm, discussed in the later part of this chapter, is to support the discovery of relevant web services.

A Formal Definition of Web Service Ontology

The semantic web service ontology can be described as follows:

$$\theta_{service}\{\alpha_{fp},\beta_{nfp}.\gamma_{ip},\delta_{o}\}$$

where

θs_{ervice} symbolizes semantic web service in a prescribed representation;

αf_p expresses functional characteristic attributes of service (it comprises of syntax attributes, static semantics which includes messages and operation semantics, service mediator and dynamic semantics;

βn_{fp} corresponds to non-functional attributes of service (it includes u*nique service identification, service name, service type, quality of service, economic properties,* and so on);

γi_p stands for a collection of interface attributes (consisting of input interfaces sets, output interfaces sets, pre-condition interfaces sets, post-condition interfaces sets, and so on) for a semantic web service; and

$\delta 0$ denotes ontology of service.

An ontology 0 comprises of six constituent parts and it can be defined as follows:

$$\delta_o\{C, A^C, R, A^R, H, X\}$$

where

C symbolizes a set of concepts;
A^c expresses a collection of attribute sets, one of each concept;
R represents a set of relationships;
A^R denotes a collection of attribute sets, one for each relationship;
H corresponds to a concept hierarchy; and
X stands for a set of axioms.

In this formalism, every concept C_i in C stands for a collection of similar object types, and can be described by the same collection of characteristic properties denoted by $A^C(C_i)$. Each relationship $r_i(c_p, c_q)$ in R denotes a binary association between concepts c_p and $c_{q,}$ and the instances of such a relationship are pairs of (c_p, c_q) concept objects. The characteristic properties of r_i can be symbolized by $A^R(r_i)$. In this representation formalism, H is a concept hierarchy derived from C and it is a set of parent-child (or superclass – subclass) relationships between concepts in C. Each axiom in X is a constraint on the concepts and relationships attribute values or a constraint on the relationships between concept objects. Each constraint can be expressed in a logic programming rule format. Contextual information that establishes relationships between the data and the real world aspects it applies to forms rich metadata. In this way, academic research has investigated approaches of semantic annotations in web services (Cardoso & Sheth, 2003) (Patil et al, 2004) and offers different semantic web service frameworks.

Semantic Web Service Frameworks

The new breed of web semantic annotated web service is ushering the realization process of having data on the Web defined and linked in such a way that it can be used by matching not just for display purposes, but for automation, integration, and reuse of data across various applications. In this section, three main approaches, to bring semantics to web services, are discussed: WSDL-S, OWL-S, and WSMO.

WSDL-S

Initially this approach was originated by a research group at the University of Georgia, USA. In this approach, the expressivity of web service description (WSDL specification) is augmented with semantics by employing ontological concepts; and it is termed as WSDL-S (WSDL-S, 2005). The idea of establishing mappings between service, task, or activity descriptions and ontological concepts was first proposed by Cardoso and Sheth (Cardoso & Sheth, 2003). In this approach, one can specifically define the semantics of a web service for an area of interest. With the help of ontologies, the semantics or the meaning of service data and functionality can be described. In this way, integration can be accomplished in an automated way and with a higher degree of success. The WSDL elements that can be marked up with metadata are operations, messages, preconditions and effects, since all the elements are specifically described in a WSDL description.

- **Operations**: Each WSDL description may have a number of operations with different functionalities. In order to add semantics, the operations must be mapped to ontological concepts to describe their functionality.
- **Message**: Message parts, which are input and output parameters of operations, are defined in WSDL using the XML Schema. Ontologies – which are more expressive than the XML Schema – can be used to annotate WSDL message parts.
- **Preconditions and Effects**: Each WSDL operation may have a number of preconditions and effects. The preconditions are usually logical conditions, which must be evaluated to be true in order to execute a specific operation. Effects are changes in the world that occur after the execution of an operation.

OWL-S

OWL-S (formally DAML-S) is emerging as a description language that semantically describes web services using OWL ontologies. OWL-S consists of three parts expressed with OWL ontologies: the service profile, the service model, and the service grounding. The profile is used to describe "what a service does", with advertisement and discovery as its objective. The service model describes "how a service works", to enable invocation, enactment, composition, monitoring and recovery. Finally, the grounding maps the constructs of the process model onto detailed specifications of message formats and protocols. In this approach, the ontology itself defines the top-level concept "Service" and three OWL-S sub-ontologies known as the "Service Profile" (SP), "Service Model" (SM), and "Service Grounding" (SG), as shown in Figure-5.

Service Profile (SP)

Every instance of the service class *presents* zero or more service profiles. A service profile expresses the purposes of advertising and serves as a template for service requests, thus enabling service discovery and matchmaking in a better way. The profile consists of non-functional properties - such as references to existing categorization schemes or ontologies, service provider information, and the quality rating of the service. In addition, the specification of functionality of the service is the most important information in the service profile.

Figure 5. OWL-S conceptual model

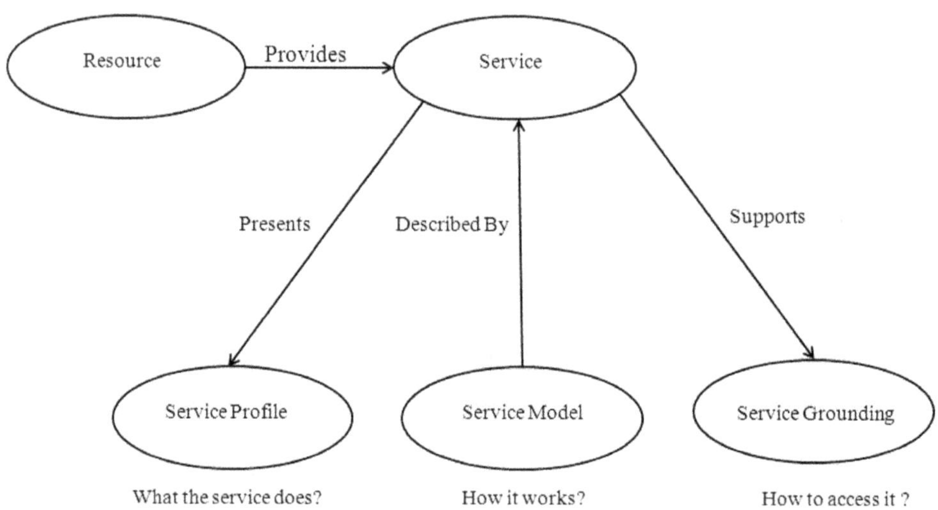

Service Model (SM)

A service capability needs to be described by a service model which tells "how a service works". The essential purpose of a service model is to enable invocation, enactment, composition, monitoring, and recovery. The service model views the interactions of the service as a process. A process is not necessarily a program to be executed, but rather, a specification of ways in which a client may interact with a service.

Service Grounding (SG)

The grounding of a given OWL-S service description provides a pragmatic binding between the logic-based and XMLS-based service definitions for the purpose of facilitating service execution. In order to map to the web service world, an OWL service can support a grounding which maps the constructs of the process model to detailed specifications of message formats, protocols, and so on. Unlike OWL-S, WSDL cannot be used to express pre-conditions or effects of executing services. Any atomic or composite OWL-S service with a grounding in WSDL is executable either by direct invocation of the (service) program that is referenced in the WSDL file, or by a BPEL engine, which processes the WSDL groundings of semantic web services.

WSMO

The third approach, Web Service Modelling Ontology (WSMO), provides ontological specifications for the description of semantic web services. WSMO has been developed by the Digital Enterprise Research Institute (DERI), a European research organization that targets the integration of the semantic web with web services. The WSMO approach is based on the Web Service Modeling Framework (WSMF) (Fensel & Bussler, 2002), a framework that provides the appropriate conceptual model for developing and describing web services and their composition.

Web service modelling ontology discovery framework (WSMO-DF) is based on the WSMO framework (Roman et al, 2005) for web service discovery. In WSMO-DF, a web service is a computational entity which is able, by invocation, to achieve a goal. A *service,* in contrast, is the actual value provided by this invocation, to achieve a goal. Therefore, there are abstract web service and concrete service descriptions. The former describes web services in terms of its abstract functionality, whereas the latter contains more detailed information about the service. For example, a metal trading merchant offers an abstract service for supplying different types of metals, and requesters provide concrete descriptions of their requirements, e.g. number of pallets of a particular metal, its dimensions, quality specification, date of requirement to a particular manufacturing plant, and so on.

Web Service Description of a Business Scenario

In an inventory management system, different materials need to be procured for manufacturing supply chain management purposes. Material attribute ontology design can be viewed from higher perspectives, such as semantic meanings or logical reasoning. However, in this chapter, the main focus is on one pragmatic perspective: as a definition of concepts (or taxonomies) in the domain and associated relations. To illustrate the functionalities of domain ontologies, a simple business scenario has been used to demonstrate the activities.

Business Scenario

Table 1 presents four web services advertisements using the complex concepts and the OWL-S service profile approach. The advertisement one (i.e. adv1) is classified in

Table 1. Web service description examples using description logic syntax.

Domain Ontology Axioms
$Order \sqsubseteq Costing \sqcap \exists StockItem.\top \sqcap \exists account.\top \sqcap \exists material.\top \sqcap \exists to.\top,$ $Search \sqsubseteq Resource \sqcap \exists StockItem. \sqcap \exists StockItem.\top,$ $Costing \sqsubseteq Profile, Resource \sqsubseteq Profile, MetalBar \sqsubseteq Material,$ $CeramicsPallet \sqsubseteq Material, sa : Country, uk : Country,$
Complex Concept
[1] $adv1 \equiv Order \sqcap stockitem.StockItem \sqcap \forall material.MetalBar \sqcap \forall account.ProcurementOfficer \sqcap \exists to.\{sa\}$ [2] $adv2 \equiv Order \sqcap stockitem.StockItem \sqcap \forall material.CeramicsPallet \sqcap \forall account.ProcurementOfficer \sqcap \exists to.\{sa\}$ [3] $adv3 \equiv Order \sqcap stockitem.StockItem \sqcap \forall material.CeramicsPallet \sqcap \forall account.ProcurementOfficer \sqcap \exists to.\{sa\}$ [4] $adv4 \equiv Search \sqcap \forall stockitem.StockItem \sqcap \forall material.MetalBar$
OWL-S Service Profile Instances
[1] $adv1 : Order, < adv1, StockItem >: hasInput,$ $< adv1, ProcurementOfficer >: hasInput, < adv1, MetalBar >: hasOutput, < adv1, sa >: to$ [2] $adv2 : Order, < adv2, StockItem >: hasInput,$ $< adv2, ProcurementOfficer >: hasInput, < adv2, CeramicPallet >: hasOutput, < adv2, sa >: to$ [3] $adv3 : Order, < adv3, StockItem >: hasInput,$ $< adv3, ProcurementOfficer >: hasInput, < adv3, CeramicPallet >: hasOutput, < adv3, uk >: to$ [4] $adv4 : Search, < adv4, StockItem >: hasInput, < adv4, Metal >: hasOutput$

the Order class and requires a description and an account as inputs in order to return a *metal bar* that can be sent to South Africa (SA). In a similar way, the advertisement two (i.e. adv2) is classified in the Order class and requires a description and an account in order to return a *ceramics pallet* that can be sent to South Africa. The advertisement three (i.e. adv3) is also classified in the Order class and requires a *stock item* and an account in order to return a *ceramics pallet* that can be sent to UK. Finally, the advertisement four (i.e. adv4) is classified in the Search class and returns a *metal bar* based on the *stock item*. The above characteristic properties are expressed in the complex concept model by defining appropriate classes that describe services as a whole, whereas in the OWL-S service profile model each advertisement is expressed as an instance of the appropriate Profile subclass.

The scheme, as shown in Table 1, provides skeletons of instances for web services in material management of a global supply chain. In SWSDF, object-oriented structural matching techniques have been used in the domain of Structural Case-Based Reasoning (Bergmann & Schaaf, 2003), with Description Logic (DL) based reasoning over Profile instances. Structural CBR (S-CBR) and ontology based semantic web service management are widely used by the research community.

Semantic Web Services and Case Based Reasoning

Semantic web service initiatives define information systems infrastructure, which enrich the human-readable data on the Web with machine-readable annotations thereby allowing the Web to evolve into the world's biggest information repository which can be accessible from anywhere, at anytime. In order to achieve these objectives, one main issue would be the *markup* of web services to make them computer-interpretable. Within this markup and semantically enhanced service descriptions, powerful tools should be facilitated across the *web service lifecycle* (Papazoglou, 2012). In particular, web services lifecycle includes automatic web service discovery to find either a web service that offers a particular service, or a web service to be used that is sufficiently similar to the current service request; and automatic web service composition and interoperation that involves the run-time service selection, composition, and interoperation of appropriate web services to complete some business activity, given a high-level abstraction of service description.

At the same time, another research community has been working on similarity based *retrieval* and *adaptation* of past solutions to match new problems: two main aspects in the working semantic web service lifecycle. Case-Based Reasoning (CBR) is thriving in the applied computing community and is propagating the idea of finding a solution to a problem based on past experience of similar problems. CBR systems are a particular type of analogical reasoning system (Liang & Konsynski, 1993). It has diverse applications in many fields, such as classification systems for credit card transactions (Reategui & Campbell, 1994) and decision support systems for business acquisitions (Pal & Palmer, 1999). Attempting to imitate human reasoning, this technique solves new problems by using or adopting solutions of previously-solved old problems. A CBR system consists of a case base, which is the set of all previously solved cases that are known to the system. The case base can be thought of as a specific kind of knowledge that contains only *cases* and their *solutions*. There are four main stages in the CBR life cycle and they are:

- **Case Representation**: A case is a contextualized piece of knowledge representing an experience. Since a problem is solved by recalling a past experience suitable for solving the new problem at hand, the case search and matching processes need to be both effective and reasonably time efficient. Moreover, since the experience from a problem just solved has to be retained in some way, these need to apply to the method of integrating a new case into the case collection, too. In this way, CBR is heavily dependent on the structure and content of its collection of cases.
- **Case Storage and Indexing**: Cases are assigned indices that express information about their content, then stored in a case library. This is an important aspect for the design of CBR systems because it reflects the conceptual view of what is represented in the case. The indexing problem is central and a much focused problem in CBR.
- **Case Retrieval**: An important step in the CBR cycle is the retrieval of previous cases that can be used to solve the target problem. Whenever a new problem needs to be solved, the case library index is searched for cases which can be a potential solution. The first phase of this search is case retrieval with the aim of finding the cases which are contextually similar to the new problem. The case retrieval task starts with a problem description, and ends when a suitable matching previous case has been found. Its subtasks are referred to as Identify Features, Search, and Select best possible cases from the system's repository.
- **Case Matchmaking and Use**: Matchmaking performs comparison between the similar cases and the new request to verify if the possible solution is the one applied to prior cases. The past solutions may be reused, directly or through adaptation, in the current situation.

CBR systems typically apply retrieval and matching algorithms to a case base of past problem-solution pairs. Many successful research and industry results are paving the way of CBR in software development and deployment practice. In recent years, *ontologies and descriptive logics* (DLs) have become systems of interest for the CBR community. Many multinational organizations (e.g. IBM, British Airways,

Volkswagen, NASA, and so on) are using CBR techniques for their knowledge intensive business operations (Watson, 1997). Moreover, some real-world CBR applications are taking advantage of the Descriptive Logics (DLs) reasoning mechanisms for the processes involved in the CBR cycle. However, among the different approaches considered, all focus on the fact that the formal semantics and the capabilities of the DLs maintain terminological taxonomy. These are interesting properties to measure similarity and to manage a case base.

In SWSDF, efforts of the semantic web services lifecycle management and CBR cycle are trying to find synergies between both of them. Given a certain requirement describing the user goals, automatic web service discovery typically uses a dedicated inference mechanism in order to answer queries conforming to the logic formalism and the terms defined in the ontology.

PROPOSED SYSTEM FRAMEWORK

This section briefly presents the overall architecture of the SWSDF system and illustrates the interplay of the different components. The computational framework of SWSDF is shown in Figure 4. It uses a relational similarity assessment measure between implicitly stated concepts. The proposed framework accepts the service consumer request which consists of the requirements of a new service (e.g. input, output, precondition, and so on). Next, the user requirement information is parsed for further processing; and finally semantically ranked web services are presented to the consumer. The dynamics of SWSDF are as follows:

- Initially, the service repository is populated with semantically enriched web service descriptions for specific application areas within a supply chain.
- The service requester inputs the service requirements using SWSDF's interface.
- The service matchmaking module takes the retrieved cases and the annotation of the problem description from the semantic description generator module (within the system framework), runs them through a matchmaking algorithm and forwards the closest match web service to the requester.

The ontologically enhanced web service descriptions are manually encoded in the SWSDF service repository. In the processing of ontological concept matching, when dealing with similarity between concepts, it not only considers inheritance (i.e. the relationship between supper-class and subclass) relations, but also considers the distance relationship between concepts. In SWSDF, on the basis of the comprehensive consideration of the inheritance relations and semantic distance between concepts, a concept similarity matching method based on semantic distance has been used. The SWSDF uses structural case-based reasoning (S-CBR) for services and the relevant ontological concepts storage purpose; and it uses a rule-based reasoning (RBR) for service similarity assessment. The algorithm, as shown in Figure 5, is used to discover semantic web services advertised within SWSDF.

Model of Concept Similarity for SWSDF

This section describes the method for measuring the degree of similarity of two OWL concepts. This measure will then be used in the next section for determining the degree of functional similarity of two services.

Definition 1 (*Concept Similarity*): A similarity σ: $C \times \mathbf{C} \rightarrow [0,1]$ is a function from a pair of concepts to a real number between zero and one expressing the degree of similarity between two concepts such that:

$$(1)\ \forall x \in C, \sigma(x,x) = 1$$

$$(2)\ \forall x,y \in C, \sigma(x,y) = \sigma(y,x)$$

$$(3)\ \forall x,y,z:\ \textit{if } SimDistance(x,y) > SimDistance(x,z),\ \textit{then } \sigma(x,y) < \sigma(x,z)$$

Figure 6. Diagrammatic representation of the SWSDF

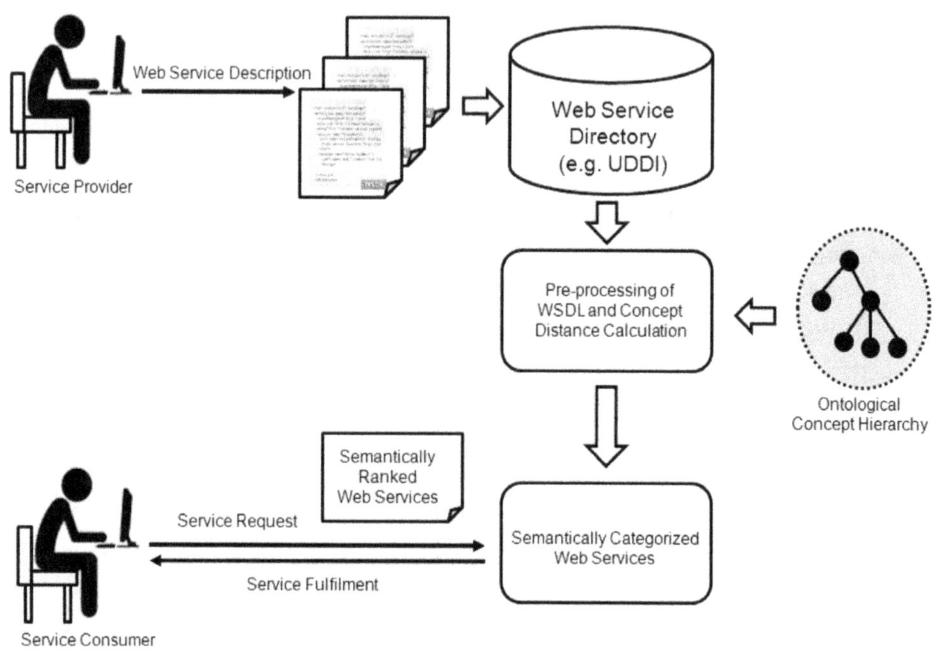

The above properties provide the range of semantic similarity function $\sigma(x, x)$. For exactly similar concepts the similarity is $\sigma(\mathbf{x},x)=1$; and when two concepts have nothing in common, their similarity is $\sigma(\mathbf{x},\mathbf{y})=0$. In this way, the output of similarity function should be in closed interval [0,1] and it is a reflexive relation. In SWSDF, the following semantic similarity function has been used for computation purposes:

$$f_{similarity} = p^{SimDistance+1}$$

In the above similarity function, the value of $p(0<p\leq 1)$ and *SimDistance* decide the impact degree of semantic distance to semantic similarity. In SWSDF, the similarity between two ontological concepts C_i and C_j can be expressed by a number S_{ij} which can be expressed by the semantic distance among any two concepts. Given two concepts C_i and C_j, the SWSDF calculates the distance as weight allocation function as follows:

$$\omega[sub(C_i \text{ and } C_j)] = 1 + \frac{1}{k^{depth(c_j)}}$$

where depth (C_i) represents the depth of concept (C_j) from the root concept to node C_j in ontology hierarchy, and k is a predefined factor larger than 1 showing the rate at which the weight values decrease along the ontology hierarchy.

Table 2. Algorithm for semantic distance computation

ALGORITHM1: similarity measure of two concepts (C_1, C_2)
INPUT: concepts C_1 and C_2 OUTPUT: Similarity Distance (SimDistance between C_1 and C_2)
BEGIN
IF C_1 and C_2 are exactly same concept THEN
SimDistance (C_1, C_2) = 0
ELSE
IF there exist any indirect path relations between (C_1 and C_2) THEN
SimDistance (C_1, C_2) = Weight [sub (C_1, C_2)]
ELSE SimDistance (C_1, C_2) = $\sum_{C \in SPath(C_1, C_2)} (Weight[sub(C_1, C_2)]$
ELSE SimDistance (C_1, C_2) = min {SimDistance (C_1, C_0)} + + min {SimDistance (C_2, C_0)}
END

The above function has got two important properties: (1) the semantic differences between higher concepts are more in comparison to lower level concepts, and (2) the distance between sibling concepts is greater than the distance between parent and child concepts. In particular, the depth of topmost concept is considered be zero, and the lower level other concepts are related to their path length to root concept node.

The algorithm, as shown in Figure 5, takes two concepts as input and computes a semantic similarity as output based on the ALGORITHM1.

Experimental Evaluation

The part of the type hierarchy in the matchmaker ontology and all instances used in this example are shown in Figure 6. In the experimental comparison, semantic similarity among Copper, Glass, Metal, Steel and Material are considered.

In Table 2, (a) tabulates the results of synonymy similarity (Giunchiglia et al, 2004), (b) tabulates the results of Jian and Conrath similarity (Jiang & Conrath, 1997) results, (c) tabulates the results of path similarity (Varelas et al, 2005), and (d) tabulates the results of algorithm used in SWSDF – concept similarity measure based on semantic distance.

Figure 7. The hierarchical concept relationships

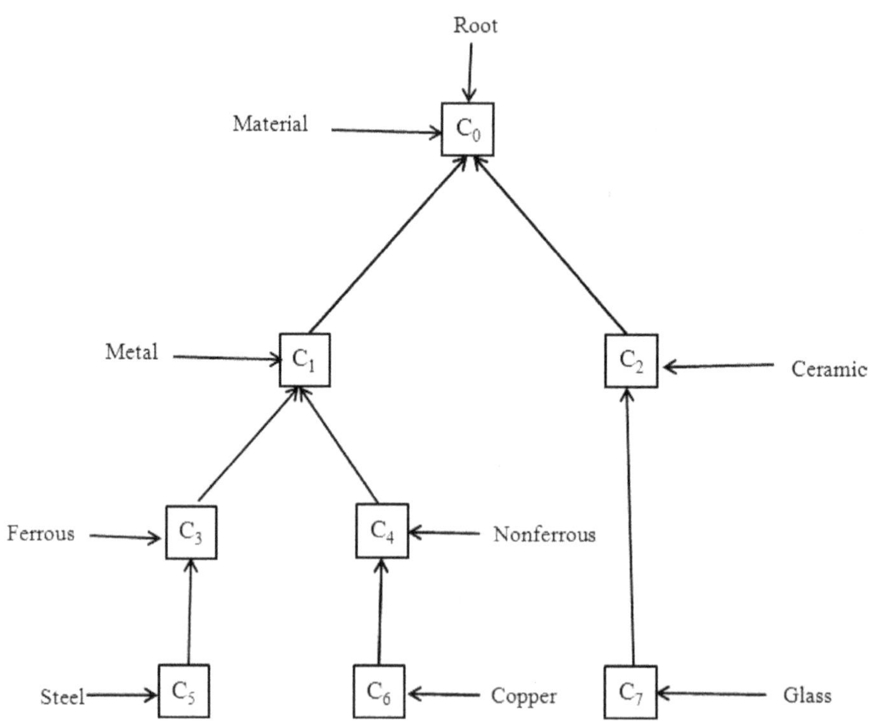

Table 3. The results of various similarity measures

$C_1 \rightarrow C_2$ C_3 C_4 C_5 C_1 1.00 0.00 0.00 0.00 0.00 C_2 0.00 1.00 0.00 0.00 0.00 C_3 0.00 0.00 1.00 0.00 0.00 C_4 0.00 0.00 0.00 1.00 0.00 C_5 0.00 0.00 0.00 0.00 1.00	$C_1 \rightarrow C_2$ C_3 C_4 C_5 C_1 1.00 0.60 0.41 0.97 0.52 C_2 0.42 1.00 0.81 0.60 0.36 C_3 0.97 0.81 1.00 0.68 0.44 C_4 0.60 0.60 0.68 1.00 0.53 C_5 0.52 0.36 0.44 0.53 1.00
(a) Synonymy similarity	*(b) Jian and Conrath similarity*
$C_1 \rightarrow C_2$ C_3 C_4 C_5 C_1 1.00 0.25 0.50 0.20 0.20 C_2 0.25 1.00 0.50 0.33 0.16 C_3 0.50 0.50 1.00 0.25 0.16 C_4 0.20 0.33 0.25 1.00 0.20 C_5 0.20 0.16 0.16 0.20 1.00	$C_1 \rightarrow C_2$ C_3 C_4 C_5 C_1 1.0 0.48 0.65 0.51 0.38 C_2 0.48 1.0 0.65 0.51 0.38 C_3 0.65 0.65 1.0 0.71 0.48 C_4 0.51 0.51 0.71 1.0 0.59 C_5 0.38 0.38 0.48 0.59 1.0
(c) Path similarity	*(d) The proposed method*

As shown in Tablc 2, the synonymy similarity measure can only find similarity between the same concepts, and Jian and Conrath' similarity measure is better than the synonymy similarity measure. The path similarity measure and SWSDF's used method are better than the above two methods. The path similarity measure can find the semantic similarity between concepts, but the similarity score is low. The SWSDF's similarity method can also get the semantic similarity between concepts, and the similarity score is high.

RELATED RESEARCH WORK

The semantic web approaches to web services give business communities the ability to describe the semantics of web services and their capabilities in a formal and machine-processable manner. A majority of the current approaches (e.g. OWL-S, WSDL-S, and WSMO) enhancing web services using semantic tagged descriptions. However, these approaches have several limitations. First, it is impractical to expect all new services to have semantic tagged descriptions. Second, descriptions of the vast majority of existing web services are specified using WSDL and do not have associated semantics. Also, from the service requestor's perspective, the requestor may not be aware of all the knowledge that constitutes the domain. Specifically, the service requestor may not be aware of all the terms related to the service request.

As a result, many services relevant to the request may not be considered in the service discovery process. Akkiraju and his research group (Akkiraju et al, 2005), conjectured an attempt to design a system which can create semantic web services is by mapping concepts in a web service description (WSDL specification) to ontological concepts. This approach is known as WSDL-S. The idea of establishing mappings between service, task, or activity description and its enrichment using domain specific ontological concepts was first introduced by Cardoso (Cardoso & Sheth, 2003). Martin has also concentrated on enhancement of service descriptions, in work with other researchers on OWL-S (Martin et al, 2007), which is an important attempt to use lightweight web service description based on inputs, outputs and non-functional properties, in order to find an initial set of candidate web services for a request. Fensel has also concentrated on service enrichment and modelling, in work with Bussler on the system WSMF (Fensel & Bussler, 2002), a framework that provides the appropriate conceptual model for developing and describing web services and their composition.

Web service modelling ontology discovery framework (WSMO-DF), also contributed to semantic enrichment of web services, and is based on the WSMO framework (Roman et al, 2005) for web service discovery. In the semantic web service paradigm, discovery is performed over semantic descriptions of web services. WSMO-DF and OWL-S SP (service profile) are two frameworks that are generally used for service description purposes.

While these are a few main styles of service enrichment in semantic web service descriptions, they are by no means the only research conducted in the recent past. Later work by Pengwei and his colleagues on their semantic enhancement web service research (Wang et al, 2008) has used WSMO-DF for rich web service representation purposes. In contrast to Pengwei and his research partners (Weang et al, 2008) work, SWSDF follows the Service Profile (SP) model and uses structural ontology information.

In IRS-III (Domingue et al, 2008), an extended approach of the WSMO conceptual model is used, where OCML (Options Configuration Modelling Language) has provided internal description of service and an appropriate OCML reasoner. In contrast to SWSDF, IRS-III follows an enhanced WSMO model and a frame-based rule language for representing domain ontologies.

Li and his colleagues advocated the use of a mechanism based on the Rough sets theory to discover grid services (Li et al, 2008). The implemented software system, known as ROSSE, builds on the Rough sets theory to dynamically reduce uncertain properties when matching grid services. The evaluation results have shown that ROSSE significantly improves the precision and recall of services compared with keyword-based service matching techniques and OWL-S matching. The novelty of ROSSE is in its capability to deal with uncertain properties, that is, properties that are explicitly used by one advertisement but do not appear in another service of the same category. In SWSDF, only the common properties of an advertisement have been used.

Li and Horrocks have distinguished a number of things in a service matchmaking research porotype (Li & Horrocks, 2003), which uses a DL reasoner to match service advertisements and requests based on ontology enhanced service descriptions. In this particular project, web service descriptions are defined as Complex Concepts (CCs) in OWL and the matchmaking mechanism examines the subsumption relationships. FC-MATCH research project (Bianchini et al, 2006) uses a similar type of approach, performing text similarity matching using WordNet. In some research (Grimm et al., 2006), a software framework has been used to annotate web services using DLs. Similar to SWSDF, it follows the abstract web service model.

In the DAML-S/UDDI matchmaker (Sycara et al, 2003), OWL-S SP advertisements and requests refers to DAML concepts and the matching process that performs inferences on the subsumption hierarchy. It uses a different definition of web service filters from SWSDF and it does not consider profile taxonomies, roles or group filtering.

LARKS (Sycara et al, 2002) uses both syntactic and semantic matching. It uses five matchmaking filters, namely context matching, profile comparison, similarity matching, signature matching and constant matching. LARKS uses its own capability description and DL language in contrast to the SWSDF approach.

OWLS-MX (Klusch et al, 2008) utilizes both logic-based reasoning and content-based IR techniques for web services in OWL-S. It cannot handle profile taxonomies and it follows the static SP paradigm, unable to use dynamic ontology roles. iMatcher2 (Kiefer & Bernstein, 2008) follows the OWLS-MX approach, also applying learning algorithms in order to predict similarities. Like OWLS-MX, it uses a DL reasoner in order to unfold the annotation concepts, creating a vector on which the IR techniques are applied. iMatcher2 does not follow a standard matchmaking algorithm, which is defined through an iSPARQL strategy. WSMO-MX (Kaufer & Klusch, 2006) is a hybrid approach based on rich WSMO service descriptions.

In the DAML-S/UDDI matchmaker (Sycara et al, 2003), OWL-S SP advertisements and requests refers to DAML concepts and the matching process performs inferences on the subsumption hierarchy. It uses a different definition of web service filters from SWSDF and it does not consider profile taxonomies, roles or group filtering.

LARKS (Sycara et al, 2002) use both syntactic and semantic matching. It uses five matchmaking filters, namely context matching, profile comparison, similarity matching, signature matching and constant matching. LARKS uses its own capability description and DL language in contrast to the SWSDF approach.

In a hybrid semantic web service matchmaker for OWL-S services, known as OWLS-MX (Klusch et al, 2008), researchers have used both logic-based reasoning and content-based information retrieval techniques. Experimental evaluation results show strong justification in favor of the proposition that the performance of logic-based matchmaking can be considerably improved by incorporating non-logic based information retrieval techniques into the matchmaking algorithms. However, OWLS-MX cannot handle profile taxonomies and it follows the static SP paradigm, unable to use dynamic ontology roles. iMatcher2 (Kiefer & Bernstein, 2008) follows the OWLS-MX approach, applying also learning algorithms in order to predict similarities. Like OWLS-MX, it uses a DL reasoner in order to unfold the annotation concepts, creating a vector on which the IR techniques are applied. iMatcher2 does not follow a standard matchmaking algorithm, which is defined through an iSPARQL strategy. WSMO-MX (Kaufer & Klusch, 2006) is a hybrid approach based on rich WSMO service descriptions.

There are plenty of other approaches that are based on inputs/outputs, for example (Cardoso, 2006) (Pathak et al, 2005) (Skoutas et al, 2007). These approaches retrieve directly the input/output annotations and any taxonomical knowledge from special properties, such as service categorization. Moreover, they do not consider roles, using static annotation concepts, and do not apply further filtering on results (group filtering). METEROR-S (Verma et al, 2005) follows the WSDL-S approach, where WSDL constructs point to ontology concepts.

Thakker, Osman and Al-Dabass have reported their research in which the web service execution experiences are modeled as cases that represent the web service properties in a specific area described using OWL semantic description (Osman et al, 2006a) (Osman et al, 2006b). In this research, the service repository administrator performs the storing of service descriptions using ontology enhanced semantics for case representation. This representation is used to semantically annotate the users' queries looking for adequate services as well as the web service execution experiences in the given area. The proposed system uses frame structures to model its cases. These structures are not generalized and depend heavily on the application domain so that the constituent elements of these structures more precisely 'slots' differ from one application to another.

Lamjmi and co-researchers have proposed the WeSCo_CBR approach based mainly on ontologies and case-based reasoning meant for the web service composition (Lajmi et al, 2006a) (Lajmi et al, 2006b). They have created an ontology that describes various features of a web service using OWL representation formalism in order to bring a semi-automatic guidance for the user. In order to facilitate the processing, they proceed by transforming the user's query into an ontological formulation combining a set of ontology concepts. For each received new query, the reuse process consists on retrieving similar prior stored cases and eventually evaluating and storing the new case. In WeSCo_CBR, a case comprises the following three elements: a problem, a solution and an evaluation. The discovery of web service meeting the client's needs is accomplished by using similarity measures designed in accordance with the formalization of the problem. The most relevant case is usually determined according to its similarity with the new problem case.

In order to improve the web service discovery, Wan and Cao (Wang & Cao, 2007) have introduced an additional case-based reasoning component called CBR/OWL-S Matching Engine (Wang & Cao, 2007). In order to find out the desired web service, this matching engine uses ontologies for semantic similarity measure.

The SWSDF work has been motivated by object-oriented structural matching techniques that are used in the domain of Structural Case-Based Reasoning (SCBR) (Bergman & Schaaf, 2003), with the use of a DL reasoner to handle semantic web service descriptions and to apply an extended matchmaking algorithm. In addition, the method of allocating the weight value to concept node has been used for similarity assessment purposes.

CONCLUSION

This chapter reviews some of the business and technology challenges that companies are facing today in supply chain information sharing between business partners, and describes how a number of these difficulties could be overcome with the use of semantic web service. However, in order for semantic web service to be adopted within a global supply chain network there must be tools, which will help to automate heterogeneous data sources existing in this networked enterprise. In this chapter, a supply chain information sharing architecture between business partners is described using the semantic web service framework. The architecture is based on a hybrid knowledge-based service matchmaking framework, which uses Structural Case-Based Reasoning (S-CBR) and Rule-Based Reasoning (RBR). It uses ontology enhanced web service descriptions; object-oriented S-CBR knowledge representation, description logic (DL) for service formalization, and an algorithm to measure ontological concept similarity based on semantic distance. This algorithm considers not only the inheritance relation between concepts, but also the level of concepts in the ontology hierarchy. An experimental evaluation of the proposed algorithm is presented. In this architecture, ontological concepts play an important role in the development of the semantic web as a means for defining shared terms in web resources in SCM automation. Today, business partners within global supply chains are generating huge amounts of raw-data; and they are collecting some of this data for business intelligence purposes. This data is commonly referred to as 'big data' – because of its *volume*, the *velocity* with which it arrives in global supply chain environments, and the *variety* of forms it takes. Big data is ushering in a new era of corporate business intelligence promise; but one of main bottlenecks is how to capture this raw-data and analyze it to generate meaningful information. In the future, this research will extend the current concept-based ontological reasoning framework and investigate additional mapping techniques in order to express service descriptions in a much more enhanced form. This will allow a richer service discovery for globalized supply chain world. Particularly, one of the challenging tasks is how to handle *big data* in global supply chain environments, and how to use these untapped corporate *cyber-physical* resources to come up with better service provisions for its stakeholders. Cyber-physical systems enable new types of interconnected information service provisions by connecting networked systems with services of the automated system infrastructure. This in turn enables interaction with extended capabilities of physical business world through computation, communication and control. This infrastructure is going to be the source of next generation big data driven global supply chain information systems integration and coordination of global power houses.

REFERENCES

Akkiraju, R., Farrell, J., Miller, J., Nagarajan, M., Schmidt, M., Sheth, A., & Verma, K. (2005). *Web Service Semantics - WSDL-S*. A joint UGA-IBM Technical Note, version 1.0. http://lsdis.cs.uga.edu/projects/METEOR-S/WSDL-S

Antoniou, G., & Harmelen, F. V. (2008). *A Semantic Web Primer*. The MIT Press.

Baader, F., & Nutt, W. (2003). *Basic Description Logics, The description logic handbook*. Cambridge University Press.

Bergmann, R., & Schaaf, M. (2003). Structural Case-Based Reasoning and Ontology-Based Knowledge Management: A Perfect Match? *Journal of Universal Computer Science, UCS*, *9*(7), 608–626.

Berners-Lee, T., Hendler, J., & Lassila, O. (2001). The Semantic Web. *Scientific American, 284*(May), 34–43. doi:10.1038cientificamerican0501-34 PMID:11323639

Bianchini, D., Antonellis, V. A., Melchiori, M., & Salvi, D. (2006). Semantic Enriched Service Discovery. *International Conference in Data Engineering Workshop*, 38.

Cai, M. Zhang, W. Y., Zhang, K. & Li, S. T. (2010). SWMRD: A Semantic Web-based manufacturing resource discovery system for cross-enterprise collaboration. *International Journal of Production Research, 48*(12), 3445-3460.

Cardoso, J. (2006). Discovering Semantic Web Services with and without a Common Ontology Commitment. *IEEE Service Computing Workshop*, 183-190.

Cardoso, J., & Sheth, A. (2003). Semantic e-Workflow Composition. *Journal of Intelligent Information Systems*, *21*(3), 191–225. doi:10.1023/A:1025542915514

Cliche, Taghipour, & Canel. (2020). An Improved Forecasting Approach to Reduce Inventory-Levels in Decentralized Supply Chains. *European Journal of Operational Research*, *287*(2), 511–527.

Copacino, W., & Anderson, D. (2003). Connecting with the Bottom Line: A Global Study of Supply Chain Leadership and its Contribution to the High Performance Business. *Accenture, 1*.

Domingue, J., Cabral, L., Galizia, S., Tanasescu, V., Gugliotta, A., Norton, B., & Pedrinaci, C. (2008). IRS-III: A Broker-based Approach to Semantic Web Service. *Journal of Web Semantics*, *6*(2), 109–132. doi:10.1016/j.websem.2008.01.001

Fensel, D., & Bussler, C. (2002). The Web Service Modeling Framework WSMF. *Electronic Commerce Research and Applications*, *1*(2), 113–137. doi:10.1016/S1567-4223(02)00015-7

Fugate, B., Sahin, F., & Mentzer, J. T. (2006). Supply Chain Management Coordination Mechanisms. *Journal of Business Logistics, 27*(2), 129–161. doi:10.1002/j.2158-1592.2006.tb00220.x

Ganeshan, R., & Harrison, T. P. (1995). An introduction to supply chain management. *Supply Chain Management.* Available from http://silmaril.smeal.psu.edu/misc/supply_chain_ intro.html

Giunchiglia, F., Shvaiko, P., & Yatskevich, M. (2004). S-Match: an algorithm and an implementation of semantic matching. *Proceedings of 1st European Semantic Web Symposium (ESWS)*, 3053, 61-75. 10.1007/978-3-540-25956-5_5

Grimm, S., Monk, B., & Preist, C. (2006). Matching Semantic Service Descriptions with Local Closed-World Reasoning. *European Semantic Web Conference*, 575-589. 10.1007/11762256_42

Gruber, T. R. (1993). *A Translation Approach to Portable Ontology Specifications.* Stanford University, Computer Science Department, Knowledge Systems Laboratory, Technical Report KSL 92-71.

Guarino, N., & Giaretta, P. (1995). *Ontologies and Knowledge Base: Towards a Terminological Classification Toward Very Large Knowledge Base: Knowledge Building and Knowledge Sharing.* IOS Press.

Jiang, J. J., & Conrath, D. W. (1997). Semantic Similarity Based on Corpus Statistics and Lexical Taxonomy. *Proceedings of International Conference Research on Computational Linguistics.*

Kalakota, R., & Whiston, A. (1997). *Electronic commerce: a manager's guide.* Addison Wesley.

Kaufer, F., & Klusch, M. (2006). WSMO-MX: A Logic Programming Based Hybrid Service Matchmaker. *European Conference on Web Services*, 161-170. 10.1109/ECOWS.2006.39

Kiefer, C., & Bernstein, A. (2008). The Creation and Evaluation of iSPARQL Strategies for Matchmaking. *European Semantic Web Conference*, 463-477. 10.1007/978-3-540-68234-9_35

Klusch, M., Fries, B., & Sycara, K. (2008). OWLS-MX: A Hybrid Semantic Web Service Matchmaker for OWL-S Services. *Journal of Web Semantics.*

Lajmi, S., Ghedira, C., & Ghedira, K. (2006a). How to apply CBR method in web service composition. In *Second International Conference on Signal-Image Technology and Internet Based Systems (SITI'2006).* Springer Verlag.

Lajmi, S., Ghedira, C., Ghedira, K., & Benslimane, D. (2006b). Web_CBR: How to compose web service via case based reasoning. *IEEE International Symposium on Service-Oriented Applications, Integration and Collaboration held with the IEEE International Conference on eBusiness Engineering (ICEBE 2006).*

Laliwala, Z., Khosla, R., Majumdar, P., & Chaudhary, S. (2006). Semantic and Rule Based Event-Driven Dynamic Web Service Composition for Automation of Business Processes. *Proceedings of the IEEE Service Computing Workshop (SCW06).*

Lambert, D. M., & Cooper, M. C. (2000). Issues in Supply Chain Management. *Industrial Marketing Management, 29*(1), 65–83. doi:10.1016/S0019-8501(99)00113-3

Li, J., Sikora, R., Shaw, M. J., & Woo Tan, G. A. (2006). Strategic analysis of inter-organizational information sharing. *Decision Support Systems, 42*(1), 251–266. doi:10.1016/j.dss.2004.12.003

Li, L., & Horrocks, I. (2003). A Software Framework for Matchmaking Based on Semantic Web Technology. *International Conference in World Wide Web*, 331-339. 10.1145/775152.775199

Li, M., Yu, B., Rana, O. F., & Wang, Z. (2008). Grid Service Discovery with Rough Sets. *IEEE Transactions on Knowledge and Data Engineering, 20*(6), 851–862. doi:10.1109/TKDE.2007.190744

Li, S. H. (2002). *An Integrated Model for Supply Chain Management Practice, Performance and Competitive Advantage* (PhD Dissertation). University of Toledo, Toledo, OH.

Liang, T., & Konsynski, B. R. (1993). Modeling by analogy: Use of analogical reasoning in model management systems. *Decision Support Systems, 9*(1), 113–125. doi:10.1016/0167-9236(93)90026-Y

Martin, D., Burstein, M., Mcdermott, D., Mcilraith, S., Paolucci, M., Sycara, K., Mcguinness, D. L., Sirin, E., & Srinivasan, N. (2007). Bringing Semantics to Web Services with OWL-S. *World Wide Web (Bussum), 10*(3), 243–277. doi:10.100711280-007-0033-x

Martin, D., Paolucci, M., McIlraith, S., Burstein, M., McDermott, D., McGunness, D., Barsia, B., Payne, T., Sabou, M., Solanki, M., Srinivasan, N., & Sycara, K. (2004). Bringing Semantics to Web Services: The OWL-S Approach. *Proceeding of First International Workshop Semantic Web Services and Web Process Composition.*

Matskin, M., Maigre, R., & Tyugu, E. (2007). Computational logical semantics for business process language. *Proceedings of second international conference on Internet and Web applications and services (ICIW 2007)*, 526-531.

McIlraith, S., & Martin, D. (2003). Bringing Semantics to Web Services. *IEEE Intelligent Systems, 18*(1), 90–93. doi:10.1109/MIS.2003.1179199

OASIS. (2004). *Introduction to UDDI: Important Features and Functional Concepts*. Organization for the Advancement of Structured Information Standards.

OMG. (2009). *Business Process Model and Notation*. https://www.omg.org/spec/BPMN/1.2/(2009)

Osman, T., Thakker, D., & Al-Dabass, D. (2006a). Semantic-Driven Matching of Web services using Case-Based Reasoning. *Fourth IEEE International Conference on Web Services (ICWS 2006)*, 29-36.

Osman, T., Thakker, D., & Al-Dabass, D. (2006b). S-CBR: Semantic Case Based Reasoner for Web services discovery and matchmaking. *20th European Conference on Modeling and Simulation (ECMS2006)*, 723-729.

Pal, K., & Karakostas, B. (2014). A Multi Agent-based Service Framework for supply Chain Management. *Procedia Computer Science, 32*, 53-60.

Pal, K., & Palmer, O. (2000). A decision-support systems for business acquisition. *Decision Support Systems, 27*(4), 411–429. doi:10.1016/S0167-9236(99)00083-4

Papazoglou, M. (2012). *Web Services and SOA: Principles and Technology*. Pearson.

Pathak, J., Koul, N., Caragea, D., & Honavar, V. G. (2005). A Framework for Semantic Web Services Discovery. *ACM International Workshop on Web Information and Data Management*, 45-50. 10.1145/1097047.1097057

Patil, A., Oundhaka, S., Sheth, A., & Verma, K. (2004). METEOR-S Web service Annotation Framework. *The Proceedings of the Thirteenth International World Wide Web Conference*, 553-562.

Radhoui, Taghipour, & Canel. (2018). *The distribution and pickup of goods- a literature review and survey in Hierarchical Planning and Information Sharing Techniques in Supply Chain Management.* IGI Global.

Reategui, E. B., & Campbell, J. A. (1995). A Classification System for Credit Card Transactions. In *Advances in Case-Based Reasoning: Second European Workshop (EWCBR-94)*. Springer. 10.1007/3-540-60364-6_43

Roman, D., Keller, U., Lausen, H., de Bruijn, J., Lara, R., Stollberg, M., Polleres, A., Feier, C., Bussler, C., & Fensel, D. (2005). Web service modeling ontology. *Applied Ontology*, *1*(1), 77–106.

Roman, D., Kopecky, J., Vitvar, T., Domingue, J., & Fensel, D. (2015). WSMO-Lite and hRESTS: Lightweight semantic annotations for Web services and RESTful APIs. *Journal of Web Semantics*, *31*, 39–58. doi:10.1016/j.websem.2014.11.006

Shingo, S. (1988). *Non-Stock Production*. Productivity Press.

Skoutas, D., Simitsis, A., & Sellis, T. (2007). A Ranking Mechanism for Semantic Web Service Discovery. *IEEE Congress on Services*, 41-48. 10.1109/SERVICES.2007.8

Studer, R., Benjamins, V. R., & Fensel, D. (1998). Knowledge engineering: Principles and methods. *Data & Knowledge Engineering*, *25*(1-2), 161–197. doi:10.1016/S0169-023X(97)00056-6

Sycara, K., Widoff, S., Klusch, M., & Lu, J. (2002). LARKS: Dynamic Matching Among Heterogeneous Software Agents in Cyberspace. *Autonomous Agents and Multi-Agent Systems*, *5*(2), 173–203. doi:10.1023/A:1014897210525

Sycara, K. P., Paolucci, M., Ankolekar, A., & Srinivasan, N. (2003). Automated Discovery, Interaction and Computation of Semanticmweb Services. *Journal of Web Semantics*, *1*(1), 27–46. doi:10.1016/j.websem.2003.07.002

Taghipour. (2020). *Demand Forecasting and Order Planning in Supply Chains and Humanitarian Logistics*. IGI Global.

Varelas, G., Voutsakis, E., Raftopoulou, P., Petrakis, E. G. M., & Milios, E. (2005). Semantic Similarity methods in WordNet and their application to information retrieval on the Web. *Proceedings of the 7th annual ACM international workshop on web information and data management*. 10.1145/1097047.1097051

Verma, K., Sivashanmugam, K., Sheth, A., Patil, A., Oundhakar, S., & Miller, J. (2005). METEOR-S WSDI: A Scalable P2P Infrastructure of Registries for Semantic Publication and Discovery of Web Services. *Information Technology and Management*, *6*(1), 17–39. doi:10.100710799-004-7773-4

Vrijhoef, R., & Koskela, L. (1999). Role of supply chain management in construction. *Proceedings of the Seventh Annual Conference of the International Group for Lean Construction*, 133-146.

Wang, L., & Cao, J. (2007). Web Services Semantic Searching enhanced by Case Based Reasoning. *18th International Workshop on Database and Expert Systems Applications*.

Wang, P., Jin, Z., Liu, L., & Cai, G. (2008). Building Toward Capability Specifications of Web Services Based on an Environment Ontology. *IEEE Transactions on Knowledge and Data Engineering*, *20*(4), 547–561. doi:10.1109/TKDE.2007.190719

Watson, I. (1997). *Applying Case-Based Reasoning: Techniques for Enterprise Systems*. Morgan Kaufman.

Wooldridge, M., & Jennings, N. (1995). Intelligent Agents: Theory and Practice. *The Knowledge Engineering Review*, *10*(2), 115–152. doi:10.1017/S0269888900008122

WSDL-S. (2005). http://www.w3.org/Submission/WSDL-S/

Zhang, W. Y., Cai, M., Qiu, J., & Yin, J. W. (2009). Managing distributed manufacturing knowledge through multi-perspective modelling for Semantic Web applications. *International Journal of Production Research*, *47*(23), 6525–6542. doi:10.1080/00207540802311114

KEY TERMS AND DEFINITIONS

Case-Based Reasoning: Case-based reasoning (CBR) is one of the useful mechanisms for both modeling human reasoning and building intelligent software application systems. The basic principle of case-based reasoning systems is that of solving problems by adapting the solution of similar problems solved in the past. A CBR system consists of a *case base*, which is the set of all cases that are known to the system. The case base can be thought of as a specific kind of knowledge base that contains only cases. When a new case is presented to the system, it checks the case base for similar cases that are most relevant to the case in hand, in a *selection process*. If a similar case is found, then the system retrieves that particular case and attempts to modify it (if necessary) to produce a potential solution for the new case. The process is known as *adaption*.

Description Logic: Knowledge-based software system relies on its stored knowledge and decision-making mechanisms. At the time of knowledge-based system design and development stages, software engineers use different knowledge representation techniques; and one of the techniques is symbolic logic-based representation. Different symbolic logic representation is used for knowledge presentation purpose. Description Logics (DLs) are a family of knowledge representation languages that can be used to represent the knowledge of an application domain in a structured way.

Ontology: Information sharing among supply chain business partners using information system is an important enabler for supply chain management. There are different types of data to be shared across supply chain, namely – order, demand, inventory, shipment, and customer service. Consequently, information about these issues needs to be shared in order to achieve efficiency and effectiveness in supply chain management. In this way, information-sharing activities require that human and/or machine agents agree on common and explicit business related concepts (the shared conceptualizations among hardware/software agents, customers, and service providers) are known as explicit ontologies; and these help to exchange data and derived knowledge out of the data to achieve collaborative goals of business operations.

Rule-Based Reasoning: In conventional rule-based reasoning, both common sense knowledge and domain specific domain expertise are represented in the forms of plausible rules (e.g. **IF** <*precondition*(s)> **THEN** <*conclusion*(s)>). For example, an instance of a particular rule: IF {(*Sam has a driving license*) AND (*Sam is drunk*) AND (*Sam is driving a logistic distribution track*) AND (*Sam is stopped by police*)} THEN {(*Sam's driving license will be revoked by the transport authority*)}. Moreover, rule-based reasoning requires an exact match on the precondition(s) to predict the conclusion(s). This is very restrictive, as real-world situations are often fuzzy and do not match exactly with rule preconditions. Thus, there are some extensions to the basic approach that can accommodate partial degrees of matching in rule preconditions.

Semantic Web Service: The advantages of integrating and coordinating supply chain business partners' information service applications, which are loosely distributed among participants with a wide range of hardware and software capabilities, are immensely important issue from operation of global supply chain. Web service is an information technology-based solution for system interoperability; and in this technology business services are described in a standard web service description language (WSDL). Establishing the compatibility of services is an important prerequisite to service provision in web service operation. Web service has embraced the concepts of enriching distributed information systems with machine-understandable semantic metadata (known as ontology); and these new breed of web services are known as semantic web service. In this way, semantic web service provides a common framework for web-based services, which allows data to be shared and reuse across application, enterprise, and extended community boundaries.

Supply Chain Coordination: A supply chain consists of a network of key business processes and facilities, involving end users and suppliers that provide products, services and information. In this chain management, improving the efficiency of the overall chain is an important factor; and it needs at least four important strategic issues to be considered: supply chain network design, capacity planning, risk assessment and management, and performances monitoring and measurement. Moreover, the details break down of these issues need to consider in the level of individual business processes and sub-processes; and the combined performance of this chain. The coordination these huge business processes and their performances are of immense importance.

Chapter 7
Security Issues of Blockchain-Based Information System to Manage Supply Chain in a Global Crisis

Kamalendu Pal
https://orcid.org/0000-0001-7158-6481
City, University of London, UK

ABSTRACT

Global supply chain crisis management has become increasingly crucial for tackling unusual incidents (e.g., natural disaster, terrorism, pandemic). While crisis management has focused on a few organizations involved in supply chain operations (manufacturers, governments, carriers, and the consuming public), it has primarily received a functional focus. Due to their decentralized network structure, supply chains are prone to suffer from disruptive events solved by supply chain crisis management. This chapter presents the blockchain technologies' possibilities and limits used in an integrated IoT-based information system architecture. The chapter describes how the scalability limits of blockchain technology affect the proposed architecture performance that uses it. Also, the chapter presents a review of the academic literature, pointing out how some solutions use a centralization process to improve response time and security of the blockchain-based architecture. Finally, the chapter provides security threat models, which consider by blockchain protocols in IoT networks.

DOI: 10.4018/978-1-7998-6874-3.ch007

INTRODUCTION

In recent decades, many academics and practitioners have conducted empirical and conceptual research studies on various business crisis (Lagadec, 1990) (Lagadec, 1993) (Shrivastava, 1993). However, as with many new research areas, these studies lack adequate integration (Shrivastava, 1993). The interdisciplinary nature of organizational crisis has explicitly resulted in this lack of integration (Shrivastava, 1993). Mainly, organizational crisis inherently are phenomena for which psychological, social-political, and technological-structural issues act as motivational sources in their creation and management (Pauchant & Douville, 1994). Because the study of organizational crisis involves many disciplines, researchers believe that crisis must be researched and studied using a systems approach (Pauchant & Mitroff, 1992). Also, academics and practitioners believe that psychological, socio-political, and technological issues should be explicitly considered and used when studying and managing organizational crisis.

Some researchers, in their studies, wholeheartedly pursue a multidisciplinary research approach (Shrivastava, Mitroff, Miller & Miglani, 1988). However, some other researcher uses causal reasoning, and management techniques to understand organizational crisis (Shrivastava, 1993). This chapter assumes that this lack of integration has kept research on organizational crisis at the management theory periphery. To take a requireded step toward a multidisciplinary approach to the study of organizational crisis (Lagadec, 1993) (Shrivastava, 1993), the chapter illustrates an alternative view on organizational crisis by handling the situation with a scenario planning activity. This scenario planning is not a prediction about what will happen, but it represents hypotheses about what could happen and the effect on the manufacturing (e.g., apparel, automobile) business world.

This chapter serves as a beginning point to help businesses and policymakers think through the potential implications for manufacturing industry operations management and success in the marketplace. The disruption had always existed in the manufacturing supply chain network operations even before the term supply chain management (SCM) became part of today's business (Pal, 2017). Disruptions have changed their abilities and types over centuries from supply chain disruptions due to ecosystem changes, business model transformation, and security attacks in emerging information and communication technologies (ICT).

Global manufacturing supply networks' fragility is increasing due to disruption risks that directly or indirectly endanger the industry's stability and security. As an example, the spread of coronavirus globally has affected the movement of people and materials worldwide. The resulting manufacturing business network disruptions have led to delivery delays and shortages of products and essential items. Simultaneously, demands for objects utilized for pandemic control have increased dramatically, and the forecasting of demand patterns for many consumer goods has become more challenging (Taghipour, 2020) (Radhouri et al., 2018) (Cliché et al., 2020).

In addition, the apparel manufacturing industry inclines to worldwide business operations due to the economic advantage of the globalisation of product design and development. In this way, a typical apparel manufacturing network consists of organisations' sequence, facilities, functions, and activities to produce and develop an ultimate product or related services. This activity starts with raw materials purchase from selective suppliers and products produced at one or more production facilities (Pal, 2019). Next, these products are moved to intermediate collection points (e.g., warehouse, distribution centres) to store temporarily to move to the next stage of the manufacturing network and finally deliver the products to intermediate storages or retailers or customers (Pal, 2017).

The connecting path from supplier to the customer can include several intermediaries, such as warehouse, wholesalers, and retailers, depending on the ultimate products and markets. Global apparel manufacturing networks are becoming increasingly complicated due to a growing need for inter-organizational and intra-organizational connectedness, which enabled by advances in modern technologies and tightly coupled business processes. The essential strategic asset in apparel business operational information has been a critical strategic asset. Also, apparel business networks use information systems to monitor manufacturing network activities (Pal, 2020).

The new digital technologies (e.g., Internet of Things (IoT), Blockchain Technology, Service-Oriented Computing, Big Data Analytics) have attracted attention from academics and practitioners as a growing area of research (Okorie et al., 2017). This research focuses on how data derived from various manufacturing sources can produce a better product life cycle management. In this life cycle management initiative, researchers are looking for ways to increasing the manufacturing products utilization and environmental compliance of the manufacturing of the product.

A group of researchers (Pagorpoulos et al., 2017) advocated three primary information and communication technology (ICT) application areas in manufacturing: (i) integration of heterogeneous data along with the global operations, (ii) data collection, and (iii) analysis of collected data. Within heterogeneous data integration, service-oriented computing (SOC) plays a dominating role, given that intelligent perception and collection from the various computer networks of physical manufacturing resources and abilities. Also, SOC provides reliable security solutions and technologies under the wider internet environment. At the same time, new technologies have emerged. They have wide use in different manufacturing applications, such as the IoT. The data collected by Radio Frequency Identification (RFID) tags and sensors for their underlying assets can help find the circular attributes (e.g., location, condition, availability) that form the essential ingredient for the modern apparel manufacturing economy. Therefore, IoT-enabled manufacturing assets can improve their real-time data gathering abilities to act as a vital enabler for modern manufacturing.

Standard IoT systems are built on a centralised computing environment, which requires all devices to be connected and authenticated through the central server. This framework would not be able to provide the needs to outspread the IoT system in globalised operation. Therefore, moving the IoT system into the decentralised path may be the right decision. One of the popular decentralisation platforms is blockchain technology.

In simple, a blockchain technology is based on a distributed database management system which keeps recods of all business-related exchange information (i.e., transactions) that have been executed and shared among participating parties in the network. This distributed database system is known as a distributed ledger technology (DLT). Individual business exchange information is stored in the distributed ledger and must be verified by the consent of the majority of the participating-members of this network. All business realted transactions that have ever made are contained in the block. Bitcoin, the decentralised peer-to-peer (P2P) digital currency, is the most popular example that uses blockchain technology (Nakamoto, 2008).

The convergence of IoT with blockchain technology will have many advantages. The blockchain's decentralisation model will have the ability to handle processing a vast number of transactions between IoT devices, significantly reducing the cost associated with installing and maintaining large, centralised data centres and distributing computation and storage needs across the devices that form IoT networks. Besides, working with blockchain technology will eliminate the single point of failure associated with the centralised IoT architecture. In addition, convergence of blockchain with IoT will allow the P2P messaging, file distribution and autonomous coordination between IoT devices with no centralised computing model.

This chapter presents an overview of integrating blockchain with the IoT system; this involves examining the advantages resulting from the integration process and the implementation challenges encountered. The ultimate goal of this work is to provide a framework, and its description of the benefits and challenges that result from combining blockchain with IoT to decide whether to go with the decentralisation for the IoT.

Below, this chapter introduces first the basic idea of blockchain technology. Next, the chapter presents the use of blockchain technology in the manufacturing industry. This section also analyses the issues (e.g., traceability, security, flexibility, and smart contracts) related to the blockchain-based manufacturing system. The chapter presents related research work in the manufacturing industry in recent years. Then the uses of blockchain-based technology in the manufacturing industry have been discussed. Next, it discusses the critical issues that need consideration in designing industry-specific reference architecture. It also includes different secure manufacturing problems in business process automation. Finally, the chapter discusses the experimental results and concludes with the scope of future research.

INTERNET OF THINGS AND ITS APPLICATIONS IN APPAREL INDUSTRY

The IoT idea was ðrst created in 1999 by Kevin Ashton (Keertikumar et al., 2015). IoT technology uses in apparel industries for different business process automation purpose. This area of computing has recently focused on enterprise automation, and there is a handful of evidence of the successful use of this technology in supply chain operations. IoT based information system aims to improve organisational communication and collaboration activities. In recent decades, World Wide Web technologies are getting prominence for business use, and the number of Internet-based IoT services are increasing rapidly for supply chain communities. These services, which human users can access using devices. The main form of communication is human-to-human. IoT attempts to not only have humans communicating through the Internet but also have objects or devices. These things are to exchange information by themselves over the Internet, and new forms of Internet communication forms: human-to-things and things-to-things.

The apparel (i.e., textile and clothing) industry is an integral part of the world economy and society (Pal & Ul-Haque, 2020) (Pal, 2020). In recent decades, global apparel manufacturing businesses incline to worldwide activities due to the economic advantage of the globalisation of product design and development (Pal, 2020a). Global apparel supply chains are becoming increasingly heterogeneous and complicated due to a growing need for inter-organisational and intra-organizational connectedness by advances in modern technologies and tightly coupled business processes. Hence, information has been an essential strategic asset in apparel business operational management. The apparel business networks are also using information systems to monitor supply chain activities.

Despite the increasing applicability of IoT applications in supply chains, there are many challenges to using this technology. For example, IoT-related technical issues experienced when operating at the ecosystem level, such as security, authenticity, confidentiality, and privacy of all stakeholders (Tzounis et al., 2017). Academics and practitioners consider that privacy and security issues are mainly related to IoT system applications' vulnerability. Besides, problems such as physical tampering, hacking, and data theft might increase business partners' trust-related issues (Kshetri, 2017). Therefore, IoT applications must be secure against external security, particular protections that only authorised entities can access and change data in the application layer.

Moreover, most IoT devices are limited in power, data processing capability, small sizes, and low inherent design cost. Academics and practitioners are urging to design IoT devices and their protocols to data using IoT data communication network. IoT data reliability can achieve by using distributed information processing methods that execute a verification method between the parties among all its participants to ensure that data remain immutable and untampered. Considering these technical issues and realising today's blockchain technology's essential characteristics now offers several potential solutions to address known disadvantages related to IoT applications in apparel business networks.

Blockchain technology is a distributed network for orchestrating transactions, value, and assets between peers without intermediaries' assistance. Blockchain technology helps record transactions or any digital interaction designed to be secure, transparent, highly resistant to outages, auditable, and efficient. These characteristics provide impetus to blockchain-based IoT architecture for secure data processing in a distributed environment. In order words, IoT-based information systems to improve their IoT networked infrastructure to blockchain complimented technology. It is a distributed ledger managed by a peer-to-peer (P2P) network to provide internode communication and verify new blocks. A convergence of IoT and blockchain technologies can lead to a verifiable, secure, and robust mechanism of storing and managing data processed by smart connected devices. This network of connected devices will interact with their environment and make decisions without any human intervention. However, integrating blockchain technology in IoT-based information systems will enhance the security, data privacy, and reliability of IoT devices, it creates a new set of challenges.

This chapter presents how apparel businesses can leverage IoT applications in combination with blockchain technology to streamline their supply chains business information. When combined, these enabling technologies will help global textile and clothing companies to overcome difficulties related to data collection d integrity, address security challenges, and reduce information asymmetry. This chapter will demonstrate areas of disadvantages towards safety and privacy in blockchain technology. The rest of this chapter organised as follows. Section 2 presents an introduction of IoT and its applications in the apparel industry. It includes IoT applications in apparel supply chain management and IoT applications' drawbacks in the apparel supply chain. Section 3 describes blockchain technology in apparel business management applications. Section 4 explains blockchain applications for the IoT. Section 5 describes the background related to security and privacy for enterprise computing and research challenges. Then Section 6 reviews some of the threat models for blockchain technology. Finally, Section 7 concludes the chapter by discussing relevant research issues.

INTERNET OF THINGS AND ITS APPLICATIONS IN APPAREL INDUSTRY

The IoT idea was ðrst created in 1999 by Kevin Ashton (Keertikumar et al., 2015). IoT technology has used in apparel industries for different business process automation purpose. This area of computing has recently focused on enterprise automation, and there is a handful of evidence of the successful use of this technology in supply chain operations. IoT based information system aims to improve organisational communication and collaboration activities. In recent decades, World Wide Web technologies are getting prominence for business use, and the number of Internet-based IoT services are increasing rapidly for supply chain communities. These services, which human users can access using devices. The main form of communication is human-to-human. IoT attempts to not only have humans communicating through the Internet but also have objects or devices. These things are to exchange information by themselves over the Internet, and new forms of Internet communication would form human-to-things and things-to-things.

Simplistically, the IoT technology characterised by three types of visions:

1. **Things Oriented Vision**: This vision supported by the fact that this technology can track anything using sensors. The advancement and convergence of microelectronic systems technology, wireless communications and digital electronics have resulted in the development of miniature devices having the ability to sense, compute and communicate wirelessly in an effective way. The basic philosophy is uniquely identifying an object using specifications of Electronic Product Code (EPC). It is worth considering that the future of 'Things Oriented Vision' will depend upon sensor technology evolution for accurate sensing (without any error) and its capabilities to fulfil the "thing" oriented other issues.
2. **Internet Oriented Vision**: This vision realises upon the need to make smart objects which are connected.
3. **Semantic Oriented Vision**: This vision is power because the number of sensors used in the apparel industry is vast. The data that these IoT infrastructures collect is massive. Thus, the industry needs to process this data in a meaningful way to form value-added services using semantic technologies (e.g., ontology, knowledge-based reasoning), efficient, secure, scalable, and market-oriented computing.

In this way, the IoT application builds on three pillars, related to the ability of smart objects to (i) be identifiable (anything identifies itself), (ii) to communicate (anything communicates), and (iii) to interact (anything interacts) – either among themselves, building networks of interconnected objects, or with end-users or other entities in the network. Furthermore, cloud computing and fog computing provide computing resources and scalability to connect, store and analyse IoT data (often labelled as big data).

According to Barreto et al. (Barreto et al., 2017), the three distinguishing features of IoT are context, omnipresence and optimisation. The context describes IoT's capability to provide real-time monitoring, to interact, and enable an instant response to speciðc situations that are controlled. Omnipresence lies in the technology's pervasiveness and its broad applicability, while optimisation refers to the speciðc functionalities and characteristics each physical object has (Witkowski et al., 2017).

IoT Applications in Apparel Supply Chain Management

The application of IoT promises significant operational improvements in the manufacturing industry. The advantages result primarily from real-time information exchange, reducing time wastage caused by the bullwhip effect (Wang et al., 2008) (Zhou, 2012). Moreover, IoT can help to revolutionize supply chains by improving operational efficiencies and creating revenue opportunities. Three areas in the manufacturing industry that can benefit from IoT use include (1) inventory management and warehouse operations, (2) production and manufacturing operations, and (3) transportation operations (See Table 1). For example, smart forklifts and racks, and novel usage of *smart glasses* (i.e., wearable devices using sensors and camera technologies to locate objects in the warehouse), monitoring cameras, and other intelligent warehouse management software.

Also, in warehouse operations – reusable assets (e.g., inventory storage totes and pallets) can be attached to IoT-enabled tags or devices that help guide and direct the warehouse pickers to their storage locations. In this way, IoT technologies help automate the warehouses' operational activities, but they reduce human intervention (and error) linked with manual storage management. This advantage results from using industrial-grade RFID-tags and RFID-readers that send a radio signal to identify correctly tag-embedded on pallets, totes, or the product cartons leading to a reduction in the time spent in collecting, recording, and retrieving business operational data.

IoT technologies are common to use in apparel production and manufacturing activities. Apparel manufacturing processes consist of spinning and knitting. Spinning is the conversion of fibers into yarn, while knitting is a process of making fabric by

Table 1. IoT levers in apparel supply chain business

Inventory Management and Warehouse Operations	
Enablers	Processes
• Smart racks • Smart glasses • Monitoring cameras • Smart forklifts • Smart warehouse management system (SWMS)	• Route optimization, elimination of in-process collisions • Fast, cost-efficient, and flexible operations
Production and Manufacturing Operations	
Enablers	Processes
Embedded machine sensors Machine analytics	• Real-time condition monitoring • Predictive maintenance: Detection of physical stress levels, pileups, and prevention of failures • Enhancement of both machine-to-machine and machine-to-human interactions
Transportation Operations	
Enablers	Processes
GPRS sensors RFID tags Routers GPS satellites	• Real-time shipment tracking • Remote sensing (e.g., temperature, humidity, vibrations) • Maximizing fuel efficiency and optimize routing strategies.

intermeshing a series of loops of one or more yarn. It generally contains three major phases, i.e., producing raw materials, processing materials, and making clothes. Therefore, IoT-based technologies can lead to more efficient machine utilization, reduce bottlenecks in production, and optimize production planning and scheduling at varying levels within an apparel business. As a result, this improved insight into key manufacturing processes will enable more vital collaboration and value co-creation with suppliers and improved machine-to-machine and machine-to-human interaction.

Moreover, when it comes to transportation activities in apparel supply chain management, IoT-based technology can also provide potential advantages. For example, a GPS (Global Positioning System) helps to position vehicles (e.g., trucks) from remote distribution centers and optimize routing and delivery time., GPS, RFID technology, and attached sensors increase the in-transit visibility by precisely localizing vehicles on public roads or shipping port using large-scale mapping, data collection from traffic, and analysis of this data. The business processes data collected from these IoT devices will improve the forecasting of delivery times, fleet availability, and routing efficiency (Waller & Fawcett, 2013). Moreover, these devices can enhance the sharing of underutilized resources among vehicles in the parking space or on the road (Barreto et al., 2017).

Drawbacks and Threats of IoT Applications in Apparel Supply Chain

The apparel manufacturing process consists of spinning and knitting. Spinning is the conversion of fibers into yarn, while knitting is a process of making fabric by intermeshing a series of loops of one or more yarn. The use of IoT-based applications in the apparel supply chain has proved to be effective in operational efficiency. IoT technology addresses different apparel manufacturing chain challenges (i.e., the right products, at the right time, in the right place, incorrect quantity, and at the right price). In this way, as IoT systems generate massive volumes of data across the apparel network business environment, this data often resides in silos, often the potential for security and privacy-related risks.

There are different types of IoT security issues that need to be addressed, including IoT device trust, access control, data integrity, physical tampering, and user privacy. An IoT technology deployment survey concluded that 70 percentage of IoT devices are vulnerable due to encryption-related issues, unprotected interfaces, and inappropriate authorization (Lee & Lee, 2015). In highlighting different privacy and security issues, a group of researchers (Cam-Winget et al., 2016) comment on the recent system security solutions are insufficient due to scalability issues in processing and analyzing data generated from vast networks of heterogeneous IoT-based devices and the need to fulfil real-time requirements. Proper security and privacy approaches are considered unusable to IoT-based information system environment due to their dynamic topology and distributed nature. The current Internet architecture with its server-based computing platform might not be able to deal with an enormous number of devices and vast data because individual servers may pose a single point of failure for cyber-attacks and physical damage. For example, IoT devices are at risk from DDoS attacks, data theft, and remote hijacking. Also, Marjani and colleagues (Marjani et al., 2017) argue that some IoT-based applications lack a service level agreement (SLA) to safeguard 'Personally Identiðable Information' (PII) demanded by privacy laws. Therefore, it can have a negative influence on data integrity. Hence, system security may suffer in privacy protection for individuals and enterprises (Suresh et al., 2014).

Moreover, apparel supply chain business-partners may have concerns regarding the physical security and conðdentiality of product information as it moves along the enterprise value chain. Even though IoT-based information system helps supply chain exchange partners validate and verify the authenticity of items in the supply chain. There are still some concerns about IoT devices' vulnerability to counterfeiting, cloning, and fraudulent practices, access authorization, tampering with existing data, and manipulation. For instance, if RFID tags are compromised,, it may be possible to bypass security measures and introduce new vulnerabilities during automatic veriðcation processes (Kumar & Iyengar, 2017). Besides, the manual retrieval and storage of information regarding unique tag identities in a centralized database permits the reproducing or forging of this information at any time (Lin et al., 2017). Hence, it is difficult to identify counterfeit products accompanied by misleading provenance histories (Hua et al., 2018).

In the end, centralized systems may pose a disadvantage for IoT-based system deployments in the apparel manufacturing business for traceability operations. The existence of centralized business organizations may lead to mistrust, which may curb the futuristic enhancement of supply chains (Tse et al., 2017). A centralized approach for data storing and processing can lead to several business risks and operation related issues to the integrity of data, privacy, and security. For example, cloud-computing based IoT systems need to consider data privacy-related issues (Khetri, 2017) (Kamilaris et al., 2019). Moreover, these solutions may create obscurity and enhance information asymmetry between supply chain exchange partners. An additional factor is that centralised information systems act as a black box, and the collaborating business nodes do not know how their data is stored, managed, utilised, and secured (Galvez et al., 2018). Blockchain technology can help to prevent e several of these problems.

BLOCKCHAIN TECHNOLOGY IN APPAREL BUSINESS

Since the innovation of Bitcoin, a digital cryptocurrency, in 2008 (Nakamoto, 2008), blockchain technology has positioned itself as the focal point of interest among a diverse range of researchers and practitioners. Blockchain is a decentralised ledger that stores all transactions that have made on top of a peer-to-peer (P2P) network in a secure, verifiable, and transparent way. The significant advantage of blockchain over the existing technologies is that it enables the two parties to make transactions over the Internet securely without any intermediary party's interference. The omission of the intermediate party can reduce the processing cost while improving the security and efficiency of transactions.

Due to the benefits that blockchain can bring in information processing, this technology expands its applicability to new territories such as supply chain management and logistics management. Today, blockchain also stands as a gatekeeper in the emerging "trust economy", in which the global apparel supply chain operates to serve its suppliers and customers. The efficiency of a global apparel supply chain relies on trust between the different stakeholders. The integration of blockchain and IoT technologies can increase the traceability and reliability of information and the business network. The IoT technology should integrate with enterprise resource planning (ERP) and point of sales (POS) systems of apparel business to share and monitor real-time information at each stage, as shown in Figure 1.

Blockchain technology offers a mechanism to record transactions, or any digital interaction designed to secure, transparent, highly resistant to outages, auditable, and efficient. In other words, blockchain technology has introduced an effective solution to IoT based information systems security. A blockchain enhances IoT devices to send inclusion data in a shared transaction repository with the tamper-resistant record. It improves business partners to access and supply IoT data without central control and management, which creates a digital fusion.

Figure 1. RFID tagging level at different stages in the apparel manufacturing network

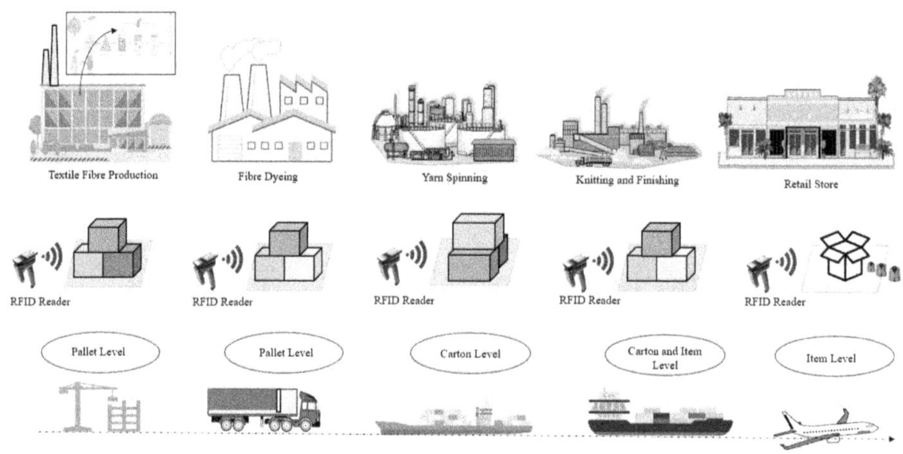

Therefore, blockchain is now a vital technology for different enterprise applications in the apparel business. A *blockchain* is a certain class of data structure used in some distributed manner (known as '*distributed ledger*' - DL) that stores and transmits data in packages called '*blocks*' connected in a digital '*chain*'. The idea of distributed ledger originated from the concept of a '*shared ledger*'. A shared ledger can be a single ledge with *layered permissions* or a distributed ledger, consisting of multiple ledgers supported by a distributed network of nodes (or *business activities*). Distributed Ledger Technology (DLT) refers to an evolving storage method and sharing data across many data stores. It helps data to record, shared, and synchronised across a distributed network of different network participants. Blockchains employ '*cryptographic*' and algorithmic methods to record and synchronise data across a network in an *'immutable manner'*. A simple diagrammatic representation of blockchain is present in Figure 2.

A blockchain is a connected list of blocks in a real-world, and each block keeps the hash function value of a previous block in the chain. The hash function computation uses a cryptographic technique to maintain the integrity of the system. Individual block also digitally signs their contents by using the hash function of their contents inside the block. An important design strategy is to create a Merkle tree (Katz & Lindell, 2007) to store and verify the hashes efficiently. Thus, each block only stores the root of the Merkle tree, as, given the root, it is easy to verify the immutability.

DLs are categorised as *'permissioned'* or *'permissionless'*, depending on whether network participants (nodes) require permission from any entity to make updates to the ledger. The DLs can be classified as *'public'* or *'private'* based on the accessibility of the participating nodes. *'Public Key Cryptography* (PKC)*'* techniques are often used in blockchain technology-based implementation. PKC is an asymmetric encryption scheme that uses two sets of keys: a public key that widely disseminates and a private key known to the owner. PKC can be used to create digital signatures and uses in a wide array of applications, such as *'HyperText Transmission Protocols'* (HTTP) used in the Internet operation, for authentication in critical applications in chip-based payment cards.

Transactions in a blockchain system are identical to their traditional database counterparts. A blockchain transaction could be visualised as a set of reading/ write operations performed on each node of a replicated distributed database in its vanilla form.

Figure 2. Basic blockchain representations

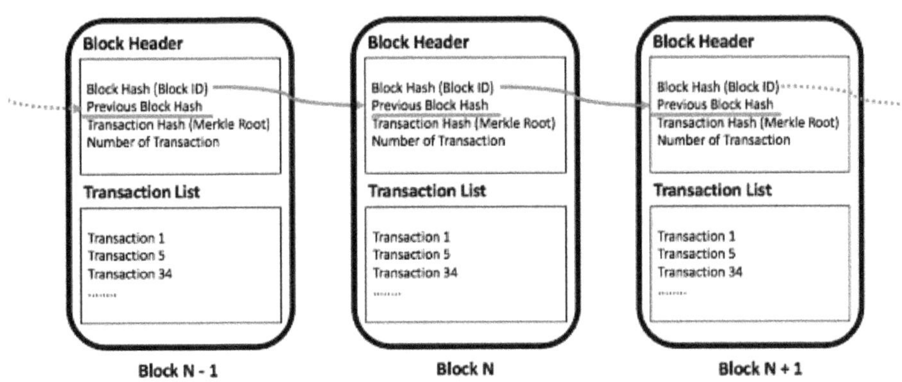

In a blockchain-based infrastructure, every node of the chain maintains a local copy of transaction information. The copy is identical to the original copy and updated in the global information sheet as it distributed within the database with well-built constancy support. Once data entered within the blockchain ledger in this database, no one can change this data in the future. However, this mechanism is known as *tamperproof*, a systematic effort required for building a *reliable* blockchain-based information infrastructure. The main features of these systematic efforts are as follows: (i) Blockchain Protocols for Commitment: The *protocol of commitment* makes sure that valid transaction from apparel business processes are committed and stored in the blockchain information storage with appropriate *validation mechanism* and within a *stipulated time*; (ii) Consensus: Consensus consists of two things: First, it permits blockchain to be updated while making sure that every block in the network is valid as well as keeping participants incentivised and second, it safeguards any single entity from controlling or crashing the whole blockchain system. The consensus aims to create a distributed network without central authorities with participants who do not necessarily need to trust each other. The consensus is an essential part of blockchain technology. Each node runs a programmed mechanism called a consensus. The consensus is how nodes agree on how to update the blockchain because of a set of transactions. Achieving consensus ensures that most network nodes have validated the same set of transactions; (iii) Security: Safety is an essential aspect of the blockchain-based transaction processes. All the data within the blockchain ecosystem needs to be secured and tamperproof. Ensures that there are no malicious nodes within the blockchain-based enterprise ecosystem. (iv) Privacy and Authenticity: Privacy in blockchain enables the client/user to perform transactions without leaking its identification information in the network; and (v) Smart Contracts: In 1994, Nick Szabo (Szabo, 1994) presented the basic concept of a smart contract.

In recent years, blockchain technology ushered a massive range of industrial applications, and many similar information exchange schemes have developed for different industrial business process automation purposes.

BLOCKCHAIN APPLICATIONS FOR THE IoT

Blockchain technology uses in different application areas in SCM. Some of these applications described in this section.

Applications in Supply Chain

Academics and practitioners identified industrial business processes, mainly supply chain and logistics management, essential for deploying IoT based information system applications (Atkore et al., 2018) (Gubbi et al., 2013). IoT-based industrial information systems can enhance enterprise competitiveness through more effective tracking of raw materials' flow, leading to improved business processes' effectiveness and efficiencies (Shroud et al., 2014). In the context of globalised business practice, with multiple collaborating-partners based supply chains, IoT-based applications enhance the sharing of more accurate and timely information relevant to production, quality control, distribution, and logistics (Chen et al., 2014). However, researchers expressed their concern regarding standalone IoT-based applications and global supply chain management (Pal, 2020). The main concerns raised on the issues of standalone IoT systems security and privacy.

The research community has proposed different hybrid information system architectures (e.g., IoT with blockchain, cloud based IoT and blockchain technology). A blockchain enhances IoT-based applications tamper-resistant characteristics. In recent years, different blockchain-based information management systems have reported by researchers. For example, IBM has developed a new blockchain-based service designed to track high-value items through complex supply chains in a secure cloud-based application system (Kim, 2016). Another exemplary industrial application is a fine-wine Provence-tracking service, known as the Chai Wine vault, developed by London-based Company Ever ledger (Finextra, 2016) in business-partnership with fine-wine expert Maureen Downey. An innovative anti-counterfeit application, called Block Verify, is designed, and deployed for tracking anti-counterfeit products (Hulse apple, 2015) to create a sustainable business world. A start-up company from Finland (i.e., Kouvola), in partnership with IBM, developed a smart tendering application for supply chain management. The reported application built on an automatic blockchain-based smart contract (Banker, 2016). Another blockchain-based smart contract, called SmartLog, launched by Kouvola in recent years (Ahlman, 2016).

In recent decades, due to globalisation, manufacturing supply chain networks are going through an evolutionary change through their business practices' continued digitisation. These global manufacturing chains evolve into value-creating networks where the value chain becomes an essential competitive advantage source. Simultaneously, developments are in progress to integrate blockchain technology with other technologies solutions (e.g., IoT-based applications, cloud-based solutions, and fog computing-based automation): modern manufacturing supply chains and holistic collaboration mechanisms value-enhancing applications for the global business.

Applications on the Internet of Things Devices Management

In IoT, devices management relates to security solutions for the physical devices, embedded software, and residing data on the devices. Internet of Things (IoT) comprises of "Things" (or IoT devices) that have remote sensing and data collecting capabalities and can exchange data with other connected devices and applications (directly or indirectly). IoT devices can collect data and process the data either locally or send them to centralize servers or cloud-based application back-ends for processing. A recent on-demand model of manufacturing that is leveraging IoT technologies is called Cloud-Based Manufacturing (CBM). It enables ubiquitous, convenient, on-demand network access to a shared pool of configurable manufacturing business processes information collection and use it service provision.

However, attackers seek to exfiltrate IoT devices' data using malicious codes in malware, especially on the open-source Android platform. Gu et al. (Gu et al., 2018) reported a malware identification system in a blockchain-based system named CB-MDEE composed of detecting consortium chain by test members and public chain users. The CB-MDEE system uses a soft-computing-based comparison technique and more than one marking function to minimise the false-positive rate and improve malware variants' identification ability. A research group (Lee et al., 2017) uses a firmware update scheme based on blockchain technology to safeguard the IoT system's embedded devices.

Applications on the Internet of Things Access Management

Access control is a mechanism in computer security that regulates access to information system. The access control systems face many problems, such as third-party, inefficiency, and lack of privacy. These problems can be address by blockchain, the technology that received significant attention in recent years, and many potentials. Jemel and other researchers (Jemel & Serhrouchni, 2017) report a couple of centralised access control systems problems. As there is a third party with access to the data, the risk of privacy leakage exists. Also, a major party is in charge to control the access, so the risk of a single point of failure also exists. This study presents an access control mechanism with a temporal dimension to solve these problems and adapts a blockchain-based solution for verifying access permissions. The attribute-based Encryption method (Sahai & Waters, 2005) also has some problems, such as privacy leakage from the private key generator (PKG) (Hur & Noh, 2011) and a single point of failure as mentioned before. Wang and colleagues (Wang et al.,2018) introduce a framework for data sharing and access control to address this problem by implementing decentralised storage.

Blockchain can be classified either as private (permission) or public (permissionless). Both classes are decentralising and provide a certain level of immunity against faulty or malicious users for blockchain technology. The significant differences between private and public blockchains lie in the consensus protocol's execution, the ledger's maintenance, and the authorisation mechanism to join the distributed network.

Recently, there has been a tremendous investment from the industries and significant interest from academia to solve significant research challenges in blockchain technologies. For example, consensus protocols are the primary building blocks of blockchain-based technologies. Therefore, the threats targeting the consensus protocols become a significant research issue in the blockchain.

BLOCKCHAIN SECURITY AND PRIVACY ISSUES

Blockchain technology offers an approach to storing information, executing transactions, performing functions, and establishing trust is secure computing without centralised authority in a networked environment. Although blockchain has received growing interest in academia and industry in recent years, blockchains' security and privacy continue to be at the centre of the debate when deploying blockchain in different industrial applications.

Key Security Risk Areas of Blockchain

The main areas of security on blockchain technology are (i) Ledger, (ii) Consensus Mechanism, (iii) Networking Infrastructure, (iv) Identity Access Management, and (v) Cryptography. A diagrammatic representation is present in the risk areas in Figure 4.

Ledger: The ledger uses to register all transactions and changes in the status of the data. The ledger distributed by smart design and shared between the blockchain participating nodes. Two challenging problems (or hazards) generally threaten the applicability of the ledger technology in blockchain applications: (a) unauthorised entry into the ledger; and (b) unauthorised (or improper, or illegal) operations on recorded ledger data.

Consensus Mechanism: A consensus mechanism is a protocol (i.e., set of rules) to ensure that all the blockchain network participants comply with the agreed rules for day-to-day operations. It makes sure that the transactions originate from a legitimate source by having every participant consent to the distributed ledger's state. The public blockchain is a decentralised technology, and no centralised authority is in place to regulate the required act. Therefore, the network requires authorisations from the network participants to verify and authenticate any blockchain network activities. The whole process is done based on the consensus of the network participants, and it makes the blockchain a trustless, secure, and reliable technology for digital transactions. Distinct consensus mechanisms follow different principles, which enables the network participants to comply with those rules. Several consensus mechanisms have introduced considering the requirements of secure digital transactions. However, proof of work (PoW), proof of stake (PoS), and delegated proof of stake (DPoS) are the few consensus protocols used by the industries. In this way, the blockchain relies on the distributed consensus mechanism to establish mutual trust. However, the consensus mechanism itself has a vulnerability, which attackers can exploit to control the entire blockchain. Although a few approaches, e.g., (Muhammad et al., 2018), are highlighted in blockchain-related research to deter and prevent attacks. Due to the inherent characteristics of openness, the PoW-based permissionless blockchain networks may not be completely secure.

Network Infrastructure: The network infrastructure requirements for both blockchain and Distributed Ledger Technology (DLT). The network infrastructure threats can detect in nodes being stopped by a malicious attacker using good anticipatory mechanisms. In August 2016, nearly 120,000 Bitcoin (over US $60mn at the time) were stolen from Bitfinex (Nagaraj & Maguire, 2017). Based in Hong Kong, Bitfinex is one of the world's largest digital and cryptocurrency exchanges. The incident exploited security vulnerabilities within individual organisations. The blockchain network itself remained fully functional and operated as envisioned. The incident may have prevented a detailed end-to-end review of security, using scenarios, meaning there would have been a higher chance of identifying risks upfront and mitigating them at that point.

Identity Access Management: Privacy in blockchain enables the client/user to perform transactions without leaking its identification information in the network. Also, blockchain technology uses numerous techniques to achieve the highest level of privacy and authenticity for transactions. As information comes from different users within the blockchain industrial ecosystem, the infrastructure needs to ensure every user privacy and authenticity. Blockchain-based information system often employs a combination of public and private key to encrypt and decrypt data securely.

Cryptography: The records on a blockchain are secured through cryptography. Network participants have their private keys assigned to the transactions they make and act as a personal digital signature. If a record is altered, the signature will become invalid, and the peer network will know right away that something has happened. However, there could be software bugs and glitches in cryptography coding. These could include anything from developers' coding mistakes, inappropriate design, and an underlying defect in the cryptography routines. Also, trained coders can make a mistake in putting together well-known and tested cryptographic tools to not secure. Hackers can take advantages of this weakness.

Figure 3. Various Security Risk Areas of Blockchain

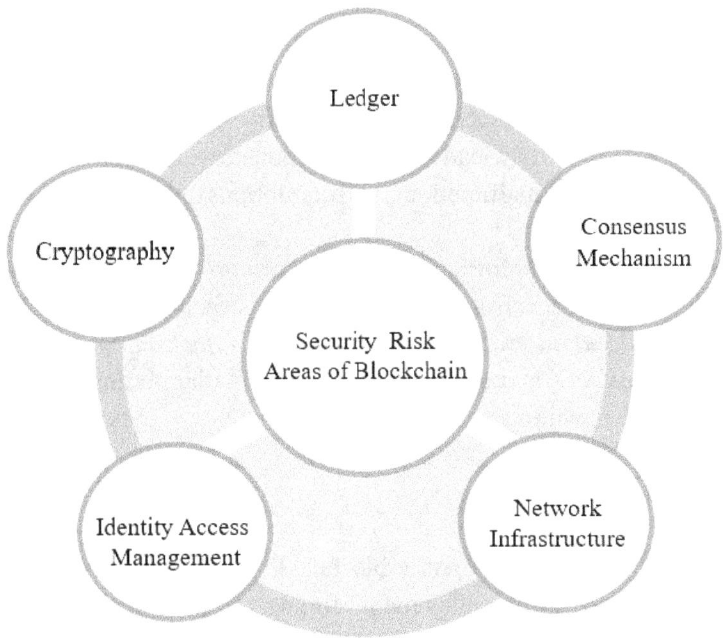

Safety is an essential aspect of blockchain-based transaction processes. All the data within the blockchain ecosystem needs to be secured and tamperproof. The security ensures that there are no malicious nodes within the blockchain-based enterprise ecosystem. As mentioned earlier, the data inserted into a public ledger or inside the blockchain is distributed to individual users, and everyone maintains their local copy of the blockchain. In that local copy, that individual cannot tamper but upgrade the data and retransmit the network's data. However, for the transaction to be validated, the other nodes should be convinced that the broadcasted information is not malicious, and the system security is ensured.

THREAT MODELS FOR BLOCKCHAIN

This section explains the threat models that are considered by the blockchain protocols in IoT networks. Threat agents are mostly malicious users whose intention is to steal assets, break functionalities, or disrupt services. However, threat agents might also be inadvertent entities, such as developers of smart contacts who unintentionally create bugs and designers of blockchain applications who make mistakes in the design or ignore some issues.

Threats facilitate various attacks on assets. Threats arise from vulnerabilities at the network, smart contracts, consensus protocol deviations or violations of consensus protocol assumptions, or application-specific vulnerabilities. Countermeasures protect owners from threats. They involve various security and safety solutions and tools, incentives, reputation techniques, best practices, and so on. Threats and their agents cause risks. They may lead to a loss of monetary assets, a loss of privacy, a loss of reputation, service malfunctions, and disruptions of services and applications (i.e., availability issues).

The blockchain-based information systems owners wish to minimise the risk caused by threats that arise from threat agents. This section presents five types of attacks: *identity-based attacks*, *manipulation-based attacks*, *cryptanalytic attacks*, *reputation-based attacks*, and *service-based attacks*. A diagrammatic representation of these attacks is shown in Figure 5.

Identity-Based Attacks

The emergence of DLT based upon a blockchain data structure has given rise to new approaches to identity management, aiming to upend dominant approaches to providing and consuming digital identities. These new approaches to identity management (IdM) propose to enhance decentralisation, transparency and user control in transactions that involve identity information. In identity-based attacks, the attacker forges identity to masquerade as an authorised user to access the system and manipulate it. Again, identity-based attacks can be broadly classified into four different types, and they are (i) Key attack, (ii) Replay attack, (iii)Impersonation attack, and Sybil attack.

Key attack: In blockchain technology, certificates and identities are validated and protected in Hyperledger Fabric by asymmetric cryptography. How each participant chooses to store and protect their private key is up to them. A wide range of wallets and management methods available as Hyperledger Fabric requires no cohesive management scheme. An outside attacker obtaining private key(s) could lead to any number of attacks. To deal with this attack, LNSC (Lightning Network and Smart Contract) protocol (Huang et al., 2018) provides an authentication mechanism between the electric vehicles and charging piles. It uses elliptic curve encryption to calculate the hash functions, ensuring resiliency against the critical leakage attack.

Replay attack: This attack aims to spoof two parties' identities, intercept their data packets, and relay them to their destinations without modiðcation. To resist this attack, LNSC (Huang et al., 2018) uses the idea of elliptic curve encryption to calculate the hash functions. On the other hand, BSein (blockchain-based system for secure mutual authentication) (Lin et al., 2018) uses a fresh one-time public/private key pair.

Impersonation attack: An attacker tries to masquerade as a legitimate user to perform unauthorised operations. As presented in Table II, three methods are proposed to protect against this attack. The elliptic curve encryption idea to calculate the hash functions is proposed by LNSC protocol (Huang et al., 2018). Wang et al. (Wang et al., 2018) propose a distributed incentive-based cooperation mechanism, which protects the user's privacy and a transaction veriðcation method. On the other hand,

BSein (Lin et al., 2018) uses the concept of attribute-based signatures (i.e., legitimate devices can produce a valid signature, and hence any impersonation attempt will be detected when its corresponding authentication operation fails.

Sybil attack: A sybil attack is when an attacker creates multiple accounts on a blockchain to deceive the other blockchain participants. A successful Sybil attack increases the reputation of some agents or lowers the reputation of others by initiating interactions in the network. These attacks should not be an issue on a permissioned blockchain since the members are clearly identified and wallets are not normally used. TrustChain (i.e., capable of creating trusted transactions among strangers without central control) (Otte et al., 2017) addresses this issue by creating an immutable chain.

Whitewashing: When an agent has a negative reputation, it can eliminate its identity and make a new one. There is no remedie to prevent this behaviour. However, it is suggested in (Otte et a., 2017) to give lower priorities to new identities agents when applying the allocation policy.

Service-based attacks: The attacker try either to make the service unavailable or make it behave differently from its speciðcations. Under this category, we can ðnd the following attacks:

DDoS/DoS attack: A distributed denial-of-service (DDOS) attack is a prevalent type of network attack against a website, a communication network node, or even a membership service provider. The objective of this attack is to slow down or crash the system. The concentrated attack and subsequent shut down of the system result in a "denial of service" for legitimate users. Denial of Service (DoS) and DDoS are common security problems. DoS attacks on the connectivity of consensus nodes may result in a loss of consensus power, thus preventing consensus nodes from being rewarded. It involves sending a huge number of requests to cause the failure of the blockchain system. CoinParty (Ziegeldorf et al., 2018) proposes the idea of decentralised mixing service. Liu et al. (Liu et al., 2018) employ a ring-based signature with the Elliptic Curve Digital Signature Algorithm (ECDSA). The resilience against DoS in BSeIn (Lin et al., 2018) is achieved by limiting the block size, and using the '*multi-receivers*' encryption technique to provide conðdentiality for authorised users.

Figure 4. Classification of threat models for blockchain

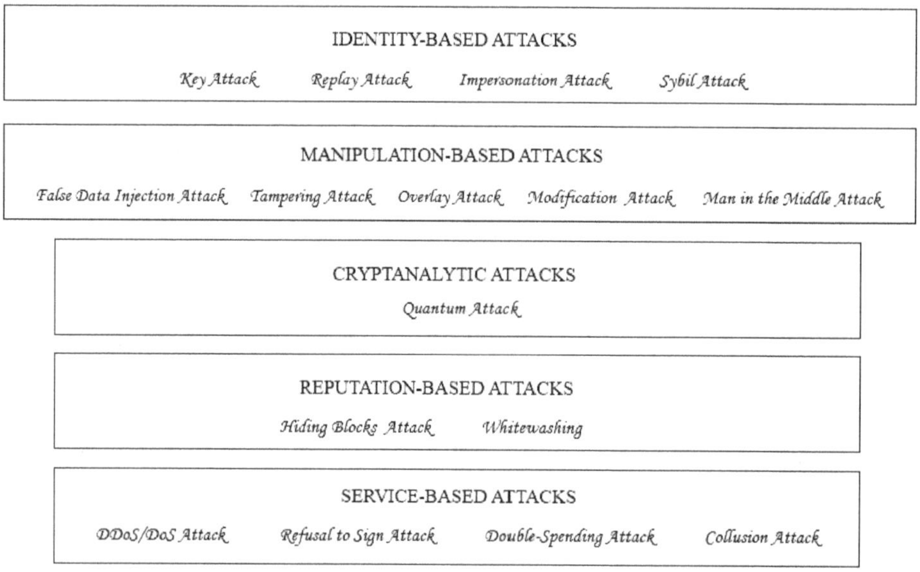

Manipulation-Based Attacks

Manipulation-based attacks can occur when the attacker is near the information system's device or data communication network. General types of physical layer attacks are as follows:

Tampering: Physical damage to device (e.g., RFID tag, Tag reader), or communication network (Andrea et al., 2015).

Malicious Code Injection: The attacker physically introduces a malicious code onto an IoT system by compromising its operation. The attacker can control the IoT system and launch attacks (Ahemd et al., 2017).

Radio Frequency Signal Interference (Jamming): The predator sends a particular type of radiofrequency signal to hinder communication in the IoT system, and it creates a denial of service (DoS) from the information system (Ahemd et al., 2017).

Fake Node Injection: The intruder creates an artificial node and the IoT-based system network and access the information from the network illegally or control data flow (Ahemd et al., 2017).

Sleep Denial Attack: The aim of the attacker is to keeps the battery-powered devices awake by sending them with inappropriate inputs, and this causes exhaustion of battery power that leads to shutting down of nodes (Ahemd et al., 2017).

Side Channel Attack: In this attack, the intruder gets hold of the encryption keys by applying malicious techniques on the devices of the IoT-based information system (Andrea et al., 2015), and by using these keys, the attacker can encrypt or decrypt confidential information from the IoT network.

Permanent Denial of Service (PDoS): In this attack, the attacker permanently damages the IoT system using hardware sabotage. The attack can be launched by damaging firmware or uploading an inappropriate BIOS using malware (Foundry, 2017).

Refusal to Sign attack: An attacker can decide not to sign a transaction that is not in his favour. Although preventing this attack is not possible, punishment measures can be taken against the refusal agents. It is proposed in (Otte Et al., 2017) to not interact with the malicious agent or split the transactions into smaller amounts. If an agent refuses to sign a transaction, the interaction is aborted.

Double-spending attack: It means that the attackers spend the same bitcoin twice to acquire extra amounts. In (Wang et al., 2017), the Timestamp and the Proof-of-Work mechanism is used. In (Aitzhan & Svetinovic, 2016), a multi-signature transaction is employed, where a minimum number of keys must sign a transaction before spending tokens.

Collusion Attack: Nodes can collide with each other and behave selðshly to maximise their proðt. In (He et al., 2018), an incentive mechanism and pricing strategy are proposed to thwart selðsh behaviours.

CONCLUSION

Today's manufacturing operation faces significant volatility, uncertainty and complexity imposed by a dynamic business environment. Changes in customer buying pattern, the demand for a low price, higher service levels, mobile commerce, and so on – necessitate customer intelligence and varying fulfilment models. These have introduced significant stress on manufacturing supply chain networks, compelling, relevant businesses to revisit their supply chain design practice. It includes the deployment of appropriate information systems that enhance supply chain execution. In such scenarios, enterprise information systems architecture plays a significant role.

The IoT-based system is a smart, more comprehensive network of interconnected objects, which through unique address schemes (e.g., EPC-based address), can cooperate and interact with their neighbours to collect data, process data, and convert it to daily business-related decisions. The data obtained from the IoT applications along manufacturing business processes can make operational decision-making much more comfortable. However, standalone IoT application systems face different security problems ranging from attacks on IoT devices to attacks on transit data that have drawn interest from academics and practitioners. The tight integration of the digital world with the physical world using automated information systems has further created IoT systems' vulnerabilities.

IoT device data often stored in the service-oriented computing storage in the cloud, but they are not protected against compromised integrity devices or tampering at the source. In contrast, the blockchain is an evolving technology that can help with IoT systems resiliency. However, the extensive use of IoT technologies and blockchain-based linked data results in new security, privacy, and policy-related problems; at the same time, they can also be part of the solution. For example, more accurate models for figuring out security issues can be built using the data's contextual semantic interpretation. Besides, the purposeful interpretation of personal data exchanged among business partners could be used to improve the ability of IoT based manufacturing network users to control over interactions, and hence better manage their online privacy. The machine-processable and machine-readable representation of data-related policies can also provide different benefits to manufacturers by automation of tasks related to policy-management.

REFERENCES

Ahemd, M. M., Shah, M. A., & Wahid, A. (2017). Iot security: a layered approach for attacks and defenses. *2017 International Conference on Communication Technologies (ComTech),* 104–110.

Ahlman, R. (2016). *Finish city partners with IBM to validate blockchain application in logistics.* https://cointelegraph.com/news/finish-city-partners-with-ibm-to-validate-blockchain-application-in-logistics

Aitzhan, N. Z. & Svetinovic, D. (2016). Security and Privacy in Decentralized Energy Trading through Multi-signatures, Blockchain and Anonymous Messaging Streams. *IEEE Transaction on Dependable and Secure Computing*, 1–1.

Andrea, I., Chrysostomou, C., & Hadjichristofi, G. (2015). Internet of things: security vulnerabilities and challenges. *2015 IEEE Symposium on Computers and Communication (ISCC),* 180–187.

Atzori, L., Iera, A., & Morabito, G. (2018). The Internet of Things: A survey. *Computer Networks*, *54*(15), 2787–2805. doi:10.1016/j.comnet.2010.05.010

Banker, S. (2016). *Will blockchain technology revolutionise supply chain applications?* https://logisticsviewpoints.com/2016/06/20/will-block-chain-technology-revolutionize-supply -chain-applications/

Barreto, L., Amaral, A., & Pereira, T. (2017). Industry 4.0 implications in logistics: An overview. *Procedia Manufacturing*, *2017*(13), 1245–1252. doi:10.1016/j.promfg.2017.09.045

Cam-Winget, N., Sadeghi, A.-R., & Jin, Y. (2016). INVITED: Can IoT be Secured: Emerging Challenges in Connecting the Unconnected. *Proceedings of the 53rd Annual Design Automation Conference (DAC '16).* 10.1145/2897937.2905004

Chen, R., Guo, J., & Bao, F. (2014). Trust management for service composition in SOA-based IoT systems. *Proceedings of the 2014 IEEE Wireless Communications and Networking Conference (WCNC)*, 3444–3449. 10.1109/WCNC.2014.6953138

Cliche, Taghipour, & Canel. (2020). An Improved Forecasting Approach to Reduce Inventory-Levels in Decentralized Supply Chains. *European Journal of Operational Research*, *287*(2), 511–527.

Cui, Y. (2018). Supply Chain Innovation with IoT. In Multi-Criteria Methods and Techniques Applied to Supply Chain Management. Intech Open. doi:10.5772/intechopen.74155

Deloitte. (2017). *Digital Procurement: New Capabilities from Disruptive Technologies*. Deloitte Development LLC.

Dorri, A., Kanhere, S. S., Jurdak, R., & Gauravaram, P. (2017). Blockchain for IoT security and privacy: The case study of a smart home. *Proceedings of the 2017 IEEE International Conference on Pervasive Computing and Communications Workshops (PerCom Workshops)*.

Finextra. (2016). *Everledger secures the first bottle of wine on the blockchain*. https://www.finextra.com/pressaritcle/67381/everledger-secures-the-first-bottle-of-wine-on-the-blockchain

Foundry, D. (2017). *What Is a Permanent Dos (Pdos) Attack?* https://www.datafoundry. com/blog/what-is-permanent-dos-pdos-attack/t

Galvez, J. F., Mejuto, J. C., & Gandara, J. S. (2018). Future challenges on the use of blockchain for food traceability analysis. *Trends in Analytical Chemistry*, *107*, 222–232. doi:10.1016/j.trac.2018.08.011

Garg, S., Gentry, C., Halevi, S., Sahai, A., & Waters, W. (2013). *Attribute-Based Encryption for Circuits from Multilinear Maps*. Academic Press. doi:10.1007/978-3-642-40084-1_27

Gu, J., Sum, B., Du, X., Wang, J., Zhuang, Y., & Wang, Z. (2018). Consortium Blockchain-Based Malware Detection in Mobile Devices. *IEEE Access: Practical Innovations, Open Solutions*, *6*, 12118–12128. doi:10.1109/ACCESS.2018.2805783

Gubbi, J., Buyya, R., Marusic, S., & Palaniswami, M. (2013). Internet of Things (IoT): A vision, architectural elements, and future directions. *Future Generation Computer Systems*, *29*(7), 1645–1660. doi:10.1016/j.future.2013.01.010

He, Y., Li, H., Cheng, X., Liu, Y., Yang, C., & Sun, L. (2018). A Blockchain based Truthful Incentive Mechanism for Distributed P2P Applications. *IEEE Access: Practical Innovations, Open Solutions*, *6*, 1–1. doi:10.1109/ACCESS.2018.2821705

Hua, J., Wang, X., Kang, M., Wang, H., & Wang, F. (2018). Blockchain based Provenance for Agricultural Products: A Distributed Platform with Duplicated and Shared Bookkeeping. *Proceedings of the IEEE Intelligent Vehicles Symposium (IV)*. 10.1109/IVS.2018.8500647

Huang, X., Xu, C., Wang, P., & Liu, H. (2018). LNSC: A security model for electric vehicle and charging pile management based on blockchain ecosystem. *IEEE Access: Practical Innovations, Open Solutions*, *6*, 13565–13574. doi:10.1109/ACCESS.2018.2812176

Hulse Apple, C. (2015). *Block Verify uses blockchains to end counterfeiting and making world more honest.* https://cointelegraph.com/news/block-verify-uses-blockchains-to-end-counterfeiting-and-make-world-more-honest

Hur, J., & Noh, D. K. (2011). Attribute-based access control with efficient revocation in data outsourcing systems. *IEEE Transactions on Parallel and Distributed Systems*, *22*(7), 1214–1221. doi:10.1109/TPDS.2010.203

Jemel, M., & Serhrouchni, A. (2017). Decentralised access control mechanism with temporal dimension based on blockchain. *2017 IEEE 14th International Conference on e-Business Engineering (ICEBE),* 177–182.

Kamilaris, A., Fonts, A., & Prenafeta-Boldv, F. X. (2019). The rise of blockchain technology in agriculture and food supply chain. *Trends in Food Science & Technology*, *91*, 640–652. doi:10.1016/j.tifs.2019.07.034

Katz, J., & Lindell, Y. (2007). *Digital Signature Schemes. In Introduction to Modern Cryptography*. Chapman & Hall/ CBC Press. doi:10.1201/9781420010756

Keertikumar, M., Shubham, M., & Banakar, R. M. (2015). Evolution of IoT in smart vehicles: An overview. *Proceedings of the International Conference on Green Computing and Internet of Things (ICGCIoT)*, 804–809. 10.1109/ICGCIoT.2015.7380573

Kim, N. (2016). IBM pushes blockchain into the supply chain. *Wall Street Journal.*

Kshetri, N. (2017). Can Blockchain Strengthen the Internet of Things? *IEEE IT Professional*, *19*(4), 68–72. doi:10.1109/MITP.2017.3051335

Kumanduri, R., & Romero, C. (1998). *Number Theory with Computer Applications*. Prentice Hall.

Kumar, M. V., & Iyengar, N. C. S. N. (2017). A Framework for blockchain technology in rice supply chain management. *Advanced Science and Technology Letters*, *146*, 125–130. doi:10.14257/astl.2017.146.22

Lagadec, P. (1990). Communication strategies in crisis situations. *Industrial Crisis Quarterly*, *1*, 19–26.

Lagadec, P. (1993). *Preventing chaos in a crisis*. McGraw-Hill.

Lee, B., & Lee, J. H. (2017). Blockchain-based secure firmware update for embedded devices in an Internet of Things environment. *The Journal of Supercomputing*, *73*(3), 1152–1167. doi:10.100711227-016-1870-0

Lee, I., & Lee, K. (2015). The Internet of Things (IoT): Applications, investments, and challenges for enterprises. *Business Horizons*, *58*(4), 431–440. doi:10.1016/j.bushor.2015.03.008

Liang, G., Weller, S. R., Luo, F., Zhao, J., & Dong, Z. Y. (2018). Distributed Blockchain-Based Data Protection Framework for Modern Power Systems against Cyber Attacks. *IEEE Transactions on Smart Grid*, 1–1.

Lin, C., He, D., Huang, X., Choo, K. K. R., & Vasilakos, A. V. (2018). Bsein: A blockchain-based secure mutual authentication with ðne-grained access control system for industry 4.0. *Journal of Network and Computer Applications*, *116*, 42–52. doi:10.1016/j.jnca.2018.05.005

Lin, I. C., Shin, H., Liu, J. C., & Jie, Y. X. (2017). Food traceability system using blockchain. *Proceedings of the 79th IASTEM International Conference*.

Liu, Y., Liu, X., Tang, C., Wang, J., & Zhang, L. (2018). Unlinkable Coin Mixing Scheme for Transaction Privacy Enhancement of Bitcoin. *IEEE Access: Practical Innovations, Open Solutions*, *6*, 23261–23270. doi:10.1109/ACCESS.2018.2827163

Mahjabin, T., Xiao, Y., Sun, G., & Jiang, W. (2017). A survey of distributed denial-of-service attack, prevention, and mitigation techniques. *International Journal of Distributed Sensor Networks*, *13*(12), 155014771774146. doi:10.1177/1550147717741463

Muhammad, S., Aziz, M., Charles, K., Kevin, H., & Laurent, N. (2018). Countering double spending in next-generation blockchains. IEEE ICC 2018.

Nagaraj, K., & Maguire, E. (2017). *Securing the Chain*. KPMG International. https://assets.kpmg.com/content/dam/kpmg/xx/pdf/2017/05/securing-the-chain.pdf

Okorie, O., Turner, C., Charnley, F., Moreno, M., & Tiwari, A. (2017). A review of data driven approaches for circular economy in manufacturing. *Proceedings of the 18th European Roundtable for Sustainable Consumption and Production.*

Otte, P., de Vos, M., & Pouwelse, J. (2017, Sept.). TrustChain: A Sybil-resistant scalable blockchain. *Future Generation Computer Systems*.

Paillisse, J., Subira, J., Lopez, L., Rodriguez-Natal, A., Ermagan, V., Maino, F., & Cabellos, A. (2019). *Distributed Access Control with Blockchain*. Academic Press.

Pal, K. & Ul-Haque, A. (2020). Internet of Things and Blockchain Technology in Apparel Manufacturing Supply Chain Data Management. *Proceeding of 11th International Conference on Ambient Systems, Networks and Technologies (ANT-2020)*.

Pal, K. (2017). Supply Chain Coordination Based on Web Services. In H. K. Chan, N. Subramanian, & M. D. Abdulrahman (Eds.), *Supply Chain Management in the Big Data Era* (pp. 137–171). IGI Global Publication. doi:10.4018/978-1-5225-0956-1.ch009

Pal, K. (2017). *A Semantic Web Service Architecture for Supply Chain Management*. The 8th International Conference on Ambient Systems, Networks and Technologies, Portugal.

Pal, K. (2019). Algorithmic Solutions for RFID Tag Anti-Collision Problem in Supply Chain Management. *Procedia Computer Science*, 929-934.

Pal, K. (2020). Information sharing for manufacturing supply chain management based on blockchain technology. In *Cross-Industry Use of Blockchain Technology and Opportunities for the Future*. IGI Global.

Pal, K. (2020a). Ontology-Assisted Enterprise Information Systems Integration in Manufacturing Supply Chain. In Handbook of Research on Developments and Trends in Industrial and Material Engineering. IGI Global.

Pal, K. (2020b). Information Sharing for Manufacturing Supply Chain Management Based on Blockchain Technology. In Cross-industry Use of Blockchain Technology and Opportunities for the Future. IGI Global.

Pal, K., & Yasar, A. (2020). Internet of Things and blockchain technology in apparel manufacturing supply chain data management. *Procedia Computer Science*, *170*, 450–457.

Pauchant, T., & Mitroff, I. (1992). *Transforming the crisis-prone organization*. Jossey-Bass.

Pauchant, T. C., & Douville, R. (1994). Recent research in crisis management: A study of 24 authors' publications from 1986 to 1991. *Industrial and Environmental Crisis Quarterly*, *7*, 43–61.

Radhoui, Taghipour, & Canel. (2018). *The distribution and pickup of goods- a literature review and survey in Hierarchical Planning and Information Sharing Techniques in Supply Chain Management.* IGI Global.

Rejeb, A. (2018). Blockchain Potential in Tilapia Supply Chain in Ghana. *Acta Tech. Jaurinensis*, *11*(2), 104–118. doi:10.14513/actatechjaur.v11.n2.462

Sahai, A., & Waters, B. (2005). Fuzzy identity-based encryption. In *Annual International Conference on the Theory and Applications of Cryptographic Techniques*. Springer.

Sharma, P. K., Singh, S., Jeong, Y. S., & Park, J. H. (2017). DistBlockNet: A Distributed Blockchains-Based Secure SDN Architecture for IoT Networks. *IEEE Communication Management*, *55*(9), 78–85. doi:10.1109/MCOM.2017.1700041

Shrivastava, P. (1993). Crisis theory/practice: Towards a sustainable future. *Industrial and Environmental Crisis Quarterly*, *7*, 23–42.

Shrivastava, P., Mitroff, I., Miller, D., & Miglani, A. (1988). Understanding industrial crises. *Journal of Management Studies*, *25*, 285–303.

Shrouf, F., Ordieres, J., & Miragliotta, G. (2014). Smart factories in Industry 4.0: A review of the concept and of energy management approached in production based on the Internet of Things paradigm. *Proceedings of the IEEE International Conference on Industrial Engineering and Engineering Management*, 679–701. 10.1109/IEEM.2014.7058728

Szabo, N. (1994). *Smart Contracts*. Available online: https://archive.is/zQ1p8

Taghipour. (2020). *Demand Forecasting and Order Planning in Supply Chains and Humanitarian Logistics*. IGI Global.

Tse, D., Zhang, B., Yang, Y., Cheng, C., & My, H. (2017). Blockchain application in food supply information security. *Proceedings of the IEEE International Conference on Industrial Engineering and Engineering Management (IEEM 2017)*, 1357–1361. 10.1109/IEEM.2017.8290114

Tzounis, A., Katsoulas, N., Bartzanas, T., & Kittas, C. (2017). Internet of things in agriculture, recent advances, and future challenges. *Biosystems Engineering*, *164*, 31–48. doi:10.1016/j.biosystemseng.2017.09.007

Waller, M. A., & Fawcett, S. E. (2013). Data science, predictive analytics, and big data: A revolution that will transform supply chain design and management. *Journal of Business Logistics*, *34*(2), 77–84. doi:10.1111/jbl.12010

Wang, Q., Qin, B., Hu, J., & Xiao, F. (2017, Sept.). Preserving transaction privacy in bitcoin. *Future Generation Computer Systems*.

Wang, S., Zhang, Y., & Zhang, Y. (2018). A blockchain-based framework for data sharing with fine-grained access control in decentralised storage systems. *IEEE Access: Practical Innovations, Open Solutions*, *6*, 38437–38450. doi:10.1109/ACCESS.2018.2851611

Wang, S. J., Liu, S. F., & Wang, W. L. (2008). The simulated impact of RFID-enabled supply chain on pull-based inventory replenishment in TFT-LCD industry. *International Journal of Production Economics*, *112*(2), 570–586. doi:10.1016/j.ijpe.2007.05.002

Washington, L. C. (2008). *Elliptic Curves: Number Theory and Cryptography* (2nd ed.). Chapman & Hall/CRC. doi:10.1201/9781420071474

Witkowski, K. (2017). Internet of Things, Big Data, Industry 4.0 - Innovative Solutions in Logistics and Supply Chains Management. *Procedia Engineering*, *2017*(182), 763–769. doi:10.1016/j.proeng.2017.03.197

Yan-e, D. (2011). Design of intelligent agriculture management information system based on IoT. *Proceedings of the 2011 Fourth International Conference on Intelligent Computation Technology and Automation*, 1, 1045–1049. 10.1109/ICICTA.2011.262

Yin, W., Wen, Q., Li, W., Zhang, H., & Jin, Z. (2018). An Anti-Quantum Transaction Authentication Approach in Blockchain. *IEEE Access: Practical Innovations, Open Solutions*, *6*, 5393–5401. doi:10.1109/ACCESS.2017.2788411

Zhou, Z. (2012). Applying RFID to reduce bullwhip effect in a FMCG supply chain. *Proceedings of the Advances in Computational Environment Science*.

Ziegeldorf, J. H., Matzutt, R., Henze, M., Grossmann, F., & Wehrle, K. (2018). Secure and anonymous decentralized Bitcoin mixing. *Future Generation Computer Systems*, *80*, 448–466. doi:10.1016/j.future.2016.05.018

Chapter 8
The Perspectives of Supply Chain Management Using Natural Knowledge From 3D Blockchain Technologies and Avatar-Based and Geographic Information Systems (GIS)

Vardan Mkrttchian
HHH University, Australia

Dmitry Davydov
Penza State University, Russia

Viacheslav Voronin
https://orcid.org/0000-0001-8114-6383
Moscow State Technological University "Stankin", Russia

ABSTRACT

The blockchain restores control and ownership of information back to its rightful owner, thus eliminating dependencies on central authorities and third parties. These material chains are immensely complex; they can be subject to the laws and regulations of more than 200 countries and territories, and they are heavily influenced by many different factors ranging from freight consolidation to the timing of hundreds of concurrent shipments. This chapter is about algorithmic modeling of supply chain management using natural knowledge from a 3D-hybrid blockchain as a dragon chain.

DOI: 10.4018/978-1-7998-6874-3.ch008

INTRODUCTION

The Production supply chain consists of many participants like Producer, Consumer (people who buy the product and consume them), Wholesalers and Retailers. This system consists of many levels of mediator parties as well which have different policies of commission. Due to the difference in these policies, the Producers do not get their fair share of price. Due to the varying prices, consumers also suffer as they do not get the right quality of product for the right price (Tliche, Taghipour, & Canel, 2020). There are no central records maintained regarding the transactions between the participants which could lead to many serious problems. To tackle the above-mentioned issues, we need a holistic approach which can provide solutions to most of the above issues. Here, Blockchain based solution can be used to achieve: Traceability (we can trace the whereabouts of the product, origin of the product, etc.), Transparency (so that a sense of trust is achieved), Fairness (by removing the intermediaries), Assurance of products safety and pricing (so that nobody has to bear the loss). Digital Signature is a cryptographic approach to provide authenticity and integrity of the data. Here data can be anything software, images, videos, etc. (Radhoui, Taghipour, & Canel, 2018). With the above-mentioned services, it also provides one more important service, non-repudiation which was previously unknown to us. Non-repudiation in layman's terms means that if I send a document to person X, then after some time I cannot deny sending the document.

The Digital Signature is divided into three main parts, Key Generation Algorithm, Signing Algorithm and Signature Verification Algorithm. The basic functionality of Digital Signature as mentioned above is providing authenticity, integrity, and non-repudiation. We will understand the process of Digital Signature through the following steps (Mahfod, Khoury, Depitre, & Taghipour, 2020):

1. Firstly, we compute the hash of the data to be signed. The used hash function is mentioned in the information of Digital Signature as it will be used by the receiver as well.
2. Then we encrypt this hash using our private key which is also called the Signature Key. The encrypted hash along with other information is the digital signature of that data. This is appended with the data and is sent.
3. The receiver receives the data along with its digital signature. The data itself is encrypted but let's not get into that for now.
4. Receiver decrypts the received Digital Signature using the public key of the sender and gets the hash of the data.
5. Then using the algorithm mentioned in the information, the receiver computes the hash of the data sent. If this hash matches the one obtained from decryption, then we can guarantee that the data is not changed.

BACKGROUND

As we saw all the background details required to understand the blockchain technology, we will now see the various types of blockchain that exist which have been classified according to their uses and their properties. Two main types of blockchain are Permissioned Blockchain and Permission-less Blockchain as a 3D Blockchain (Mkrttchian et al., 2019, 2020).

Permissioned 3D Blockchain

Also known as Private 3D Blockchain, this act as a closed ecosystem where access is restricted to a group of people only. The transactions made by these people are not visible to the outside world. Typically, these types of blockchain are used within an organization where it thinks that the data is too sensitive to be public. To verify the transactions made in these types of blockchain you are required to have the permission of a central authority controlling that blockchain. Thus, because of the presence of a central entity, these blockchain are more centralized in nature.

Ripple can be thought of a perfect example of a permissioned blockchain. Also, hyper ledger and Corday are private 3D Blockchain.

There are certain advantages of using a private blockchain, which are as follows,

1. This 3D Blockchain have more scalability as compared to the public 3D Blockchain.
2. Due to the presence of central authority, various levels or steps of governance can be implemented according to the rules of that particular organization.
3. Clearly, because of a smaller number of participants, the speed of the overall blockchain network is high and thus more efficient performance.

Permission Less 3D Blockchain

Also known as public 3D Blockchain are the open source variant of 3D Blockchain where anyone is allowed to participate as full nodes, light nodes, community members, etc. Here, all the transactions made are fully transparent in nature. Anyone from the outside world can view the transaction. These 3D Blockchain are fully decentralized in nature unlike the private ones and so do not have any central authority controlling them. Now, because of the absence of a central authority, this 3D Blockchain need to have some sort of tokens (currency of that blockchain) to incentivize and reward the participants. Now, certain characteristics of public blockchain are as follows:

1. Currency / Token Requirement: As mentioned earlier, public 3D Blockchain require incentives or rewards as there is no central entity and the verification part is to be done by the participants only. One purpose served by introducing a token is that trust can be built in the blockchain network.
2. Transparency: This property states that the participants can know every detail in the system. Let us take an example of Bitcoin to understand the transparency in it. To access any Bitcoin account, you need to have private keys (related to each of the accounts) with you, without which the access is not possible. So, we can consider this as a default, which needs to be provided to the users in any case. But transparency here enables the users to also get addresses (of accounts) and see all the transactions that have been done till that point of time.
3. Presence of Decentralization: There is no central entity present in this type of blockchain as mentioned earlier. So theoretically to modify any protocol, make any changes to the network, or for any sort of malicious activity, 51% of the users need to agree on it, which is very difficult practically.

Now, as we saw the major characteristics/advantages of the two types of 3D Blockchain (Public and Private), there are also a few disadvantages of both. From the above points we can note that we not only require privacy from the Private or Permissioned one, but also transparency and security from the Public one. So, to combine the above benefits, there exists a Hybrid blockchain. A perfect example of a hybrid blockchain is Dragon chain. This provides the businesses with significant flexibility (Mkrttchian, et al., 2021).

WORKING OF THE SYSTEM

In this section, we will look at the detailed working of the system including all the algorithms. It also gives a basic idea about the process flows happening between different participants in the system (Atour Taghipour, Phuong Hoang and Xue Cao,2020). As mentioned in the diagram, the various participants in the system are producers (producing the goods), wholesaler, end consumer, retailer and the APMCs. Here, APMCs is the government appointed committee which trades in certain products based on the acts issued by the government. Here, transaction is defined by the following entities (Figure 1):

We can divide the process of communication between all these entities into three main parts:

1. Producer - APMC process flow

2. APMC - Wholesaler process flow
3. Seller - Buyer Process Flow

Figure 1. Corrected diagram of linked list of sliding mode(Mkrttchian & Aleshina, 2017)

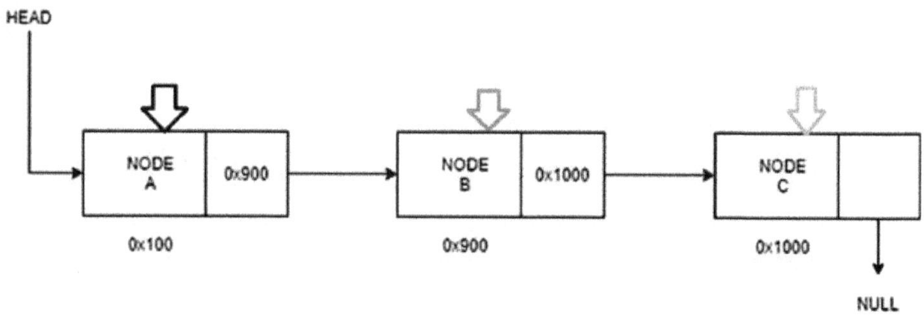

This part depicts the communication between the producer and APMC admin and also with the other entities in the APMC, which include Publisher, Assaying Operator and Entry Operator (Figure 2).

Figure 2. Algorithm 1: sending product details

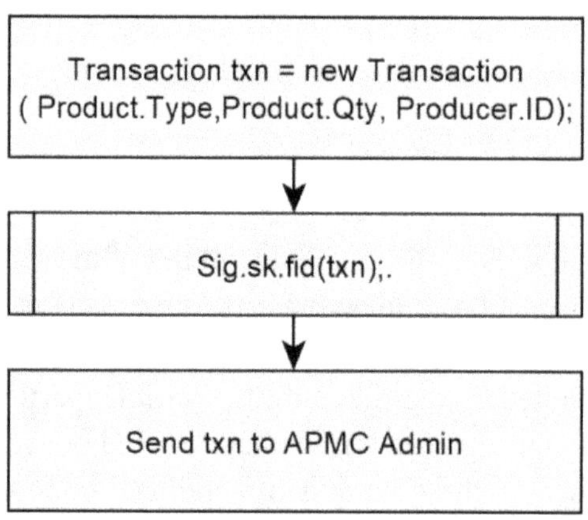

Here, whenever a producer wants his products to be published so that they get purchased, he will need to advertise it first by sending the details to APMC Admin. This is done by the Sending Product Details algorithm. Here, the producer supplies the required information associated with the product like Type of the Product,

Quantity of the product produced, and ID of the producer. This is converted into a transaction and is digitally signed using Producer's ID. We have already seen what Digital Signature is and how it is used. Then this will be sent to the APMC Admin (Figure 3).

Figure 3. Algorithm 2: send for entry

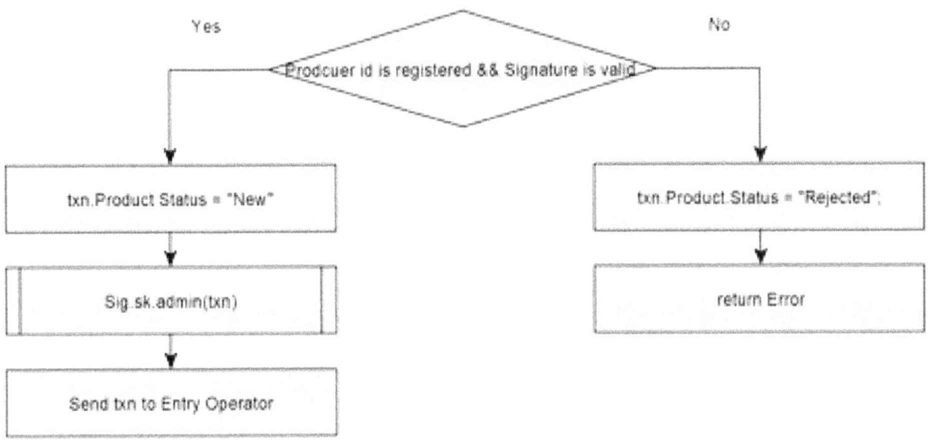

Now, once the producer has sent the details of the product he wishes to sell, it needs to be verified. This is to avoid any fraudulent transactions. So, the APMC Admin executes this algorithm to verify the transaction. APMC Admin checks whether the provided ID is registered, and the signature is valid, if both check out, Admin labels the transaction as New and sends it to the Entry Operator. If either the ID is not registered, or the signature is not valid then the transaction is rejected and error is returned. As a result, the product is not entered, and the transaction is invalid. As mentioned earlier, this is a necessary precaution to curb malicious activities (Figure 4).

Now, once the transaction is sent to the Entry Operator after verification, the Entry Operator would carry out the necessary steps like vehicle entry management (for the producer's actual vehicle), Producer's ID verification. Then Entry Operator will generate a Product ID which will be associated with the product as a unique identifier. Product ID is a hash of product details and producer ID. SHA_{256} is used here. Then the relevant status is associated with the product. If successful, signature of Entry Operator will be marked on the transaction and then the transaction is forwarded to the Assaying Operator (Figure 5).

Figure 4. Algorithm 3: generate entry

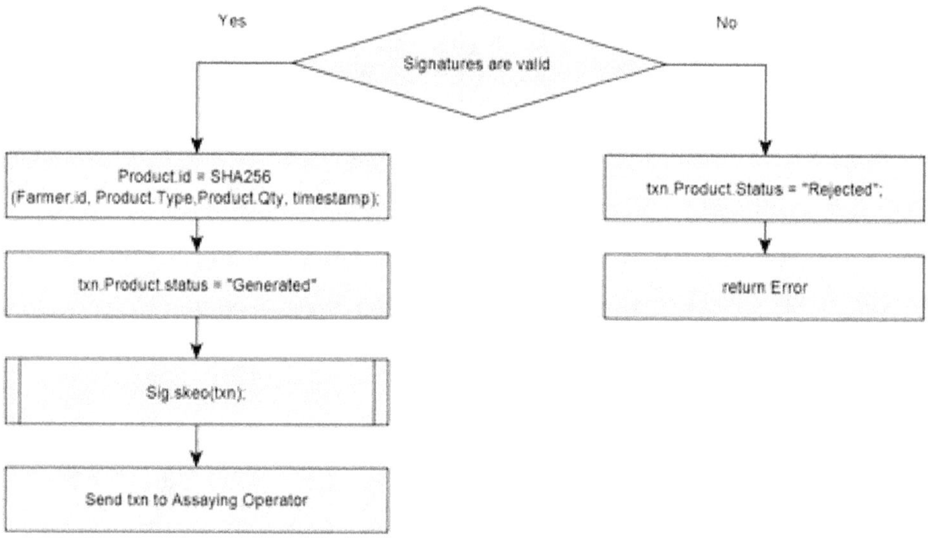

Figure 5. Algorithm 4: assess product

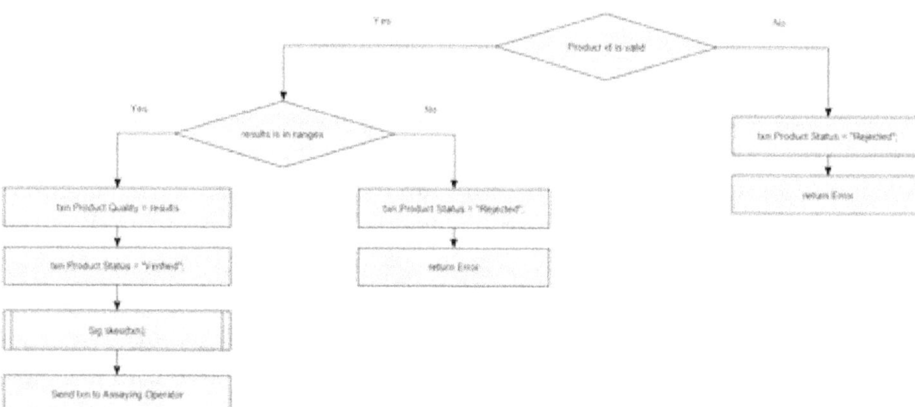

When the Assaying Operator receives the product from the Entry Operator, he needs to check the quality of the product so that the product is compatible with the quality guidelines. To do so, the Assaying Operator will get a sample of the product and perform the required quality tests in the APMC premises itself. The values will be compared with predefined ranges for acceptance. If the value obtained from the sample is within the predefined ranges, then it is accepted and the required parameters like Quality and Status are updated. The status here is updated to "Verified". Then to prove that the Assaying Operator was indeed genuine, his signature is also captured in the transaction. Then this transaction is forwarded to the Sales Operator (Figure 6).

Figure 6. Algorithm 5: sales approval

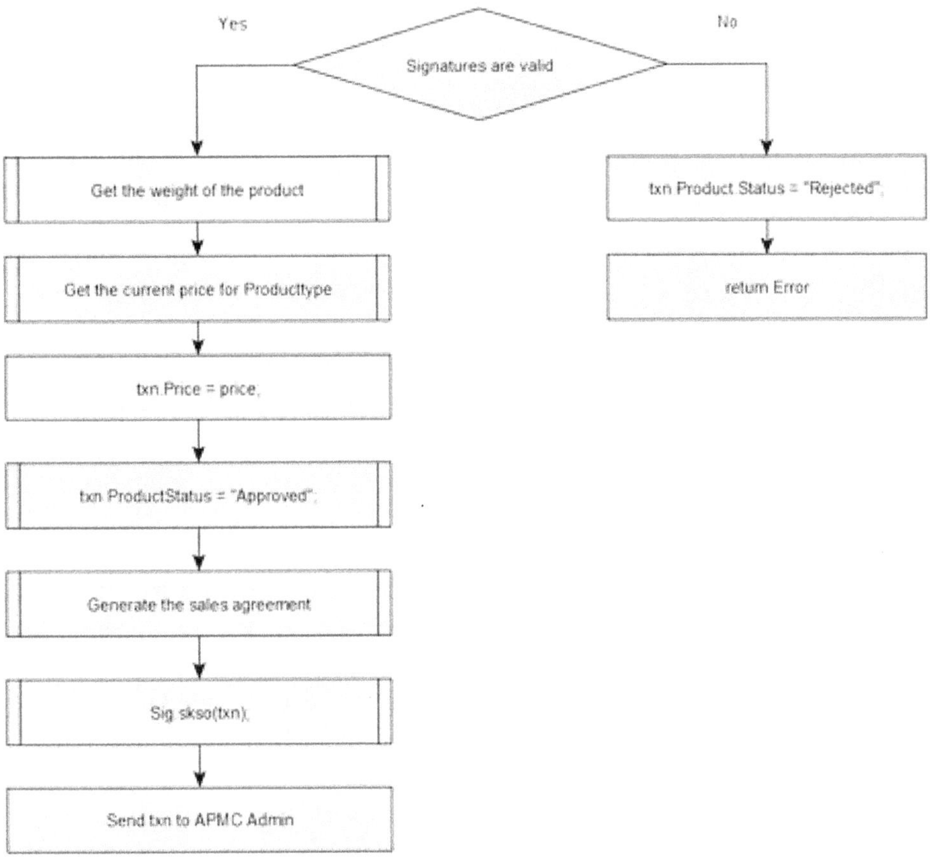

Once the Sales Operator receives the transaction from the Assaying Operator, the Sales Operator would calculate the weight of the product and acquire the price details of the product. This information would be updated into the transaction. Then the status of the product would be updated as "Approved". After updating the status, an agreement would be generated between buyer and the seller of the product. Once again to verify the identity of the operator, his signature is captured into the transaction. Then this transaction is sent to APMC Admin for approval. If the rest of the signatures from the previous processes are not valid, then this transaction is "Rejected" (Figure 7).

Figure 7. Algorithm 6: publish transaction

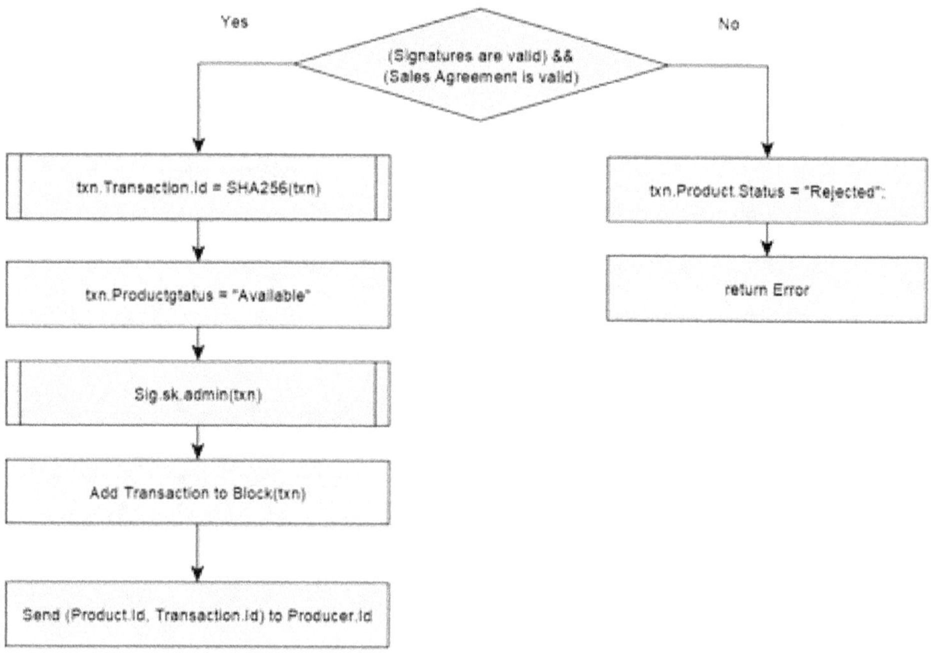

After completion of all the above steps, the APMC receives the transaction with all the required details including Sales Agreement. APMC Admin verifies the signatures of all the entities. It also verifies the Sales Agreement made in the last algorithm. If all the details check out, APMC Admin updates the product transaction to "Available" and signs the transaction. Then this is added to the block which will be eventually added to the blockchain. Then the transaction status is sent to the producer.

Now coming to the APMC - Wholesaler process flow.

This subsection of algorithms gives an idea about the basic process flow which takes place from APMC to the wholesaler who wants to buy the product. In order to do so, the details can be obtained from the blockchain. Then a buy request is generated. The step by step explanation of this process will be given as algorithms implemented to do their respective functions. The name of the algorithm will be intuitive enough to just like the ones mentioned in the previous subsection of the algorithms (Figure 8).

Now as introduced, to buy the product, the wholesaler needs to fetch the data from the blockchain. To do so, the wholesaler gives the input as product $_{ID}$ and it creates a new transaction. Then the product is searched in the blockchain and details of it are sent to the APMC admin. As usually done, the transaction is signed with the Buyer's signature (Figure 9).

Figure 8. Algorithm 7: buy request

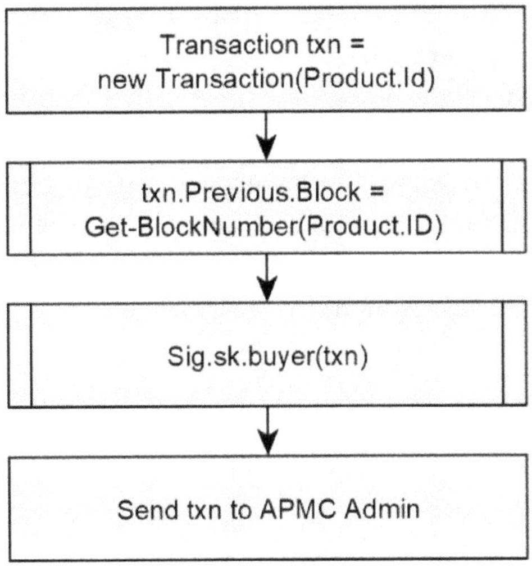

Figure 9. Algorithm 8: sales operator approve

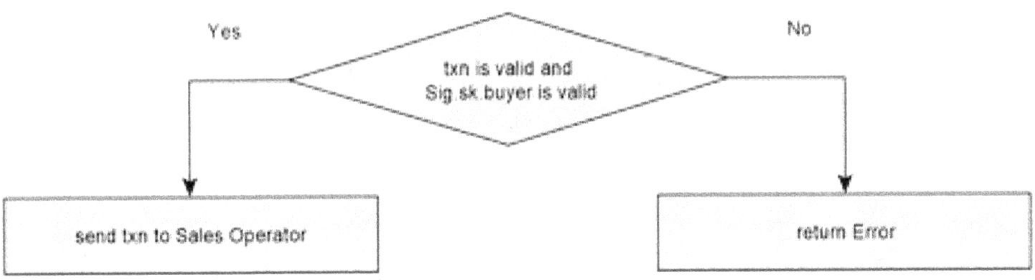

Figure 10. Algorithm 9: sales operator verification

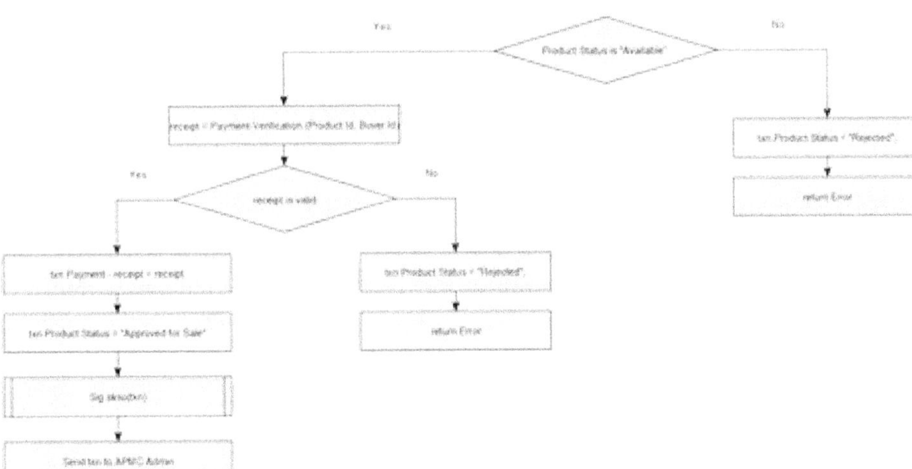

Now, APMC admin will receive the newly created transaction from the previous algorithm and will verify the signature of Buyer (wholesaler) and sends it further to the Sales Operator (Figure 10).

The main aim of this algorithm is to verify whether the payment done is genuine and valid or not. To verify, the Sales Operator will call the payment module and get the receipt of the payment. Now if the payment is verified, the operator would update the same in the transaction. Operator also changes the status of the transaction to "Approved for Sale". Now operator signature is included like the previous algorithms, and then it is sent to APMC Admin (Figure 11).

Figure 11. Algorithm 10: payment verification

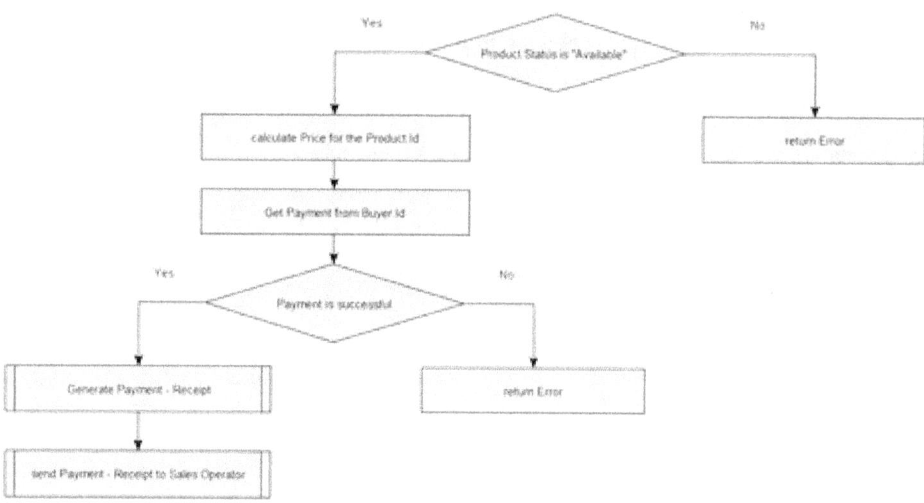

This is the payment verification module that we talked about in the previous algorithm. The input to this algorithm will be the Product and the Buyer. This module will first check the availability of the product and get the current price for the product from the market. Then that amount will be debited from the buyer's account and a receipt will be generated. This receipt will be sent to APMC Admin which will be used by it for the verification (Figure 12).

Now after the "Sales Operator Verification" algorithm, it sends the signed transaction to APMC Admin. Admin would verify all the signatures included in the transactions and change the transaction status to "SOLD-TO-WHOLESALER (ID)". The transaction will be signed by the APMC Admin and then added to the blockchain. The transaction details will be sent to the buyer. As covered in the last subsections of algorithms, the product now is available with the wholesaler. Here, the wholesaler is the one who has direct contact with the producer of the product. After that, the wholesaler can supply it to anybody right from retailers to industries using it as a raw material. To do so, the buyer needs to get the product details from the blockchain. Both the participants of the transaction have A Mutual Agreement signed between them. This Mutual Agreement will be available in the transaction itself. The next subsection of algorithms will depict how these processes are carried out.

Figure 12. Algorithm 11: publish transaction

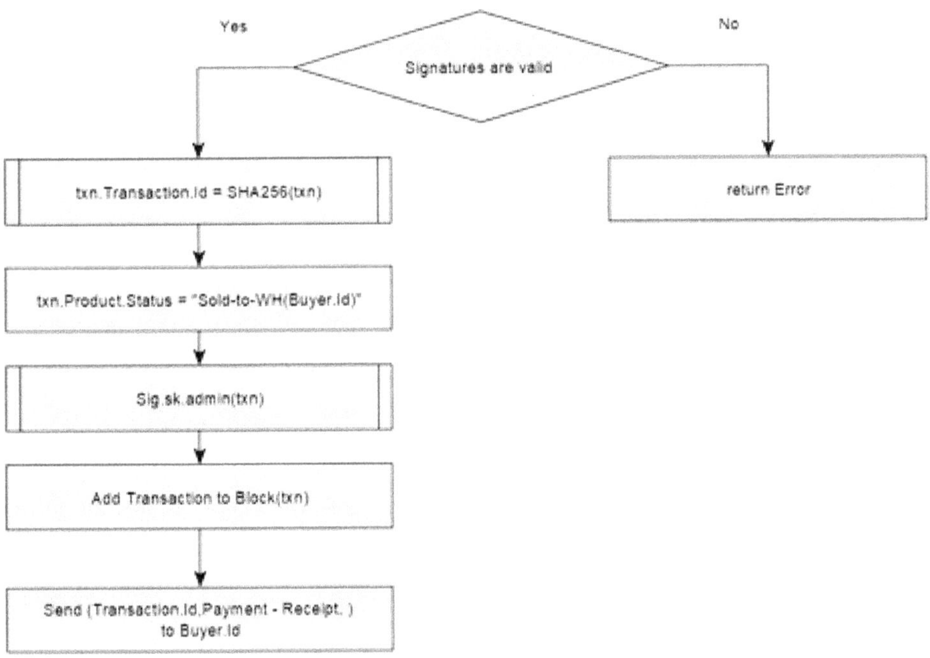

Figure 13. Algorithm 12: buyer buy request

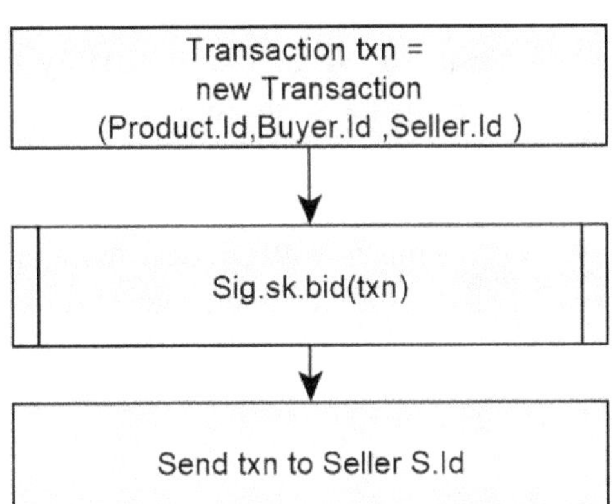

As mentioned above, to buy the product, the buyer would fetch the details of the product from the blockchain. So, the input to this algorithm will be Product. Now as mentioned in the algorithm, a new transaction will be created which will have the details of the product, buyer and seller. This transaction will also include the signature of the buyer. This transaction is further sent to the Seller (Figure 14).

Figure 14. Algorithm 13: seller response

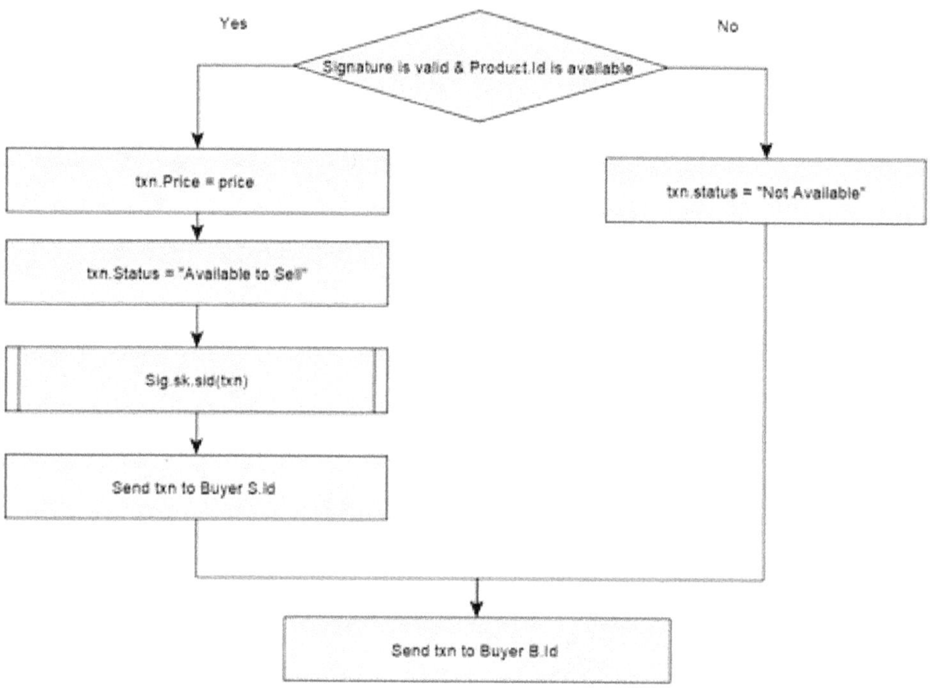

When the seller receives the request forwarded in the last transaction, it updates the price of the product based on the current price in the market. It will subsequently also update the status of the product to "Available to Sell (Buyer ID)". The transaction will also include the signature of the Seller and will be sent back to the Buyer (Figure 15).

After the Buyer receives the details related to the product from the Seller, the details are verified by the Buyer. If they match with the ones mentioned in the transaction, then the transaction is forwarded to the wholesaler network for approval (Figure 16).

Figure 15. Algorithm 14: buyer approval

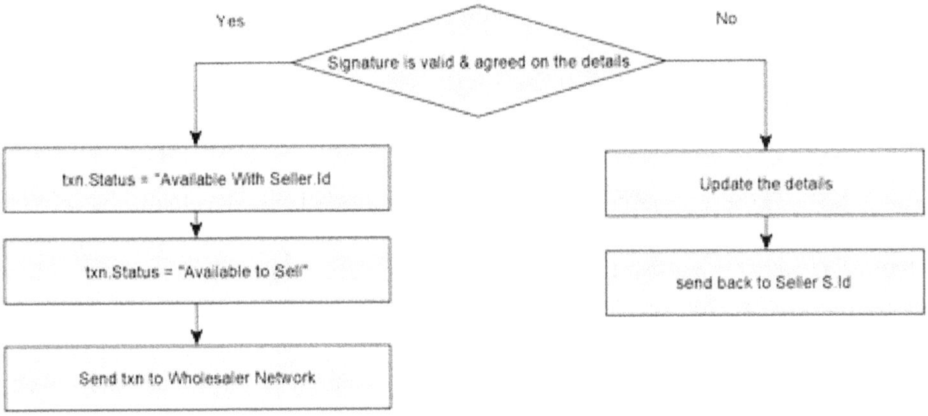

Figure 16. Algorithm 15: wholesaler approval

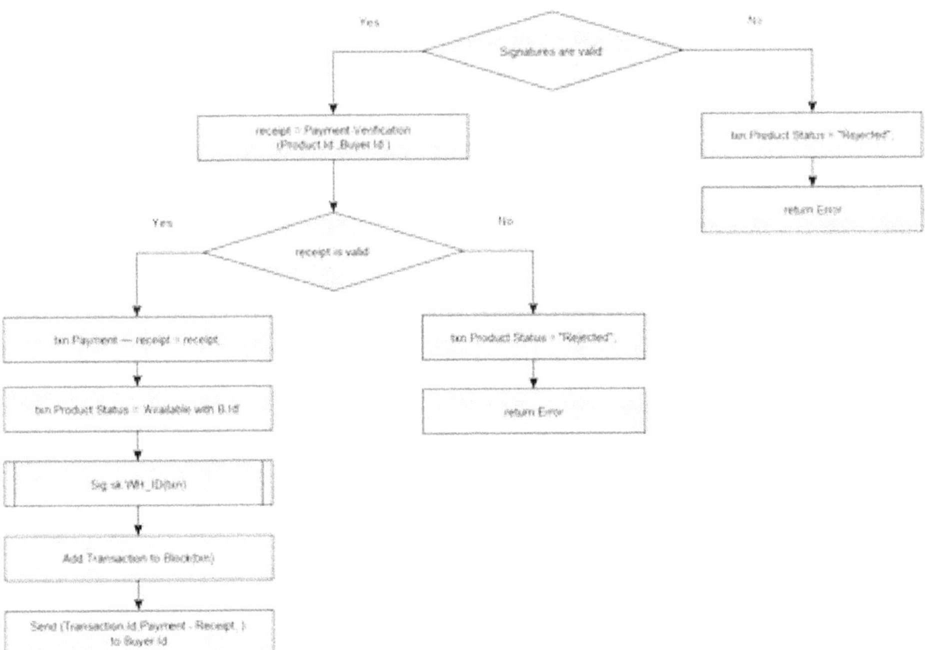

This is the last part of the process before the product is owned by the Buyer. The wholesaler will verify all the signatures on the transaction and will check for the payment by the Buyer. After the payment is confirmed, the ownership of the product will be changed to the Buyer. Also, the amount transferred by the Buyer will be credited into the Seller's account.

CONCLUSION

So, in this chapter we saw how the traditional agricultural supply chain suffers and how Blockchain overcomes the problems associated with the existing supply chain. To learn more about the Blockchain technology, we saw a detailed overview of all the basics required to understand how Blockchain technology works. We also saw the three main branches contributing to Blockchain technology. Then we saw different types of 3D Blockchain and which of them is relevant for our system. The next section gives us a basic idea about the operation flow of transactions and participant entities. In this section we saw a detailed overview of all the algorithms present in the system, its participants, and its input outputs. We also saw the detailed components of hyper ledger Fabric and their uses. We tried to conclude the implementation part by giving a step wise description of how the system will work. Smooth and concise interface of each participant can be developed using key exchange in the existing system.

Transparency, Traceability and Fairness are the most prominent challenge in the existing agricultural supply chain. So, this chapter presents process flows and algorithms which help to address the above challenges faced by different participants in the system. These algorithms make use of Blockchain technology which can solve most of the problems related to unfair pricing, lack of transparency in the system, etc. The implementation of algorithms is done here in Hyper ledger Fabric.

REFERENCES

Mahfod, Khoury, Depitre, & Taghipour. (2020). Logistics providers in Syria humanitarian operations. In *Demand Forecasting and Order Planning in Supply Chains and Humanitarian Logistics*. IGI Global.

Mkrttchian, Vertakova, & Symonyan. (2021). Data Integrity Management for Laboratory of the Control of Lifecycle of Domestic Russian Tour Products. In *Book Data Integrity and Quality*. doi:10.5772/intechopen.96071

Mkrttchian, V. (2019a). New Tools for Cyber Security Using Blockchain Technology and Avatar-Based Management Technique. In Machine Learning and Cognitive Science Applications in Cyber Security (pp. 105-122). IGI Global. DOI: doi:10.4018/978-1-5225-8100-0.ch004

Mkrttchian, V. (2019b). Machine Learning With Avatar-Based Management of Sleptsov Net-Processor Platform to Improve Cyber Security. In Machine Learning and Cognitive Science Applications in Cyber Security (pp. 139-153). IGI Global, DOI: doi:10.4018/978-1-5225-8100-0.ch004

Mkrttchian, V. (2020). Human Capital Management in the Context of the Implementation of Digital Intelligent Decision Support Systems and Knowledge Management: Theoretical and Methodological Aspects. In Knowledge Management, Innovation, and Entrepreneurship in a Changing World (pp. 123-148). IGI Global. doi:10.4018/978-1-7998-2355-1.ch006

Mkrttchian, V. (2021a). Avatars-Based Decision Support System Using Blockchain and Knowledge Sharing for Processes Simulation a Natural Intelligence: Implementation of the Multi Chain Open Source Platform. *International Journal of Knowledge Management*, *17*(1), 5. Advance online publication. doi:10.4018/IJKM.2021010105

Mkrttchian, V., & Aleshina, E. (2017). *Sliding Mode in Intellectual Control and Communication: Emerging Research and Opportunities*. IGI Global. doi:10.4018/978-1-5225-2292-8

Mkrttchian, V., & Chernyshenko, S. (2021b). Digital Intelligent Design of Avatar-Based Control with Application to Human Capital Management. *International Journal of Human Capital and Information Technology Professionals*, *12*(1), 2. Advance online publication. doi:10.4018/IJHCITP.2021010102

Radhoui, H., Taghipour, A., & Canel, B. (2018). Vehicle routing problem with delivery and pickup of goods in general transport system: A literature review and survey. *Transport Reviews*.

Taghipour, A., Hoang, P., & Cao, X. (2020). Just in Time/Lean Purchasing Approach: An investigation for research and applications. *Journal of Advanced Management Science*, *8*(2), 2020.

Tliche, Taghipour, & Canel. (2020). Exploring a downstream demand inference strategy in a decentralized two-level supply chain. In *Demand Forecasting and Order Planning in Supply Chains and Humanitarian Logistics*. IGI Global.

ADDITIONAL READING

Alguliyev, R. M., Aliguliyev, R. M., & Sukhostat, L. V. (2020). Efficient algorithm for big data clustering on single machine. *CAAI Trans Intell Technol*, *5*(1), 9–14.

Antonopoulos, A. M. (2014). *Mastering bitcoin: unlocking digital crypto-currencies*. O'Reilly Media Inc.

Ash, J. S., Berg, M., & Coiera, E. (2004). Some unintended consequences of information technology in health care: The nature of patient care information system-related errors. *Journal of the American Medical Informatics Association*, *11*(2), 104–112.

Chang, X., & Han, F. (2016). *Block chain: From digital currency to credit society*. China Citic Press.

Devi, D., Namasudra, S., & Kadry, S. (2020). A boosting-aided adaptive cluster-based undersampling approach for treatment of class imbalance problem. *International Journal of Data Warehousing and Mining*, *16*(3).

Ho, D. C. K., Au, K. F., & Newton, E. (2002). Empirical research on supply chain management: A critical review and recommendations. *International Journal of Production Research*, *40*(17), 4415–4430.

Huang, G. Q., Lau, J. S. K., & Mak, K. L. (2003). The impacts of sharing production information on supply chain dynamics: A review of the literature. *International Journal of Production Research*, *41*(7), 1483–1517.

Hwang, J., Choi, M., Lee, T., Jeon, S., Kim, S., Park, S., & Park, S. (2017). Energy prosumer business model using blockchain system to ensure transparency and safety. *Energy Procedia*, *141*, 194–198.

Kshetri, N. (2017). Cybersecurity in India: Regulations, governance, institutional capacity and market mechanisms. *Asian Research Policy*, *8*(1), 64–76.

Li, S., Wang, G., & Yang, J. (2019). Survey on cloud model based similarity measure of uncertain concepts. *CAAI Trans Intell Technol*, *4*(4), 223–230.

Ming, Z., Jun, C., Yuqing, W., Yuanfei, L., Yongqi, Y., & Jinyue, D. (2017). The primarily research for multi module cooperative autonomous mode of energy internet under blockchain framework. *Zhongguo Dianji Gongcheng Xuebao*, *37*(13), 3672–3681.

Namasudra, S. (2018). Taxonomy of DNA-based security models. In S. Namasudra & G. C. Deka (Eds.), *Advances of dna computing in cryptography* (pp. 53–68). Springer.

Namasudra, S. (2018). Cloud computing: A new era. *J Fundam Appl Sci*, *10*(2), 113–135.

Namasudra, S., Chakraborty, R., Majumder, A., & Moparthi, N. R. (2020). *Securing multimedia by using DNA based encryption in the cloud computing environment.* ACM T Multi Comput Commun Appl.

Namasudra, S., & Deka, G. C. (2018). *Advances of DNA computing in cryptography*. Taylor & Francis.

Namasudra, S., & Deka, G. C. (2018). Introduction of DNA computing in cryptography. In S. Namasudra & D. C. Deka (Eds.), *Advances of dna computing in cryptography* (pp. 27–34). Springer.

Namasudra, S., Deka, G. C., & Bali, R. (2018). Applications and future trends of DNA computing. In S. Namasudra & G. C. Deka (Eds.), *Advances of DNA computing in cryptography* (pp. 181–192). Taylor & Francis.

Namasudra, S., Devi, D., Choudhary, S., Patan, R., & Kallam, S. (2018). Security, privacy, trust, and anonymity. In S. Namasudra & G. C. Deka (Eds.), *Advances of DNA computing in cryptography* (pp. 153–166). Taylor & Francis.

Namasudra, S., Devi, D., Kadry, S., Sundarasekar, R., & Shanthini, A. (2020). Towards DNA based data security in the cloud computing environment. *Computer Communications*, *151*, 539–547.

Namasudra, S., & Roy, P. (2016). Secure and efficient data access control in cloud computing environment: A survey. *Multiagent Grid Sys Int J*, *12*(2), 69–90.

Namasudra, S., & Roy, P. (2017). Time saving protocol for data accessing in cloud computing. *IET Communications*, *11*(10), 1558–1565.

Namasudra, S., & Roy, P. (2018). PpBAC: Popularity based access control model for cloud computing. *Journal of Organizational and End User Computing*, *30*(4), 14–31.

Namasudra, S., Roy, P., Vijayakumar, P., Audithan, S., & Balusamy, B. (2017). Time efficient secure DNA based access control model for cloud computing environment. *Future Generation Computer Systems*, *73*, 90–105.

Sarkar, M., Saha, K., Namasudra, S., & Roy, P. (2015). An efficient and time saving web service based android application. *SSRG Int J Comput Sci Eng*, *2*(8), 18–21.

Williams, A. (2016). *IBM to open first blockchain innovation centre in Singapore, to create applications and grow new markets in finance and trade*. The Straits Times Singapore Press Holdings Ltsd. Co.

Wood, G. (2014). *Ethereum: a secure decentralised generalised transaction ledger*. Ethereum Project Yellow Paper.

Xue, T., Hongbin, S., & Qinglai, G. (2016). Electricity transactions and congestion management based on blockchain in energy internet. *Power Syst Technol*, *40*(12), 3630–3638.

Zhao, X., Li, R., & Zuo, X. (2019). Advances on QoS-aware web service selection and composition with nature-inspired computing. *CAAI Trans Intell Technol*, *4*(3), 159–174.

Zheng, Z., Xie, S., Dai, H. N., & Wang, H. (2016). Blockchain challenges and opportunities: A survey. *International Journal of Web and Grid Services*, *14*(4), 314–335.

Compilation of References

. Bouwman, H., Nikou, S., Molina-Castillo, F. J., & de Reuver, M. (2018). The impact of digitalization on business models. *Digital Policy, Regulation and Governance*.

Abdul-Muhmin, A. G. (2005). Instrumental and interpersonal determinants of relationship satisfaction and commitment in industrial markets. *Journal of Business Research*, *58*(5), 619–628. doi:10.1016/j.jbusres.2003.08.004

Ageron, B., Bentahar, O., & Gunasekaran, A. (2020, July). Digital Supply Chain: Challenges and future directions. *Supply Chain Forum International Journal (Toronto, Ont.)*, *21*(3), 133–138.

Agrawal, P., & Narain, R. (2018). Digital supply chain management: An Overview. *IOP Conference Series. Materials Science and Engineering*, *455*(1).

Ahemd, M. M., Shah, M. A., & Wahid, A. (2017). Iot security: a layered approach for attacks and defenses. *2017 International Conference on Communication Technologies (ComTech)*, 104–110.

Ahlman, R. (2016). *Finish city partners with IBM to validate blockchain application in logistics*. https://cointelegraph.com/news/finish-city-partners-with-ibm-to-validate-blockchain-application-in-logistics

Ahmed, P. K., & Rafiq, M. (2003). Internal marketing issues and challenges. *European Journal of Marketing*, *37*(9), 1177–1186. doi:10.1108/03090560310498813

Aitzhan, N. Z. & Svetinovic, D. (2016). Security and Privacy in Decentralized Energy Trading through Multi-signatures, Blockchain and Anonymous Messaging Streams. *IEEE Transaction on Dependable and Secure Computing*, 1–1.

Akkiraju, R., Farrell, J., Miller, J., Nagarajan, M., Schmidt, M., Sheth, A., & Verma, K. (2005). *Web Service Semantics - WSDL-S*. A joint UGA-IBM Technical Note, version 1.0. http://lsdis.cs.uga.edu/projects/METEOR-S/WSDL-S

Aldrighetti, R., Zennaro, I., Finco, S., & Battini, D. (2019). Healthcare supply chain simulation with disruption considerations: A case study from Northern Italy. *Global Journal of Flexible Systems Managment*, *20*(1), 81–102. doi:10.100740171-019-00223-8

Alipour, M., & Hallaj Mohammadi, M. (2011). The effect of Customer Relationship Management (CRM) on achieving competitive advantage of manufacturing tractor. *Global Journal of Management and Business Research, 11*(5).

Alldredge, K., Newaskar, P., & Ungerman, K. (2015). *The digital future of consumer-packaged-goods companies*. McKinsey & Co., White Paper.

Alrubaiee, L., Alshaibi, H., & Al-bayati, Y. (2012). Relationship between B2B e-commerce benefits, e-marketplace usage and supply chain management. *Global Journal of Management and Business Research, 12*(9).

Amiri-Aref, M., Farahani, R. Z., Hewitt, M., & Klibi, W. (2019). Equitable location of facilities in a region with probabilistic barriers to travel. *Transportation Research Part E, Logistics and Transportation Review, 127*, 66–85. doi:10.1016/j.tre.2019.04.010

Andrea, I., Chrysostomou, C., & Hadjichristofi, G. (2015). Internet of things: security vulnerabilities and challenges. *2015 IEEE Symposium on Computers and Communication (ISCC),* 180–187.

Antoniou, G., & Harmelen, F. V. (2008). *A Semantic Web Primer*. The MIT Press.

Arasli, H. (2012). Towards business excellence in the hospitality industry: A case for 3-, 4-, and 5-star hotels in Iran. *Total Quality Management & Business Excellence, 23*(5-6), 573–590. doi: 10.1080/14783363.2012.669539

Atzori, L., Lera, A., & Morabito, G. (2010). The internet of things: A survey. *Computer Networks, 54*(16), 2787–2805. doi:10.1016/j.comnet.2010.05.010

Baader, F., & Nutt, W. (2003). *Basic Description Logics, The description logic handbook*. Cambridge University Press.

Bag, Wood, Xu, Dhamija, & Kayikc. (2020). Big data analytics as an operational excellence approach to enhance sustainable supply chain performance. *Resources, Conservation and Recycling*, 153.

Bal, S., & Tact, B. (2012). Clouds for Different Services. *IJCSI International Journal of Computer Science, 9*, 273–277.

Banker, S. (2016). *Will blockchain technology revolutionise supply chain applications?* https://logisticsviewpoints.com/2016/06/20/will-block-chain-technology-revolutionize-supply -chain-applications/

Barreto, L., Amaral, A., & Pereira, T. (2017). Industry 4.0 implications in logistics: An overview. *Procedia Manufacturing, 2017*(13), 1245–1252. doi:10.1016/j.promfg.2017.09.045

Bass, F. M. (1969). A new product growth model for consumer durable. *Management Science, 15*(5).

Behret, H., & Korugan, A. (2009). Performance analysis of the hybrid system under quality impacts of returns. *Computers & Industrial Engineering, 56*(2), 507–520.

Bergmann, R., & Schaaf, M. (2003). Structural Case-Based Reasoning and Ontology-Based Knowledge Management: A Perfect Match? *Journal of Universal Computer Science, UCS*, *9*(7), 608–626.

Berners-Lee, T., Hendler, J., & Lassila, O. (2001). The Semantic Web. *Scientific American*, *284*(May), 34–43. doi:10.1038cientificamerican0501-34 PMID:11323639

Bianchini, D., Antonellis, V. A., Melchiori, M., & Salvi, D. (2006). Semantic Enriched Service Discovery. *International Conference in Data Engineering Workshop*, 38.

Bittner, A. K. (2011). *Managing change: Innovation and trade unionism in the news industry*. EFJ.

Blinder, S. (1986). Can the Production Smoothing Model of Inventory Behavior be Saved? *The Quarterly Journal of Economics*, *101*(3), 431–440. doi:10.2307/1885691

Boccaletti, S., Ditto, W., Mindlin, G., & Atangana, A. (2020). Modeling and forecasting of epidemic spreading: The case of Covid-19 and beyond. *Chaos, Solitons, and Fractals*, *135*, 109794. doi:10.1016/j.chaos.2020.109794 PMID:32288357

Bouranta, N., Psomas, E., Suárez-Barraza, M. F., & Jaca, C. (2019). The key factors of total quality management in the service sector: A cross-cultural study. *Benchmarking*, *26*(3), 893–921. doi:10.1108/BIJ-09-2017-0240

Büyüközkan, G., & Göçer, F. (2018). Digital supply chain: Literature review and a proposed framework for future research. *Computers in Industry*, *97*, 157–177. doi:10.1016/j.compind.2018.02.010

Cai, M. Zhang, W. Y., Zhang, K. & Li, S. T. (2010). SWMRD: A Semantic Web-based manufacturing resource discovery system for cross-enterprise collaboration. *International Journal of Production Research, 48*(12), 3445-3460.

Cambrra-Fierro, J. J., & Polo-Redondo, Y. (2008). Creating satisfaction in the demand-supply chain: The buyers' perspective. *Supply Chain Management*.

Cam-Winget, N., Sadeghi, A.-R., & Jin, Y. (2016). INVITED: Can IoT be Secured: Emerging Challenges in Connecting the Unconnected. *Proceedings of the 53rd Annual Design Automation Conference (DAC '16)*. 10.1145/2897937.2905004

Canetta, L., Salvade, A., Schnegg, P. A., Müller, E., & Lanini, M. (2011). RFID-ERP Key data integration challenges. In L. Canetta, C. Redaelli, & M. Flores (Eds.), *Digital Factory for Human-Oriented Production Systems* (pp. 73–95). Springer. doi:10.1007/978-1-84996-172-1_5

Cardoso, J. (2006). Discovering Semantic Web Services with and without a Common Ontology Commitment. *IEEE Service Computing Workshop*, 183-190.

Cardoso, J., & Sheth, A. (2003). Semantic e-Workflow Composition. *Journal of Intelligent Information Systems*, *21*(3), 191–225. doi:10.1023/A:1025542915514

Carter, P. L., Monczka, R. M., Ragatz, G. L., & Jennings, P. L. (2009). Supply chain integration: Challenges and good practices. *CAPS Research*, 95-99.

Casadesus-Masanell, R., & Ricart, J. E. (2010). From strategy to business models and onto tactics. *Long Range Planning*, *43*(2-3), 195–215. doi:10.1016/j.lrp.2010.01.004

Cauchois, R., Taghipour, A., Kang, D., Zoghlami, N., & Abed, M. (2017). Advanced Solutions for a Supply Chain with Stochastic Information. *Journal of Advanced Management Science, 5*(1).

Chan, F. T. S. (2003). Performance measurement in a supply chain. *International Journal of Advanced Manufacturing Technology*, *21*(7), 534–548. doi:10.1007001700300063

Chang, E., West, M., & Hanzic, M. (2006). A digital ecosystem for extended logistics enterprises. *e-Networks in an Increasingly Volatile World Proceedings of the 11th International Workshop on Telework*, 32-40.

Chen, Finkenstaedt, & Liu. (2019). Maintenance Repair and Operations Parts Inventory Management in the Era of Industry 4.0. *IFAC-PapersOnLine*, *52*(13), 171–176.

Chen, R., Guo, J., & Bao, F. (2014). Trust management for service composition in SOA-based IoT systems. *Proceedings of the 2014 IEEE Wireless Communications and Networking Conference (WCNC)*, 3444–3449. 10.1109/WCNC.2014.6953138

Chesbrough, H., & Rosenbloom, R. S. (2002). The role of business model in capturing value from innovation: Evidence from Xerox Corporation's technology spin-off companies. *Industrial and Corporate Change*, *11*(3), 529–555. doi:10.1093/icc/11.3.529

Christopher, M., & Holweg, M. (2017). Supply chain 2.0 revisited: A framework for managing volatility-induced risk in the supply chain. *International Journal of Physical Distribution & Logistics Management*, *47*(1), 2–17. doi:10.1108/IJPDLM-09-2016-0245

Christopher, M., & Towill, D. R. (2000). Supply chain migration from lean and functional to agile and customized. *Supply Chain Management*, *5*(4), 206–213. doi:10.1108/13598540010347334

Cliche, Taghipour, & Canel. (2020). An Improved Forecasting Approach to Reduce Inventory-Levels in Decentralized Supply Chains. *European Journal of Operational Research*, *287*(2), 511–527.

Colakovic, A., & Hadzialic, M. (2018). Internet of Things (IoT): A review of enabling technologies, challenges, and open research issues. *Computer Networks*, *144*, 17–39. doi:10.1016/j.comnet.2018.07.017

Columbus L. (2015). 10 Ways Analytics Are Accelerating Digital Manufacturing. *Forbes*.

Copacino, W., & Anderson, D. (2003). Connecting with the Bottom Line: A Global Study of Supply Chain Leadership and its Contribution to the High Performance Business. *Accenture, 1*.

Corkery, M., & Yaffe-Bellany, D. U. S. (2020). Food Supply Chain Is Strained as Virus Spreads. *The New York Times*.

Croom, S. R. (2005). The impact of e-business on supply chain management. *International Journal of Operations & Production Management*, *25*(1), 55–73. doi:10.1108/01443570510572240

Cui, Y. (2018). Supply Chain Innovation with IoT. In Multi-Criteria Methods and Techniques Applied to Supply Chain Management. Intech Open. doi:10.5772/intechopen.74155

Currie, C. S., Fowler, J. W., Kotiadis, K., Monks, T., Onggo, B. S., Robertson, D. A., & Tako, A. A. (2020). How simulation modelling can help reduce the impact of COVID-19. *Journal of Simulation*, *14*(2), 83–97. doi:10.1080/17477778.2020.1751570

Da Xu, L., He, W., & Li, S. (2014). Internet of things in industries: A survey. *IEEE Transactions on Industrial Informatics*, *10*(4), 2233–2243. doi:10.1109/TII.2014.2300753

Degryse, C. (2016). *Digitalisation of the economy and its impact on labour markets.* ETUI research paper-working paper.

Deloitte. (2017). *Digital Procurement: New Capabilities from Disruptive Technologies.* Deloitte Development LLC.

Deniaud, I., Marmier, F., & Michalak, J. L. (2020). Méthodologie et outil de diagnostic 4.0: Définir sa stratégie de transition 4.0 pour le management de la chaîne logistique. *Logistique & Management*, *28*(1), 4–17. doi:10.1080/12507970.2019.1693914

Derrouiche, R., & Lamouri, S. (2020). *Numéro spécial: Supply Chain 4.0.* Academic Press.

Dev, N. K., Shankar, R., & Choudhary, A. (2017). Strategic design for inventory and production planning in a closed-loop hybrid system. *International Journal of Production Economics*, *183*, 345–353. doi:10.1016/j.ijpe.2016.06.017

Domingue, J., Cabral, L., Galizia, S., Tanasescu, V., Gugliotta, A., Norton, B., & Pedrinaci, C. (2008). IRS-III: A Broker-based Approach to Semantic Web Service. *Journal of Web Semantics*, *6*(2), 109–132. doi:10.1016/j.websem.2008.01.001

Dorri, A., Kanhere, S. S., Jurdak, R., & Gauravaram, P. (2017). Blockchain for IoT security and privacy: The case study of a smart home. *Proceedings of the 2017 IEEE International Conference on Pervasive Computing and Communications Workshops (PerCom Workshops).*

Dubey, A. D., & Tripathi, S. (2020). Analysing the sentiments towards work-from-home experience during covid-19 pandemic. *Journal of Innovation Management*, *8*(1), 13–19. doi:10.24840/2183-0606_008.001_0003

Dubey, R., Altay, N., Gunasekaran, A., Blome, C., Papadopoulos, T., & Childe, S. J. (2018). Supply chain agility, adaptability and alignment: Empirical evidence from the Indian auto components industry. *International Journal of Operations & Production Management*, *38*(1), 129–148. doi:10.1108/IJOPM-04-2016-0173

Eckstein, D., Goellner, M., Blome, C., & Henke, M. (2015). The performance impact of supply chain agility and supply chain adaptability: The Moderating Effect of Product Complexity. *International Journal of Production Research*, *53*(10), 3028–3046. doi:10.1080/00207543.2014.970707

El Nemr, Canel, & Taghipour. (2021). The Determinants of Hotel Room Rates in Beirut: A Hedonic Pricing Model. *International Journal of Trade, Economics and Finance*, *12*(2).

El Nemr, N., Canel, B., & Taghipour, A. (2020). Luxury Hotels' Eco-Friendly Activities & Customers' Preferences and Willingness to Pay for Green Hotels. *Journal of Advanced Management Science*, *8*(1). Advance online publication. doi:10.18178/joams.8.1.7-14

Ellram, L. M., & Murfield, M. L. U. (2019). Supply chain management in industrial marketing–Relationships matter. *Industrial Marketing Management*, *79*, 36–45. doi:10.1016/j.indmarman.2019.03.007

Engelhardt & Nowitzki. (2012). Improving value chain flexibility and adaptability in build-to-order environments. *International Journal of Physical Distribution & Logistics Management*, *42*, 318–337.

Eng, T. Y. (2004). The role of e-marketplaces in supply chain management. *Industrial Marketing Management*, *33*(2), 97–105. doi:10.1016/S0019-8501(03)00032-4

Fadaki, M., Rahman, S., & Chan, C. (2020). Leagile supply chain: Design drivers and business performance implications. *International Journal of Production Research*, *58*(18), 5601–5623. doi:10.1080/00207543.2019.1693660

Fair, R. C. (1989). The production-smoothing model is alive and well. *Journal of Monetary Economics*, *24*(3), 353–370.

Fel, F., Cayla, J., & Carbone, V. (2020). L'industrie 4.0 peut-elle favoriser une relocalisation de la production en France? *Logistique & Management*, *28*(1), 18–28. doi:10.1080/12507970.2019.1683477

Fensel, D., & Bussler, C. (2002). The Web Service Modeling Framework WSMF. *Electronic Commerce Research and Applications*, *1*(2), 113–137. doi:10.1016/S1567-4223(02)00015-7

Finextra. (2016). *Everledger secures the first bottle of wine on the blockchain.* https://www.finextra.com/pressaritcle/67381/everledger-secures-the-first-bottle-of-wine-on-the-blockchain

Fitzgerald, J. (2017). Using autonomous robots to drive supply chain innovation. *Deloitte Perspective*, 215–227.

Flyvbjerg, B. (2006). Five misunderstandings about case-study research. *Qualitative Inquiry*, *12*(2), 219–245. doi:10.1177/1077800405284363

Ford, M. (2015). *Rise of the robots: technology and the threat of a jobless future*. Basic Books.

Formentini, M., & Romano, P. (2016). Towards supply chain collaboration in B2B pricing. *International Journal of Operations & Production Management*, *36*(7), 734–756. doi:10.1108/IJOPM-03-2015-0124

Fotopoulos, C. B., & Psomas, E. L. (2009). The impact of "soft" and "hard" TQM elements on quality management results. *International Journal of Quality & Reliability Management*, *26*(2), 150–163. doi:10.1108/02656710910928798

Foundry, D. (2017). *What Is a Permanent Dos (Pdos) Attack?* https://www.datafoundry. com/blog/what-is-permanent-dos-pdos-attack/t

Fugate, B., Sahin, F., & Mentzer, J. T. (2006). Supply Chain Management Coordination Mechanisms. *Journal of Business Logistics*, *27*(2), 129–161. doi:10.1002/j.2158-1592.2006.tb00220.x

Galvez, J. F., Mejuto, J. C., & Gandara, J. S. (2018). Future challenges on the use of blockchain for food traceability analysis. *Trends in Analytical Chemistry*, *107*, 222–232. doi:10.1016/j.trac.2018.08.011

Gandhi, S., Thota, B., Kuchembuck, R., & Swartz, J. (2018). Demystifying data monetization. *MIT Sloan Management Review*, 1–9.

Ganeshan, R., & Harrison, T. P. (1995). An introduction to supply chain management. *Supply Chain Management.* Available from http://silmaril.smeal.psu.edu/misc/supply_chain_intro.html

Gao, Y., Li, Z., Taghipour, A., Canel, B., & Kang, D. S. (2018). Supply Chain Coordination: A Review. *Journal of Advanced Management Science*, *6*(4), 213–217. doi:10.18178/joams.6.4.213-217

Garay-Rondero, C. L., Martinez-Flores, J. L., Smith, N. R., Morales, S. O. C., & Aldrette-Malacara, A. (2019). Digital supply chain model in Industry 4.0. *Journal of Manufacturing Technology Management*, *31*(5), 887–933. doi:10.1108/JMTM-08-2018-0280

Garg, S., Gentry, C., Halevi, S., Sahai, A., & Waters, W. (2013). *Attribute-Based Encryption for Circuits from Multilinear Maps*. Academic Press. doi:10.1007/978-3-642-40084-1_27

Geunes, J., Romeijn, H. E., & van den Heuvel, W. (2016). Improving the efficiency of decentralized supply chains with fixed ordering costs. *European Journal of Operational Research*, *252*(3), 815–828. doi:10.1016/j.ejor.2016.02.004

Ghadimi, P., Toosi, F. G., & Heavey, C. (2018). Multi-agent systems approach for sustainable supplier selection and order allocation in a partnership supply chain. *European Journal of Operational Research*, *269*(1), 286–301.

Ghadimi, & Wang, Lime, & Heavey. (2019). Intelligent sustainable supplier selection using multi-agent technology: Theory and application for Industry 4.0 supply chains. *Computers & Industrial Engineering*, *127*, 588–600.

Giannoccaro, I. (2018). Centralized vs. decentralized supply chains: The importance of decision maker's cognitive ability and resistance to change. *Industrial Marketing Management*, *73*, 59–69. doi:10.1016/j.indmarman.2018.01.034

Giunchiglia, F., Shvaiko, P., & Yatskevich, M. (2004). S-Match: an algorithm and an implementation of semantic matching. *Proceedings of 1st European Semantic Web Symposium (ESWS)*, 3053, 61-75. 10.1007/978-3-540-25956-5_5

Gligor, D. M., & Holcomb, M. (2014). The road to supply chain agility: An RBV perspective on the role of logistics capabilities. *International Journal of Logistics Management*, *14*(25), 160–179.

Gnimpieba, Z. D. R., Nait-Sidi-Moh, A., Durand, D., & Fortin, J. (2015). Using the Internet of Things technologies for a collaborative supply chain: Application to tracking of pallets and containers. *Procedia Computer Science*, *56*, 550–557.

Golan, M., Cohen, Y., & Singer, G. (2019). A framework for the operator– workstation interaction in Industry 4. *International Journal of Production Research*, *58*(8), 2421–2432.

Goldsby, T. J., Griffis, S. E., & Roath, A. S. (2006). Modeling lean, agile, and leagile supply chain strategies. *Journal of Business Logistics*, *27*(1), 57–80. doi:10.1002/j.2158-1592.2006.tb00241.x

Govindan, K., Mina, H., & Alavi, B. (2020). A decision support system for demand management in healthcare supply chains considering the epidemic outbreaks: A case study of coronavirus disease 2019 (COVID-19). *Transportation Research Part E, Logistics and Transportation Review*, *138*, 101967. doi:10.1016/j.tre.2020.101967 PubMed

Grimm, S., Monk, B., & Preist, C. (2006). Matching Semantic Service Descriptions with Local Closed-World Reasoning. *European Semantic Web Conference*, 575-589. 10.1007/11762256_42

Gruber, T. R. (1993). *A Translation Approach to Portable Ontology Specifications*. Stanford University, Computer Science Department, Knowledge Systems Laboratory, Technical Report KSL 92-71.

Guarino, N., & Giaretta, P. (1995). *Ontologies and Knowledge Base: Towards a Terminological Classification Toward Very Large Knowledge Base: Knowledge Building and Knowledge Sharing*. IOS Press.

Gubbi, J., Buyya, R., Marusic, S., & Palaniswami, M. (2013). Internet of Things (IoT): A vision, architectural elements, and future directions. *Future Generation Computer Systems*, *29*(7), 1645–1660. doi:10.1016/j.future.2013.01.010

Gu, J., Sum, B., Du, X., Wang, J., Zhuang, Y., & Wang, Z. (2018). Consortium Blockchain-Based Malware Detection in Mobile Devices. *IEEE Access: Practical Innovations, Open Solutions*, *6*, 12118–12128. doi:10.1109/ACCESS.2018.2805783

Gunasekaran, A., Tiwari, M. K., Dubey, R., & Wamba, S. F. (2016). Big data and predictive analytics applications in supply chain management. *Computers & Industrial Engineering*, *101*, 525–527. doi:10.1016/j.cie.2016.10.020

Hadjikhani, A., & LaPlaca, P. (2013). Development of B2B marketing theory. *Industrial Marketing Management*, *42*(3), 294–305. doi:10.1016/j.indmarman.2013.03.011

Hall, D., Lister, J., & Mercer, H. (2020). *Privatised and Unprepared: The NHS Supply Chain*. Academic Press.

Handfield, R. B., Straube, F., Pfohl, H. C., & Wieland, A. (2013). *Trends and Strategies in Logistics and Supply Chain Management: Embracing Global Logistics Complexity to Drive Market Advantage*. DVV Media Group.

Hartmann, B., King, W. P., & Narayanan, S. (2015). *Digital Manufacturing: the revolution will be virtualized*. McKinsey.

He, Y., Li, H., Cheng, X., Liu, Y., Yang, C., & Sun, L. (2018). A Blockchain based Truthful Incentive Mechanism for Distributed P2P Applications. *IEEE Access: Practical Innovations, Open Solutions*, *6*, 1–1. doi:10.1109/ACCESS.2018.2821705

High-Level, U. S. G. S. (2019). *Panel on Digital Cooperation*. The Age of Digital Interdependence Report.

Hines, T. (2004). *Supply chain strategies: Customer driven and customer focused*. Routledge.

Hoover, W. E. Jr, Eloranta, E., Holmstrom, J., & Huttunen, K. (2002). *Managing the Demand-Supply Chain: Value Innovations for Customer Satisfaction*. John Wiley & Sons.

Hua, J., Wang, X., Kang, M., Wang, H., & Wang, F. (2018). Blockchain based Provenance for Agricultural Products: A Distributed Platform with Duplicated and Shared Bookkeeping. *Proceedings of the IEEE Intelligent Vehicles Symposium (IV)*. 10.1109/IVS.2018.8500647

Huang, X., Xu, C., Wang, P., & Liu, H. (2018). LNSC: A security model for electric vehicle and charging pile management based on blockchain ecosystem. *IEEE Access: Practical Innovations, Open Solutions*, *6*, 13565–13574. doi:10.1109/ACCESS.2018.2812176

Hulse Apple, C. (2015). *Block Verify uses blockchains to end counterfeiting and making world more honest*. https://cointelegraph.com/news/block-verify-uses-blockchains-to-end-counterfeiting-and-make-world-more-honest

Hur, J., & Noh, D. K. (2011). Attribute-based access control with efficient revocation in data outsourcing systems. *IEEE Transactions on Parallel and Distributed Systems*, *22*(7), 1214–1221. doi:10.1109/TPDS.2010.203

Hurley, R. F., & Hult, G. T. M. (1998). Innovation, market orientation, and organizational learning: An integration and empirical examination. *Journal of Marketing*, *62*(3), 42–54. doi:10.1177/002224299806200303

Iddris, F. (2018). Digital supply chain: Survey of the literature. *International Journal of Business Research and Management*, *9*(1), 47–61.

Ilcus, M. A. (2018). Impact of Digitalization in Business World. *Revista de Management Comparat International*, *19*(4), 350–358. doi:10.24818/RMCI.2018.4.350

Inderfurth, K. (2005). Impact of uncertainties on recovery behavior in a remanufacturing environment: A numerical analysis. *International Journal of Physical Distribution & Logistics Management, 35*(5), 318–336.

iNNOVAHEALTH. (2012). *Building on Open Innovation Ecosystem in Europe for Healthcare.* Cyprus EU Presidency.

Irani, L. (2019). Justice for Data Janitors. In *Think in Public* (pp. 23–40). Columbia University Press. doi:10.7312/marc19008-003

Ivanov, D. (2020). Viable supply chain model: Integrating agility, resilience and sustainability perspectives—lessons from and thinking beyond the COVID-19 pandemic. *Annals of Operations Research*, 1–21. doi:10.100710479-020-03640-6 PMID:32836614

Ivanov, D., & Das, A. (2020). Coronavirus (COVID-19/SARS-CoV-2) and supply chain resilience: A research note. *International Journal of Integrated Supply Management, 13*(1), 90–102. doi:10.1504/IJISM.2020.107780

Ivanov, D., & Dolgui, A. (2020). Viability of intertwined supply networks: Extending the supply chain resilience angles towards survivability. A position paper motivated by COVID-19 outbreak. *International Journal of Production Research, 58*(10), 2904–2915. doi:10.1080/00207543.2020.1750727

Jemel, M., & Serhrouchni, A. (2017). Decentralised access control mechanism with temporal dimension based on blockchain. *2017 IEEE 14th International Conference on e-Business Engineering (ICEBE),* 177–182.

Jianga, Z., Zhou, T., & Zhang, H. (2016, November). Reliability and cost optimization for remanufacturing process planning. *Journal of Cleaner Production, 135*(1), 1602–1610.

Jiang, J. J., & Conrath, D. W. (1997). Semantic Similarity Based on Corpus Statistics and Lexical Taxonomy. *Proceedings of International Conference Research on Computational Linguistics.*

Johnson, M. W., Christensen, C. M., & Kagermann, H. (2008). Reinventing your business model. *Harvard Business Review, 86*(12), 57–68.

Jung, H., Chen, F. F., & Jeong, B. (2008). Decentralized supply chain planning framework for third party logistics partnership. *Computers & Industrial Engineering, 55*(2), 348–364. doi:10.1016/j.cie.2007.12.017

Jyoti, J., Kour, S., & Sharma, J. (2017). Impact of total quality services on financial performance: Role of service profit chain. *Total Quality Management & Business Excellence, 28*(7-8), 897–929. doi:10.1080/14783363.2016.1274649

Kalakota, R., & Whiston, A. (1997). *Electronic commerce: a manager's guide.* Addison Wesley.

Kamilaris, A., Fonts, A., & Prenafeta-Boldv, F. X. (2019). The rise of blockchain technology in agriculture and food supply chain. *Trends in Food Science & Technology, 91*, 640–652. doi:10.1016/j.tifs.2019.07.034

Katz, J., & Lindell, Y. (2007). *Digital Signature Schemes. In Introduction to Modern Cryptography*. Chapman & Hall/ CBC Press. doi:10.1201/9781420010756

Kaufer, F., & Klusch, M. (2006). WSMO-MX: A Logic Programming Based Hybrid Service Matchmaker. *European Conference on Web Services*, 161-170. 10.1109/ECOWS.2006.39

Keertikumar, M., Shubham, M., & Banakar, R. M. (2015). Evolution of IoT in smart vehicles: An overview. *Proceedings of the International Conference on Green Computing and Internet of Things (ICGCIoT)*, 804–809. 10.1109/ICGCIoT.2015.7380573

Keller, K. L., & Lehmann, D. R. (2006). Brands and branding: Research findings and future priorities. *Marketing Science*, *25*(6), 740–759. doi:10.1287/mksc.1050.0153

Kiefer, C., & Bernstein, A. (2008). The Creation and Evaluation of iSPARQL Strategies for Matchmaking. *European Semantic Web Conference*, 463-477. 10.1007/978-3-540-68234-9_35

Kilpatrick, J., & Barter, L. (2020). *COVID-19: Managing supply chain risk and disruption*. Deloitte.

Kilpi, J., Töyli, J., & Vepsäläinen, A. (2009). Cooperative strategies for the availability service of repairable aircraft components. *International Journal of Production Economics*, *117*(2), 360–370.

Kim, N. (2016). IBM pushes blockchain into the supply chain. *Wall Street Journal*.

Kirk, R. (2015). Cars of the future: The Internet of Things in the automotive industry. *Network Security*, *9*, 16–18.

Klusch, M., Fries, B., & Sycara, K. (2008). OWLS-MX: A Hybrid Semantic Web Service Matchmaker for OWL-S Services. *Journal of Web Semantics*.

Kouedeu, A. F., Kenné, J.-P., Dejax, P., Songmene, V., & Polotski, V. (2014). Production Planning of a Failure-Prone manufacturing/Remanufacturing System with production-Dependent Failure Rates. *Applied Mathematics*, *5*(10), 10. doi:10.4236/am.2014.510149

Kowalski, W. (2015, July). The European digital agenda: Unambitious and too narrow. *Social Europe*, *6*. https://www.socialeurope.eu/2015/07/european-digitalagenda-unambitious-narrow

Kozlenkova, I. V., Hult, G. T. M., Lund, D. J., Mena, J. A., & Kekec, P. (2015). The role of marketing channels in supply chain management. *Journal of Retailing*, *91*(4), 586–609. doi:10.1016/j.jretai.2015.03.003

KPMG International Cooperative. (2020). *Building supply chain resilience through digital transformation*. Retrieved from https://assets.kpmg/content/dam/kpmg/xx/pdf/2020/06.

Kshetri, N. (2017). Can Blockchain Strengthen the Internet of Things? *IEEE IT Professional*, *19*(4), 68–72. doi:10.1109/MITP.2017.3051335

Kumanduri, R., & Romero, C. (1998). *Number Theory with Computer Applications*. Prentice Hall.

Kumar, A., & Rahman, S. (2014). RFID-enabled process re-engineering of closed-loop supply chains in the health care industry of Singapore. *Journal of Cleaner Production*, *85*, 382–394.

Kumar, M. V., & Iyengar, N. C. S. N. (2017). A Framework for blockchain technology in rice supply chain management. *Advanced Science and Technology Letters, 146*, 125–130. doi:10.14257/astl.2017.146.22

Lagadec, P. (1990). Communication strategies in crisis situations. *Industrial Crisis Quarterly, 1*, 19–26.

Lagadec, P. (1993). *Preventing chaos in a crisis*. McGraw-Hill.

Lajmi, S., Ghedira, C., & Ghedira, K. (2006a). How to apply CBR method in web service composition. In *Second International Conference on Signal-Image Technology and Internet Based Systems (SITI'2006)*. Springer Verlag.

Lajmi, S., Ghedira, C., Ghedira, K., & Benslimane, D. (2006b). Web_CBR: How to compose web service via case based reasoning. *IEEE International Symposium on Service-Oriented Applications, Integration and Collaboration held with the IEEE International Conference on eBusiness Engineering (ICEBE 2006).*

Laliwala, Z., Khosla, R., Majumdar, P., & Chaudhary, S. (2006). Semantic and Rule Based Event-Driven Dynamic Web Service Composition for Automation of Business Processes. *Proceedings of the IEEE Service Computing Workshop (SCW06).*

Lambert, D. M., & Cooper, M. C. (2000). Issues in Supply Chain Management. *Industrial Marketing Management, 29*(1), 65–83. doi:10.1016/S0019-8501(99)00113-3

Lambert, D. M., & Enz, M. G. (2017). Issues in supply chain management: Progress and potential. *Industrial Marketing Management, 62*, 1–16. doi:10.1016/j.indmarman.2016.12.002

Larson, R. C., & Nigmatulina, K. R. (2009). Engineering responses to pandemics. *Information, Knowledge, Systems Management, 8*(1-4), 311–339. doi:10.3233/IKS-2009-0145 PMID:20543252

Lavassani, K., Movahedi, B., & Kumar, V. (2008, May). Transition to B2B e-Marketplace enabled supply chain: Readiness assessment and success factors. In CONF-IRM 2008 Proceedings (p. 59). Academic Press.

Lebosse, S., Taghipour, A., & Canel-Depitre, B. (2017). Quick response to fluctuations in supply chains: A review. *Journal of Advanced Management Science, 5*(5).

Lebosse, S., Taghipour, A., & Canel-Depitre, B. (2017). Quick Response to Fluctuations in Supply Chains: A Review. *Journal of Advanced Management Science, 5*(5), 394–400.

Lee, B., & Lee, J. H. (2017). Blockchain-based secure firmware update for embedded devices in an Internet of Things environment. *The Journal of Supercomputing, 73*(3), 1152–1167. doi:10.100711227-016-1870-0

Lee, H. L. (2004). The tripple-A supply chain. *Harvard Business Review, 82*(10), 102–112. PMID:15559579

Lee, H. L., & Billington, C. (1993). Material management in decentralized supply chains. *Operations Research*, *41*(5), 835–847. doi:10.1287/opre.41.5.835

Lee, H., & Whang, S. (1999). Decentralized multi-echelon supply chains: Incentives and information. *Management Science*, *45*(5), 633–640. doi:10.1287/mnsc.45.5.633

Lee, I., & Lee, K. (2015). The Internet of Things (IoT): Applications, investments, and challenges for enterprises. *Business Horizons*, *58*(4), 431–440.

Li, S. H. (2002). *An Integrated Model for Supply Chain Management Practice, Performance and Competitive Advantage* (PhD Dissertation). University of Toledo, Toledo, OH.

Liang, G., Weller, S. R., Luo, F., Zhao, J., & Dong, Z. Y. (2018). Distributed Blockchain-Based Data Protection Framework for Modern Power Systems against Cyber Attacks. *IEEE Transactions on Smart Grid*, 1–1.

Liang, T., & Konsynski, B. R. (1993). Modeling by analogy: Use of analogical reasoning in model management systems. *Decision Support Systems*, *9*(1), 113–125. doi:10.1016/0167-9236(93)90026-Y

Li, J., Sikora, R., Shaw, M. J., & Woo Tan, G. A. (2006). Strategic analysis of inter-organizational information sharing. *Decision Support Systems*, *42*(1), 251–266. doi:10.1016/j.dss.2004.12.003

Li, L., & Horrocks, I. (2003). A Software Framework for Matchmaking Based on Semantic Web Technology. *International Conference in World Wide Web*, 331-339. 10.1145/775152.775199

Li, M., Yu, B., Rana, O. F., & Wang, Z. (2008). Grid Service Discovery with Rough Sets. *IEEE Transactions on Knowledge and Data Engineering*, *20*(6), 851–862. doi:10.1109/TKDE.2007.190744

Lin, C., He, D., Huang, X., Choo, K. K. R., & Vasilakos, A. V. (2018). Bsein: A blockchain-based secure mutual authentication with ðne-grained access control system for industry 4.0. *Journal of Network and Computer Applications*, *116*, 42–52. doi:10.1016/j.jnca.2018.05.005

Lin, I. C., Shin, H., Liu, J. C., & Jie, Y. X. (2017). Food traceability system using blockchain. *Proceedings of the 79th IASTEM International Conference*.

Liu, L., Parlar, M., & Zhu, S. X. (2007). Pricing and lead time decisions in decentralized supply chains. *Management Science*, *53*(5), 713–725. doi:10.1287/mnsc.1060.0653

Liu, Y., Liu, X., Tang, C., Wang, J., & Zhang, L. (2018). Unlinkable Coin Mixing Scheme for Transaction Privacy Enhancement of Bitcoin. *IEEE Access: Practical Innovations, Open Solutions*, *6*, 23261–23270. doi:10.1109/ACCESS.2018.2827163

Li, Y., & Zobel, C. W. (2020). Exploring supply chain network resilience in the presence of the ripple effect. *International Journal of Production Economics*, *228*, 107693. doi:10.1016/j.ijpe.2020.107693

Loivet, W., Taghipour, A., & Kang, D. S. (2020). The Rise of Green Supply Chain Management: Between Complexity and Necessity. *Journal of Economics, Business and Management, 8*(1), 1–7.

Loivet, W., Taghipour, A., & Kang, D.-S. (2020). The Rise of Green Supply Chain Management: Between Complexity and Necessity, Journal of Economics. *Business and Management, 8*(1), 1–7.

Lu, S. Y., Lau, H. Y., & Yiu, C. K. (2012). A hybrid solution to collaborative decision-making in a decentralized supply-chain. *Journal of Engineering and Technology Management, 29*(1), 95–111. doi:10.1016/j.jengtecman.2011.09.008

Mahfod, Khoury, Depitre, & Taghipour. (2020). Logistics providers in Syria humanitarian operations. In *Demand Forecasting and Order Planning in Supply Chains and Humanitarian Logistics.* IGI Global.

Mahfod, J., Canel-Depitre, B., & Taghipour, A. (2019). Quality Function Deployment in Supplier Evaluation. *Journal of Advanced Management Science, 7*(4), 131–135. doi:10.18178/joams.7.4.131-135

Mahjabin, T., Xiao, Y., Sun, G., & Jiang, W. (2017). A survey of distributed denial-of-service attack, prevention, and mitigation techniques. *International Journal of Distributed Sensor Networks, 13*(12), 155014771774146. doi:10.1177/1550147717741463

Mahmood, S., & Ahmed, A. (2014). Relationship between TQM dimensions and organizational performance. *Pakistan Journal of Commerce and Social Sciences, 8*(3), 662–679.

Martin, D., Burstein, M., Mcdermott, D., Mcilraith, S., Paolucci, M., Sycara, K., Mcguinness, D. L., Sirin, E., & Srinivasan, N. (2007). Bringing Semantics to Web Services with OWL-S. *World Wide Web (Bussum), 10*(3), 243–277. doi:10.100711280-007-0033-x

Martin, D., Paolucci, M., McIlraith, S., Burstein, M., McDermott, D., McGunness, D., Barsia, B., Payne, T., Sabou, M., Solanki, M., Srinivasan, N., & Sycara, K. (2004). Bringing Semantics to Web Services: The OWL-S Approach. *Proceeding of First International Workshop Semantic Web Services and Web Process Composition.*

Matskin, M., Maigre, R., & Tyugu, E. (2007). Computational logical semantics for business process language. *Proceedings of second international conference on Internet and Web applications and services (ICIW 2007)*, 526-531.

Matthyssens, P., Vandenbempt, K., & Berghman, L. (2006). Value innovation in business markets: Breaking the industry recipe. *Industrial Marketing Management, 35*(6), 751–761. doi:10.1016/j.indmarman.2005.05.013

Mbiatem, J., Taghipour, A., & Canel-Depitre, B. (2018, August). Supplier Selection Approaches for Decision Makers. In *Proceedings of the 8th International Conference on Information Communication and Management* (pp. 108-112). Academic Press.

McIlraith, S., & Martin, D. (2003). Bringing Semantics to Web Services. *IEEE Intelligent Systems, 18*(1), 90–93. doi:10.1109/MIS.2003.1179199

McKenzie, B. (2020). Beyond COVID-19: Supply chain resilience holds key to recovery. *Retrieved*, *24*, 2020.

Mihardjo, L., Sasmoko, S., Alamsjah, F., & Elidjen, E. (2019). The influence of digital customer experience and electronic word of mouth on brand image and supply chain sustainable performance. *Uncertain Supply Chain Management*, *7*(4), 691–702. doi:10.5267/j.uscm.2019.4.001

Mkrttchian, V. (2019a). New Tools for Cyber Security Using Blockchain Technology and Avatar-Based Management Technique. In Machine Learning and Cognitive Science Applications in Cyber Security (pp. 105-122). IGI Global. DOI: doi:10.4018/978-1-5225-8100-0.ch004

Mkrttchian, V. (2020). Human Capital Management in the Context of the Implementation of Digital Intelligent Decision Support Systems and Knowledge Management: Theoretical and Methodological Aspects. In Knowledge Management, Innovation, and Entrepreneurship in a Changing World (pp. 123-148). IGI Global. doi:10.4018/978-1-7998-2355-1.ch006

Mkrttchian, Vertakova, & Symonyan. (2021). Data Integrity Management for Laboratory of the Control of Lifecycle of Domestic Russian Tour Products. In *Book Data Integrity and Quality*. doi:10.5772/intechopen.96071

Mkrttchian, V. (2021a). Avatars-Based Decision Support System Using Blockchain and Knowledge Sharing for Processes Simulation a Natural Intelligence: Implementation of the Multi Chain Open Source Platform. *International Journal of Knowledge Management*, *17*(1), 5. Advance online publication. doi:10.4018/IJKM.2021010105

Mkrttchian, V., & Aleshina, E. (2017). *Sliding Mode in Intellectual Control and Communication: Emerging Research and Opportunities*. IGI Global. doi:10.4018/978-1-5225-2292-8

Mkrttchian, V., & Chernyshenko, S. (2021b). Digital Intelligent Design of Avatar-Based Control with Application to Human Capital Management. *International Journal of Human Capital and Information Technology Professionals*, *12*(1), 2. Advance online publication. doi:10.4018/IJHCITP.2021010102

Montori, Bedogni, Di Felice, & Bononi. (2018). Machine-to-machine wireless communication technologies for the Internet of Things: Taxonomy, comparison and open issues. *Pervasive and Mobile Computing*, *50*, 56–81.

Mudambi, S. M., Doyle, P., & Wong, V. (1997). An exploration of branding in industrial markets. *Industrial Marketing Management*, *26*(5), 433–446. doi:10.1016/S0019-8501(96)00151-4

Muhammad, S., Aziz, M., Charles, K., Kevin, H., & Laurent, N. (2018). Countering double spending in next-generation blockchains. IEEE ICC 2018.

Mülling, D., Neutzling, A. L., Seuring, S., & do Nascimentod, L. F. M. (2018). Linking sustainability-oriented innovation to supply chain relationship integration. *Journal of Cleaner Production*, *172*, 3448–3458. doi:10.1016/j.jclepro.2017.11.091

Nadia, E. N., Beatrice, C. D., & Atour, T. (2021). The Determinants of Hotel Room Rates in Beirut: A Hedonic Pricing Model. *International Journal of Trade, Economics and Finance*, *12*(2).

Nagaraj, K., & Maguire, E. (2017). *Securing the Chain*. KPMG International. https://assets.kpmg.com/content/dam/kpmg/xx/pdf/2017/05/securing-the-chain.pdf

OASIS. (2004). *Introduction to UDDI: Important Features and Functional Concepts*. Organization for the Advancement of Structured Information Standards.

Okorie, O., Turner, C., Charnley, F., Moreno, M., & Tiwari, A. (2017). A review of data driven approaches for circular economy in manufacturing. *Proceedings of the 18th European Roundtable for Sustainable Consumption and Production.*

OMG. (2009). *Business Process Model and Notation*. https://www.omg.org/spec/BPMN/1.2/(2009)

Ornig, H. J. (2016). *Leading into the Future: The so What? on Exponential Technology and Leadership*. Balboa Press.

Osman, T., Thakker, D., & Al-Dabass, D. (2006a). Semantic-Driven Matching of Web services using Case-Based Reasoning. *Fourth IEEE International Conference on Web Services (ICWS 2006)*, 29-36.

Osman, T., Thakker, D., & Al-Dabass, D. (2006b). S-CBR: Semantic Case Based Reasoner for Web services discovery and matchmaking. *20th European Conference on Modeling and Simulation (ECMS2006)*, 723-729.

Otte, P., de Vos, M., & Pouwelse, J. (2017, Sept.). TrustChain: A Sybil-resistant scalable blockchain. *Future Generation Computer Systems*.

Owen, J. M. (2007). *The Scientific Article in the Age of Digitization*. Springer.

Padmos, D., Alexander, M., Brody, P., Chadam, J., Cookson, C., Little, J., & Meadows, B. (2016). *Digital supply chain: it's all about that data*. Ernst and Young.

Paillisse, J., Subira, J., Lopez, L., Rodriguez-Natal, A., Ermagan, V., Maino, F., & Cabellos, A. (2019). *Distributed Access Control with Blockchain*. Academic Press.

Pal, K. & Ul-Haque, A. (2020). Internet of Things and Blockchain Technology in Apparel Manufacturing Supply Chain Data Management. *Proceeding of 11th International Conference on Ambient Systems, Networks and Technologies (ANT-2020).*

Pal, K. (2017). *A Semantic Web Service Architecture for Supply Chain Management*. The 8th International Conference on Ambient Systems, Networks and Technologies, Portugal.

Pal, K. (2019). Algorithmic Solutions for RFID Tag Anti-Collision Problem in Supply Chain Management. *Procedia Computer Science*, 929-934.

Pal, K. (2020a). Ontology-Assisted Enterprise Information Systems Integration in Manufacturing Supply Chain. In Handbook of Research on Developments and Trends in Industrial and Material Engineering. IGI Global.

Pal, K. (2020b). Information Sharing for Manufacturing Supply Chain Management Based on Blockchain Technology. In Cross-industry Use of Blockchain Technology and Opportunities for the Future. IGI Global.

Pal, K., & Karakostas, B. (2014). A Multi Agent-based Service Framework for supply Chain Management. *Procedia Computer Science, 32*, 53-60.

Pal, K. (2017). Supply Chain Coordination Based on Web Services. In H. K. Chan, N. Subramanian, & M. D. Abdulrahman (Eds.), *Supply Chain Management in the Big Data Era* (pp. 137–171). IGI Global Publication. doi:10.4018/978-1-5225-0956-1.ch009

Pal, K. (2020). Information sharing for manufacturing supply chain management based on blockchain technology. In *Cross-Industry Use of Blockchain Technology and Opportunities for the Future*. IGI Global.

Pal, K., & Palmer, O. (2000). A decision-support systems for business acquisition. *Decision Support Systems, 27*(4), 411–429. doi:10.1016/S0167-9236(99)00083-4

Pal, K., & Yasar, A. (2020). Internet of Things and blockchain technology in apparel manufacturing supply chain data management. *Procedia Computer Science, 170*, 450–457.

Pankaj, Ansari, & Kant. (2020). A Pythagorean fuzzy AHP approach and its application to evaluating the enablers of sustainable supply chain innovation. *Sustainable Production and Consumption, 23*, 77-93.

Papazoglou, M. (2012). *Web Services and SOA: Principles and Technology*. Pearson.

Parasuraman, A. (2004). Assessing and improving service performance for maximum impact: Insights from a two-decade-long research journey. *Performance Measurement and Metrics, 5*(2), 45–52. doi:10.1108/14678040410546064

Pathak, J., Koul, N., Caragea, D., & Honavar, V. G. (2005). A Framework for Semantic Web Services Discovery. *ACM International Workshop on Web Information and Data Management*, 45-50. 10.1145/1097047.1097057

Patil, A., Oundhaka, S., Sheth, A., & Verma, K. (2004). METEOR-S Web service Annotation Framework. *The Proceedings of the Thirteenth International World Wide Web Conference*, 553-562.

Pauchant, T. C., & Douville, R. (1994). Recent research in crisis management: A study of 24 authors' publications from 1986 to 1991. *Industrial and Environmental Crisis Quarterly, 7*, 43–61.

Pauchant, T., & Mitroff, I. (1992). *Transforming the crisis-prone organization*. Jossey-Bass.

Paul, S., & Venkateswaran, J. (2020). Designing robust policies under deep uncertainty for mitigating epidemics. *Computers & Industrial Engineering, 140*, 106221. doi:10.1016/j.cie.2019.106221

Pedersen, E. R. G., Henriksen, M. H., Frier, C., Søby, J., & Jennings, V. (2013). Stakeholder thinking in sustainability management: The case of Novozymes. *Social Responsibility Journal, 9*(4), 500–515. doi:10.1108/SRJ-08-2012-0101

Penthin, S., & Dillman, R. (2015). *Digital SCM*. Academic Press.

Porter, M. (1985). *The value chain. The Value Chain and Competitive advantage: creating and sustaining superior performance*. Academic Press.

Pournader, M., Kach, A., & Talluri, S. (2020). A review of the existing and emerging topics in the supply chain risk management literature. *Decision Sciences*, *51*(4), 867–919. doi:10.1111/deci.12470

Prajogo, D. I. (2005). The comparative analysis of TQM practices and quality performance between manufacturing and service firms. *International Journal of Service Industry Management*, *16*(3), 217–228. doi:10.1108/09564230510601378

Prater, E., Biehl, M., & Smith, M. A. (2001). International supply chain agility—Tradeoffs between flexibility and uncertainty. *International Journal of Operations & Production Management*, *21*, 823–839.

Psomas, E. L., & Jaca, C. (2016). The impact of total quality management on service company performance: Evidence from Spain. *International Journal of Quality & Reliability Management*, *33*(3), 380–398. doi:10.1108/IJQRM-07-2014-0090

Qrunfleh, S., & Tarafdar, M. (2013). Lean and agile supply chain strategies and supply chain responsiveness: The role of strategic supplier partnership and postponement. *Supply Chain Management*, *18*, 571–582.

Queiroz, M. M., Ivanov, D., Dolgui, A., & Wamba, S. F. (2020). Impacts of epidemic outbreaks on supply chains: Mapping a research agenda amid the COVID-19 pandemic through a structured literature review. *Annals of Operations Research*, 1–38. PMID:32836615

Radhoui, Taghipour, & Canel. (2018). *The distribution and pickup of goods- a literature review and survey in Hierarchical Planning and Information Sharing Techniques in Supply Chain Management.* IGI Global.

Radhoui, H., Taghipour, A., & Canel, B. (2018). Vehicle routing problem with delivery and pickup of goods in general transport system: A literature review and survey. *Transport Reviews*.

Ramanathan, R. (2007). Supplier selection problem: Integrating DEA with the approaches of the total cost of ownership and AHP. *Supply Chain Management*, *12*, 258–261.

Reategui, E. B., & Campbell, J. A. (1995). A Classification System for Credit Card Transactions. In *Advances in Case-Based Reasoning: Second European Workshop (EWCBR-94)*. Springer. 10.1007/3-540-60364-6_43

Rejeb, A. (2018). Blockchain Potential in Tilapia Supply Chain in Ghana. *Acta Tech. Jaurinensis*, *11*(2), 104–118. doi:10.14513/actatechjaur.v11.n2.462

Ren, Z., Taghipour, A., & Canel-Depitre, B. (2016, October). Information sharing in supply chain under uncertainty. In *2016 6th International Conference on Information Communication and Management (ICICM)* (pp. 67-71). IEEE. 10.1109/INFOCOMAN.2016.7784217

Ribeiro da Silva, E., Shinohara, A. C., Pinheiro de Lima, E., Angelis, J., & Machado, C. G. (2019). Reviewing Digital Manufacturing concept in the Industry 4.0 paradigm. *Procedia CIRP*, *81*, 240–245.

Richey, R. G. Jr, Morgan, T. R., Lindsey-Hall, K., & Adams, F. G. (2016). A global exploration of big data in the supply chain. *International Journal of Physical Distribution & Logistics Management*, *46*(8), 710–739. doi:10.1108/IJPDLM-05-2016-0134

Ritter, T., & Pedersen, C. L. (2020). Digitization capability and the digitalization of business models in business-to-business firms: Past, present, and future. *Industrial Marketing Management*, *86*, 180–190. doi:10.1016/j.indmarman.2019.11.019

Roman, D., Keller, U., Lausen, H., de Bruijn, J., Lara, R., Stollberg, M., Polleres, A., Feier, C., Bussler, C., & Fensel, D. (2005). Web service modeling ontology. *Applied Ontology*, *1*(1), 77–106.

Roman, D., Kopecky, J., Vitvar, T., Domingue, J., & Fensel, D. (2015). WSMO-Lite and hRESTS: Lightweight semantic annotations for Web services and RESTful APIs. *Journal of Web Semantics*, *31*, 39–58. doi:10.1016/j.websem.2014.11.006

Roubini, N. (2015). *Labor in the Digital Age (Part 1 and Part 2)*. Roubini Global Economics.

Ryals, L. J., & Humphries, A. S. (2007). Managing key business-to-business relationships: What marketing can learn from supply chain management. *Journal of Service Research*, *9*(4), 312–326. doi:10.1177/1094670507299380

Saaty, T. L. (1980). *The Analytic Hierarchy Process: Planning, Priority Setting, Resource Allocation*. McGraw-Hill International Book Co.

Sahai, A., & Waters, B. (2005). Fuzzy identity-based encryption. In *Annual International Conference on the Theory and Applications of Cryptographic Techniques*. Springer.

Schrauf, S., & Berttram, P. (2016). *Industry 4.0: How digitization makes the supply chain more efficient, agile, and customer-focused*. Strategy & Recuperado de https://www. strategyand. pwc. com/media/file/Industry4.0.pdf

Scuotto, V., Caputo, F., Villasalero, M., & Del Giudice, M. (2017). A multiple buyer–supplier relationship in the context of SMEs' digital supply chain management. *Production Planning and Control*, *28*(16), 1378–1388. doi:10.1080/09537287.2017.1375149

Sharma, M. K., & Bhagwat, R. (2007). An integrated BSC-AHP approach for supply chain management evaluation. *Measuring Business Excellence*, *11*, 57–68.

Sharma, P. K., Singh, S., Jeong, Y. S., & Park, J. H. (2017). DistBlockNet: A Distributed Blockchains-Based Secure SDN Architecture for IoT Networks. *IEEE Communication Management*, *55*(9), 78–85. doi:10.1109/MCOM.2017.1700041

Shaw, K., Shankar, R., Yadav, S. S., & Thakur, L. S. (2012). Supplier selection using fuzzy AHP and fuzzy multi-objective linear programming for developing the low carbon supply chain. *Expert Systems with Applications*, *39*, 8182–8192.

Shingo, S. (1988). *Non-Stock Production*. Productivity Press.

Shivajee, V., Singh, R. K., & Rastogi, S. (2019). Manufacturing conversion cost reduction using quality control tools and digitization of real-time data. *Journal of Cleaner Production*, *237*, 117678.

Shiyong, W. S., Wan, J., Li, D., & Zhang, C. (2016). Implementing smart factory of industry 4.0: An outlook. *International Journal of Distributed Sensor Networks*, *12*(1), 3159805. doi:10.1155/2016/3159805

Shrivastava, P. (1993). Crisis theory/practice: Towards a sustainable future. *Industrial and Environmental Crisis Quarterly*, *7*, 23–42.

Shrivastava, P., Mitroff, I., Miller, D., & Miglani, A. (1988). Understanding industrial crises. *Journal of Management Studies*, *25*, 285–303.

Shrouf, F., Ordieres, J., & Miragliotta, G. (2014). Smart factories in Industry 4.0: A review of the concept and of energy management approached in production based on the Internet of Things paradigm. *Proceedings of the IEEE International Conference on Industrial Engineering and Engineering Management*, 679–701. 10.1109/IEEM.2014.7058728

Siggelkow, N. (2007). Persuasion with case studies. *Academy of Management Journal*, *50*(1), 20–24. doi:10.5465/amj.2007.24160882

Silvestro, R. (1998). The manufacturing TQM and service quality literatures: Synergistic or conflicting paradigms? *International Journal of Quality & Reliability Management*, *15*(3), 303–328. doi:10.1108/02656719810198917

Simon, H., & Schumann, H. (2001). *Pricing opportunities in the digital age.* Academic Press.

Singh, K., & Singh Ahuja, I. (2014). Effectiveness of TPM implementation with and without integration with TQM in Indian manufacturing industries. *Journal of Quality in Maintenance Engineering*, *20*(4), 415–435. doi:10.1108/JQME-01-2013-0003

Singh, P. J., Feng, M., & Smith, A. (2006). ISO 9000 series of standards: Comparison of manufacturing and service organizations. *International Journal of Quality & Reliability Management*, *23*(2), 122–142. doi:10.1108/02656710610640916

Skoutas, D., Simitsis, A., & Sellis, T. (2007). A Ranking Mechanism for Semantic Web Service Discovery. *IEEE Congress on Services*, 41-48. 10.1109/SERVICES.2007.8

Studer, R., Benjamins, V. R., & Fensel, D. (1998). Knowledge engineering: Principles and methods. *Data & Knowledge Engineering*, *25*(1-2), 161–197. doi:10.1016/S0169-023X(97)00056-6

Sun, C. (2012). Application of RFID technology for logistics on the internet of things. *AASRI Procedia*, *1*, 106–111.

Sung, T. K. (2018). Industry 4.0: A Korea perspective. *Technological Forecasting and Social Change*, *132*, 40–45.

Sureshchandar, G. S., Rajendran, C., & Anantharaman, R. N. (2001). A conceptual model for total quality management in service organizations. *Total Quality Management, 12*(3), 343–363. doi:10.1080/09544120120034492

Syam, N., & Sharma, A. (2018). Waiting for a sales renaissance in the fourth industrial revolution: Machine learning and artificial intelligence in sales research and practice. *Industrial Marketing Management, 69*, 135–146. doi:10.1016/j.indmarman.2017.12.019

Sycara, K. P., Paolucci, M., Ankolekar, A., & Srinivasan, N. (2003). Automated Discovery, Interaction and Computation of Semanticmweb Services. *Journal of Web Semantics, 1*(1), 27–46. doi:10.1016/j.websem.2003.07.002

Sycara, K., Widoff, S., Klusch, M., & Lu, J. (2002). LARKS: Dynamic Matching Among Heterogeneous Software Agents in Cyberspace. *Autonomous Agents and Multi-Agent Systems, 5*(2), 173–203. doi:10.1023/A:1014897210525

Szabo, N. (1994). *Smart Contracts*. Available online: https://archive.is/zQ1p8

Taghipour, A. (2009). Évaluation de la collaboration dans une chaîne d'approvisionnement. *Revue française de gestion industrielle, 28*(1), 25-42.

Taghipour, A. (2012). *Supply Chain Management: Coordination of Operations Planning*. Lambert Academic Publishing.

Taghipour. (2018). *Operations, and Management Science, Hierarchical Planning and Information Sharing Techniques in Supply Chain Management*. IGI Global. . doi:10.4018/978-1-5225-7299-2

Taghipour. (2020). *Demand Forecasting and Order Planning in Supply Chains and Humanitarian Logistics*. IGI Global.

Taghipour, A. (2014). Production Network Planning Based on Constraint Relaxation and Discount Approach. *Lecture Notes on Information Theory, 02*(03), 279–282. doi:10.12720/lnit.2.3.279-282

Taghipour, A. (2014a, June). Globally improvement of upstream planning in manufacturing networks. In *2014 International Conference on Logistics Operations Management* (pp. 15-19). IEEE. 10.1109/GOL.2014.6887441

Taghipour, A. (2014b). Improving the Plan of a Manufacturing Network with Non-Integrated Business Units. *International Journal of Applied Logistics, 5*(2), 1–11. doi:10.4018/ijal.2014040101

Taghipour, A. (2017). *Contemporary Approaches and Strategies for Applied Logistics: A contemporary approach to plan independent logistics actors*. IGI Global.

Taghipour, A. (2018). A Contemporary Approach to Plan Independent Logistics Actors. In *Contemporary Approaches and Strategies for Applied Logistics* (pp. 337–364). IGI Global. doi:10.4018/978-1-5225-5273-4.ch014

Taghipour, A., & Frayret, J. M. (2011). A new heuristic search with local optimization to manage a supply chain. *Meta*, 15.

Taghipour, A., & Frayret, J. M. (2012). Mutual adju tment search with incentive for supply chain planning coordination. *International Journal of Computer Integrated Manufacturing*, *25*(10), 946–962. doi:10.1080/0951192X.2011.646307

Taghipour, A., & Frayret, J. M. (2013). Coordination of operations planning in supply chains: A review. *International Journal of Business Performance and Supply Chain Modelling*, *5*(3), 272–307. doi:10.1504/IJBPSCM.2013.055729

Taghipour, A., & Frayret, J. M. (2013). Dynamic mutual adjustment search for supply chain operations planning co-ordination. *International Journal of Production Research*, *51*(9), 2715–2739. doi:10.1080/00207543.2012.737952

Taghipour, A., Hoang, P., & Cao, X. (2020). Just in Time/Lean Purchasing Approach: An investigation for research and applications. *Journal of Advanced Management Science*, *8*(2), 2020.

Talib, F. (2013). An overview of total quality management: Understanding the fundamentals in service organization. *International Journal of Advanced Quality Management*, *1*(1), 1–20.

Tang, C. S., & Zhou, S. (2012). Research advances in environmentally and socially sustainable operations. *European Journal of Operational Research*, *223*(3), 585–594.

Tang, S. Y., Gurnani, H., & Gupta, D. (2014). Managing disruptions in decentralized supply chains with endogenous supply process reliability. *Production and Operations Management*, *23*(7), 1198–1211. doi:10.1111/poms.12160

Telukdarie, A., Buhula, E., Baga, S., Gupta, S., & Luo, Z. (2018). Industry 4.0 implementation for multinationals. *Process Safety and Environmental Protection*, *118*, 316–329. doi:10.1016/j.psep.2018.06.030

Tliche, Taghipour, & Canel. (2018). *Anticipation of Demand in Supply Chains in Hierarchical Planning and Information Sharing Techniques in Supply Chain Management*. IGI Global.

Tliche, Taghipour, & Canel. (2020). Exploring a downstream demand inference strategy in a decentralized two-level supply chain. In *Demand Forecasting and Order Planning in Supply Chains and Humanitarian Logistics*. IGI Global.

Tliche, Y., Taghipour, A., & Canel-Depitre, B. (2019). Anticipation of Demand in Supply Chains. In *Hierarchical Planning and Information Sharing Techniques in Supply Chain Management* (pp. 1–45). IGI Global. doi:10.4018/978-1-5225-7299-2.ch001

Tliche, Y., Taghipour, A., & Canel-Depitre, B. (2019). Downstream Demand Inference in decentralized supply chains. *European Journal of Operational Research*, *274*(1), 65–77. doi:10.1016/j.ejor.2018.09.034

Tliche, Y., Taghipour, A., & Canel-Depitre, B. (2020). An improved forecasting approach to reduce inventory levels in decentralized supply chains. *European Journal of Operational Research*, *287*(2), 511–527. doi:10.1016/j.ejor.2020.04.044

Tse, D., Zhang, B., Yang, Y., Cheng, C., & My, H. (2017). Blockchain application in food supply information security. *Proceedings of the IEEE International Conference on Industrial Engineering and Engineering Management (IEEM 2017)*, 1357–1361. 10.1109/IEEM.2017.8290114

Tyrrell, D. A. J., & Bynoe, M. L. (1966). Cultivation of viruses from a high proportion of patients with colds. *Lancet*, *287*(7428), 76–77. doi:10.1016/S0140-6736(66)92364-6 PMID:4158999

Tzounis, A., Katsoulas, N., Bartzanas, T., & Kittas, C. (2017). Internet of things in agriculture, recent advances, and future challenges. *Biosystems Engineering*, *164*, 31–48. doi:10.1016/j.biosystemseng.2017.09.007

UN Capital Development Fund (UNCDF). (n.d.). Available online: https://www.uncdf.org/financial-inclusion)

United Nations Conference on Trade and Development (UNCTAD). (2015). *Information Economy Report 2015 Unlocking the Potential of E-Commerce for Developing Countries*. https://unctad.org/en/PublicationsLibrary/ier2015_en.pdf

Urbach, N., & Ahlemann, F. (2019). *IT Management in the Digital Age: A Roadmap for the IT Department of the Future*. Springer., doi:10.1007/978-3-319-96187-3

Utterback, J. M., & Abernathy, W. J. (1975). A dynamic model of process and product innovation. *Omega*, *3*(6), 639–656. doi:10.1016/0305-0483(75)90068-7

Varelas, G., Voutsakis, E., Raftopoulou, P., Petrakis, E. G. M., & Milios, E. (2005). Semantic Similarity methods in WordNet and their application to information retrieval on the Web. *Proceedings of the 7th annual ACM international workshop on web information and data management*. 10.1145/1097047.1097051

Vargo, S. L., & Lusch, R. F. (2011). It's all B2B… and beyond: Toward a systems perspective of the market. *Industrial Marketing Management*, *40*(2), 181–187. doi:10.1016/j.indmarman.2010.06.026

Verma, K., Sivashanmugam, K., Sheth, A., Patil, A., Oundhakar, S., & Miller, J. (2005). METEOR-S WSDI: A Scalable P2P Infrastructure of Registries for Semantic Publication and Discovery of Web Services. *Information Technology and Management*, *6*(1), 17–39. doi:10.100710799-004-7773-4

Vosooghidizaji, M., Taghipour, A., & Canel-Depitre, B. (2020). Supply chain coordination under information asymmetry: A review. *International Journal of Production Research*, *58*(6), 1805–1834. doi:10.1080/00207543.2019.1685702

Vosooghidizaji, M., Taghipour, A., & Canel-Depitre, B. (2020, December). Information Asymmetry in Supply Chain Coordination: State of the Art. *Journal of Industrial and Intelligent Information*, *8*(2), 38–43. doi:10.18178/jiii.8.2.38-43

Vrijhoef, R., & Koskela, L. (1999). Role of supply chain management in construction. *Proceedings of the Seventh Annual Conference of the International Group for Lean Construction*, 133-146.

Waller, M. A., & Fawcett, S. E. (2013). Data science, predictive analytics, and big data: A revolution that will transform supply chain design and management. *Journal of Business Logistics, 34*(2), 77–84. doi:10.1111/jbl.12010

Walsh, W. E., & Wellman, M. P. (2003). Decentralized supply chain formation: A market protocol and competitive equilibrium analysis. *Journal of Artificial Intelligence Research, 19*, 513–567. doi:10.1613/jair.1213

Wang, Q., Qin, B., Hu, J., & Xiao, F. (2017, Sept.). Preserving transaction privacy in bitcoin. *Future Generation Computer Systems*.

Wang, L., & Cao, J. (2007). Web Services Semantic Searching enhanced by Case Based Reasoning. *18th International Workshop on Database and Expert Systems Applications*.

Wang, P., Jin, Z., Liu, L., & Cai, G. (2008). Building Toward Capability Specifications of Web Services Based on an Environment Ontology. *IEEE Transactions on Knowledge and Data Engineering, 20*(4), 547–561. doi:10.1109/TKDE.2007.190719

Wang, S. J., Liu, S. F., & Wang, W. L. (2008). The simulated impact of RFID-enabled supply chain on pull-based inventory replenishment in TFT-LCD industry. *International Journal of Production Economics, 112*(2), 570–586. doi:10.1016/j.ijpe.2007.05.002

Wang, S., Zhang, Y., & Zhang, Y. (2018). A blockchain-based framework for data sharing with fine-grained access control in decentralised storage systems. *IEEE Access: Practical Innovations, Open Solutions, 6*, 38437–38450. doi:10.1109/ACCESS.2018.2851611

Wang, W., Wang, Y., Mo, D., & Tseng, M. M. (2017). Managing component reuse in remanufacturing under product diffusion dynamics. *International Journal of Production Economics, 183*, 551–560.

Washington, L. C. (2008). *Elliptic Curves: Number Theory and Cryptography* (2nd ed.). Chapman & Hall/CRC. doi:10.1201/9781420071474

Watson, I. (1997). *Applying Case-Based Reasoning: Techniques for Enterprise Systems*. Morgan Kaufman.

Wieland, A., Handfield, R. B., & Durach, C. F. (2016). Mapping the landscape of future research themes in supply chain management. *Journal of Business Logistics, 37*, 205–212.

Witkowski, K. (2017). Internet of Things, Big Data, Industry 4.0 - Innovative Solutions in Logistics and Supply Chains Management. *Procedia Engineering, 2017*(182), 763–769. doi:10.1016/j.proeng.2017.03.197

Wooldridge, M., & Jennings, N. (1995). Intelligent Agents: Theory and Practice. *The Knowledge Engineering Review, 10*(2), 115–152. doi:10.1017/S0269888900008122

Woon, K. C. (2000). TQM implementation: Comparing Singapore's service and manufacturing leaders. *Managing Service Quality, 10*(5), 318–331. doi:10.1108/09604520010345777

World Bank Group. (2016). *World development report 2016: digital dividends*. World Bank Publications.

WSDL-S. (2005). http://www.w3.org/Submission/WSDL-S/

Xu, J. (2014). *Managing digital enterprise: ten essential topics*. Springer. doi:10.2991/978-94-6239-094-2

Yan-e, D. (2011). Design of intelligent agriculture management information system based on IoT. *Proceedings of the 2011 Fourth International Conference on Intelligent Computation Technology and Automation*, 1, 1045–1049. 10.1109/ICICTA.2011.262

Yi, C. Y., Ngai, E. W. T., & Moon, K. L. (2011). Supply chain flexibility in an uncertain environment: Exploratory from five case studies. *Supply Chain Management*, *16*, 271–283.

Yin, W., Wen, Q., Li, W., Zhang, H., & Jin, Z. (2018). An Anti-Quantum Transaction Authentication Approach in Blockchain. *IEEE Access: Practical Innovations, Open Solutions*, *6*, 5393–5401. doi:10.1109/ACCESS.2017.2788411

Yongquan, S., Xi, C., He, R., Yingchao, J., & Quanwu, L. (2016). Ordering decision-making methods on spare parts for a new aircraft fleet based on a two-sample prediction. *Reliability Engineering & System Safety*, *156*, 40–50.

Zhang, W. Y., Cai, M., Qiu, J., & Yin, J. W. (2009). Managing distributed manufacturing knowledge through multi-perspective modelling for Semantic Web applications. *International Journal of Production Research*, *47*(23), 6525–6542. doi:10.1080/00207540802311114

Zhang, Y., Qu, T., Ho, O., & Huang, G. Q. (2011). Real-time work-in-progress management for the smart object-enabled ubiquitous shop-floor environment. *International Journal of Computer Integrated Manufacturing*, *24*(5), 431–445.

Zheng, M., & Wu, K. (2017). Smart spare parts management systems in semiconductor manufacturing. *Industrial Management & Data Systems*, *117*(4), 754–763.

Zhong, R. Y., Huang, G. Q., Lan, S., Dai, Q. Y., Chen, X., & Zhang, T. (2015). A big data approach for logistics trajectory discovery from RFID-enabled production data. *International Journal of Production Economics*, *165*, 260–272.

Zhou, Z. (2012). Applying RFID to reduce bullwhip effect in a FMCG supply chain. *Proceedings of the Advances in Computational Environment Science*.

Zhu, S. X. (2015). Integration of capacity, pricing, and lead-time decisions in a decentralized supply chain. *International Journal of Production Economics*, *164*, 14–23. doi:10.1016/j.ijpe.2015.02.026

Ziegeldorf, J. H., Matzutt, R., Henze, M., Grossmann, F., & Wehrle, K. (2018). Secure and anonymous decentralized Bitcoin mixing. *Future Generation Computer Systems*, *80*, 448–466. doi:10.1016/j.future.2016.05.018

Related References

To continue our tradition of advancing information science and technology research, we have compiled a list of recommended IGI Global readings. These references will provide additional information and guidance to further enrich your knowledge and assist you with your own research and future publications.

Abtahi, M. S., Behboudi, L., & Hasanabad, H. M. (2017). Factors Affecting Internet Advertising Adoption in Ad Agencies. *International Journal of Innovation in the Digital Economy*, *8*(4), 18–29. doi:10.4018/IJIDE.2017100102

Agrawal, S. (2017). The Impact of Emerging Technologies and Social Media on Different Business(es): Marketing and Management. In O. Rishi & A. Sharma (Eds.), *Maximizing Business Performance and Efficiency Through Intelligent Systems* (pp. 37–49). Hershey, PA: IGI Global. doi:10.4018/978-1-5225-2234-8.ch002

Alnoukari, M., Razouk, R., & Hanano, A. (2016). BSC-SI: A Framework for Integrating Strategic Intelligence in Corporate Strategic Management. *International Journal of Social and Organizational Dynamics in IT*, *5*(2), 1–14. doi:10.4018/IJSODIT.2016070101

Alnoukari, M., Razouk, R., & Hanano, A. (2016). BSC-SI, A Framework for Integrating Strategic Intelligence in Corporate Strategic Management. *International Journal of Strategic Information Technology and Applications*, *7*(1), 32–44. doi:10.4018/IJSITA.2016010103

Altındağ, E. (2016). Current Approaches in Change Management. In A. Goksoy (Ed.), *Organizational Change Management Strategies in Modern Business* (pp. 24–51). Hershey, PA: IGI Global. doi:10.4018/978-1-4666-9533-7.ch002

Alvarez-Dionisi, L. E., Turner, R., & Mittra, M. (2016). Global Project Management Trends. *International Journal of Information Technology Project Management, 7*(3), 54–73. doi:10.4018/IJITPM.2016070104

Anantharaman, R. N., Rajeswari, K. S., Angusamy, A., & Kuppusamy, J. (2017). Role of Self-Efficacy and Collective Efficacy as Moderators of Occupational Stress Among Software Development Professionals. *International Journal of Human Capital and Information Technology Professionals, 8*(2), 45–58. doi:10.4018/IJHCITP.2017040103

Aninze, F., El-Gohary, H., & Hussain, J. (2018). The Role of Microfinance to Empower Women: The Case of Developing Countries. *International Journal of Customer Relationship Marketing and Management, 9*(1), 54–78. doi:10.4018/IJCRMM.2018010104

Arsenijević, O. M., Orčić, D., & Kastratović, E. (2017). Development of an Optimization Tool for Intangibles in SMEs: A Case Study from Serbia with a Pilot Research in the Prestige by Milka Company. In M. Vemić (Ed.), *Optimal Management Strategies in Small and Medium Enterprises* (pp. 320–347). Hershey, PA: IGI Global. doi:10.4018/978-1-5225-1949-2.ch015

Aryanto, V. D., Wismantoro, Y., & Widyatmoko, K. (2018). Implementing Eco-Innovation by Utilizing the Internet to Enhance Firm's Marketing Performance: Study of Green Batik Small and Medium Enterprises in Indonesia. *International Journal of E-Business Research, 14*(1), 21–36. doi:10.4018/IJEBR.2018010102

Atiku, S. O., & Fields, Z. (2017). Multicultural Orientations for 21st Century Global Leadership. In N. Baporikar (Ed.), *Management Education for Global Leadership* (pp. 28–51). Hershey, PA: IGI Global. doi:10.4018/978-1-5225-1013-0.ch002

Atiku, S. O., & Fields, Z. (2018). Organisational Learning Dimensions and Talent Retention Strategies for the Service Industries. In N. Baporikar (Ed.), *Global Practices in Knowledge Management for Societal and Organizational Development* (pp. 358–381). Hershey, PA: IGI Global. doi:10.4018/978-1-5225-3009-1.ch017

Ávila, L., & Teixeira, L. (2018). The Main Concepts Behind the Dematerialization of Business Processes. In M. Khosrow-Pour, D.B.A. (Ed.), Encyclopedia of Information Science and Technology, Fourth Edition (pp. 888-898). Hershey, PA: IGI Global. doi:10.4018/978-1-5225-2255-3.ch076

Bartens, Y., Chunpir, H. I., Schulte, F., & Voß, S. (2017). Business/IT Alignment in Two-Sided Markets: A COBIT 5 Analysis for Media Streaming Business Models. In S. De Haes & W. Van Grembergen (Eds.), *Strategic IT Governance and Alignment in Business Settings* (pp. 82–111). Hershey, PA: IGI Global. doi:10.4018/978-1-5225-0861-8.ch004

Bashayreh, A. M. (2018). Organizational Culture and Organizational Performance. In W. Lee & F. Sabetzadeh (Eds.), *Contemporary Knowledge and Systems Science* (pp. 50–69). Hershey, PA: IGI Global. doi:10.4018/978-1-5225-5655-8.ch003

Bedford, D. A. (2018). Sustainable Knowledge Management Strategies: Aligning Business Capabilities and Knowledge Management Goals. In N. Baporikar (Ed.), *Global Practices in Knowledge Management for Societal and Organizational Development* (pp. 46–73). Hershey, PA: IGI Global. doi:10.4018/978-1-5225-3009-1.ch003

Benmoussa, F., Nakara, W. A., & Jaouen, A. (2016). The Use of Social Media by SMEs in the Tourism Industry. In I. Lee (Ed.), *Encyclopedia of E-Commerce Development, Implementation, and Management* (pp. 2159–2170). Hershey, PA: IGI Global. doi:10.4018/978-1-4666-9787-4.ch155

Berger, R. (2016). Indigenous Management and Bottom of Pyramid Countries: The Role of National Institutions. In U. Aung & P. Ordoñez de Pablos (Eds.), *Managerial Strategies and Practice in the Asian Business Sector* (pp. 107–123). Hershey, PA: IGI Global. doi:10.4018/978-1-4666-9758-4.ch007

Bharwani, S., & Musunuri, D. (2018). Reflection as a Process From Theory to Practice. In M. Khosrow-Pour, D.B.A. (Ed.), Encyclopedia of Information Science and Technology, Fourth Edition (pp. 1529-1539). Hershey, PA: IGI Global. doi:10.4018/978-1-5225-2255-3.ch132

Bhatt, G. D., Wang, Z., & Rodger, J. A. (2017). Information Systems Capabilities and Their Effects on Competitive Advantages: A Study of Chinese Companies. *Information Resources Management Journal*, *30*(3), 41–57. doi:10.4018/IRMJ.2017070103

Bhushan, M., & Yadav, A. (2017). Concept of Cloud Computing in ESB. In R. Bhadoria, N. Chaudhari, G. Tomar, & S. Singh (Eds.), *Exploring Enterprise Service Bus in the Service-Oriented Architecture Paradigm* (pp. 116–127). Hershey, PA: IGI Global. doi:10.4018/978-1-5225-2157-0.ch008

Bhushan, S. (2017). System Dynamics Base-Model of Humanitarian Supply Chain (HSCM) in Disaster Prone Eco-Communities of India: A Discussion on Simulation and Scenario Results. *International Journal of System Dynamics Applications*, *6*(3), 20–37. doi:10.4018/IJSDA.2017070102

Biswas, A., & De, A. K. (2017). On Development of a Fuzzy Stochastic Programming Model with Its Application to Business Management. In S. Trivedi, S. Dey, A. Kumar, & T. Panda (Eds.), *Handbook of Research on Advanced Data Mining Techniques and Applications for Business Intelligence* (pp. 353–378). Hershey, PA: IGI Global. doi:10.4018/978-1-5225-2031-3.ch021

Bücker, J., & Ernste, K. (2018). Use of Brand Heroes in Strategic Reputation Management: The Case of Bacardi, Adidas, and Daimler. In A. Erdemir (Ed.), *Reputation Management Techniques in Public Relations* (pp. 126–150). Hershey, PA: IGI Global. doi:10.4018/978-1-5225-3619-2.ch007

Bureš, V. (2018). Industry 4.0 From the Systems Engineering Perspective: Alternative Holistic Framework Development. In R. Brunet-Thornton & F. Martinez (Eds.), *Analyzing the Impacts of Industry 4.0 in Modern Business Environments* (pp. 199–223). Hershey, PA: IGI Global. doi:10.4018/978-1-5225-3468-6.ch011

Buzady, Z. (2017). Resolving the Magic Cube of Effective Case Teaching: Benchmarking Case Teaching Practices in Emerging Markets – Insights from the Central European University Business School, Hungary. In D. Latusek (Ed.), *Case Studies as a Teaching Tool in Management Education* (pp. 79–103). Hershey, PA: IGI Global. doi:10.4018/978-1-5225-0770-3.ch005

Campatelli, G., Richter, A., & Stocker, A. (2016). Participative Knowledge Management to Empower Manufacturing Workers. *International Journal of Knowledge Management, 12*(4), 37–50. doi:10.4018/IJKM.2016100103

Căpusneanu, S., & Topor, D. I. (2018). Business Ethics and Cost Management in SMEs: Theories of Business Ethics and Cost Management Ethos. In I. Oncioiu (Ed.), *Ethics and Decision-Making for Sustainable Business Practices* (pp. 109–127). Hershey, PA: IGI Global. doi:10.4018/978-1-5225-3773-1.ch007

Carneiro, A. (2016). Maturity in Health Organization Information Systems: Metrics and Privacy Perspectives. *International Journal of Privacy and Health Information Management, 4*(2), 1–18. doi:10.4018/IJPHIM.2016070101

Chan, R. L., Mo, P. L., & Moon, K. K. (2018). Strategic and Tactical Measures in Managing Enterprise Risks: A Study of the Textile and Apparel Industry. In K. Strang, M. Korstanje, & N. Vajjhala (Eds.), *Research, Practices, and Innovations in Global Risk and Contingency Management* (pp. 1–19). Hershey, PA: IGI Global. doi:10.4018/978-1-5225-4754-9.ch001

Chandan, H. C. (2016). Motivations and Challenges of Female Entrepreneurship in Developed and Developing Economies. In N. Baporikar (Ed.), *Handbook of Research on Entrepreneurship in the Contemporary Knowledge-Based Global Economy* (pp. 260–286). Hershey, PA: IGI Global. doi:10.4018/978-1-4666-8798-1.ch012

Charlier, S. D., Burke-Smalley, L. A., & Fisher, S. L. (2018). Undergraduate Programs in the U.S: A Contextual and Content-Based Analysis. In J. Mendy (Ed.), *Teaching Human Resources and Organizational Behavior at the College Level* (pp. 26–57). Hershey, PA: IGI Global. doi:10.4018/978-1-5225-2820-3.ch002

Chaudhuri, S. (2016). Application of Web-Based Geographical Information System (GIS) in E-Business. In U. Panwar, R. Kumar, & N. Ray (Eds.), *Handbook of Research on Promotional Strategies and Consumer Influence in the Service Sector* (pp. 389–405). Hershey, PA: IGI Global. doi:10.4018/978-1-5225-0143-5.ch023

Choudhuri, P. S. (2016). An Empirical Study on the Quality of Services Offered by the Private Life Insurers in Burdwan. In U. Panwar, R. Kumar, & N. Ray (Eds.), *Handbook of Research on Promotional Strategies and Consumer Influence in the Service Sector* (pp. 31–55). Hershey, PA: IGI Global. doi:10.4018/978-1-5225-0143-5.ch002

Dahlberg, T., Kivijärvi, H., & Saarinen, T. (2017). IT Investment Consistency and Other Factors Influencing the Success of IT Performance. In S. De Haes & W. Van Grembergen (Eds.), *Strategic IT Governance and Alignment in Business Settings* (pp. 176–208). Hershey, PA: IGI Global. doi:10.4018/978-1-5225-0861-8.ch007

Damnjanović, A. M. (2017). Knowledge Management Optimization through IT and E-Business Utilization: A Qualitative Study on Serbian SMEs. In M. Vemić (Ed.), *Optimal Management Strategies in Small and Medium Enterprises* (pp. 249–267). Hershey, PA: IGI Global. doi:10.4018/978-1-5225-1949-2.ch012

Daneshpour, H. (2017). Integrating Sustainable Development into Project Portfolio Management through Application of Open Innovation. In M. Vemić (Ed.), *Optimal Management Strategies in Small and Medium Enterprises* (pp. 370–387). Hershey, PA: IGI Global. doi:10.4018/978-1-5225-1949-2.ch017

Daniel, A. D., & Reis de Castro, V. (2018). Entrepreneurship Education: How to Measure the Impact on Nascent Entrepreneurs. In A. Carrizo Moreira, J. Guilherme Leitão Dantas, & F. Manuel Valente (Eds.), *Nascent Entrepreneurship and Successful New Venture Creation* (pp. 85–110). Hershey, PA: IGI Global. doi:10.4018/978-1-5225-2936-1.ch004

David, F., van der Sijde, P., & van den Besselaar, P. (2016). Enterpreneurial Incentives, Obstacles, and Management in University-Business Co-Operation: The Case of Indonesia. In J. Saiz-Álvarez (Ed.), *Handbook of Research on Social Entrepreneurship and Solidarity Economics* (pp. 499–518). Hershey, PA: IGI Global. doi:10.4018/978-1-5225-0097-1.ch024

David, R., Swami, B. N., & Tangirala, S. (2018). Ethics Impact on Knowledge Management in Organizational Development: A Case Study. In N. Baporikar (Ed.), *Global Practices in Knowledge Management for Societal and Organizational Development* (pp. 19–45). Hershey, PA: IGI Global. doi:10.4018/978-1-5225-3009-1.ch002

Delias, P., & Lakiotaki, K. (2018). Discovering Process Horizontal Boundaries to Facilitate Process Comprehension. *International Journal of Operations Research and Information Systems*, *9*(2), 1–31. doi:10.4018/IJORIS.2018040101

Denholm, J., & Lee-Davies, L. (2018). Success Factors for Games in Business and Project Management. In *Enhancing Education and Training Initiatives Through Serious Games* (pp. 34–68). Hershey, PA: IGI Global. doi:10.4018/978-1-5225-3689-5.ch002

Deshpande, M. (2017). Best Practices in Management Institutions for Global Leadership: Policy Aspects. In N. Baporikar (Ed.), *Management Education for Global Leadership* (pp. 1–27). Hershey, PA: IGI Global. doi:10.4018/978-1-5225-1013-0.ch001

Deshpande, M. (2018). Policy Perspectives for SMEs Knowledge Management. In N. Baporikar (Ed.), *Knowledge Integration Strategies for Entrepreneurship and Sustainability* (pp. 23–46). Hershey, PA: IGI Global. doi:10.4018/978-1-5225-5115-7.ch002

Dezdar, S. (2017). ERP Implementation Projects in Asian Countries: A Comparative Study on Iran and China. *International Journal of Information Technology Project Management*, *8*(3), 52–68. doi:10.4018/IJITPM.2017070104

Domingos, D., Martinho, R., & Varajão, J. (2016). Controlled Flexibility in Healthcare Processes: A BPMN-Extension Approach. In M. Cruz-Cunha, I. Miranda, R. Martinho, & R. Rijo (Eds.), *Encyclopedia of E-Health and Telemedicine* (pp. 521–535). Hershey, PA: IGI Global. doi:10.4018/978-1-4666-9978-6.ch040

Domingos, D., Respício, A., & Martinho, R. (2017). Reliability of IoT-Aware BPMN Healthcare Processes. In C. Reis & M. Maximiano (Eds.), *Internet of Things and Advanced Application in Healthcare* (pp. 214–248). Hershey, PA: IGI Global. doi:10.4018/978-1-5225-1820-4.ch008

Dosumu, O., Hussain, J., & El-Gohary, H. (2017). An Exploratory Study of the Impact of Government Policies on the Development of Small and Medium Enterprises in Developing Countries: The Case of Nigeria. *International Journal of Customer Relationship Marketing and Management, 8*(4), 51–62. doi:10.4018/IJCRMM.2017100104

Durst, S., Bruns, G., & Edvardsson, I. R. (2017). Retaining Knowledge in Smaller Building and Construction Firms. *International Journal of Knowledge and Systems Science, 8*(3), 1–12. doi:10.4018/IJKSS.2017070101

Edvardsson, I. R., & Durst, S. (2017). Outsourcing, Knowledge, and Learning: A Critical Review. *International Journal of Knowledge-Based Organizations, 7*(2), 13–26. doi:10.4018/IJKBO.2017040102

Edwards, J. S. (2018). Integrating Knowledge Management and Business Processes. In M. Khosrow-Pour, D.B.A. (Ed.), Encyclopedia of Information Science and Technology, Fourth Edition (pp. 5046-5055). Hershey, PA: IGI Global. doi:10.4018/978-1-5225-2255-3.ch437

Ejiogu, A. O. (2018). Economics of Farm Management. In *Agricultural Finance and Opportunities for Investment and Expansion* (pp. 56–72). Hershey, PA: IGI Global. doi:10.4018/978-1-5225-3059-6.ch003

Ekanem, I., & Abiade, G. E. (2018). Factors Influencing the Use of E-Commerce by Small Enterprises in Nigeria. *International Journal of ICT Research in Africa and the Middle East, 7*(1), 37–53. doi:10.4018/IJICTRAME.2018010103

Ekanem, I., & Alrossais, L. A. (2017). Succession Challenges Facing Family Businesses in Saudi Arabia. In P. Zgheib (Ed.), *Entrepreneurship and Business Innovation in the Middle East* (pp. 122–146). Hershey, PA: IGI Global. doi:10.4018/978-1-5225-2066-5.ch007

El Faquih, L., & Fredj, M. (2017). Ontology-Based Framework for Quality in Configurable Process Models. *Journal of Electronic Commerce in Organizations, 15*(2), 48–60. doi:10.4018/JECO.2017040104

El-Gohary, H., & El-Gohary, Z. (2016). An Attempt to Explore Electronic Marketing Adoption and Implementation Aspects in Developing Countries: The Case of Egypt. *International Journal of Customer Relationship Marketing and Management, 7*(4), 1–26. doi:10.4018/IJCRMM.2016100101

Entico, G. J. (2016). Knowledge Management and the Medical Health Librarians: A Perception Study. In J. Yap, M. Perez, M. Ayson, & G. Entico (Eds.), *Special Library Administration, Standardization and Technological Integration* (pp. 52–77). Hershey, PA: IGI Global. doi:10.4018/978-1-4666-9542-9.ch003

Faisal, M. N., & Talib, F. (2017). Building Ambidextrous Supply Chains in SMEs: How to Tackle the Barriers? *International Journal of Information Systems and Supply Chain Management, 10*(4), 80–100. doi:10.4018/IJISSCM.2017100105

Fernandes, T. M., Gomes, J., & Romão, M. (2017). Investments in E-Government: A Benefit Management Case Study. *International Journal of Electronic Government Research, 13*(3), 1–17. doi:10.4018/IJEGR.2017070101

Fouda, F. A. (2016). A Suggested Curriculum in Career Education to Develop Business Secondary Schools Students' Career Knowledge Management Domains and Professional Thinking. *International Journal of Technology Diffusion, 7*(2), 42–62. doi:10.4018/IJTD.2016040103

Gallardo-Vázquez, D., & Pajuelo-Moreno, M. L. (2016). How Spanish Universities are Promoting Entrepreneurship through Your Own Lines of Teaching and Research? In L. Carvalho (Ed.), *Handbook of Research on Entrepreneurial Success and its Impact on Regional Development* (pp. 431–454). Hershey, PA: IGI Global. doi:10.4018/978-1-4666-9567-2.ch019

Gao, S. S., Oreal, S., & Zhang, J. (2018). Contemporary Financial Risk Management Perceptions and Practices of Small-Sized Chinese Businesses. In I. Management Association (Ed.), Global Business Expansion: Concepts, Methodologies, Tools, and Applications (pp. 917-931). Hershey, PA: IGI Global. doi:10.4018/978-1-5225-5481-3.ch041

Garg, R., & Berning, S. C. (2017). Indigenous Chinese Management Philosophies: Key Concepts and Relevance for Modern Chinese Firms. In B. Christiansen & G. Koc (Eds.), *Transcontinental Strategies for Industrial Development and Economic Growth* (pp. 43–57). Hershey, PA: IGI Global. doi:10.4018/978-1-5225-2160-0.ch003

Gencer, Y. G. (2017). Supply Chain Management in Retailing Business. In U. Akkucuk (Ed.), *Ethics and Sustainability in Global Supply Chain Management* (pp. 197–210). Hershey, PA: IGI Global. doi:10.4018/978-1-5225-2036-8.ch011

Giacosa, E. (2016). Innovation in Luxury Fashion Businesses as a Means for the Regional Development. In L. Carvalho (Ed.), *Handbook of Research on Entrepreneurial Success and its Impact on Regional Development* (pp. 206–222). Hershey, PA: IGI Global. doi:10.4018/978-1-4666-9567-2.ch010

Giacosa, E. (2018). The Increasing of the Regional Development Thanks to the Luxury Business Innovation. In L. Carvalho (Ed.), *Handbook of Research on Entrepreneurial Ecosystems and Social Dynamics in a Globalized World* (pp. 260–273). Hershey, PA: IGI Global. doi:10.4018/978-1-5225-3525-6.ch011

Gianni, M., & Gotzamani, K. (2016). Integrated Management Systems and Information Management Systems: Common Threads. In P. Papajorgji, F. Pinet, A. Guimarães, & J. Papathanasiou (Eds.), *Automated Enterprise Systems for Maximizing Business Performance* (pp. 195–214). Hershey, PA: IGI Global. doi:10.4018/978-1-4666-8841-4.ch011

Gianni, M., Gotzamani, K., & Linden, I. (2016). How a BI-wise Responsible Integrated Management System May Support Food Traceability. *International Journal of Decision Support System Technology*, *8*(2), 1–17. doi:10.4018/IJDSST.2016040101

Glykas, M., & George, J. (2017). Quality and Process Management Systems in the UAE Maritime Industry. *International Journal of Productivity Management and Assessment Technologies*, *5*(1), 20–39. doi:10.4018/IJPMAT.2017010102

Glykas, M., Valiris, G., Kokkinaki, A., & Koutsoukou, Z. (2018). Banking Business Process Management Implementation. *International Journal of Productivity Management and Assessment Technologies*, *6*(1), 50–69. doi:10.4018/IJPMAT.2018010104

Gomes, J., & Romão, M. (2017). The Balanced Scorecard: Keeping Updated and Aligned with Today's Business Trends. *International Journal of Productivity Management and Assessment Technologies*, *5*(2), 1–15. doi:10.4018/IJPMAT.2017070101

Gomes, J., & Romão, M. (2017). Aligning Information Systems and Technology with Benefit Management and Balanced Scorecard. In S. De Haes & W. Van Grembergen (Eds.), *Strategic IT Governance and Alignment in Business Settings* (pp. 112–131). Hershey, PA: IGI Global. doi:10.4018/978-1-5225-0861-8.ch005

Grefen, P., & Turetken, O. (2017). Advanced Business Process Management in Networked E-Business Scenarios. *International Journal of E-Business Research*, *13*(4), 70–104. doi:10.4018/IJEBR.2017100105

Haider, A., & Saetang, S. (2017). Strategic IT Alignment in Service Sector. In S. Rozenes & Y. Cohen (Eds.), *Handbook of Research on Strategic Alliances and Value Co-Creation in the Service Industry* (pp. 231–258). Hershey, PA: IGI Global. doi:10.4018/978-1-5225-2084-9.ch012

Haider, A., & Tang, S. S. (2016). Maximising Value Through IT and Business Alignment: A Case of IT Governance Institutionalisation at a Thai Bank. *International Journal of Technology Diffusion*, *7*(3), 33–58. doi:10.4018/IJTD.2016070104

Hajilari, A. B., Ghadaksaz, M., & Fasghandis, G. S. (2017). Assessing Organizational Readiness for Implementing ERP System Using Fuzzy Expert System Approach. *International Journal of Enterprise Information Systems*, *13*(1), 67–85. doi:10.4018/IJEIS.2017010105

Haldorai, A., Ramu, A., & Murugan, S. (2018). Social Aware Cognitive Radio Networks: Effectiveness of Social Networks as a Strategic Tool for Organizational Business Management. In H. Bansal, G. Shrivastava, G. Nguyen, & L. Stanciu (Eds.), *Social Network Analytics for Contemporary Business Organizations* (pp. 188–202). Hershey, PA: IGI Global. doi:10.4018/978-1-5225-5097-6.ch010

Hall, O. P. Jr. (2017). Social Media Driven Management Education. *International Journal of Knowledge-Based Organizations*, *7*(2), 43–59. doi:10.4018/IJKBO.2017040104

Hanifah, H., Halim, H. A., Ahmad, N. H., & Vafaei-Zadeh, A. (2017). Innovation Culture as a Mediator Between Specific Human Capital and Innovation Performance Among Bumiputera SMEs in Malaysia. In N. Ahmad, T. Ramayah, H. Halim, & S. Rahman (Eds.), *Handbook of Research on Small and Medium Enterprises in Developing Countries* (pp. 261–279). Hershey, PA: IGI Global. doi:10.4018/978-1-5225-2165-5.ch012

Hartlieb, S., & Silvius, G. (2017). Handling Uncertainty in Project Management and Business Development: Similarities and Differences. In Y. Raydugin (Ed.), *Handbook of Research on Leveraging Risk and Uncertainties for Effective Project Management* (pp. 337–362). Hershey, PA: IGI Global. doi:10.4018/978-1-5225-1790-0.ch016

Hass, K. B. (2017). Living on the Edge: Managing Project Complexity. In Y. Raydugin (Ed.), *Handbook of Research on Leveraging Risk and Uncertainties for Effective Project Management* (pp. 177–201). Hershey, PA: IGI Global. doi:10.4018/978-1-5225-1790-0.ch009

Hassan, A., & Privitera, D. S. (2016). Google AdSense as a Mobile Technology in Education. In J. Holland (Ed.), *Wearable Technology and Mobile Innovations for Next-Generation Education* (pp. 200–223). Hershey, PA: IGI Global. doi:10.4018/978-1-5225-0069-8.ch011

Hassan, A., & Rahimi, R. (2016). Consuming "Innovation" in Tourism: Augmented Reality as an Innovation Tool in Digital Tourism Marketing. In N. Pappas & I. Bregoli (Eds.), *Global Dynamics in Travel, Tourism, and Hospitality* (pp. 130–147). Hershey, PA: IGI Global. doi:10.4018/978-1-5225-0201-2.ch008

Hawking, P., & Carmine Sellitto, C. (2017). Developing an Effective Strategy for Organizational Business Intelligence. In M. Tavana (Ed.), *Enterprise Information Systems and the Digitalization of Business Functions* (pp. 222–237). Hershey, PA: IGI Global. doi:10.4018/978-1-5225-2382-6.ch010

Hawking, P., & Sellitto, C. (2017). A Fast-Moving Consumer Goods Company and Business Intelligence Strategy Development. *International Journal of Enterprise Information Systems, 13*(2), 22–33. doi:10.4018/IJEIS.2017040102

Hawking, P., & Sellitto, C. (2017). Business Intelligence Strategy: Two Case Studies. *International Journal of Business Intelligence Research, 8*(2), 17–30. doi:10.4018/IJBIR.2017070102

Haynes, J. D., Arockiasamy, S., Al Rashdi, M., & Al Rashdi, S. (2016). Business and E Business Strategies for Coopetition and Thematic Management as a Sustained Basis for Ethics and Social Responsibility in Emerging Markets. In M. Al-Shammari & H. Masri (Eds.), *Ethical and Social Perspectives on Global Business Interaction in Emerging Markets* (pp. 25–39). Hershey, PA: IGI Global. doi:10.4018/978-1-4666-9864-2.ch002

Hee, W. J., Jalleh, G., Lai, H., & Lin, C. (2017). E-Commerce and IT Projects: Evaluation and Management Issues in Australian and Taiwanese Hospitals. *International Journal of Public Health Management and Ethics, 2*(1), 69–90. doi:10.4018/IJPHME.2017010104

Hernandez, A. A. (2018). Exploring the Factors to Green IT Adoption of SMEs in the Philippines. *Journal of Cases on Information Technology, 20*(2), 49–66. doi:10.4018/JCIT.2018040104

Hernandez, A. A., & Ona, S. E. (2016). Green IT Adoption: Lessons from the Philippines Business Process Outsourcing Industry. *International Journal of Social Ecology and Sustainable Development, 7*(1), 1–34. doi:10.4018/IJSESD.2016010101

Hollman, A., Bickford, S., & Hollman, T. (2017). Cyber InSecurity: A Post-Mortem Attempt to Assess Cyber Problems from IT and Business Management Perspectives. *Journal of Cases on Information Technology, 19*(3), 42–70. doi:10.4018/JCIT.2017070104

Igbinakhase, I. (2017). Responsible and Sustainable Management Practices in Developing and Developed Business Environments. In Z. Fields (Ed.), *Collective Creativity for Responsible and Sustainable Business Practice* (pp. 180–207). Hershey, PA: IGI Global. doi:10.4018/978-1-5225-1823-5.ch010

Ilahi, L., Ghannouchi, S. A., & Martinho, R. (2016). A Business Process Management Approach to Home Healthcare Processes: On the Gap between Intention and Reality. In M. Cruz-Cunha, I. Miranda, R. Martinho, & R. Rijo (Eds.), *Encyclopedia of E-Health and Telemedicine* (pp. 439–457). Hershey, PA: IGI Global. doi:10.4018/978-1-4666-9978-6.ch035

Iwata, J. J., & Hoskins, R. G. (2017). Managing Indigenous Knowledge in Tanzania: A Business Perspective. In P. Jain & N. Mnjama (Eds.), *Managing Knowledge Resources and Records in Modern Organizations* (pp. 198–214). Hershey, PA: IGI Global. doi:10.4018/978-1-5225-1965-2.ch012

Jabeen, F., Ahmad, S. Z., & Alkaabi, S. (2016). The Internationalization Decision-Making of United Arab Emirates Family Businesses. In N. Zakaria, A. Abdul-Talib, & N. Osman (Eds.), *Handbook of Research on Impacts of International Business and Political Affairs on the Global Economy* (pp. 1–22). Hershey, PA: IGI Global. doi:10.4018/978-1-4666-9806-2.ch001

Jain, P. (2017). Ethical and Legal Issues in Knowledge Management Life-Cycle in Business. In P. Jain & N. Mnjama (Eds.), *Managing Knowledge Resources and Records in Modern Organizations* (pp. 82–101). Hershey, PA: IGI Global. doi:10.4018/978-1-5225-1965-2.ch006

Jamali, D., Abdallah, H., & Matar, F. (2016). Opportunities and Challenges for CSR Mainstreaming in Business Schools. *International Journal of Technology and Educational Marketing*, *6*(2), 1–29. doi:10.4018/IJTEM.2016070101

James, S., & Hauli, E. (2017). Holistic Management Education at Tanzanian Rural Development Planning Institute. In N. Baporikar (Ed.), *Management Education for Global Leadership* (pp. 112–136). Hershey, PA: IGI Global. doi:10.4018/978-1-5225-1013-0.ch006

Janošková, M., Csikósová, A., & Čulková, K. (2018). Measurement of Company Performance as Part of Its Strategic Management. In R. Leon (Ed.), *Managerial Strategies for Business Sustainability During Turbulent Times* (pp. 309–335). Hershey, PA: IGI Global. doi:10.4018/978-1-5225-2716-9.ch017

Jean-Vasile, A., & Alecu, A. (2017). Theoretical and Practical Approaches in Understanding the Influences of Cost-Productivity-Profit Trinomial in Contemporary Enterprises. In A. Jean Vasile & D. Nicolò (Eds.), *Sustainable Entrepreneurship and Investments in the Green Economy* (pp. 28–62). Hershey, PA: IGI Global. doi:10.4018/978-1-5225-2075-7.ch002

Jha, D. G. (2016). Preparing for Information Technology Driven Changes. In S. Tiwari & L. Nafees (Eds.), *Innovative Management Education Pedagogies for Preparing Next-Generation Leaders* (pp. 258–274). Hershey, PA: IGI Global. doi:10.4018/978-1-4666-9691-4.ch015

Joia, L. A., & Correia, J. C. (2018). CIO Competencies From the IT Professional Perspective: Insights From Brazil. *Journal of Global Information Management, 26*(2), 74–103. doi:10.4018/JGIM.2018040104

Juma, A., & Mzera, N. (2017). Knowledge Management and Records Management and Competitive Advantage in Business. In P. Jain & N. Mnjama (Eds.), *Managing Knowledge Resources and Records in Modern Organizations* (pp. 15–28). Hershey, PA: IGI Global. doi:10.4018/978-1-5225-1965-2.ch002

K., I., & A, V. (2018). Monitoring and Auditing in the Cloud. In K. Munir (Ed.), *Cloud Computing Technologies for Green Enterprises* (pp. 318-350). Hershey, PA: IGI Global. doi:10.4018/978-1-5225-3038-1.ch013

Kabra, G., Ghosh, V., & Ramesh, A. (2018). Enterprise Integrated Business Process Management and Business Intelligence Framework for Business Process Sustainability. In A. Paul, D. Bhattacharyya, & S. Anand (Eds.), *Green Initiatives for Business Sustainability and Value Creation* (pp. 228–238). Hershey, PA: IGI Global. doi:10.4018/978-1-5225-2662-9.ch010

Kaoud, M. (2017). Investigation of Customer Knowledge Management: A Case Study Research. *International Journal of Service Science, Management, Engineering, and Technology, 8*(2), 12–22. doi:10.4018/IJSSMET.2017040102

Kara, M. E., & Fırat, S. Ü. (2016). Sustainability, Risk, and Business Intelligence in Supply Chains. In M. Erdoğdu, T. Arun, & I. Ahmad (Eds.), *Handbook of Research on Green Economic Development Initiatives and Strategies* (pp. 501–538). Hershey, PA: IGI Global. doi:10.4018/978-1-5225-0440-5.ch022

Katuu, S. (2018). A Comparative Assessment of Enterprise Content Management Maturity Models. In N. Gwangwava & M. Mutingi (Eds.), *E-Manufacturing and E-Service Strategies in Contemporary Organizations* (pp. 93–118). Hershey, PA: IGI Global. doi:10.4018/978-1-5225-3628-4.ch005

Khan, M. A. (2016). MNEs Management Strategies in Developing Countries: Establishing the Context. In M. Khan (Ed.), *Multinational Enterprise Management Strategies in Developing Countries* (pp. 1–33). Hershey, PA: IGI Global. doi:10.4018/978-1-5225-0276-0.ch001

Khan, M. A. (2016). Operational Approaches in Organizational Structure: A Case for MNEs in Developing Countries. In M. Khan (Ed.), *Multinational Enterprise Management Strategies in Developing Countries* (pp. 129–151). Hershey, PA: IGI Global. doi:10.4018/978-1-5225-0276-0.ch007

Kinnunen, S., Ylä-Kujala, A., Marttonen-Arola, S., Kärri, T., & Baglee, D. (2018). Internet of Things in Asset Management: Insights from Industrial Professionals and Academia. *International Journal of Service Science, Management, Engineering, and Technology*, *9*(2), 104–119. doi:10.4018/IJSSMET.2018040105

Klein, A. Z., Sabino de Freitas, A., Machado, L., Freitas, J. C. Jr, Graziola, P. G. Jr, & Schlemmer, E. (2017). Virtual Worlds Applications for Management Education. In L. Tomei (Ed.), *Exploring the New Era of Technology-Infused Education* (pp. 279–299). Hershey, PA: IGI Global. doi:10.4018/978-1-5225-1709-2.ch017

Kożuch, B., & Jabłoński, A. (2017). Adopting the Concept of Business Models in Public Management. In M. Lewandowski & B. Kożuch (Eds.), *Public Sector Entrepreneurship and the Integration of Innovative Business Models* (pp. 10–46). Hershey, PA: IGI Global. doi:10.4018/978-1-5225-2215-7.ch002

Kumar, J., Adhikary, A., & Jha, A. (2017). Small Active Investors' Perceptions and Preferences Towards Tax Saving Mutual Fund Schemes in Eastern India: An Empirical Note. *International Journal of Asian Business and Information Management*, *8*(2), 35–45. doi:10.4018/IJABIM.2017040103

Lassoued, Y., Bouzguenda, L., & Mahmoud, T. (2016). Context-Aware Business Process Versions Management. *International Journal of e-Collaboration*, *12*(3), 7–33. doi:10.4018/IJeC.2016070102

Lavassani, K. M., & Movahedi, B. (2017). Applications Driven Information Systems: Beyond Networks toward Business Ecosystems. *International Journal of Innovation in the Digital Economy*, *8*(1), 61–75. doi:10.4018/IJIDE.2017010104

Lazzareschi, V. H., & Brito, M. S. (2017). Strategic Information Management: Proposal of Business Project Model. In G. Jamil, A. Soares, & C. Pessoa (Eds.), *Handbook of Research on Information Management for Effective Logistics and Supply Chains* (pp. 59–88). Hershey, PA: IGI Global. doi:10.4018/978-1-5225-0973-8.ch004

Lederer, M., Kurz, M., & Lazarov, P. (2017). Usage and Suitability of Methods for Strategic Business Process Initiatives: A Multi Case Study Research. *International Journal of Productivity Management and Assessment Technologies*, *5*(1), 40–51. doi:10.4018/IJPMAT.2017010103

Lee, I. (2017). A Social Enterprise Business Model and a Case Study of Pacific Community Ventures (PCV). In V. Potocan, M. Ünğan, & Z. Nedelko (Eds.), *Handbook of Research on Managerial Solutions in Non-Profit Organizations* (pp. 182–204). Hershey, PA: IGI Global. doi:10.4018/978-1-5225-0731-4.ch009

Lee, L. J., & Leu, J. (2016). Exploring the Effectiveness of IT Application and Value Method in the Innovation Performance of Enterprise. *International Journal of Enterprise Information Systems*, *12*(2), 47–65. doi:10.4018/IJEIS.2016040104

Lee, Y. (2016). Alignment Effect of Entrepreneurial Orientation and Marketing Orientation on Firm Performance. *International Journal of Customer Relationship Marketing and Management*, *7*(4), 58–69. doi:10.4018/IJCRMM.2016100104

Leon, L. A., Seal, K. C., Przasnyski, Z. H., & Wiedenman, I. (2017). Skills and Competencies Required for Jobs in Business Analytics: A Content Analysis of Job Advertisements Using Text Mining. *International Journal of Business Intelligence Research*, *8*(1), 1–25. doi:10.4018/IJBIR.2017010101

Leu, J., Lee, L. J., & Krischke, A. (2016). Value Engineering-Based Method for Implementing the ISO14001 System in the Green Supply Chains. *International Journal of Strategic Decision Sciences*, *7*(4), 1–20. doi:10.4018/IJSDS.2016100101

Levy, C. L., & Elias, N. I. (2017). SOHO Users' Perceptions of Reliability and Continuity of Cloud-Based Services. In M. Moore (Ed.), *Cybersecurity Breaches and Issues Surrounding Online Threat Protection* (pp. 248–287). Hershey, PA: IGI Global. doi:10.4018/978-1-5225-1941-6.ch011

Levy, M. (2018). Change Management Serving Knowledge Management and Organizational Development: Reflections and Review. In N. Baporikar (Ed.), *Global Practices in Knowledge Management for Societal and Organizational Development* (pp. 256–270). Hershey, PA: IGI Global. doi:10.4018/978-1-5225-3009-1.ch012

Lewandowski, M. (2017). Public Organizations and Business Model Innovation: The Role of Public Service Design. In M. Lewandowski & B. Kożuch (Eds.), *Public Sector Entrepreneurship and the Integration of Innovative Business Models* (pp. 47–72). Hershey, PA: IGI Global. doi:10.4018/978-1-5225-2215-7.ch003

Lhannaoui, H., Kabbaj, M. I., & Bakkoury, Z. (2017). A Survey of Risk-Aware Business Process Modelling. *International Journal of Risk and Contingency Management, 6*(3), 14–26. doi:10.4018/IJRCM.2017070102

Li, J., Sun, W., Jiang, W., Yang, H., & Zhang, L. (2017). How the Nature of Exogenous Shocks and Crises Impact Company Performance?: The Effects of Industry Characteristics. *International Journal of Risk and Contingency Management, 6*(4), 40–55. doi:10.4018/IJRCM.2017100103

Lu, C., & Liu, S. (2016). Cultural Tourism O2O Business Model Innovation-A Case Study of CTrip. *Journal of Electronic Commerce in Organizations, 14*(2), 16–31. doi:10.4018/JECO.2016040102

Machen, B., Hosseini, M. R., Wood, A., & Bakhshi, J. (2016). An Investigation into using SAP-PS as a Multidimensional Project Control System (MPCS). *International Journal of Enterprise Information Systems, 12*(2), 66–81. doi:10.4018/IJEIS.2016040105

Malega, P. (2017). Small and Medium Enterprises in the Slovak Republic: Status and Competitiveness of SMEs in the Global Markets and Possibilities of Optimization. In M. Vemić (Ed.), *Optimal Management Strategies in Small and Medium Enterprises* (pp. 102–124). Hershey, PA: IGI Global. doi:10.4018/978-1-5225-1949-2.ch006

Malewska, K. M. (2017). Intuition in Decision-Making on the Example of a Non-Profit Organization. In V. Potocan, M. Ünğan, & Z. Nedelko (Eds.), *Handbook of Research on Managerial Solutions in Non-Profit Organizations* (pp. 378–399). Hershey, PA: IGI Global. doi:10.4018/978-1-5225-0731-4.ch018

Maroofi, F. (2017). Entrepreneurial Orientation and Organizational Learning Ability Analysis for Innovation and Firm Performance. In N. Baporikar (Ed.), *Innovation and Shifting Perspectives in Management Education* (pp. 144–165). Hershey, PA: IGI Global. doi:10.4018/978-1-5225-1019-2.ch007

Martins, P. V., & Zacarias, M. (2017). A Web-based Tool for Business Process Improvement. *International Journal of Web Portals, 9*(2), 68–84. doi:10.4018/IJWP.2017070104

Matthies, B., & Coners, A. (2017). Exploring the Conceptual Nature of e-Business Projects. *Journal of Electronic Commerce in Organizations, 15*(3), 33–63. doi:10.4018/JECO.2017070103

McKee, J. (2018). Architecture as a Tool to Solve Business Planning Problems. In M. Khosrow-Pour, D.B.A. (Ed.), Encyclopedia of Information Science and Technology, Fourth Edition (pp. 573-586). Hershey, PA: IGI Global. doi:10.4018/978-1-5225-2255-3.ch050

McMurray, A. J., Cross, J., & Caponecchia, C. (2018). The Risk Management Profession in Australia: Business Continuity Plan Practices. In N. Bajgoric (Ed.), *Always-On Enterprise Information Systems for Modern Organizations* (pp. 112–129). Hershey, PA: IGI Global. doi:10.4018/978-1-5225-3704-5.ch006

Meddah, I. H., & Belkadi, K. (2018). Mining Patterns Using Business Process Management. In R. Hamou (Ed.), *Handbook of Research on Biomimicry in Information Retrieval and Knowledge Management* (pp. 78–89). Hershey, PA: IGI Global. doi:10.4018/978-1-5225-3004-6.ch005

Mendes, L. (2017). TQM and Knowledge Management: An Integrated Approach Towards Tacit Knowledge Management. In D. Jaziri-Bouagina & G. Jamil (Eds.), *Handbook of Research on Tacit Knowledge Management for Organizational Success* (pp. 236–263). Hershey, PA: IGI Global. doi:10.4018/978-1-5225-2394-9.ch009

Mnjama, N. M. (2017). Preservation of Recorded Information in Public and Private Sector Organizations. In P. Jain & N. Mnjama (Eds.), *Managing Knowledge Resources and Records in Modern Organizations* (pp. 149–167). Hershey, PA: IGI Global. doi:10.4018/978-1-5225-1965-2.ch009

Mokoqama, M., & Fields, Z. (2017). Principles of Responsible Management Education (PRME): Call for Responsible Management Education. In Z. Fields (Ed.), *Collective Creativity for Responsible and Sustainable Business Practice* (pp. 229–241). Hershey, PA: IGI Global. doi:10.4018/978-1-5225-1823-5.ch012

Muniapan, B. (2017). Philosophy and Management: The Relevance of Vedanta in Management. In P. Ordóñez de Pablos (Ed.), *Managerial Strategies and Solutions for Business Success in Asia* (pp. 124–139). Hershey, PA: IGI Global. doi:10.4018/978-1-5225-1886-0.ch007

Muniapan, B., Gregory, M. L., & Ling, L. A. (2016). Marketing Education in Sarawak: Looking at It from the Employers' Viewpoint. In B. Smith & A. Porath (Eds.), *Global Perspectives on Contemporary Marketing Education* (pp. 112–130). Hershey, PA: IGI Global. doi:10.4018/978-1-4666-9784-3.ch008

Murad, S. E., & Dowaji, S. (2017). Using Value-Based Approach for Managing Cloud-Based Services. In A. Turuk, B. Sahoo, & S. Addya (Eds.), *Resource Management and Efficiency in Cloud Computing Environments* (pp. 33–60). Hershey, PA: IGI Global. doi:10.4018/978-1-5225-1721-4.ch002

Mutahar, A. M., Daud, N. M., Thurasamy, R., Isaac, O., & Abdulsalam, R. (2018). The Mediating of Perceived Usefulness and Perceived Ease of Use: The Case of Mobile Banking in Yemen. *International Journal of Technology Diffusion*, *9*(2), 21–40. doi:10.4018/IJTD.2018040102

Naidoo, V. (2017). E-Learning and Management Education at African Universities. In N. Baporikar (Ed.), *Management Education for Global Leadership* (pp. 181–201). Hershey, PA: IGI Global. doi:10.4018/978-1-5225-1013-0.ch009

Naidoo, V., & Igbinakhase, I. (2018). Opportunities and Challenges of Knowledge Retention in SMEs. In N. Baporikar (Ed.), *Knowledge Integration Strategies for Entrepreneurship and Sustainability* (pp. 70–94). Hershey, PA: IGI Global. doi:10.4018/978-1-5225-5115-7.ch004

Nayak, S., & Prabhu, N. (2017). Paradigm Shift in Management Education: Need for a Cross Functional Perspective. In N. Baporikar (Ed.), *Management Education for Global Leadership* (pp. 241–255). Hershey, PA: IGI Global. doi:10.4018/978-1-5225-1013-0.ch012

Ndede-Amadi, A. A. (2016). Student Interest in the IS Specialization as Predictor of the Success Potential of New Information Systems Programmes within the Schools of Business in Kenyan Public Universities. *International Journal of Information Systems and Social Change*, *7*(2), 63–79. doi:10.4018/IJISSC.2016040104

Nedelko, Z., & Potocan, V. (2016). Management Practices for Processes Optimization: Case of Slovenia. In G. Alor-Hernández, C. Sánchez-Ramírez, & J. García-Alcaraz (Eds.), *Handbook of Research on Managerial Strategies for Achieving Optimal Performance in Industrial Processes* (pp. 545–561). Hershey, PA: IGI Global. doi:10.4018/978-1-5225-0130-5.ch025

Nedelko, Z., & Potocan, V. (2017). Management Solutions in Non-Profit Organizations: Case of Slovenia. In V. Potocan, M. Ünğan, & Z. Nedelko (Eds.), *Handbook of Research on Managerial Solutions in Non-Profit Organizations* (pp. 1–22). Hershey, PA: IGI Global. doi:10.4018/978-1-5225-0731-4.ch001

Nedelko, Z., & Potocan, V. (2017). Priority of Management Tools Utilization among Managers: International Comparison. In V. Wang (Ed.), *Encyclopedia of Strategic Leadership and Management* (pp. 1083–1094). Hershey, PA: IGI Global. doi:10.4018/978-1-5225-1049-9.ch075

Nedelko, Z., Raudeliūnienė, J., & Črešnar, R. (2018). Knowledge Dynamics in Supply Chain Management. In N. Baporikar (Ed.), *Knowledge Integration Strategies for Entrepreneurship and Sustainability* (pp. 150–166). Hershey, PA: IGI Global. doi:10.4018/978-1-5225-5115-7.ch008

Nguyen, H. T., & Hipsher, S. A. (2018). Innovation and Creativity Used by Private Sector Firms in a Resources-Constrained Environment. In S. Hipsher (Ed.), *Examining the Private Sector's Role in Wealth Creation and Poverty Reduction* (pp. 219–238). Hershey, PA: IGI Global. doi:10.4018/978-1-5225-3117-3.ch010

Nycz, M., & Pólkowski, Z. (2016). Business Intelligence as a Modern IT Supporting Management of Local Government Units in Poland. *International Journal of Knowledge and Systems Science*, *7*(4), 1–18. doi:10.4018/IJKSS.2016100101

Obaji, N. O., Senin, A. A., & Olugu, M. U. (2016). Supportive Government Policy as a Mechanism for Business Incubation Performance in Nigeria. *International Journal of Information Systems and Social Change*, *7*(4), 52–66. doi:10.4018/IJISSC.2016100103

Obicci, P. A. (2017). Risk Sharing in a Partnership. In *Risk Management Strategies in Public-Private Partnerships* (pp. 115–152). Hershey, PA: IGI Global. doi:10.4018/978-1-5225-2503-5.ch004

Obidallah, W. J., & Raahemi, B. (2017). Managing Changes in Service Oriented Virtual Organizations: A Structural and Procedural Framework to Facilitate the Process of Change. *Journal of Electronic Commerce in Organizations*, *15*(1), 59–83. doi:10.4018/JECO.2017010104

Ojasalo, J., & Ojasalo, K. (2016). Service Logic Business Model Canvas for Lean Development of SMEs and Start-Ups. In N. Baporikar (Ed.), *Handbook of Research on Entrepreneurship in the Contemporary Knowledge-Based Global Economy* (pp. 217–243). Hershey, PA: IGI Global. doi:10.4018/978-1-4666-8798-1.ch010

Ojo, O. (2017). Impact of Innovation on the Entrepreneurial Success in Selected Business Enterprises in South-West Nigeria. *International Journal of Innovation in the Digital Economy*, *8*(2), 29–38. doi:10.4018/IJIDE.2017040103

Okdinawati, L., Simatupang, T. M., & Sunitiyoso, Y. (2017). Multi-Agent Reinforcement Learning for Value Co-Creation of Collaborative Transportation Management (CTM). *International Journal of Information Systems and Supply Chain Management*, *10*(3), 84–95. doi:10.4018/IJISSCM.2017070105

Ortner, E., Mevius, M., Wiedmann, P., & Kurz, F. (2016). Design of Interactional Decision Support Applications for E-Participation in Smart Cities. *International Journal of Electronic Government Research*, *12*(2), 18–38. doi:10.4018/IJEGR.2016040102

Pal, K. (2018). Building High Quality Big Data-Based Applications in Supply Chains. In A. Kumar & S. Saurav (Eds.), *Supply Chain Management Strategies and Risk Assessment in Retail Environments* (pp. 1–24). Hershey, PA: IGI Global. doi:10.4018/978-1-5225-3056-5.ch001

Palos-Sanchez, P. R., & Correia, M. B. (2018). Perspectives of the Adoption of Cloud Computing in the Tourism Sector. In J. Rodrigues, C. Ramos, P. Cardoso, & C. Henriques (Eds.), *Handbook of Research on Technological Developments for Cultural Heritage and eTourism Applications* (pp. 377–400). Hershey, PA: IGI Global. doi:10.4018/978-1-5225-2927-9.ch018

Parry, V. K., & Lind, M. L. (2016). Alignment of Business Strategy and Information Technology Considering Information Technology Governance, Project Portfolio Control, and Risk Management. *International Journal of Information Technology Project Management, 7*(4), 21–37. doi:10.4018/IJITPM.2016100102

Pashkova, N., Trujillo-Barrera, A., Apostolakis, G., Van Dijk, G., Drakos, P. D., & Baourakis, G. (2016). Business Management Models of Microfinance Institutions (MFIs) in Africa: A Study into Their Enabling Environments. *International Journal of Food and Beverage Manufacturing and Business Models, 1*(2), 63–82. doi:10.4018/IJFBMBM.2016070105

Patiño, B. E. (2017). New Generation Management by Convergence and Individual Identity: A Systemic and Human-Oriented Approach. In N. Baporikar (Ed.), *Innovation and Shifting Perspectives in Management Education* (pp. 119–143). Hershey, PA: IGI Global. doi:10.4018/978-1-5225-1019-2.ch006

Pawliczek, A., & Rössler, M. (2017). Knowledge of Management Tools and Systems in SMEs: Knowledge Transfer in Management. In A. Bencsik (Ed.), *Knowledge Management Initiatives and Strategies in Small and Medium Enterprises* (pp. 180–203). Hershey, PA: IGI Global. doi:10.4018/978-1-5225-1642-2.ch009

Pejic-Bach, M., Omazic, M. A., Aleksic, A., & Zoroja, J. (2018). Knowledge-Based Decision Making: A Multi-Case Analysis. In R. Leon (Ed.), *Managerial Strategies for Business Sustainability During Turbulent Times* (pp. 160–184). Hershey, PA: IGI Global. doi:10.4018/978-1-5225-2716-9.ch009

Perano, M., Hysa, X., & Calabrese, M. (2018). Strategic Planning, Cultural Context, and Business Continuity Management: Business Cases in the City of Shkoder. In A. Presenza & L. Sheehan (Eds.), *Geopolitics and Strategic Management in the Global Economy* (pp. 57–77). Hershey, PA: IGI Global. doi:10.4018/978-1-5225-2673-5.ch004

Pereira, R., Mira da Silva, M., & Lapão, L. V. (2017). IT Governance Maturity Patterns in Portuguese Healthcare. In S. De Haes & W. Van Grembergen (Eds.), *Strategic IT Governance and Alignment in Business Settings* (pp. 24–52). Hershey, PA: IGI Global. doi:10.4018/978-1-5225-0861-8.ch002

Perez-Uribe, R., & Ocampo-Guzman, D. (2016). Conflict within Colombian Family Owned SMEs: An Explosive Blend between Feelings and Business. In J. Saiz-Álvarez (Ed.), *Handbook of Research on Social Entrepreneurship and Solidarity Economics* (pp. 329–354). Hershey, PA: IGI Global. doi:10.4018/978-1-5225-0097-1.ch017

Pérez-Uribe, R. I., Torres, D. A., Jurado, S. P., & Prada, D. M. (2018). Cloud Tools for the Development of Project Management in SMEs. In R. Perez-Uribe, C. Salcedo-Perez, & D. Ocampo-Guzman (Eds.), *Handbook of Research on Intrapreneurship and Organizational Sustainability in SMEs* (pp. 95–120). Hershey, PA: IGI Global. doi:10.4018/978-1-5225-3543-0.ch005

Petrisor, I., & Cozmiuc, D. (2017). Global Supply Chain Management Organization at Siemens in the Advent of Industry 4.0. In L. Saglietto & C. Cezanne (Eds.), *Global Intermediation and Logistics Service Providers* (pp. 123–142). Hershey, PA: IGI Global. doi:10.4018/978-1-5225-2133-4.ch007

Pierce, J. M., Velliaris, D. M., & Edwards, J. (2017). A Living Case Study: A Journey Not a Destination. In N. Silton (Ed.), *Exploring the Benefits of Creativity in Education, Media, and the Arts* (pp. 158–178). Hershey, PA: IGI Global. doi:10.4018/978-1-5225-0504-4.ch008

Radosavljevic, M., & Andjelkovic, A. (2017). Multi-Criteria Decision Making Approach for Choosing Business Process for the Improvement: Upgrading of the Six Sigma Methodology. In J. Stanković, P. Delias, S. Marinković, & S. Rochhia (Eds.), *Tools and Techniques for Economic Decision Analysis* (pp. 225–247). Hershey, PA: IGI Global. doi:10.4018/978-1-5225-0959-2.ch011

Radovic, V. M. (2017). Corporate Sustainability and Responsibility and Disaster Risk Reduction: A Serbian Overview. In M. Camilleri (Ed.), *CSR 2.0 and the New Era of Corporate Citizenship* (pp. 147–164). Hershey, PA: IGI Global. doi:10.4018/978-1-5225-1842-6.ch008

Raghunath, K. M., Devi, S. L., & Patro, C. S. (2018). Impact of Risk Assessment Models on Risk Factors: A Holistic Outlook. In K. Strang, M. Korstanje, & N. Vajjhala (Eds.), *Research, Practices, and Innovations in Global Risk and Contingency Management* (pp. 134–153). Hershey, PA: IGI Global. doi:10.4018/978-1-5225-4754-9.ch008

Raman, A., & Goyal, D. P. (2017). Extending IMPLEMENT Framework for Enterprise Information Systems Implementation to Information System Innovation. In M. Tavana (Ed.), *Enterprise Information Systems and the Digitalization of Business Functions* (pp. 137–177). Hershey, PA: IGI Global. doi:10.4018/978-1-5225-2382-6.ch007

Rao, Y., & Zhang, Y. (2017). The Construction and Development of Academic Library Digital Special Subject Databases. In L. Ruan, Q. Zhu, & Y. Ye (Eds.), *Academic Library Development and Administration in China* (pp. 163–183). Hershey, PA: IGI Global. doi:10.4018/978-1-5225-0550-1.ch010

Ravasan, A. Z., Mohammadi, M. M., & Hamidi, H. (2018). An Investigation Into the Critical Success Factors of Implementing Information Technology Service Management Frameworks. In K. Jakobs (Ed.), *Corporate and Global Standardization Initiatives in Contemporary Society* (pp. 200–218). Hershey, PA: IGI Global. doi:10.4018/978-1-5225-5320-5.ch009

Renna, P., Izzo, C., & Romaniello, T. (2016). The Business Process Management Systems to Support Continuous Improvements. In W. Nuninger & J. Châtelet (Eds.), *Handbook of Research on Quality Assurance and Value Management in Higher Education* (pp. 237–256). Hershey, PA: IGI Global. doi:10.4018/978-1-5225-0024-7.ch009

Rezaie, S., Mirabedini, S. J., & Abtahi, A. (2018). Designing a Model for Implementation of Business Intelligence in the Banking Industry. *International Journal of Enterprise Information Systems*, *14*(1), 77–103. doi:10.4018/IJEIS.2018010105

Riccò, R. (2016). Diversity Management: Bringing Equality, Equity, and Inclusion in the Workplace. In J. Prescott (Ed.), *Handbook of Research on Race, Gender, and the Fight for Equality* (pp. 335–359). Hershey, PA: IGI Global. doi:10.4018/978-1-5225-0047-6.ch015

Romano, L., Grimaldi, R., & Colasuonno, F. S. (2017). Demand Management as a Success Factor in Project Portfolio Management. In L. Romano (Ed.), *Project Portfolio Management Strategies for Effective Organizational Operations* (pp. 202–219). Hershey, PA: IGI Global. doi:10.4018/978-1-5225-2151-8.ch008

Rostek, K. B. (2016). Risk Management: Role and Importance in Business Organization. In D. Jakóbczak (Ed.), *Analyzing Risk through Probabilistic Modeling in Operations Research* (pp. 149–178). Hershey, PA: IGI Global. doi:10.4018/978-1-4666-9458-3.ch007

Rouhani, S., & Savoji, S. R. (2016). A Success Assessment Model for BI Tools Implementation: An Empirical Study of Banking Industry. *International Journal of Business Intelligence Research*, *7*(1), 25–44. doi:10.4018/IJBIR.2016010103

Ruan, Z. (2016). A Corpus-Based Functional Analysis of Complex Nominal Groups in Written Business Discourse: The Case of "Business". *International Journal of Computer-Assisted Language Learning and Teaching*, *6*(2), 74–90. doi:10.4018/IJCALLT.2016040105

Ruhi, U. (2018). Towards an Interdisciplinary Socio-Technical Definition of Virtual Communities. In M. Khosrow-Pour, D.B.A. (Ed.), Encyclopedia of Information Science and Technology, Fourth Edition (pp. 4278-4295). Hershey, PA: IGI Global. doi:10.4018/978-1-5225-2255-3.ch371

Ryan, J., Doster, B., Daily, S., & Lewis, C. (2016). A Case Study Perspective for Balanced Perioperative Workflow Achievement through Data-Driven Process Improvement. *International Journal of Healthcare Information Systems and Informatics*, *11*(3), 19–41. doi:10.4018/IJHISI.2016070102

Safari, M. R., & Jiang, Q. (2018). The Theory and Practice of IT Governance Maturity and Strategies Alignment: Evidence From Banking Industry. *Journal of Global Information Management*, *26*(2), 127–146. doi:10.4018/JGIM.2018040106

Sahoo, J., Pati, B., & Mohanty, B. (2017). Knowledge Management as an Academic Discipline: An Assessment. In B. Gunjal (Ed.), *Managing Knowledge and Scholarly Assets in Academic Libraries* (pp. 99–126). Hershey, PA: IGI Global. doi:10.4018/978-1-5225-1741-2.ch005

Saini, D. (2017). Relevance of Teaching Values and Ethics in Management Education. In N. Baporikar (Ed.), *Management Education for Global Leadership* (pp. 90–111). Hershey, PA: IGI Global. doi:10.4018/978-1-5225-1013-0.ch005

Sambhanthan, A. (2017). Assessing and Benchmarking Sustainability in Organisations: An Integrated Conceptual Model. *International Journal of Systems and Service-Oriented Engineering*, *7*(4), 22–43. doi:10.4018/IJSSOE.2017100102

Sambhanthan, A., & Potdar, V. (2017). A Study of the Parameters Impacting Sustainability in Information Technology Organizations. *International Journal of Knowledge-Based Organizations*, *7*(3), 27–39. doi:10.4018/IJKBO.2017070103

Sánchez-Fernández, M. D., & Manríquez, M. R. (2018). The Entrepreneurial Spirit Based on Social Values: The Digital Generation. In P. Isaias & L. Carvalho (Eds.), *User Innovation and the Entrepreneurship Phenomenon in the Digital Economy* (pp. 173–193). Hershey, PA: IGI Global. doi:10.4018/978-1-5225-2826-5.ch009

Sanchez-Ruiz, L., & Blanco, B. (2017). Process Management for SMEs: Barriers, Enablers, and Benefits. In M. Vemić (Ed.), *Optimal Management Strategies in Small and Medium Enterprises* (pp. 293–319). Hershey, PA: IGI Global. doi:10.4018/978-1-5225-1949-2.ch014

Sanz, L. F., Gómez-Pérez, J., & Castillo-Martinez, A. (2018). Analysis of the European ICT Competence Frameworks. In V. Ahuja & S. Rathore (Eds.), *Multidisciplinary Perspectives on Human Capital and Information Technology Professionals* (pp. 225–245). Hershey, PA: IGI Global. doi:10.4018/978-1-5225-5297-0.ch012

Sarvepalli, A., & Godin, J. (2017). Business Process Management in the Classroom. *Journal of Cases on Information Technology, 19*(2), 17–28. doi:10.4018/JCIT.2017040102

Satpathy, B., & Muniapan, B. (2016). Ancient Wisdom for Transformational Leadership and Its Insights from the Bhagavad-Gita. In U. Aung & P. Ordoñez de Pablos (Eds.), *Managerial Strategies and Practice in the Asian Business Sector* (pp. 1–10). Hershey, PA: IGI Global. doi:10.4018/978-1-4666-9758-4.ch001

Saygili, E. E., Ozturkoglu, Y., & Kocakulah, M. C. (2017). End Users' Perceptions of Critical Success Factors in ERP Applications. *International Journal of Enterprise Information Systems, 13*(4), 58–75. doi:10.4018/IJEIS.2017100104

Saygili, E. E., & Saygili, A. T. (2017). Contemporary Issues in Enterprise Information Systems: A Critical Review of CSFs in ERP Implementations. In M. Tavana (Ed.), *Enterprise Information Systems and the Digitalization of Business Functions* (pp. 120–136). Hershey, PA: IGI Global. doi:10.4018/978-1-5225-2382-6.ch006

Seidenstricker, S., & Antonino, A. (2018). Business Model Innovation-Oriented Technology Management for Emergent Technologies. In M. Khosrow-Pour, D.B.A. (Ed.), Encyclopedia of Information Science and Technology, Fourth Edition (pp. 4560-4569). Hershey, PA: IGI Global. doi:10.4018/978-1-5225-2255-3.ch396

Senaratne, S., & Gunarathne, A. D. (2017). Excellence Perspective for Management Education from a Global Accountants' Hub in Asia. In N. Baporikar (Ed.), *Management Education for Global Leadership* (pp. 158–180). Hershey, PA: IGI Global. doi:10.4018/978-1-5225-1013-0.ch008

Sensuse, D. I., & Cahyaningsih, E. (2018). Knowledge Management Models: A Summative Review. *International Journal of Information Systems in the Service Sector, 10*(1), 71–100. doi:10.4018/IJISSS.2018010105

Sensuse, D. I., Wibowo, W. C., & Cahyaningsih, E. (2016). Indonesian Government Knowledge Management Model: A Theoretical Model. *Information Resources Management Journal, 29*(1), 91–108. doi:10.4018/irmj.2016010106

Seth, M., Goyal, D., & Kiran, R. (2017). Diminution of Impediments in Implementation of Supply Chain Management Information System for Enhancing its Effectiveness in Indian Automobile Industry. *Journal of Global Information Management, 25*(3), 1–20. doi:10.4018/JGIM.2017070101

Seyal, A. H., & Rahman, M. N. (2017). Investigating Impact of Inter-Organizational Factors in Measuring ERP Systems Success: Bruneian Perspectives. In M. Tavana (Ed.), *Enterprise Information Systems and the Digitalization of Business Functions* (pp. 178–204). Hershey, PA: IGI Global. doi:10.4018/978-1-5225-2382-6.ch008

Shaikh, A. A., & Karjaluoto, H. (2016). On Some Misconceptions Concerning Digital Banking and Alternative Delivery Channels. *International Journal of E-Business Research, 12*(3), 1–16. doi:10.4018/IJEBR.2016070101

Shams, S. M. (2016). Stakeholder Relationship Management in Online Business and Competitive Value Propositions: Evidence from the Sports Industry. *International Journal of Online Marketing, 6*(2), 1–17. doi:10.4018/IJOM.2016040101

Shamsuzzoha, A. (2016). Management of Risk and Resilience within Collaborative Business Network. In R. Addo-Tenkorang, J. Kantola, P. Helo, & A. Shamsuzzoha (Eds.), *Supply Chain Strategies and the Engineer-to-Order Approach* (pp. 143–159). Hershey, PA: IGI Global. doi:10.4018/978-1-5225-0021-6.ch008

Shaqrah, A. A. (2018). Analyzing Business Intelligence Systems Based on 7s Model of McKinsey. *International Journal of Business Intelligence Research, 9*(1), 53–63. doi:10.4018/IJBIR.2018010104

Sharma, A. J. (2017). Enhancing Sustainability through Experiential Learning in Management Education. In N. Baporikar (Ed.), *Management Education for Global Leadership* (pp. 256–274). Hershey, PA: IGI Global. doi:10.4018/978-1-5225-1013-0.ch013

Shetty, K. P. (2017). Responsible Global Leadership: Ethical Challenges in Management Education. In N. Baporikar (Ed.), *Innovation and Shifting Perspectives in Management Education* (pp. 194–223). Hershey, PA: IGI Global. doi:10.4018/978-1-5225-1019-2.ch009

Sinthupundaja, J., & Kohda, Y. (2017). Effects of Corporate Social Responsibility and Creating Shared Value on Sustainability. *International Journal of Sustainable Entrepreneurship and Corporate Social Responsibility*, *2*(1), 27–38. doi:10.4018/IJSECSR.2017010103

Škarica, I., & Hrgović, A. V. (2018). Implementation of Total Quality Management Principles in Public Health Institutes in the Republic of Croatia. *International Journal of Productivity Management and Assessment Technologies*, *6*(1), 1–16. doi:10.4018/IJPMAT.2018010101

Smuts, H., Kotzé, P., Van der Merwe, A., & Loock, M. (2017). Framework for Managing Shared Knowledge in an Information Systems Outsourcing Context. *International Journal of Knowledge Management*, *13*(4), 1–30. doi:10.4018/IJKM.2017100101

Soares, E. R., & Zaidan, F. H. (2016). Information Architecture and Business Modeling in Modern Organizations of Information Technology: Professional Career Plan in Organizations IT. In G. Jamil, J. Poças Rascão, F. Ribeiro, & A. Malheiro da Silva (Eds.), *Handbook of Research on Information Architecture and Management in Modern Organizations* (pp. 439–457). Hershey, PA: IGI Global. doi:10.4018/978-1-4666-8637-3.ch020

Sousa, M. J., Cruz, R., Dias, I., & Caracol, C. (2017). Information Management Systems in the Supply Chain. In G. Jamil, A. Soares, & C. Pessoa (Eds.), *Handbook of Research on Information Management for Effective Logistics and Supply Chains* (pp. 469–485). Hershey, PA: IGI Global. doi:10.4018/978-1-5225-0973-8.ch025

Spremic, M., Turulja, L., & Bajgoric, N. (2018). Two Approaches in Assessing Business Continuity Management Attitudes in the Organizational Context. In N. Bajgoric (Ed.), *Always-On Enterprise Information Systems for Modern Organizations* (pp. 159–183). Hershey, PA: IGI Global. doi:10.4018/978-1-5225-3704-5.ch008

Steenkamp, A. L. (2018). Some Insights in Computer Science and Information Technology. In *Examining the Changing Role of Supervision in Doctoral Research Projects: Emerging Research and Opportunities* (pp. 113–133). Hershey, PA: IGI Global. doi:10.4018/978-1-5225-2610-0.ch005

Studdard, N., Dawson, M., Burton, S. L., Jackson, N., Leonard, B., Quisenberry, W., & Rahim, E. (2016). Nurturing Social Entrepreneurship and Building Social Entrepreneurial Self-Efficacy: Focusing on Primary and Secondary Schooling to Develop Future Social Entrepreneurs. In Z. Fields (Ed.), *Incorporating Business Models and Strategies into Social Entrepreneurship* (pp. 154–175). Hershey, PA: IGI Global. doi:10.4018/978-1-4666-8748-6.ch010

Sun, Z. (2016). A Framework for Developing Management Intelligent Systems. *International Journal of Systems and Service-Oriented Engineering*, *6*(1), 37–53. doi:10.4018/IJSSOE.2016010103

Swami, B., & Mphele, G. T. (2016). Problems Preventing Growth of Small Entrepreneurs: A Case Study of a Few Small Entrepreneurs in Botswana Sub-Urban Areas. In N. Baporikar (Ed.), *Handbook of Research on Entrepreneurship in the Contemporary Knowledge-Based Global Economy* (pp. 479–508). Hershey, PA: IGI Global. doi:10.4018/978-1-4666-8798-1.ch020

Tabach, A., & Croteau, A. (2017). Configurations of Information Technology Governance Practices and Business Unit Performance. *International Journal of IT/Business Alignment and Governance*, *8*(2), 1–27. doi:10.4018/IJITBAG.2017070101

Talaue, G. M., & Iqbal, T. (2017). Assessment of e-Business Mode of Selected Private Universities in the Philippines and Pakistan. *International Journal of Online Marketing*, *7*(4), 63–77. doi:10.4018/IJOM.2017100105

Tam, G. C. (2017). Project Manager Sustainability Competence. In *Managerial Strategies and Green Solutions for Project Sustainability* (pp. 178–207). Hershey, PA: IGI Global. doi:10.4018/978-1-5225-2371-0.ch008

Tambo, T. (2018). Fashion Retail Innovation: About Context, Antecedents, and Outcome in Technological Change Projects. In I. Management Association (Ed.), Fashion and Textiles: Breakthroughs in Research and Practice (pp. 233-260). Hershey, PA: IGI Global. doi:10.4018/978-1-5225-3432-7.ch010

Tambo, T., & Mikkelsen, O. E. (2016). Fashion Supply Chain Optimization: Linking Make-to-Order Purchasing and B2B E-Commerce. In S. Joshi & R. Joshi (Eds.), *Designing and Implementing Global Supply Chain Management* (pp. 1–21). Hershey, PA: IGI Global. doi:10.4018/978-1-4666-9720-1.ch001

Tandon, K. (2016). Innovative Andragogy: The Paradigm Shift to Heutagogy. In S. Tiwari & L. Nafees (Eds.), *Innovative Management Education Pedagogies for Preparing Next-Generation Leaders* (pp. 238–257). Hershey, PA: IGI Global. doi:10.4018/978-1-4666-9691-4.ch014

Tantau, A. D., & Frăţilă, L. C. (2018). Information and Management System for Renewable Energy Business. In *Entrepreneurship and Business Development in the Renewable Energy Sector* (pp. 200–244). Hershey, PA: IGI Global. doi:10.4018/978-1-5225-3625-3.ch006

Teixeira, N., Pardal, P. N., & Rafael, B. G. (2018). Internationalization, Financial Performance, and Organizational Challenges: A Success Case in Portugal. In L. Carvalho (Ed.), *Handbook of Research on Entrepreneurial Ecosystems and Social Dynamics in a Globalized World* (pp. 379–423). Hershey, PA: IGI Global. doi:10.4018/978-1-5225-3525-6.ch017

Trad, A., & Kalpić, D. (2016). The E-Business Transformation Framework for E-Commerce Architecture-Modeling Projects. In I. Lee (Ed.), *Encyclopedia of E-Commerce Development, Implementation, and Management* (pp. 733–753). Hershey, PA: IGI Global. doi:10.4018/978-1-4666-9787-4.ch052

Trad, A., & Kalpić, D. (2016). The E-Business Transformation Framework for E-Commerce Control and Monitoring Pattern. In I. Lee (Ed.), *Encyclopedia of E-Commerce Development, Implementation, and Management* (pp. 754–777). Hershey, PA: IGI Global. doi:10.4018/978-1-4666-9787-4.ch053

Trad, A., & Kalpić, D. (2018). The Business Transformation Framework, Agile Project and Change Management. In M. Khosrow-Pour, D.B.A. (Ed.), Encyclopedia of Information Science and Technology, Fourth Edition (pp. 620-635). Hershey, PA: IGI Global. doi:10.4018/978-1-5225-2255-3.ch054

Trad, A., & Kalpić, D. (2018). The Business Transformation and Enterprise Architecture Framework: The Financial Engineering E-Risk Management and E-Law Integration. In B. Sergi, F. Fidanoski, M. Ziolo, & V. Naumovski (Eds.), *Regaining Global Stability After the Financial Crisis* (pp. 46–65). Hershey, PA: IGI Global. doi:10.4018/978-1-5225-4026-7.ch003

Turulja, L., & Bajgoric, N. (2018). Business Continuity and Information Systems: A Systematic Literature Review. In N. Bajgoric (Ed.), *Always-On Enterprise Information Systems for Modern Organizations* (pp. 60–87). Hershey, PA: IGI Global. doi:10.4018/978-1-5225-3704-5.ch004

van Wessel, R. M., de Vries, H. J., & Ribbers, P. M. (2016). Business Benefits through Company IT Standardization. In K. Jakobs (Ed.), *Effective Standardization Management in Corporate Settings* (pp. 34–53). Hershey, PA: IGI Global. doi:10.4018/978-1-4666-9737-9.ch003

Vargas-Hernández, J. G. (2017). Professional Integrity in Business Management Education. In N. Baporikar (Ed.), *Management Education for Global Leadership* (pp. 70–89). Hershey, PA: IGI Global. doi:10.4018/978-1-5225-1013-0.ch004

Vasista, T. G., & AlAbdullatif, A. M. (2017). Role of Electronic Customer Relationship Management in Demand Chain Management: A Predictive Analytic Approach. *International Journal of Information Systems and Supply Chain Management, 10*(1), 53–67. doi:10.4018/IJISSCM.2017010104

Vergidis, K. (2016). Rediscovering Business Processes: Definitions, Patterns, and Modelling Approaches. In P. Papajorgji, F. Pinet, A. Guimarães, & J. Papathanasiou (Eds.), *Automated Enterprise Systems for Maximizing Business Performance* (pp. 97–122). Hershey, PA: IGI Global. doi:10.4018/978-1-4666-8841-4.ch007

Vieru, D., & Bourdeau, S. (2017). Survival in the Digital Era: A Digital Competence-Based Multi-Case Study in the Canadian SME Clothing Industry. *International Journal of Social and Organizational Dynamics in IT, 6*(1), 17–34. doi:10.4018/IJSODIT.2017010102

Vijayan, G., & Kamarulzaman, N. H. (2017). An Introduction to Sustainable Supply Chain Management and Business Implications. In M. Khan, M. Hussain, & M. Ajmal (Eds.), *Green Supply Chain Management for Sustainable Business Practice* (pp. 27–50). Hershey, PA: IGI Global. doi:10.4018/978-1-5225-0635-5.ch002

Vlachvei, A., & Notta, O. (2017). Firm Competitiveness: Theories, Evidence, and Measurement. In A. Vlachvei, O. Notta, K. Karantininis, & N. Tsounis (Eds.), *Factors Affecting Firm Competitiveness and Performance in the Modern Business World* (pp. 1–42). Hershey, PA: IGI Global. doi:10.4018/978-1-5225-0843-4.ch001

von Rosing, M., Fullington, N., & Walker, J. (2016). Using the Business Ontology and Enterprise Standards to Transform Three Leading Organizations. *International Journal of Conceptual Structures and Smart Applications, 4*(1), 71–99. doi:10.4018/IJCSSA.2016010104

von Rosing, M., & von Scheel, H. (2016). Using the Business Ontology to Develop Enterprise Standards. *International Journal of Conceptual Structures and Smart Applications, 4*(1), 48–70. doi:10.4018/IJCSSA.2016010103

Walczak, S. (2016). Artificial Neural Networks and other AI Applications for Business Management Decision Support. *International Journal of Sociotechnology and Knowledge Development, 8*(4), 1–20. doi:10.4018/IJSKD.2016100101

Wamba, S. F., Akter, S., Kang, H., Bhattacharya, M., & Upal, M. (2016). The Primer of Social Media Analytics. *Journal of Organizational and End User Computing, 28*(2), 1–12. doi:10.4018/JOEUC.2016040101

Wang, C., Schofield, M., Li, X., & Ou, X. (2017). Do Chinese Students in Public and Private Higher Education Institutes Perform at Different Level in One of the Leadership Skills: Critical Thinking?: An Exploratory Comparison. In V. Wang (Ed.), *Encyclopedia of Strategic Leadership and Management* (pp. 160–181). Hershey, PA: IGI Global. doi:10.4018/978-1-5225-1049-9.ch013

Wang, F., Raisinghani, M. S., Mora, M., & Wang, X. (2016). Strategic E-Business Management through a Balanced Scored Card Approach. In I. Lee (Ed.), *Encyclopedia of E-Commerce Development, Implementation, and Management* (pp. 361–386). Hershey, PA: IGI Global. doi:10.4018/978-1-4666-9787-4.ch027

Wang, J. (2017). Multi-Agent based Production Management Decision System Modelling for the Textile Enterprise. *Journal of Global Information Management, 25*(4), 1–15. doi:10.4018/JGIM.2017100101

Wiedemann, A., & Gewald, H. (2017). Examining Cross-Domain Alignment: The Correlation of Business Strategy, IT Management, and IT Business Value. *International Journal of IT/Business Alignment and Governance, 8*(1), 17–31. doi:10.4018/IJITBAG.2017010102

Wolf, R., & Thiel, M. (2018). Advancing Global Business Ethics in China: Reducing Poverty Through Human and Social Welfare. In S. Hipsher (Ed.), *Examining the Private Sector's Role in Wealth Creation and Poverty Reduction* (pp. 67–84). Hershey, PA: IGI Global. doi:10.4018/978-1-5225-3117-3.ch004

Wu, J., Ding, F., Xu, M., Mo, Z., & Jin, A. (2016). Investigating the Determinants of Decision-Making on Adoption of Public Cloud Computing in E-government. *Journal of Global Information Management, 24*(3), 71–89. doi:10.4018/JGIM.2016070104

Xu, L., & de Vrieze, P. (2016). Building Situational Applications for Virtual Enterprises. In I. Lee (Ed.), *Encyclopedia of E-Commerce Development, Implementation, and Management* (pp. 715–724). Hershey, PA: IGI Global. doi:10.4018/978-1-4666-9787-4.ch050

Yablonsky, S. (2018). Innovation Platforms: Data and Analytics Platforms. In *Multi-Sided Platforms (MSPs) and Sharing Strategies in the Digital Economy: Emerging Research and Opportunities* (pp. 72–95). Hershey, PA: IGI Global. doi:10.4018/978-1-5225-5457-8.ch003

Yusoff, A., Ahmad, N. H., & Halim, H. A. (2017). Agropreneurship among Gen Y in Malaysia: The Role of Academic Institutions. In N. Ahmad, T. Ramayah, H. Halim, & S. Rahman (Eds.), *Handbook of Research on Small and Medium Enterprises in Developing Countries* (pp. 23–47). Hershey, PA: IGI Global. doi:10.4018/978-1-5225-2165-5.ch002

Zanin, F., Comuzzi, E., & Costantini, A. (2018). The Effect of Business Strategy and Stock Market Listing on the Use of Risk Assessment Tools. In *Management Control Systems in Complex Settings: Emerging Research and Opportunities* (pp. 145–168). Hershey, PA: IGI Global. doi:10.4018/978-1-5225-3987-2.ch007

Zgheib, P. W. (2017). Corporate Innovation and Intrapreneurship in the Middle East. In P. Zgheib (Ed.), *Entrepreneurship and Business Innovation in the Middle East* (pp. 37–56). Hershey, PA: IGI Global. doi:10.4018/978-1-5225-2066-5.ch003

About the Contributors

Atour Taghipour is a professor and the head of two international management master programs at Normandy University (Le Havre) in France. He holds a PhD in Industrial Engineering from the Polytechnic School of Montreal in Canada. He received two masters' degrees, one in Management, Logistics & Strategy and other in Industrial Engineering. He has more than ten years of experiences as a manager in automobile industries. He has published four books and many research papers in international journals. His areas of research are supply chain and operations management.

* * *

Dmitry Davydov is Master's student in Penza State University.

Youssef Elhaoussine is a researcher and professional from France. He has a scientific background in Physic-Chemistry and Analytic Chemistry as well as Marketing and Entrepreneurship. He has been working in China for more than 5 years as a production manager for a French printing consumable retailer, developing a manufacturer network and monitoring the production in China and Europe. In 2013, he decided to turn to a more academic career. His research focused on consumer behavior in China. After that, he became a researcher for the Sun Yat-sen International School of Business and Finance specializing in B2B Branding strategies for Chinese factories and the Belt Road Initiative. He currently works as an Assistant Lecturer in Beijing Normal University-Hong Kong Baptist University United International College and he is regularly invited by trade organization to provide the latest development on brand strategies.

Md. Masudul Hassan is currently serving as an assistant professor and Coordinator. He has published many research articles in well-known journals abroad and also published a book chapter 'Cross-Border E-Commerce Marketing and Management' from IGI Global (academic publisher), USA. He also received a "Research & Development Fellowship" from the Ministry of Science and Technology, Peoples' Republic of Bangladesh to perform Agribusiness related research. He worked on a number of research projects financed by FAO, SNV (Netherland development organization), and Govt. His educational background is MBA in Finance from Bangladesh University of Professionals (BUP), BBA in Agribusiness from Sher-e-Bangla Agricultural University, PGD in HRM from Bangladesh Institute of Human Resource Management (BIHRM). He is a reviewer of various foreign journals including Elsevier. He is active in research on Agribusiness, Human Resource Management, Finance, and the development of rooftop agriculture in urban areas. He has been engaged in various voluntary activities.

Mohammed Merimi is a student at the Normandie University in the Faculty of International Business.

Vardan Mkrttchian graduated from State Engineering University of Armenia, the Faculty of Cybernetics as an Electronics Engineer & received his Doctorate of Sciences (Engineering) in Control Systems from Lomonosov Moscow State University (former USSR). Dr. Vardan Mkrttchian taught for undergraduate and graduate student's courses of control system, information sciences and technology, at the Astrakhan State University (Russian Federation), where he was is the Professor of the Information Systems (www.aspu.ru) six years. Now he is full professor CAD&Economy departments of Penza State University (www.pnzgu.ru). He is currently chief executive of HHH University, Australia and team leader of the international academics (www.hhhuniversity.com). He also serves as executive director of the HHH Technology Incorporation. Professor Vardan Mkrttchian has authored over 400 refereed publications. He is the author of over twenty books published of IGI Global, included ten books indexed of SCOPUS in IT, Control System, Digital Economy, and Education Technology, and 43 works in SCOPUS and 47 in WoS. He also is Editor-in-Chief of International Journal of Applied Research in Bioinformatics (IJARB).

Kiran Mysore has completed his graduation (B.E.) from the University of Mysore in 1987. He did his post-graduation (M.E.) in Production Engineering from P.S.G. College of Technology (1991) and Doctoral degree (Ph.D.), in Surface Metrology from the Indian Institute of Technology (I.I.T.), Madras in 1997. He has Industry/Research/Teaching experience of 25 years. Currently working as Associate Professor in the Mechanical Engineering Department, School of Technology, Pandit Deendayal

Petroleum University. He has published technical papers in many reputed national/ international journals and conferences. He is a member of the Project management Institute (P.M.I.), U.S.A. He is a certified project manager (P.M.P.) from P.M.I. He has completed many mission-critical projects. He has conducted many trainings for working executives.

Kamalendu Pal is with the Department of Computer Science, School of Mathematics, Computer Science and Engineering, City University London. Kamalendu received his BSc (Hons) degree in Physics from Calcutta University, India, Postgraduate Diploma in Computer Science from Pune, India, MSc degree in Software Systems Technology from Sheffield University, Postgraduate Diploma in Artificial Intelligence from Kingston University, MPhil degree in Computer Science from University College London, and MBA degree from the University of Hull, United Kingdom. He has published widely in the scientific community with research articles in the ACM SIGMIS Database, Expert Systems with Applications, Decision Support Systems, and conferences. His research interests include knowledge-based systems, decision support systems, blockchain technology, software engineering, and service-oriented computing. He is on the editorial board in an international computer science journal. He is a member of the British Computer Society, the Institution of Engineering and Technology, and the IEEE Computer Society.

Subhasis Ray is Professor at Xavier Institute of Management XIMB, Xavier University Bhubaneswar, India. His research interests are in the are of business sustainability, marketing, social innovation and entrepreneurship and corporate social responsibility.

Samira Islam Resmi is serving as an Assistant Professor in the Department of Agribusiness. She has published many research articles in well-known international journals. Her educational background is MBA in Finance, awarded with Chancellor Gold Medal from Bangladesh University of Professionals (BUP), BBA in Agribusiness from Sher-e-Bangla Agricultural University, PGD in HRM from Bangladesh Institute of Human Resource Management (BIHRM). She is also a reviewer of various foreign journals. She has experienced related to leadership, direction, and management of the finance and accounting team. She has enough experience in the formulation of the business's strategy. She is involved in agribusiness, agriculture, Management, social, and SME development research.

Viacheslav Voronin is the head of the Center for Cognitive Technology and Machine Vision at Moscow State University of Technology "STANKIN," Moscow, Russian Federation. He received his BS (2006), MS (2008) in the communication system from the South-Russian State University of Economics and Service, and his Ph.D. in technics from Southern Federal University (2009). Voronin is a member of the Program Committee of the conference SPIE. His research interests include image processing, inpainting, and computer vision.

Index

3D Blockchain 174, 176-177, 188

A

artificial intelligence 6, 26, 28, 39, 47, 49, 52, 91, 93

B

B2B marketing 46-47, 49-50
Big Data 5-6, 28-29, 35-36, 88-89, 92-93, 95, 133-134, 145, 150
Big Data Analytics 92-93, 145
Blockchain Technology 24, 143, 145-146, 148-149, 153-154, 156-160, 162, 176, 188
Buying Centre 48, 53-54, 56, 58, 63

C

Case-Based Reasoning 123, 126, 132-133, 140
Chinese manufacturers 69
Covid-19 1-4, 6-7, 9, 11-12, 14, 26-27, 29-31, 37, 41
Crisis Management 143
CRM 75-76, 112

D

Data Analysis 24
Decentralized Supply Chain 46-47, 50, 55, 63
Decision Support Systems 124
Description Logic 112-113, 123, 133, 140
Digital supply chain 5, 40-41, 49, 51, 99
Digitalization 1-2, 4-7, 11, 14-15, 19, 24-29, 32-35, 37, 40-41, 49, 51, 59
Digitization 4, 19, 36, 47, 49, 81-82, 85, 90-91

E

Efficient Supply Chain 24, 52
Empirical Research 1, 7, 24

G

Geographic Information Systems 174
Global Crises 1

I

Industrial Buying 46, 54-55, 59, 63
Industry 4.0 6, 49, 81-82, 86, 88-93, 96, 98-99
Information System 75, 115, 140, 143, 147, 149, 152, 157-158, 160, 164-165
Interactive marketing 74-75
Internal marketing 74-75

N

New Buy 53-54, 63

O

Ontology 112-113, 115-118, 120-123, 125, 127-128, 130-133, 140-141
operations management 26, 144
organizational buying process 46, 48, 53

R

Radio Frequency Identification 98, 110, 145
Random Programming 5, 24
Rule-Based Reasoning 112-113, 126, 133, 141

S

sales and marketing 47
Semantic Web Service 112-113, 117-119, 123, 130-131, 133, 141
Service marketing 73-74
Supply Chain 1-7, 9-15, 19, 24-27, 29, 32, 34, 37-41, 46-47, 49-53, 55, 57, 59, 63, 73, 81-88, 92, 95-96, 98-99, 107-112, 116-117, 122-123, 133-134, 140-141, 143-144, 147-153, 157, 165, 174-175, 188
Supply Chain Coordination 141
Supply chain management 4, 6, 11, 26, 37, 41, 49-50, 52, 81, 84, 98, 108, 111, 122, 140-141, 144, 148, 150-151, 153, 157, 174
supply channels 25-26

T

Technological Innovations 25-26
The Perspectives of Supply Chain Management 174
TQM 77

W

Web Service Composition 107, 123, 132

www.ingramcontent.com/pod-product-compliance
Lightning Source LLC
LaVergne TN
LVHW061537290926
849162LV00004B/821
9781799868743